TYO
497965

A

JAPAN AIR LINES

FLIGHT NO./DATE

001

TYO
TO **TOKYO**

AUSTRIAN AIR

A

OS   52 79 27

CW01024555

AUCKLAND

NAC

SWISSAIR

SR 58 63 31 **A**

To

TLS

Airline/Flight

AF 1679

To

GVA

Airline/Flight

SR 110

機内持込手荷物
IDENTIFICATION TAG

JC4H   LON

MARTIN TURNER

 日本航空
JAPAN AIR LINES

B

Weight this piece

kg

to

GVA

airline / flight

SR 242

to

Ze4

airline / flight

SS3

ANSETT AIRLINES OF AUSTRALIA

SYDNEY

Printed in Australia

A

AIR FRANCE

AF 68-80-71

PARIS

PAR

Vol/Flight

AF 731

JAPAN AIR LINES

FLIGHT NO./DATE

W3

LON
TO **LONDON**

AI   LON

AIR·INDIA

LONDON
LON

AI.   № 122374

SORTING SYMBOL ➡ **B**

MARTIN TURNER

NO EASY ROAD

My life and times with Wishbone Ash and beyond

Dedicated to
Kim Turner

MARTIN TURNER

My life and times with
Wishbone Ash and beyond

NEASY ROAD

Researched and edited by Gary Carter
Foreword by Ted Turner

No Easy Road
My Life and Times with Wishbone Ash and Beyond
First published in 2012 by Dirty Dog Books,
An imprint of Dirty Dog Discs

Second Edition - November 2012

contact@wishboneash.co.uk
www.wishboneash.co.uk

Printed and bound by Berforts Information Press - Stevenage

Cover Illustration, design and back cover photograph by Michael Inns

Artwork by Karen Gladwell

This book is printed on demand, so no copies will
be remaindered or pulped.

ISBN 978-0-9572478-0-2

*Photographs are from Martin Turner's personal collection. In some cases it has
not been possible to ascertain or trace original photo copyright holders. The
publishers would be grateful to hear from the photographers concerned.*

*The views expressed are those of Martin Turner himself, except where otherwise
stated, and do not necessarily reflect the views of the editor, the other members
of Wishbone Ash and Martin Turner's Wishbone Ash past and present, or their
respective managements.*

Contents

	Dedication	*ii*
	Acknowledgements	*vi*
	Foreword	*vii*
	No Easy Road	*ix*
CHAPTER ONE:	**Like a Child**	1
CHAPTER TWO:	**New Rising Star**	17
CHAPTER THREE:	**Leaving To Search For Something New**	45
CHAPTER FOUR:	**First Light**	71
CHAPTER FIVE:	**Warriors**	91
CHAPTER SIX:	**At The Airport; On The Plane...**	125
CHAPTER SEVEN:	**Tonight I Saw The Magic In Your Eyes**	147
CHAPTER EIGHT:	**In New England**	171
	Photographic section	*207-222*
CHAPTER NINE:	**Carry Me a Little Closer Home**	223
CHAPTER TEN:	**Outward Bound**	243
CHAPTER ELEVEN:	**In The Skin**	265
CHAPTER TWELVE:	**Broken Wings Can Heal and Mend Again**	283
CHAPTER THIRTEEN:	**This Strange Affair**	307
CHAPTER FOURTEEN:	**The Sky is Changing**	329
CHAPTER FIFTEEN:	**Walking The Reeperbahn**	353
CHAPTER SIXTEEN:	**Phoenix Rising**	371
CHAPTER SEVENTEEN:	**Through The Looking Glass**	395
CHAPTER EIGHTEEN:	**Life Begins**	419
	Post Script	*435*

Acknowledgements

I would like to thank all who have joined me on my musical journey – in particular the various members of the Empty Vessels, Wishbone Ash, the Wolfgang, the Blue Bishops and MTWA as well as everyone who has been involved behind the scenes through the years.

Special thanks to archivist Gary Carter for his assistance in researching and editing the material contained within these pages and for his invaluable support over many years. Thanks also to those who have shared their memories and provided archival material for this book.

Thanks to my manager Martin Darvill and team at QEDG Management, and also Don McKay at Rhino Agency.

A special mention also to my wonderful family – Ed and Eileen, Glenn and Kim, Susie, Maurn, Annalise, Jessica, Andrew, Grace, Tom, Melody – for many years of love and support.

Martin Turner
Guildford, 2012

Foreword
BY TED TURNER

There are times when forces come together, energies collide, inspiration abounds! Such a moment happened meeting with Martin Turner.

The driving force behind Wishbone Ash in the early stages of our development, he recognized my ability, brought me into the band and with his encouragement, skill and patience, we explored new territory in music.

His guidance was essential in preparation and arranging the harmony so integral to our sound. His vision resulted in the foundation of Argus, all of this achieved by a young man in his twenties.

The following pages will reveal the achievements made by Martin during his career and life – explained with a humour that is typical from this independent mind and, like most of us, a life described full of twists and turns with interest and keen eye.

Forty three years have passed since we first met. The legacy of Wishbone lives on. I am proud of our accomplishments together. More importantly through the decades our friendship has remained close.

"My mate, my brother", I wish you well.

Love and light!
Ted.

No Easy Road

Rock 'n' roll keeps dragging me
Where I don't know and you can't see
Cities rolling by and by
They twist my arm and sting my eye

Point me in the right direction
Stamp your feet and shout
We can laugh and play around
And be best friends right now

Watch me join the circus
Watch me steal the show
There ain't no easy money
There ain't no easy road

Buy me, pay me, wonder why
We stumble across the land
Don't fail for you, you can't fail for me
We start to understand

Rock 'n' roll keeps dragging me
Where I don't know and you can't see
Cities rolling by and by
They twist my arm and sting my eye

Watch me join the circus
Watch me steal the show
There ain't no easy money
There ain't no easy road

Martin Turner, 1972

CHAPTER ONE

Like a Child

I WAS born Martin Robert Turner on 1 October 1947, in the West Country seaside resort of Torquay on the English Riviera – the eldest of three children born to my parents Edwin and Eileen Turner. During my early years we lived in a block of flats in the centre of town, above the old fire station. I was the kind of kid who was quite happy to roam off in search of adventure at any time and within my first couple of years I had fallen down a set of stone steps with my pregnant mother, leaving me with a hefty scar above one eye which was eventually covered by one of my substantial eyebrows. Also around this time my Dad hauled me in from a window ledge where a small crowd had gathered in the street several floors below. I also used to go exploring with some girls, who were a couple of years older, up onto some cliffs that were close to home and which my parents had to come and rescue me from. I thought I was having a great time.

*My parents – Ed and Eileen Turner
– on their wedding day*

School photo, 1953

Eventually my parents came up on the list to move to a new council estate that had been built in Shiphay and we arrived there in the early fifties to find a fascinating collection of folks from all over. In our street there were people from the north east, from London, Ireland, Greece, France and all kinds of other places. The estate contained a large central park area where, when we were a little older, we met other gangs of youths and played football and cricket together, fought together, threw knives around and got up to all kinds of mischief like scrumping apples and plums and anything else we could get our hands on – this is, of course, now known as theft!. We did actually steal cigarettes when, as twelve year old lads, we did paper rounds for local shops and regarded the fags as compensation for the poor remuneration we received for our toil. We also used to go into this guy's garage and steal cider. The park was the main "hanging out" area and later became the place where Elvis and sixties music generally was listened to on "transistor radios" at the same time as we began the awkward but exciting challenge of early teenage relationships with the "opposite" sex.

The estate was surrounded by countryside so I had plenty of opportunity to walk for miles and discovered how to track birds and seek out their nests. As a small boy I amassed a collection of birds eggs – I only took one from a nest – which involved patience, guile and an ability to climb trees. I found out that even a tiny wren would attack you when you threaten its nest. We caught lizards, we dammed streams, we train spotted, we made "camps", we picked flowers and sold them to old ladies, we found wild mushrooms, we caught live rabbits, we played "Jerrys and English" - a popular post-war game with kids of that era - and as we grew older it seemed that we sought out ever more dangerous pursuits – bike riding, bows and arrows, air rifles and shot guns and, of course, explosives, as we found it easy to make bombs with weed killer (sodium chlorate) and icing sugar. It would be a quiet Sunday afternoon in the village and suddenly there would be a huge explosion and this massive clump of earth would shoot across the road, narrowly missing the Co-Op window.

Together with my mate Chisel and Irish Kev, we were the leaders of the gang, always outside looking for adventure/trouble. Chisel had a Dad who was in the merchant Navy and came home after months at sea, with loads of money, went out, got pissed and beat his mother up. Even after she obtained a court order he did it again and Chisel had sworn to him he would shoot him if he ever repeated his behaviour and kept a twelve-bore shotgun under his bed for that purpose – his Dad left and never came back.

Chisel was definitely a troubled soul – bit of a psycho even. He would kill the rabbits with his bare hands and on one occasion he persuaded us to get even with a bloke who lived in a house nearby. This chap had called the cops when we were making a noise in the public convenience close by. We all legged it – Chisel got caught. Anyway, it was a cold November evening close to bonfire night and, as we half heartedly threw small lumps of mud across the street at the house, Chisel suddenly pushed through the gang with a whole brick that he hurled straight through the lounge window. It was most unexpected and over the top, but as we all ran for our lives we could not stop laughing at the sheer mind-boggling audacity of Chisel's revenge.

Kev had an Irish Dad from the south who clearly had a chip on his shoulder about the English and I generally gave him a wide berth, although Kev's older sister was lovely. I always felt guilt about having been the one who mixed the explosives that took the front of Kev's face off in an accident, although thankfully he did fully recover.

On one little Sunday school outing organised by the local Church we all went off onto Dartmoor in a coach. We had all been cooped up in this vehicle for quite a while when one of the old girls in charge decided to stop unknowingly at a location which was right near an Army firing range. Of course we lads discovered all these unexploded mortar bombs embedded in the field and smuggled them back on board along with a huge toad hidden in a Lyons cake box. We loved tossing these "real" bombs around on the concrete road back at the estate as part of our Germans versus English re-enactments, until one of our younger gang members borrowed one to take home for the night. It turned out his Dad was ex-army and took one look and uttered the obvious question, "Where the hell did you get that?" The lad told him exactly where, and his Dad called the cops. I was in my PJ's just off to bed when my Mum asked me to come and talk to this helmeted officer who asked, "Do you have some mortar bombs?" I took him around to the back of the house where they were stashed in a cardboard box and as I went to pick it up he uttered, "Don't touch that box". I was a bit baffled as we had been chucking them around for weeks, but he arranged for an army bomb disposal squad to come and pick them up, and we heard that they had been taken away and detonated. Hmmmm, we were quite a proud gang when we got a mention on the six o clock news on television, which was still black and white back then. I suppose we can only be thankful that we didn't end up black and white as well.

Looking back on all of this, it seems to me now that we were actually a bunch of little fuck-heads, although it really seemed like just good fun back at that time. Of course, if kids did these things now there would be an armed response unit sent out, but it was not all bad stuff. I did take on a few duties that helped the family such as digging the garden, so my Dad could grow stuff – great blackcurrants, beans, radishes, beetroot, etc. I also quite enjoyed cleaning boots and shoes and especially being taught to use an axe to make kindling wood for lighting fires – all stuff that I still do nowadays on occasion.

Growing up on a council estate was pretty rough and I was always getting involved in fights as a young boy. I used to get picked on quite a bit because I was a bit "pretty" and "girly". My way of dealing with that was to get straight in the face of anyone who gave me a hard time and be as mean and nasty as I could. On many occasions I'd end up getting involved in fist-fights and would get smacked around, ending up with a bleeding nose or a busted lip – I actually used to quite like a bit of blood. I guess it's teenage male instinct, but you soon learn that there's always somebody bigger and harder than you, although that didn't matter either. As long as I could give them some pain, it didn't matter whether I lost or won – it was the doing of it that was important. Those years were tough going, but I remember them with affection.

When I was not out gallivanting around I was making early connections with music. In fact, the very earliest childhood memories I can recall are connected with music, which I grew up surrounded by. My mother had been a singer and dancer who, with her mother who played piano, used to go out to entertain the troops during the Second World War. We would often walk over to my grandmother's house, a couple of miles away, where she had a piano in the front room. While everyone else was chatting in the kitchen or lounge, I'd often slither off into the back room, where I knew the piano was. I must have been about three years old at the time and I would sit at the piano. I had no idea what I was doing, but I'd be in a trance, tinkling away, making up little tunes for hours on end. I was in my own fantasy world, fuelled by the music I was making. It probably sounded like a bunch of twaddle, but I'd let my imagination run free and I loved the opportunity to be creative and get lost in music. My other grandmother – my father's mother – also played piano and we often used to have a song and dance with her as well.

My Dad didn't play an instrument but was still a complete and utter music nut. He had a radiogram – a bloody great piece of furniture with big speakers – and he would play music at a very loud volume. I must have picked up this from him because I still do the same thing at my home. We'd skip and dance around the house, playing the same tunes over and over again – it was brilliant. My father used to play all kinds of music – opera, country, rock 'n' roll, be-bop, jazz, classical. When it got too cold to go out we would sit there with a fire burning and classical music playing. Gradually the light would die away and I'd be sat there with my Dad listening to Mozart or Tchaikovsky. It's quite unusual really for a small lad to be able to do that, but I just loved the mental freedom to be able to respond naturally to all the emotions that came to me through the music. It was wonderful and since then I've always been very open to all kinds of music. In our house it was music, music, music – all the time. When I was a little older, Mum encouraged me to go to the local church and join the choir. This helped get me over my early shyness – I really enjoyed it and to this day I still love religious music and classical music.

Everyone knew my father as Ed - that's what we all called him and that is how I shall refer to him from here on. Ed was an ex-Naval man. He'd been on a destroyer in the Mediterranean – they'd been torpedoed and he'd had a rough time. He came back and got a job as a fireman and spent the rest of his working life in the fire brigade. That was a heavy old job for sure – firemen do a lot more than just putting out fires. People assume that police and ambulance services deal with things like motor accidents, but firemen do a hell of a lot too. Ed would end up having to cut dead bodies out of car wrecks and would be depressed for weeks over it. Ed also crashed the fire engine on one occasion and we heard about it on the news. I was very young at the time and had to go up to the top of our road to telephone the station to see if Ed was alright. It turned out they'd actually hit a bridge and ended up hanging over the railway line. Fortunately he was exonerated from blame because he had put in a report a few weeks earlier saying the tyres were bald and needed replacing, but this had not been done. I used to love going down to the fire station, where the guys – a right bunch of cowboys – would all be playing snooker or cards, because obviously there would be a lot of time when they were sat around waiting for something to happen.

Back in 1952 Ed was one of the fire service crew that was sent to Lynmouth in North Devon to help with the flood that had smashed the town, with thousands of gallons of water so powerful it carried boulders through the streets. They spent several days and nights wading through water, recovering dead bodies and setting up pumps to get the water level down. He was awake for thirty-six hours when he first got there and on his arrival home, after several days, was exhausted. He went down with pneumonia pretty soon but managed to rest and recover eventually. He must have been a fairly tough chap because he survived another bout of pneumonia years later, following all night fire fighting. This time the hospital had given him antibiotics that he suffered an allergic reaction to. He was put into intensive care and we were told that there was nothing more they could do – it was down to him to fight back, which fortunately he was gradually able to do. I seem to have inherited his high stamina levels and I recognise that it is easy for guys made like this to push themselves so far that sickness is the only thing that can slow them down.

Politically, Ed was very left-wing, socialist even. As I grew older and formulated my own views on the world, I'd have a lot of political arguments with him. I wouldn't consider myself right-wing but I would often adopt an argument to counter his political leanings which were extremely left-wing, and we used to really enjoy talking politics.

During the early years of Wishbone Ash's success on one brief weekend visit to see my parents in Torquay, I found myself sitting in a bar, having a drink with Ed. During the course of our conversation I heard the wicked little monster inside my brain suggesting that I freak Ed out a bit, so I said to him, "Ed, I think I am going to sue Mum". "What on earth do you want to do that for?" he responded. "Well," I explained. "I am contemplating legal action for sexual molestation, and I want the bit back that she had removed from my body." Ed replied, "No, I really wouldn't bother with all that". I asked "Why not?" to which he replied "Well, you see, when they circumcised you they threw away the wrong piece." We both collapsed in hysterics. I seem to come from a family with a wacky sense of humour. As I have mentioned, Ed was a fireman and that dark humour would get those guys through some very heavy situations.

My mother was in a minority in our house, as she was the only female - there was Ed, my two brothers and myself. It was a little bit out of balance and I think I grew up without a great deal of experience with females and so by the time I got to my teenage years I was itching to get to know as many girls as I could – which I did!

My brother Glenn was two years younger than me and as a child my mother instilled it in me that I had look out for him. He was asthmatic and also had eczema pretty badly. My mother had taken a fall when she was pregnant with him and we always surmised that had been the cause of Glenn's childhood illness. From birth he'd been very delicate and as a child he was rushed to hospital a couple of times and nearly died. When we were old enough to be out on the street, I used to look out for him and if anyone messed with my brother I'd immediately be at their throats – it was just something that became second nature to me. Although a little younger than me, Glenn shared my interest in music.

> **GLENN TURNER:** *I was into music from a very early age – I loved the Shadows and the Everly Brothers. There was always a lot of music around our house. Dad had a very eclectic taste and, unlike a lot of parents, ours were actually quite trendy – they loved the rock 'n' roll music of the day and used to go to dances with Dad wearing the rock 'n' roll regalia. We would listen to records like 'Rock Around The Clock' and 'Tutti Frutti' around the house.*

The arrival of my youngest brother Kim, when I was about nine years old, was fairly major. Up until then we'd all thought the family was complete, but then Mum became pregnant again. She had always wanted a girl – I would have been Martina, Glenn would have been Glenda – so when she got pregnant again she thought "Okay, this is definitely the girl that I've always wanted". That was why he was called Kim, because in her mind, it was a "she". So, Kim was born – another little willy – and my mother just tilted. She became very depressed and got very poorly and we all had to take up the slack, in the way that families do. Ed would say, "Mart, baby's nappy needs changing – your turn," and I would say "No, no, I can't deal with that – no, no, please!" So he would go "Come on, mate, I'll pay you sixpence," to which I would reply "I've got homework to do – make it a shilling!" – he would actually pay me to change the nappy. I thought Kim was a gorgeous little thing and I'd come home from school and feed him, change his clothes and his nappy and generally take care of him like a mother. This created a really strong bond between Kim and I, which lasted right up until he passed away in 2003. By the time Kim was about eighteen months old, we had to convey to my mother that this was a boy, not a girl, because she wouldn't cut his hair and she'd dress him in girly clothes. One day Ed just took the bull by the horns and cut all his hair off – my mother was in tears. We all had to get over it and move on, and I think we coped with the situation pretty well.

When I was about seven years old I got very poorly. Mum called the doctor and I was diagnosed with what he referred to as "congestion of the lungs". After the illness he told us that he did not want to use the word "pneumonia" because he knew that my Mum would worry herself stupid because my father had contracted it a few times through getting cold and wet working on the fire brigade. This illness was a particularly traumatic experience for me. I'm not sure whether it was my illness, or the drugs I was prescribed to cure it, but I found myself hallucinating. I'd be laying there and the ceiling would turn into a huge great raindrop that would plop down onto the bed. There would be hundreds of vermin, things running around in the room, pillows would turn into a bunch of sticks – it was awful. When I eventually got over it I was left feeling very depressed; almost like I was locked in a glass case. People would be talking to me and I would hardly be able to hear them – I didn't have any desire to want to engage in conversation. Possibly that's a natural protection mechanism when you've been seriously ill, but it made me feel very depressed and isolated. It was very unpleasant and I felt very lonely. This lasted for a few weeks. Eventually it lifted but every so many years it would come back if

I was poorly or run down and I would find myself back in this glass case again – it was a horrible feeling. As a kid I hadn't known quite how ill I'd really been. Illnesses are a double-edged sword – they're very depressing and threatening but when you've been through an illness you gain a new perspective on life, having lived to see another day. That whole episode gave me a new perspective and I would say it was a pivotal point in me becoming what I later became, although I'd blanked it from my mind until quite recently, because it was such a heavy unpleasant experience.

As a teenager, I was into the usual things that interested young guys – football, girls, fighting. I was quite keen on stock-car racing and to this day I like nothing more than to get down to Plough Lane in Wimbledon and watch all these brave madmen drive around a track in bangers, crashing into each other. It's anarchic, it's an enactment of complete madness, but I love it. I would love to have driven one of those cars myself. My brother Kim did, but I never got around to it – I've always loved motor racing.

Above anything else music was my main love and I was prepared to listen to anything and everything. I can remember going to Shiphay Youth Club, which was affiliated to the church where I had been a choir boy, and sipping my very first ever taste of Coca-Cola. Just as I did that the Shadows came on with 'Apache' – it was a synchronistic moment. It was magic, and I thought "Wow, this is something else." The Shadows, for any teenage kid growing up in the sixties, were quite an influence. Later there were the Beatles, the Kinks, the Who – lots of great bands. I used to think Adam Faith was great because he wore a pair of white winkle-pickers. What am I doing now in 2012? Going onstage every night in a pair of white winkle-pickers! I also listened to a lot of blues – Muddy Waters, Howlin' Wolf, Buddy Guy – as well as jazz artists like Jack McDuff. I also discovered Woody Guthrie when I got into Bob Dylan and heard that he was a fan. I always loved the fact that he wrote songs about real life and nitty gritty emotional issues and social comment. I also loved the genuine sincerity that came through in the way the guy sang.

As for learning to play an instrument myself, it all started as a result of doing a paper round. Towards the end of my paper round lived a kid I knew from Grammar School called Micky Pring. Both he and his brother Bob played guitar. Micky was pretty good and one day I asked him if he would show me a few things on the guitar. I used to finish my paper round, knock on his door and we'd sit around playing guitar. He had a Harmony guitar, which was a copy of a Gibson 335 – a great guitar. I used to play his brother's acoustic, which only had five strings on it. Soon after that I got my own semi-acoustic guitar, and then a little later I bought a Harmony six-string, although it was not quite as posh a model as Micky had. Over a period of about a year, Micky taught me the basics and by that time I was pretty decent on guitar. I could listen to Beatles albums and work out the chords and what was going on. Of course, this was not the first musical tuition I had received. When I'd been in the church choir, I'd learned to sing and was taught to read from sheet music, but I don't particularly subscribe to that written language of music. Obviously prior to the advent of tape recorders, the only way to record music was to write it down, but for me it became irrelevant once there was a tape recorder, because you could express and store your ideas onto that medium. My brother Glenn also began to play guitar.

> **GLENN TURNER:** *I had a girlfriend when I was about twelve years old who had a nice guitar, which I would play at lunch breaks. I eventually joined the school band – I was surprised to be asked as I didn't think I was good enough. I pretty much taught myself to play and had no formal tuition, although Martin and I did used to study a book called 500 Chords For the Guitar.*

Glenn and I would play together, learning the Shadows and Beatles hits of the day, and that really was the birth of our first band, The Torinoes, which was formed in November 1963. The first gig we ever played was at Foxhole Youth Club, Paignton. Someone at the youth club had heard that we could play and asked us to do a "booking", so we said "Yeah, of course." They asked "You have got a group and all the equipment, haven't you?" to which we replied "Yeah, sure we do." We actually had an amp between us and no drummer, so we had to quickly get our act together and find a drummer. Glenn and I both played guitar, but when it came to forming a band, I switched to bass, so we at least had two elements of the band in place. We had no microphones or PA system, so Glenn made a microphone stand in woodwork at school, and we borrowed Ed's Grundig tape recorder microphone and taped it onto the wooden stand – it was ridiculous and the stand kept falling over because it didn't have a heavy enough base, but it got us off the ground. We got a guy called Phil Hesketh to play drums. We borrowed him from another band and he ended up joining us. Operating as a three-piece we started to play youth clubs. It started off with about one gig a month and gradually built from there. We used to have to get Ed to drive us there as none of us could drive – I was sixteen years old, Glenn was even younger. Ed used to take us in his Ford Cortina and we'd have gear in the boot, on the roof rack, and on our laps. Eventually, as work picked up, we got our own van. Whilst Ed was still travelling with us one night, he came into the dressing room and told us that he had met a couple of girls out front of house that were enthusiastic about his lad's band. We responded by saying "Well you could have at least brought 'em back to say hi", so next time out he did precisely that, and the conversation on the home journey went: "Ed, if you're gonna bring girlies backstage, please try and find the slinky babes out there, will you". Next gig he is learning fast, and developed a real ability to encourage highly attractive young beauties that they really needed to pop back and meet "the band". My brother went out with one girl for months that Ed had chatted up for us. Fun times.

My first bass guitar was a Futurama. It was made of chipboard and had plastic screwed onto the front with a funny little grate in the middle that looked quite cosmic. It was a horrible little thing but it was cheap and got me going. A little later I bought a bass guitar off a guy in another band. It was a home-made instrument, but was quite nicely put together, being quite dainty and petite – I paid him five quid for it and eventually painted it in a psychedelic finish which was the order of the day at that time. I used it right through the sixties, up to the early days of Wishbone Ash. A couple of years ago, I actually rang up Mike Kent, who sold it to me, and said "Do you remember that guitar I bought off you in the sixties?" and he said, "Yeah". So I said "Well, I'm about to take it to the tip, so I thought I'd better call you to see if you wanted it back". He said "Are you crazy? Of course I want it back – don't throw it away". So I said "Okay, I'll bring to down next time I come to Torquay, but I need my fiver back!"

As far as favourite bass players around that time go, I can remember being very fond of Jet Harris of the Shadows. I loved him, not so much because of his bass playing but because of his hairstyle and the fact that he looked really moody. Then there was Bill Wyman, whose laconic style I admired, even though I never based my playing on him. We're total opposites stylistically, but I liked him as a character and he was a fellow bass player I could look up to. I loved the Merseybeats, with Johnny Gustafson on bass. They were one of the first bands I saw live and he was using a Gibson Thunderbird bass, which I absolutely fell in love with on the spot, although it would be a few years before I eventually got my hands on one. Paul McCartney was a great bass player in the melodic sense and I probably picked up quite a lot from him. Later, there was John Entwistle of The Who and also Jack Bruce from Cream – guys who brought the bass more to the forefront, instead of it just being a background instrument.

We were still at school when we first started gigging. In fact, I can remember my Grammar school headmaster, who was a really dour, straight-laced fuddy-duddy who had thrashed me a couple of times in his office, finally giving consent, after three years of battering, to allow a "pop group" performance at the school hall. I was really nervous walking on stage in front of this headmaster, who sat there with a look of sheer horror on his face as we started playing. It was brilliant – the old school dudes being confronted with the outrageous youth of today with their haircuts, pointy shoes and tight trousers. It must have sent a shiver down his spine, but that was fine by me – that was exactly what I wanted to do.

I left Grammar school having under-achieved. The second year at Grammar school I had become top of the class, but after that it was all downhill. From then on it was music, fashion, haircuts and girls. I had no incentive whatsoever to be academic or make an effort at school, although there were certain masters who I liked and would make a token effort for. I was very good at Maths, English, Geography and Art, which equipped me to do what I wanted to do, but I can remember really disliking history. Funny enough, in later years, I have become very interested in history. I left school with not too many qualifications and went through a succession of jobs.

While still at school I'd had a holiday job working in the kitchen at a hotel during the summer and Christmas periods. Obviously there are a lot of hotels in Torquay and they hired and fired people on a fairly regular basis – you could always get a job in a hotel in Torquay. I was shown down to the kitchen, which was in the bowels of the building and was all hot and

Sherwell Valley School, 1957 – future rock star fourth from right, second row from back. Original Empty Vessels drummer Phil Hesketh is also pictured front row, fourth from left.

steamy, and I was put in charge of washing pots and pans. The commis chef said to me "Can you smell something bad?" I said "Yeah, it stinks!" He said "Find it and destroy it." So, I had to find this disgusting smell which turned out to be a saucepan full of peeled potatoes that had been shoved under a shelf and had gone rotten – how disgusting was that? The head chef was a pirate – the first guy I'd seen with a gold tooth, an earring and long hair, tied in a bow. Quite often he'd throw a knife across the kitchen, landing it in a wooden cupboard – he was a pretty intense individual. His girlfriend was one of the chambermaids – they had a very on/off relationship and were always busting up with each other. One afternoon, during the late afternoon break before the evening shift, everyone else had left the kitchen but I had to stay to empty the dishwasher, so I was the last one in there. In the back was a bedroom where we all used to hang out on occasion and in there was a fridge with some ice cream that we could help ourselves to. So I walked into this room to get some ice cream and to my utter astonishment there were these two girls in bed naked, one of whom was the head chef's girlfriend, in the midst of some "lesbanian" encounter. At fifteen years old this was quite educational. I said "Excuse me, ladies, I just wanted to get the ice cream" and made a fairly hasty retreat.

I used to enjoy working in the hotel and it gave me some decent money – that was how I'd earned enough to buy my first guitar. The Christmas bash there was always good. One year the chef did hog's head in aspic as part of the Christmas celebration. They'd been working on it for days – it was a work of art, with peaches for the eyes, piped cream all round it and covered in this jelly. The people in the bar were constantly sending beers down for the kitchen staff and I can remember the others saying "Should you have one, Martin?" and I'd say "Yeah, yeah!" We started at eight in the morning and by ten o'clock in the evening I was completely fried. After we'd finished clearing away we went to a party. That was quite an exciting time for me. It was like rock 'n' roll before rock 'n' roll. It was pretty intense and I loved every minute of it.

CHAPTER TWO

New Rising Star

AFTER I left school I went into an office job that I did for about a year, doing sales analysis for a builders merchants. This basically involved classifying the various goods we sold and making charts up. These charts never seemed to get checked and just sat there for the whole year that I worked for the company. Even at my young age, I could see from the analysis which aspects of the business were making money and which were not, so I went in to explain my findings to the directors of the company – two old fuddy-duddies who shared this office next to me and seemed to be more interested in chatting up the sexy young secretary all day. They gave me the sack for daring to be so precocious as to tell them how they should be running their business. I was absolutely mortified and went home and told my parents I'd been fired. I'd expected them to say "That's not very good, what did you do there?" but they actually said "Well, you don't want to work in that Dickensian old place anyway – move on". I was very appreciative of the way they supported me.

Meanwhile, my brother Glenn had begun working for a guy who built exhibition display furniture. It was only a factory job, but it was quite well paid. They needed someone they could train to make jewellery display stands – conical-shaped units which were made with red velvet and lots of chromium. I committed to staying there for a year. The guy who was the foreman was called Bill Brittan. One morning he barked at me because I arrived at quarter past eight when I should have been there at eight o'clock. He asked if I thought the rules didn't apply to me, so I said "Actually Bill, as you ask that, all the guys who work here are in mortal fear of losing their jobs, because they've all got wives and kids and mortgages. For them to lose their jobs would be serious but personally I don't give a shit – if you wanna sack me, it's no big deal, but you may have noticed that although I may arrive at quarter past eight, I'm only supposed to work until five, but sometimes I'm still here at half past five finishing what I'm doing, so it works at both ends." From that moment on he treated me with a lot more respect.

We worked by day and gigged by night and were really on the case with our repertoire. We used to play anything that people wanted to hear – we were complete and utter tarts and if somebody came up to us and said "Hey, can you play such and such?" we'd either have a go, or put it on the list of songs to learn before we did the next gig. We'd go down the local music shop that also sold records. A friend of ours worked there and we'd go down on a Tuesday afternoon and say "Dave, give us a copy of the Beatles next single", which wasn't released until the Friday, when everyone got paid and could go down there and spend their six-and-eight-pence, but which they already had behind the counter. He would say "No, it's not released until next Friday, I can't give it to you". We'd say "Sod off, Dave, just give it us!" So we'd get a copy of this single, in advance of its release, and by Tuesday evening we would have worked it out – one of us on the needle and the other on the guitar and then switching over. By Wednesday evening we would be out playing the song at a gig and people would say "How the hell can they be playing the Beatles new single? It's not even released yet!"

In the very early days our agent was a chap called Lionel Digby of LMD Entertainments. He ran his operations from the Empire Ballroom in Torquay, which was actually a great gig to play as well. Lionel was a fantastic character – he knew everyone and was well connected with all the agents and managers in London. He also used to promote all the big bands of the day at Torquay Town Hall – Freddie and the Dreamers, Gerry and the Pacemakers, the Rolling Stones, the Who. I went to Torquay Town Hall at quite a young age to see Johnny Kidd and the Pirates – the first big band I had seen live. They had a fantastic guitarist called Mick Green, who was the first guy we had ever seen bend a string on the guitar. He was very impressive and for us it was a case of "Oh my God, have we got to learn to do that now?" To help publicise the shows he promoted, Lionel would ride through the town on top of his estate car. He had a seat bolted on the top so he could sit with his legs dangled over the windscreen. He usually had some scantily-clad blonde next to him and he would be wearing tight trousers, cowboy boots and hat, and a belt of bullets, complete with a holster and gun. There would be two wooden horses bolted to either side of the vehicle, with ropes going up to the top to make it look like a stage coach. As he rode through the main street of town, he would fire his gun and speak through a loud-hailer, telling everyone about the gig that weekend. Although he was only firing blanks, it created quite a scene. Can you imagine anyone getting away with that nowadays?

There was one occasion when Lionel came to a gig with us down in darkest Cornwall. We were driving back together and we stopped off at a bowling alley in Plymouth at about 2.30 in the morning, because it was one of the few places you could get a bite to eat and a coffee. We were sitting around chatting when all of a sudden we realised we were surrounded by four burly geezers in suits wanting to have a look at Lionel's gun. The gun actually had a firing pin, so it could fire live rounds of ammunition. In fact, we were aware that he did have some live ammunition in the van. Anyway, these guys wanted to have a look at his six-shooter there in the restaurant. They turned out to be cops and promptly arrested him for not producing a gun license. So we were sat there thinking "Ughh, we've got no driver, we're stuck." We were too young to drive at that point so we waited there until about four o'clock when the cops gave Lionel a lift back to the van. Lionel got out of the cop car and was chatting to them. They had the window of the car open and Lionel's parting line was "Okay, I'll give you a ring about that gig at the Policeman's ball." He'd even managed to persuade them to book the band! Lionel was an example of a character that cannot possibly be put down. He had an enthusiasm that could not be suppressed and was always looking to make a booking. He was brilliant with music and always knew what was coming next. Another time, we came off stage at the Empire Ballroom, where we'd finally progressed to headlining the show. As we walked off to rapturous applause, there was Lionel behind the curtain that was draped across the back of the stage, with some sixteen or seventeen year old girl up against the wall, with his trousers down and I'll leave the rest to your imagination. They were crazy days – a rock 'n' roll initiation. But we loved Lionel, even though he could be a bit of nightmare at times when it came to getting money out of him. We had fantastic fun during those days.

On 2 October 1964, I joined the Musicians Union. Back then that

was something you were encouraged to do by agents to demonstrate that you were bona fide. Also, occasionally you would come up against a dodgy venue or promoter who didn't want to pay you. If you were a Musicians Union member you could report them to the union and they would take up your case for you. Generally, we didn't find we needed to call on their services too often.

In October 1965 we changed the name of our band. I was never that crazy on the Torinoes.

Progressive Mart, 1965 – taken years before the term "progressive rock"

It didn't really have any relevance to us, Torino being a town in Italy. In those days we had the name painted on the back of our van. We had changed our van and we thought we may as well have a new name for the band to paint on the new van. Empty Vessels was something I thought of and was derived from the phrase "Empty Vessels make the most noise". It gave us a sales-pitch and I really liked the name, so we changed it – new van, new name!

By the Spring of 1966, Brian Roberts had come on board as our new agent/manager. While Lionel had done a great job for us in the very early days of the band, we were looking to travel further afield and generally get more dates in the diary. Brian was based in Exeter and his agency Starline Entertainments really did help increase the band's workload. He became more than just an agent – he really was our first manager and a very good job he did too.

> **BRIAN ROBERTS:** *I worked as a projectionist at the Savoy Cinema in Exeter and we used to get lots of big stage shows in the sixties. As no agency existed in Exeter to help bands get work, I started Starline in the mid-sixties after becoming friendly with a Torquay agent called Lionel Digby. I thought I could do the same as him for Exeter groups. I started with a dozen groups and cabaret acts. The idea seemed very popular so I rented an office in Exeter city centre and hired a full time secretary to help me cope with the volume of work I was getting. I hired the Empty Vessels for some bookings and they seemed a nice bunch of guys and talented but Lionel couldn't get them a lot of work. They were the first group from outside Exeter that I thought I could manage and business was good so I was very pleased to add them to my roster of talent.*

We had also had a couple of changes in the band line-up along the way. For a brief period we experimented with a four-piece line-up with Micky Pring – the guy who had taught me to play guitar – joining us on rhythm guitar. Micky was a great rhythm player, but we eventually went back to being a three piece. Our original drummer Phil Hesketh was solid – a good guy, a good drummer. His older brother Brian was also a drummer and he was quite revered in our neck of the woods because he was in a band called the Barracudas, who had been around since the very early days and were a really good band. Phil kind of had an added kudos because of this, but he eventually got himself a girlfriend who he had met at one of our gigs at Newton Abbott rugby football club and he wanted to spend more time with her, so a guy called Adrian Smith came in. He was a bit wilder, which we liked because we were getting into groups like the Who by that point. He was good at doing that kind of high energy stuff, but he was only around for a while. He had a strange kind of relationship with his step-father, who tried to muscle in on the band's management. Glenn and I were instinctively not happy about this. It caused problems in the end and inevitably our ways parted.

> **GLENN TURNER:** *I remember Phil Hesketh as being good-humoured, reliable and rock steady as drummer, although not outstanding. I think he was under pressure from his parents who didn't like him being in a rock 'n' roll band and wanted him to go to college and learn a trade. Adrian Smith was more dynamic – like Keith Moon junior. He played with such energy that he would lose several pounds in weight through sweating on stage – he was magnetic. Unfortunately he seemed to think he was worth more money and demanded a minimum fee. This caused bad feeling as we had always split the gig fees evenly. Martin and I were not happy with his attitude and decided that we had to replace him.*

This is where Steve Upton enters the picture. Steve was born in Wrexham, Wales on 24 May 1946, but had grown up in Exeter, where he lived with his mother. He started playing drums at the age of sixteen at technical college when some of his classmates said they were forming a band and asked if anyone could play drums. Steve's first band the Scimitars became

On stage with Steve Upton – earliest known live shot, 1967.
Steve and I bonded immediately both musically and personally

fairly popular around the Torquay area, playing Shadows covers. When they eventually split, Steve joined a blues band called the Devarks, who even managed to tour the German club circuit, appearing at the famous Star Club in Hamburg, where the Beatles had played in their early days. We knew of Steve through seeing him play with the Devarks and really liked his drumming. He had an original style, partly through being right-handed but having learned to play on a friend's drum-kit, which was set up for a left-handed player. Consequently Steve always set up his drums left-handed. The Devarks broke up while in Germany and Steve returned to Exeter, where he rented a small terraced cottage and took up a day job while continuing to play with bands at night. I remember Steve telling me that whilst the Devarks were out in Germany, a German band appearing with them asked if they could help give them an English name. There were four guys in the German band so they suggested something along the lines

Empty Vessels dressing room - Glenn,
Martin and Steve 1968

of the Fortunes, the Four Seasons, etc. "How about skin?" said one of the English band members, explaining that skin was your body's covering, so the German band were delighted and promptly had the name put on their bass drum – The Four Skins.

After The Empty Vessels had played a gig at Plymtree Village Hall on 16 July 1966, we bumped into Steve at a little haunt where all the local musicians used to hang out after gigs – a café run by an old girl called Dirty Dot. She used to enjoy staying up late and so kept the doors open until whenever everyone was ready to go home at three or four o'clock in the morning. She really was "dirty" – not in the way the word is used these days but in the true meaning of the word – she really was quite unclean. We would often hang out at Dirty Dot's after gigs and on this occasion Steve came cruising in there and we began chatting. Glenn and I leaned on him to come and get involved with us. That suited him at the time as he was ready for a change.

> **GLENN TURNER:** *I spotted Steve in there within five minutes and it was me who first approached him and asked him what he was doing. I asked him if he would be interested in playing with us. He said that he had already been offered two gigs that day and so would need twenty four hours to think about it. It didn't take long for him to get back to us though.*

Steve Upton joined The Empty Vessels and we began rehearsing with him on 20 July 1966, prior to playing our first gig together at the Paulk Arms, Torquay on 23 July 1966. Steve and I gelled as a rhythm section very quickly and I instinctively knew that his addition was going to be a great asset to the band.

> **GLENN TURNER:** *Steve was a great drummer, with a style that was similar to Ginger Baker. He was jazzier than most of the drummers around at that time. His playing was very interesting and expressive, with great use of the tom-toms. I had no complaints at all with Steve's drumming, although personally I found things a little difficult with him. Martin and I had working class roots, whereas Steve seemed a bit posher. This made me feel a little alienated at times and I got the impression that Steve was not that impressed with me and, perhaps, thought I wasn't good enough.*

Just a few days after Steve had joined we found ourselves opening for the Who at major theatre shows in Barnstaple and Torquay. We loved the Who. They brought back the raw, wild energy of an English rock band that could just about play. Prior to the Who there had been a big thing about soul music – we'd played shows at Exeter Civic Hall with people like Geno Washington and the Ram Jam Band. I've got nothing against soul music at all, and was quite into it. For getting on the floor and dancing with a girl it was brilliant, but because we were a three-piece band and none of us were black, it was not easy music to play, although we did play some soul songs because we had to. When the Who burst onto the scene they really were a shot in the arm. Being essentially a three-piece with a singer, we could reproduce what they were doing and played a lot of their songs – we loved their energy. The first thing I remember about them coming on stage the first night we played with them was a coca-cola bottle that came flying across the stage, hit something and smashed into a million pieces. Everyone gasped in horror and then up like a genie out of a bottle jumped Keith Moon. They always had a certain angst about them, especially between Pete Townshend and Roger Daltrey. I also remember John Entwistle using wire-wound bass strings. At that time you couldn't buy wire-wound bass strings in the West Country, only tape-wound. On this occasion John decided to take his bass strings off and put some new ones on, because he liked his sound really twangy. I noticed that he'd just thrown the old set away, so I grabbed them and that was how I first got my hands on some wire-wound bass strings.

By this time we had decided that, rather than just playing the hits of the day, we wanted to learn to write our own songs, like the Beatles and the Stones were doing. To start with we would poach other people's ideas, but only in an effort to fire our own creativity into action. These early efforts, I have to say, were so bad it was ridiculous, but it's a bit like a siphon – unless you can start the flow you can never get to what's underneath. By the end of the sixties there were maybe three or four songs that I'd written that I actually thought were pretty good. There was one called 'Magdalene Mansions' which was a little bit, dare I say it, Hendrix-y, but maybe that was because we were a three-piece. There was another that sounded a bit like the record Status Quo ended up doing, 'Pictures of Matchstick Men'. I had one before that called 'Matchbox Man', about a guy who sold matchboxes on the street. Looking back it was probably a little naïve, but I can remember being very proud of it at the time. You have to start somewhere and as the Chinese proverb says, "Even the longest journey must start with the first step".

> **GLENN TURNER:** *To start with I was probably the keenest to get into writing our own material, but eventually Martin pursued it in a much more active way. There was also a lot of co-writing between the three of us, including Steve, with everyone throwing their ideas into the pot. The music we were writing was in the psychedelic hard rock style popular at that time. We were heavily into Cream and I was hugely influenced by Jimi Hendrix. We also tried to develop interesting harmonies.*

By this time, we had built up quite a circuit of venues to play in the West Country. You have to remember that back then a lot of areas down there didn't even have television. In those days, when there was nowhere near the amount of entertainment we have now, when a band was playing a lot of people would come out to see it. In addition to the work Brian Roberts obtained for us we also used to communicate with John White at Exonian Entertainments, another Exeter based agency.

Outside our first agent Lionel Digby's office, 1968

> **BRIAN ROBERTS:** *When I took the Empty Vessels on they were very commercial, playing all danceable material. This was part of their contract as I had to provide bands for people to dance to. I think they were not too keen on this and gradually started including their own material which, regrettably, did not go down well with the audience or the hirers and getting them bookings got harder as they strived to go their own way during the latter part of the sixties when music styles changed – Bob Dylan, Jimi Hendrix and Donavan were in the charts but people in a club couldn't dance to them. Gradually I was being told by hirers not to send them as their musical influences continued to change. This eventually led to most work drying up and a mutual decision to let them seek out their own work.*

The Lansdowne Ballroom in Torquay was a really good gig. It was right next to the police station. It was run by a couple called Ted and Wendy Richings. He was an old cigar-smoking frog-like guy who wore thick heavy tinted glasses. Together they ran a dancing school. His wife was about twenty years younger than him and was great looking, busty and always immaculately turned out. I'd even joined the dancing school when I was about thirteen years old, just for the pleasure of being able to dance with her. Eventually when they realised this ballroom dancing thing was not earning them as much money as they would have liked, they started to have "beat groups" play there on a regular basis. It was a great gig – hot and sweaty, everyone packed into the room like sardines, just a hole in the wall for a bar, and the sound in there was raw. We played it lots of times and also saw a lot of other bands there including the Downliner Sect, the Soul Agents and the Better Days, a popular Plymouth band at that time. I take my hat off to Ted and Wendy for keeping the venue going for years. I don't think their heart was really in rock music, but they loved the social aspect of it.

Newton Abbott Rugby Football Club was another gig we would play regularly, mainly because they would have us there on a Thursday evening – you could always get gigs on a Friday and Saturday but midweek gigs were harder to find. Newton Abbott was about seven miles from Torquay. It had always been a railway town and in those days it was pretty rough. We used to play in the Rugby Football Club bar, which was a long bar with a decent dance area and a stage about three inches high. There was always some incident or another there. You would have all the guys holding their pints of beer at the back of the room and then all the girls on the dance floor really getting into the music. These great big rugby player guys would look down on us with our custom clothes and back-combed hair thinking "What a bunch of poofs". We'd regularly go outside to get in the van and find that all four tyres had been let down or somebody had shoved a potato up the exhaust pipe. Fights would break out fairly regularly and there was always aggravation of some kind. I can remember on one occasion seeing a chair go up in the air, just like you see in a Wild West movie, where somebody breaks a balsa wood chair over somebody else's head. This, however, was a solid oak chair, which if you hit somebody around the head with you'd probably be looking at a murder charge. Another night this gaggle of guys came careering down through the dance-floor and onto the stage, all punching crap out of each other. They were whirling around with arms and legs flailing everywhere and one of these guys got shoved and knocked over my brand new Vox AC30 amplifier that Ed had signed a high purchase agreement for. I was absolutely furious with this guy. I threw my guitar down, went after him and punched him so hard that I dislocated a knuckle on my right hand. The follow through was so intense that I actually fell on top of him and broke his arm. Now, this was a serious fifteen-stone rugby player – not somebody that I was built to deal with – but he'd knocked my amp over so he was going to pay, as far as I was concerned. Later I heard that he was going to kill me for putting him out of action on the rugby field for three months. Fortunately his girlfriend really liked our band and she told him that he was not to lay a finger on me. So, I managed to escape that one.

I got beaten up badly at a gig that we played in Ilfracombe one New Year's Eve. I'd taken some girl back to her home in the band's van and then arrived back at the gig to find they'd locked all the doors and there was a party going on inside which was supposed to be for us and anyone else who was invited. As I pulled up, there were four squaddies outside. I was wearing an Army-type jacket which they informed me I had no right to be wearing because I was not in the Army like they were. "Take it off now", they ordered. Now, my response, as a punchy young teenager, was to tell them to "Fuck off". I was jumped on by three of them at the same time. These were kids who had been trained to fight and so I had a hell of a fight on my hands. I can remember wrestling with one of them and ending up on the floor. Then another guy kicked me in the back of the head and I started losing consciousness. The fourth guy was much bigger than the other three and he didn't actually get involved. In fact, I heard him calling the others off. He intervened and possibly saved my life. That took me a good few weeks to recover from.

Back in the sixties, the West Country was a pretty dangerous place and the Neanderthal factor was a lot higher than it is nowadays. One had to keep one's eyes open for aggravation. I learned pretty quickly that a band is a sitting target and that you cannot take issue with members of the paying public because if they don't get you personally, they'll just go outside and take it out on your vehicle or equipment. We soon learned that it was best to keep the reason we were there – to entertain people – in focus and not get involved in whatever was going on around us. This was difficult for me, because I was a punchy little sod. Time and time again I would pitch in totally fearlessly, knowing I'd probably end up with blood all over me. But I didn't give a shit – it was more important to get across to people that I deserved a bit more respect. Gradually I realised that I did have to tone down my aggressive behaviour and I have to say that rock music is a good vehicle for getting rid of that young teenage testosterone-driven energy. I recognised that with lots of other bands – The Who reeked of it when they first started. I also remember us supporting the Kinks at Torquay Town Hall on one occasion and Ray and Dave Davies were fighting in the dressing room, as brothers do.

So, as the sixties went on, I learned to control my hot head and go round a problem rather than through it. A good example would be the night we supported Christine Perfect (later Christine McVie, of Fleetwood Mac fame) at Queens Hall in Barnstaple. During the gig two local families happened to bump into each other. Somebody in one family had apparently got a daughter in the other family pregnant and one almighty fight broke out – it really was something to behold. Within twenty or thirty seconds there must have been about thirty people involved, slugging each other big time. Bouncers intervened and the fight then left the building and spilled out onto the street, followed by most of the audience. It was the end of the gig and we were packed up ready to go home. We decided that rather than stick around and watch this monkey show, we would get in the van and drive off. So we went around the other side of the building, got in the van and drove down the street. It was a one way system and as we turned the corner we ran into what only could be described as a riot. The whole main

TERMS AND CONDITIONS

The Management reserves the right to refuse admission and to change the performance or the cast without prior notification in the event of illness or any unavoidable cause.

Latecomers cannot be admitted to their seats until an interval or suitable break in performance.

Cameras, tape recorders and video equipment are not permitted. Mobile phones must be switched off in the auditoria.

Tickets cannot be refunded unless a performance is cancelled, or abandoned when less than half the performance has taken place.

Replacements cannot be provided for lost tickets sold for unreserved events.

When booking tickets you will be asked for your name, address and telephone number. This information may be used to inform you about events and other developments at our venue, including fundraising. We may also pass your details to other arts organisations that may be of interest to you. If you do not want your details used in any of these ways please inform Ticket Office.

Keep up to date with the latest information about forthcoming shows and events at Lighthouse. Call the Ticket office on 0844 406 8666 to join our mailing list or check online at www.lighthousepoole.co.uk

Poole Arts Trust Ltd is a registered charity no 275961 - VAT registered no 323 4951 65

Lighthouse
POOLE'S CENTRE FOR THE ARTS

0844 406 8666
www.lighthousepoole.co.uk

Supported using public funding by
ARTS COUNCIL
ENGLAND

Supported using public funding by
ARTS COUNCIL
ENGLAND

CUSTOMER RECEIPT
LIGHTHOUSE POOLE
21 KINGLAND ROAD , POO
DORSET BH15 1UG
21/10/2014 14:07:20
RECEIPT NO.:3563
MID:XXX65802
TID:XXXX3380
AID:A0000000031010
VISA DEBIT
XXXX XXXX XXXX 8501
PAN SEQ NO. : 03
ICC
SALE GBP4[illegible]

TOTAL GBP4[illegible]

PLEASE DEBIT MY ACCOUN
PIN VERIFIED
PLEASE KEEP THIS RECE[
FOR YOUR RECORDS
AUTH CODE: 252024

Lighthouse
POOLE'S CENTRE FOR THE ARTS

Kingland Road, Poole, Dorset BH15 1UG

Lighthouse
POOLE'S CENTRE FOR THE ARTS

street was filled with people punching the crap out of each other. Just one police car had attended – a little Morris Minor – and the cop couldn't even get out of the car. He was stuck, surrounded by this seething mass of bloodlust humanity. So, we backed up and thought "Okay, it says one-way and we only want to go one way and that's out of here", so we drove the wrong way up a one-way street and got the hell out of Barnstaple.

We went on to support lots of other name acts on their visits to the West Country. I can remember playing Torquay Town Hall, supporting P.P.Arnold, backed by the Nice, featuring Keith Emerson and Davy O'List. Keith Emerson was doing exactly the same stuff I would see him doing when Wishbone Ash played alongside Emerson, Lake and Palmer a few years later, stabbing the organ with knives and rocking it around. Many of the bands we supported contained members who would later go on to bigger and better things – acts such as Tomorrow (who featured vocalist Keith West and guitarist Steve Howe, later of Yes/Asia), Episode Six (with Ian Gillan and Roger Glover, later of Deep Purple), The Gods (with Greg Lake of ELP fame and future Uriah Heep members Ken Hensley and Lee Kerslake), and the Herd (with Peter Frampton and Andy Bown). We also supported sixties singer Tommy Quickly. He was completely drunk on stage but his backing band were great – they turned out to be Status Quo, although at this time they were known as Traffic Jam.

We played Exeter Civic Hall quite a bit, supporting various bands. We supported Fleetwood Mac there, with Peter Green, Jeremy Spencer and Danny Kirwan on guitars. By this time, we'd made friends with a guy called Les Adey who was the lighting man for Principal Edwards Magic Theatre – an outfit that mixed rock and theatre. In those days they used to do these psychedelic oil light shows. Principal Edwards had this slinky blonde gorgeous babe called Ruth. I'm not sure if she sang, but she was a fantastic dancer with a phenomenal figure. Les wanted to join us at this event, come onstage during one of our songs and physically paint Ruth, who would be dancing on stage in a bikini. This was in the era of what were described as "happenings". We were totally up for this, but rather than gently dabbing oils onto her virtually naked body with a paintbrush, it ended up with Les pouring the whole bucket of paint over her. It was fairly chaotic and Mick Fleetwood was more than a little miffed when some of the paint ended up on his drum kit.

We also supported Led Zeppelin at Exeter Civic on 19 December 1968. It was one of their first ever gigs, prior to the release of their first album, and the poster advertising the show read "Lead Zeppelin, ex-Yardbirds". At the sound-check in the afternoon Jimmy Page got really upset because his Gibson Les Paul guitar had been stolen from the dressing room. They questioned all of us because we were all sharing a dressing room and everyone had access, although it was perfectly obvious none of us had grabbed it. Jimmy was absolutely mortified because it was a really precious instrument that he was immensely fond of. He was close to tears. We never did find out what happened.

Following us on the bill was a band called Mick Farren's Social Deviants. Mick Farren was considered to be a rock poet. His band members were clad in leather and had a kind of New York vibe about them, not unlike the Ramones several years later. When the Social Deviants went on, someone in the audience didn't like them and tossed a beer glass at the stage. It didn't break but Mick Farren picked it up and threw it back into the audience, which was a fairly dangerous thing to do. Everybody just leapt out of the way and a shard of this glass went through the ankle of a friend of ours – a guy called Charlie Charlton, who was the singer in a band called the Package Deal and much later sang in a band that my brothers Glenn and Kim had called Cat Iron. Charlie had a really nasty cut on his ankle and got taken to hospital, while other members of the audience were so incensed with the act of violence that they actually stormed the stage. I can remember being in the dressing room. It was quite peaceful with just the Led Zeppelin guys and us in there, when suddenly the door burst open and the Social Deviants came scurrying into the dressing room, followed by what looked like the entire audience. There were a bunch of guys who wanted to kill the Deviants. Fortunately the bouncers got involved and managed to shove the audience back out to where they belonged, but it was a fairly scary moment. The Deviants ended up leaving the gig and going out on the street to see if they could spot some of the guys who had thrown punches. Apparently they did find some of them and then got involved in another fight. I don't think they went back on stage after the kerfuffle, so Led Zeppelin went on. They were absolutely brilliant – I'd seen very few bands in that league and Cream and the Who were the only two bands who came anywhere close to what Led Zeppelin were doing around that time. I went out and bought their first album as soon as it came out the following month.

Led Zeppelin were fantastic, but it was a crazy night. Eventually we managed to extricate ourselves from this chaotic scene of mayhem and as we walked out of the building we kind of patted ourselves on the back for having emerged unscathed. Then we got to the van and found that somebody had busted the back doors open, fished out Glenn's 4x12 speaker cabinet, slashed all of the speakers with a Stanley knife and somehow managed to stuff it underneath the back axel. They'd also let all of the tyres down. So, we didn't come out totally unscathed after all.

In those days every gig was an adventure of one kind or another. At a gig at the School Hall in Martock, Somerset, we pulled up at the hall, the other guys went off to get something to eat and I sat in the van relaxing. Suddenly there was this almighty smash. This guy had come round the bend and ploughed right into the front of our van. I got out and went over and he couldn't even get out of his car. In fact, I'm glad he didn't because there was an Alsatian dog in there that was absolutely freaking out. Anyway, the guy staggered out and could hardly stand up – I could smell alcohol on his breath. Then he accused me of being on the wrong side of the road as we'd come round the bend. I said "Mate, we weren't even moving. This vehicle is parked". He started arguing and I realised we had a major problem on our hands, so I quickly ran over to where I knew Glenn was and told him to phone the cops immediately because I thought the guy was likely to drive off. Eventually, a cop rolled up from the next town and arrested this guy. During the course of the evening the guy's son rolled up at the gig and got a little bit confrontational. Basically he just wanted to know why we'd called the police. Apparently everybody in Martock knew his Dad. He was a well known drunk. Both he and his wife were alcoholics and normally the local cop would pick him up and make sure he got home safely, but this night the local cop had been in bed with the flu and they'd sent a guy from another town. Of course, he was charged with drink driving and I had to go to court to give evidence. He pleaded not guilty and tried to slither out of it. He got his barrister to try to slander me by saying I had been in the back of the vehicle with a fourteen year old girl, which was so sleazy and totally untrue. After I'd given evidence there was a short break and when we returned the guy changed his plea to guilty. I don't think he went to jail, but he certainly got banned and received a fairly hefty fine.

Growing up in Torquay was a double-edged sword, really. In the summer Torquay was the most wonderful place on the planet – everyone would be in good spirits and there would be zillions of parties going on. In the winter, however, everyone would go home and everything would be closed up. Torquay has got to be one of the wettest places in the winter, and I couldn't wait to get out of there. The summers were great though – the place would be full of holiday makers and the population doubled, or even tripled. Then of course there were girls and lots of little holiday romances that would last for a week. There were a lot of French guys used to come over. They really had it down – they had great clothes, and used all the right smelling lotions. They were very slick operators and we used to relate to them as the "opposition". In those days there were also a lot of Swedish girls who used to come over. They were beautiful, with blonde hair, great skin, lovely white teeth and everything. There was quite a high availability there and I did make friends with quite a few of them over the years. It freaked me out one year when three of them all came back at the same time – it was like juggling plates trying to see them all. At a gig we played at St. Luke's Hall in Torquay, we arrived at five or six o'clock, set up, all ready to go. We went out through the stage door to get something to eat and arrived back about 7.30 to play the gig. We walked out on stage to find the hall was full of about two hundred Swedish girls and only about three or four blokes in the room. It was like being a fox let loose in a hen coup – I did tend to keep fairly busy on that front!

At another gig, I'd made friends with a young lady from Chelmsford who was on holiday – we got on like a house on fire. We were in the band van, which had a bench seat in the back in front of the equipment, having a "brief encounter" – I was wearing a St. Christopher and nothing else. Suddenly there was a blinding light came in through the windscreen and a voice shouted out "What's your date of birth, girl?" I realised that I was being observed by the "nipple heads", as we used to call the cops, and that I didn't have a clue how old this girl was. Fortunately she came straight back to them with her date of birth. She was sixteen, so technically was allowed to be doing what she was doing, but for me there was the realisation that these cops had probably been watching me through the windscreen. You've probably never seen a willy go limp so quickly in your life! My little brain was exploding with the thought of my mother reading on the front of the local newspaper that a rock musician had been caught with an under aged girl! It was a very scary moment, but when I heard a chuckle from this cop's mate outside I realised that even policemen have got a sense of humour, although we were told to not be seen there again. Probably the funniest thing about that little incident is that it took place in a sweet, picturesque little hamlet-come-village a couple of miles from the seafront, called Cockington.

I fell in love with a girl called Sue at a venue we played in Exeter called the Quay Club. She had been Steve Upton's girlfriend for a while – Steve and I shared a lot of things other than music. I can remember dancing on the "disco dance floor" with her to Andy Williams' record 'You're Just Too

Good to Be True' and I related to it because the lyric expressed exactly how I felt about this girl. We ended up going out for quite a long time although Steve wasn't thrilled to bits about it, needless to say. That was one of my big romances, but her father never approved of me. He wanted her to go on to university and be educated. Recognising that I was a musician, he considered me a scruffy little oik and did not encourage the relationship at all. Sue was shunted off to university and the relationship got left up in the air, which was not good, as she haunted me for many years – as I later wrote in a song.

The Quay Club was also where I met Maurn – the lady who would become my first wife. Maurn first appeared at the Empty Vessels' gigs on the arm of a mod chappie by the name of John. On the other arm was her handbag, and that was about it. John did all the talking and she just listened and said virtually nothing – she was still only 15 years of age, I later discovered. We even used to refer to her as "the dumb blonde" – not in a derogatory way but purely because she said so little and we didn't know her name. One evening I found myself at the Quay Club in Exeter, as was the tendency with unattached males in search of action in the late sixties. I was surprised when a hand reached out and a voice said "Hello", firstly because I had never seen her other than on the arm of John boy, and secondly because I now had the honour of hearing her voice – and what a voice! I was amazed at just how perceptive she was, and really about as far away from a "dumb blonde" as you could get. I don't think I'd ever said a word to her before and I'd certainly never seen her out without her boyfriend, so I said "Where's John?" She said "Oh, I finished with him". I said "What? You shoved your boyfriend?" I was quite taken aback because she always seemed so meek and mild. As we slowly got to know each other I became aware of this mighty wise old spirit in a young and petite little package. We walked and talked and became great friends who really enjoyed each other's company. It was quite a cerebral relationship, which was refreshing for me. In retrospect, I'm not very proud of my attitude to girls as a young man. I did used to get about a bit and

I treated girls fairly roughly emotionally, although never physically, but
I forged a really good relationship
with Maurn over the period of a year
or more. I was already planning on
becoming a "professional" musician
and I'd previously been apprehensive
about becoming encumbered in a
relationship that could jeopardise
my ambitions. Destiny, however, had
already swung into action.

*In the bedroom of the house shared
with Steve Upton – Exeter, 1968*

By this stage Steve Upton and I had become very close. He and I had
bonded brilliantly from the day he'd joined the band, both personally
and musically. We were both very positive thinking and had this kind of
youthful belief that we could actually programme our subconscious minds
to produce the reality that we wished for. I looked up to Steve because,
although he was only about eighteen months older than me, he was very
independent for a guy of his age. He lived on his own whereas I was still
living with my family. Steve rented a small cottage in Exeter, which he had
originally been sharing the place with a couple of guys who went to Exeter
University. When they left Steve suggested that I move in with him. It was
really basic accommodation – a three floor house with just one room on
each floor. Eventually Glenn joined us there.

> **GLENN TURNER:** *I'd gotten involved with a girl called Susie*
> *Turner who was a heroin addict. Martin and Steve felt she*
> *was a bad influence and that my relationship with her was*
> *affecting my commitment to the band. They insisted that I*
> *either give up the girl and move into the cottage with them,*
> *or leave the band, so I gave up the girl and moved in with*
> *Martin and Steve. I have happy memories of living there. We*
> *got to know a lot of art students and had a nice social scene.*

Susie Turner (not to be confused with my current wife, also named Susie Turner!) was a state-registered heroin addict who was on a methadone program. She'd been a successful model in London at a young age and was now hooked on this damn drug and was back down in Torquay. The problem was she used to collect waifs and strays. She would provide a roof for any guy who was roaming around without a place to live. It was pretty crazy stuff. One day as I was driving to a gig, Glenn was in the passenger seat and she was sitting in between us. It was late afternoon and I was feeling a little bit tired, so I yawned. The next thing I hear is "Are you feeling tired baby?" So I said "Yeah, a bit. I've had a few late nights, as usual." Then, as I'm driving along, this syringe goes into my leg, straight through my jeans, and she starts banging me up with methadone. Addicts of hard drugs generally tend to be on a mission to recruit as many people as possible because if everyone else is doing it too, it must be "okay". Actually, it never is okay and let's just say she was a misguided but loveable nut-job. Another time I picked Glenn up for a gig and he came out looking as white as a sheet. I said "Are you alright, mate?" and he responded "That fucking schizoid bitch". Apparently she had been ironing her hair to get it straight. Her and Glenn had been having a huge argument and she had thrown the iron at him – still plugged in and red hot. He'd ducked and the iron took a huge chunk of plaster out of the wall.

Steve, as the senior tenant of our house, had the top floor, I had the second floor and Glenn was on the ground floor. Although it was only about twenty miles away from Torquay, for me living away from home for the first time was a big move. Steve introduced me to a lot of grown-up things. He taught me how to go to a shop, buy my own food, bring it home and cook it – I'd never had to do that in my life. He was very important in my development as a person. Steve also eventually took over running the business side of the band. He was very well organised and very good at liaising and communicating with our agents and dealing with the day to day running of the band – something I had done in the early days.

Steve got me a job with a timber yard he was working for in Exeter. He was in the office, while I got offered a job working in the yard. I had to work on a great big bench saw. There was an old codger on one side, shoving the wood through, while I worked on the other end pulling it through off the saw. You had to be careful – one day this guy showed me where he'd sawn his thumb off. We were working outside in a shed with a tin roof and open sides. There was a mad fork lift truck driver called Stan. He'd been involved in scaffolding and apparently he'd been on the side of a lorry one day when all the scaffolding fell off the truck and crushed him. His legs were so badly bent out of shape that he ended up walking a bit like a chimpanzee. He used to call me El, because he knew I was involved in music and the only person he knew in music was Elvis Presley. He would tell me to get on the forks and he would lift me right up into the air and put me on the stack of wood which was about fifteen feet high. I'd then have to break off the wood which in the winter was sometimes frozen solid, put it on the fork lift and then go back down to the ground with it. Forget health and safety – it just didn't exist! One day Stan accidentally drove the fork lift truck in underneath one of the sheds with the forks still up and virtually knocked the shed down. There was a young guy up a ladder on the other side of the shed and he was knocked off the ladder and ended up with a broken pelvis, busted collar bone, broken arms and legs. He was in hospital for three months. Stan could be a bit dangerous. I'll never forget one day I was with him when he suddenly just leapt off the fork lift truck, with this funny chimpanzee walk, with the truck still running, gradually coming to a halt. Then he just unzipped his trousers and started sprinkling in the middle of the yard, while waving at an office block that was about 150 feet away with all the secretaries up there typing away. It was hysterically funny – these guys were complete and utter cowboys! Eventually I got transferred onto driving a small pick-up truck delivering builders materials. I was quite happy about this because it gave me a little more independence. I wasn't in the yard all day long, which could be hard work.

I was out making deliveries on what I now look back on as the "big day". On New Years Eve of 1968, going into 1969, we had been down doing a gig in Redruth, Cornwall at the Flamingo Ballroom. We all ended up at some disc jockey's house until about three in the morning, drinking and smoking cigarettes with no names. We got back to Exeter about half past six in the morning. I got in and said to Steve "I'm going to bed, I'm knackered", and he said "No, you have to go to work." I said "What, me go to work – first of January, freezing cold, no sleep, no food?" He said "If we don't show up the company will know where we were last night." So I said "It's okay for you sat in your office with your fire on, but I'm out in the trenches, mate." Anyway, I did go in. After I'd done the first couple of deliveries which were out in the country I was exhausted, so I stopped and walked down through this field where I knew there was a stream. I thought that if I washed my face in the freezing cold water it would wake me up. It was an amazing morning and the sun was shining through a low mist – you could tell it was going to turn into a nice day eventually. As I washed my face, I stood up and saw a heron flying through the mist. Silently and slowly it went right over my head and as it did so it put the hairs up on the back of my neck. This whole scene was surreal, like a vision. I seem to have some kind of affiliation with the heron – the Africans call it your "bush spirit". The heron seems to appear every time my life is about to take a major change in direction. Anyway, I got back into my van and got all of my work done by about four o'clock. I was on my way back to the yard and only had about another mile to go before I would have been parked up when I passed out at the wheel. Suddenly there was this almighty crash, with grinding metal and breaking glass. I had struck the back of a parked car, going full tilt with no seatbelt on. I smacked against the steering wheel which bent my ribs and smashed my face – my lip was busted and absolutely gushing with blood. The engine was screaming – the throttle was stuck full on. I managed to kick the door open to get out of the vehicle, but I couldn't stand up and kept falling on the floor. Eventually some people dragged me into the side of the road – it was total mayhem. A crowd of people quickly gathered around me and I was sat on this wall like a rabbit with myxomatosis, shivering with blood coming out of my mouth. Everyone was staring at me and eventually a woman came through the crowd and said she was a nurse. She told me that I'd just knocked a few teeth out and that everything would be okay. Meanwhile, someone had managed to turn the engine off and pulled the key out of the ignition. The road was blocked with debris and there were double-decker buses driving on the pavement to get by, as it was rush hour. Eventually the police and ambulance arrived at the same time from different directions and there were blue lights everywhere. The police told me that before they interviewed me I'd have to go to hospital. On the way to the hospital the ambulance guy had a go at me and said "Now, don't you go telling the police a load of lies, because they'll be able to tell from marks on the road and witnesses."

I'm sat there holding my mouth thinking "Why don't you sod off, you old git?" I got to hospital, wearing Ed's coat that was about three sizes too big for me but kept me warm. I'd been in the same clothes for about thirty six hours – I probably stank and I'm sure the doctor stitched me up at arms' length so he didn't have to smell me. Eventually they checked my ribs and said "Yeah, they're bent. Are you getting any pain there?" and I said "No" – I still have bent ribs to this day. I asked if I could go and they said "Have you spoken to the police?" I said "No, where are they?" They said "They should be outside there somewhere." Obviously the doctors and nurses were busy, so I got up, staggered out, and looked around. There were no cops so I made a run for it. I phoned Steve as soon as I got out of the hospital and he said "Yes, I've heard about it. Everyone in town knows about it. Whatever you do, don't tell the cops you've been up all night or else the company will get it in the neck." So I thought "Great. He doesn't give a shit about what kind of state I'm in. All he's worried about is the company." Anyway, I went home and slept for about twelve hours.

The next day I was at home and heard knock-knock-knock on the door. I opened it up and there was this cop stood there. He said "Are you Martin

Turner?" I replied "Yes I am, as a matter of fact." He said "I nearly got thrown out of the police force because of you." Apparently he'd been following the ambulance and collided with some woman driver who didn't see him coming. He'd written the police car off and his superintendent was going to throw him out. So, I pointed out to him that we were in somewhat similar circumstances really. I said "Why don't you come in and we'll have a cup of tea?" Of course, by this time, having slept on the situation, I'd had time to get my story straight as to the reasons for the accident. The way I told it was that there had been a load of money sitting on the passenger seat, which I had picked up from my deliveries that day and had fallen onto the floor when I'd gone over a bump. I knew there was a little panel on the floor which came off to gain access to the battery and that the money could have fallen out onto the street, so I bent down to pick up the firm's money and the next thing I knew – BANG! The police took it all down and they did believe me. I went to court and got a £60 fine and an endorsement.

It was almost like fate had contrived to create this situation and I'd got a warning of it when I'd seen the vision with the heron that morning. As a band, we'd been doing very well in the West Country. We had jobs during the day time and we were busy gigging at night, especially at weekends. We were making plenty of money and the band was very popular. We were doing great and were very happy, but that accident changed everything. One thing the police told me was that if the parked car that I'd hit had not been where it was, I was headed straight for a woman with a baby in a pram. I could have killed both of them and that aspect did my head in – I really beat myself up about that. It took a couple of months for me to recover physically, but for my nervous system to recover from the shock, I would say it took about a year. Maurn stuck by me through all that and helped me to recover and get back on my feet. The accident forced me to confront the reality that I wasn't Superman after all and that I couldn't work all night and all day as well. I came to the logical conclusion that I had to choose whether I wanted to be a professional musician or to continue working at all of these Mickey Mouse jobs that I'd been doing. The accident was the pivotal point in my life when I decided that I had to be a professional musician. From that moment I decided that there was only one place to do that – London.

Aside from gigging pretty intensely during this time, we had also managed to make some demo recordings at various studios. We had travelled to London and recorded at Regent Sound in Denmark Street and R.G. Jones in Wimbledon. In those pre-motorway days travelling up from the West Country in the van with the gear was an eight hour schlepp, but London was where you had to go if you wanted to record, although we did do one recording in Torquay, I think, when they finally got a recording studio together down there. We did eventually cut a single for a German label called Metronome. It was called 'My Son John'. We didn't write it, or the b-side 'Low Toby'. They were songs that had already been written by a tried and tested song-writing team. We would have preferred to have been recording our songs, but our attitude was that it was a foot in the door and that it may lead to something. We actually drove up to London and arrived at Landsdowne Studios in Notting Hill only to be told by the producer that it would actually be a lot quicker if we recorded the backing track with session musicians. We were really pissed off about that, but we had no option but to go along with it. Eventually, because I'd told them that I was not very happy about it, they did let us actually set up and join in and play with microphones on everything, but I suspect – certainly on the a-side – that it was mainly the session guys playing. There was probably more of our playing on the b-side. Although I sang on it and the record went out as The Empty Vessels, a lot of it wasn't really us playing, which we were very unhappy about. Nothing further came from the single deal. We'd send demos in to record companies, but in those days if you were based in the West Country and were trying to get something together in London it was very difficult. We just knew that the capital city was where we needed to be if we were to make it within the music industry and in May 1969 we finally made the move.

1968 – Looking for a route to the big time, perhaps?

CHAPTER THREE

Leaving To Search For Something New

ON 13 MAY 1969 Steve, Glenn and I packed all of our equipment together with a case full of clothes each and headed for London – with nowhere to live! We had talked about doing this for years, but we were having such a great time where we were that there had been no incentive to move. My accident on New Year's Eve changed the whole equation for me, although Steve, at the time, was a little conservative. Steve wanted to give notice and work out a month at his job. He wanted us to save some money before we went so that we would be able to get flats and generally support ourselves, and he was quite right. Steve was that bit older and more responsible whereas I tended to shoot from the hip. I remember my parents' reaction when I told them we were going to London to try to make it in the music business. My mother's reaction was that of a typical mother – "Make sure you've got enough clothes, towels and sheets, dear". Although he had come out with us on our early gigs and had generally been supportive of my interest in music, Ed was unconvinced that I was going to be able to make a career out of music and was sure I was going to be back with my tail between my legs in a couple of months. This was actually quite good for me as it actually gave me something to kick against. It gave me an absolute determination to succeed in order to prove him wrong. Years later, after I had achieved success in the music business, Ed was really quite proud of my accomplishments. He loved music and being around young people and I would send him albums and he would give me feedback. Our manager/agent Brian Roberts was fully supportive of our decision to move to London.

> **BRIAN ROBERTS:** *I was finding it quite hard to keep sending them back to the limited venues in the region. They needed to go to London if they wanted to continue, or break up if they stayed in the region. I was hopeful that they would find an audience that really appreciated them more and that they could achieve what they wanted. It was a very brave decision at the time and I knew they had no choice. They went to London with my blessing. I have fond memories of The Empty Vessels. Martin and Glenn were very keen on succeeding in the music business and were polite, friendly and eager to please. Martin was very good at organising personal things within the structure of the band and was always very diplomatic and polite with me. The boys really needed his creativeness and ambition and their subsequent success was proof of this. I remember being very impressed with Steve Upton and how well he fitted into their style. They were always a pleasure to be with and I wish now that I had been able to give them more of my time. I've no complaints at all and have fond memories of The Empty Vessels.*

When we arrived in London we knocked on the door of the only guy we knew there – Phil Dunne, a recording engineer at Advision studios. He came to the door and said "Wow, what are you guys doing here?" We said "Well, we said we were going to come to London one day and here we are." He said "Oh my God, you're kidding me? Why didn't you let me know?" Phil immediately found us a bedsit in Chalk Farm and that's where we lived for the first few months.

Shortly before we had moved to London, we'd changed the name of our band to Tanglewood. As we were going to London to start from scratch in the music business, we thought we may as well pick a new name but, with hindsight, the change was fairly pointless as the new name only lasted five minutes. Since we'd been known as the Empty Vessels for a very long time, that's how I will always think of the band.

After having come up from the West Country, where we had built up a solid reputation, had a lot of contacts and had managed to keep a pretty busy working diary, it came as quite a shock when we discovered just how difficult it was for an unknown band to get work in London. Because we were new kids in town we didn't have a huge network of contacts. Also, there were so many bands and artists starting out around that time, all trying to do the same thing as we were. Just getting a foot in the door was near impossible, although we did get a handful of gigs here and there. We knocked on a lot of doors, spoke to agents, managers and record companies. Some of them expressed interest, but nothing came of it. We even invited our old manager Brian Roberts up from the West Country to see if he could help.

> **BRIAN ROBERTS:** *Martin invited me to stay with them in London once, while they were looking for a manager. I remember feeling hopelessly inadequate on the way back to Exeter and so wished I had the finance and experience to help them while they were trying so hard to succeed in a very difficult business. I had never seen such dedication as they had and I was so pleased that their talent won through in the end. I'll always be so proud to have known them in the early days of their career. I was immensely proud of the work they put in to get what they richly deserved. The boys were the only success story from all the groups I managed and I hope they remember their early days with affection.*

> **GLENN TURNER:** *I could probably count on one hand the number of shows we did after moving to London. It was a lot harder than we could ever have imagined and we had a lot of dead time and no money. We were living not far from the Roundhouse in Camden and I would go there and see all these really good bands who I felt were so far ahead of us. I found it very daunting and could see that it was going to be a hell of a journey to get to the position that these bands were in. I found it quite depressing and eventually decided to leave the band. When I told Martin and Steve that I was leaving, it didn't go down too well and the guys clearly felt that I had let them down – Steve Upton refused talk to me! A little later I realised I had made a mistake and changed my mind. I asked Martin and Steve if I could stay but their response was "No, you've made your decision".*

One agent who did call us offered us a gig at Hampstead Country Club supporting ex-Yardbirds vocalist Keith Relf's new band Renaissance. The support band had pulled out and they needed someone at short notice. So we said "Okay, how much do we get paid?" The agent said "Ah, you don't get paid, but if you're good and the guy likes you, he'll re-book you and next time you go back there you'll get eight quid." We had a little chat about it and weren't keen on doing a gig for nothing. It was going to cost us in petrol, but as it was only a mile or so up the road, we decided we would do it. This was July 1969 and that was the night that we met our future manager Miles Copeland III.

Miles Copeland was an expatriate American. His father Miles Copeland II was a CIA agent and as a result the Copeland family had travelled quite a bit. Miles had been bought up in Beirut, but had settled in London with hopes of getting involved in the lucrative rock 'n' roll business. At the point that we first met him he had very little experience at managing groups, except for a band called Rupert's People, who had been around for a couple of years and included our future publicist Rod Lynton as its guitarist as well as keyboard player John Tout, later of Renaissance. Miles had met Rupert's People while he was in Beirut and the band had visited the country for a week of shows. Like us, Miles was just starting out in the music business and was just as eager to make contacts and meet people as we were. Miles was an unusual character as far as the rock 'n' roll business goes. I'd never met anyone quite like him. He was extremely "straight" – he didn't drink alcohol, he drank milk. I thought he was a bit of a freak, but I liked him. His attitude was really positive and he spoke a lot of sense. He was clearly of the opinion that we were a great band and could go places and offered to manage us. As we were all starting out, it was an ideal hook-up.

> **GLENN TURNER:** *I was aware that Martin and Steve had been talking to some Americans that night, but wasn't really aware of exactly what they had been talking about. The atmosphere by this stage was very strained due to me leaving the band and us all knowing that this was to be the last show and I was feeling quite alienated. Because of this the offer from Miles Copeland was somewhat unbeknown to me at the time. If I had known of this spark of hope with Miles then I would probably have pushed a lot harder to stay.*

By this time Glenn had decided he'd had enough. He was different to Steve and me, being that little bit younger. Here he was in London and he wanted to go out and enjoy himself – go clubbing at weekends and all that stuff. We were living on the bread line and Glenn was sick to death of sharing a room, having to steal food to stay alive and all the rest of it. Gradually over a period of time, there was a parting of the ways and Glenn left the band. He carried on working and enjoying life in the big metropolis, while Steve and I committed to carrying on with the band.

That whole period when Glenn quit was really upsetting for me. I'd been together with Glenn in bands semi-professionally since 1963. We started out together and it had always been that way. Because he was asthmatic and had a lot of problems as a small boy, my mother had encouraged me to look out for him. We shared a bedroom, we were in a band together and I never went out or did anything without considering Glenn. Because I was a bit bigger and stronger and more outgoing, I used to look out for him and fight some of his battles for him. When we reached a point at which we were going to be parting company, I had very mixed feelings. Part of me didn't want to carry on without him and the thought of him not being with me anymore was a bit scary. It was a tough one for me and Steve Upton was the guy who helped me through that. Steve was a great help and support to me through that time. He would say "You've got to stay positive. Everything's going to be alright." Having said that, after a while I think it was good for Glenn to stand on his own two feet and to make a life for himself. Also, as much as I loved and cared for Glenn, once he took off, I found it strangely liberating that I didn't have to look out for him and didn't have to take him into consideration in all my plans and everything I wanted to do. It was a big change for both of us.

After Glenn left the band he carried on playing guitar and spent a few years going back and forth between London and the West Country. Glenn continues to play today – he's a great guitar player and has played in a number of bands in the West Country.

> **GLENN TURNER:** *After leaving the band I stayed in London for about a year, working for a music publisher in Denmark. I spent a lot of time drifting around and got heavily into drugs. I lost a lot of weight and gradually got quite burned out. I returned to Torquay in 1970 in order to recuperate, which I eventually did. By 1971 I had formed a band with my brother Kim on drums called Cat Iron, which also featured Alan "Charlie" Charlton (vocals), Mick Jacques (guitar) and Tony Brinsley (bass). Tony was eventually replaced by John McCoy, later known for his work with Ian Gillan. I hassled Miles Copeland to get us a record deal, which he eventually*

did. We did a lot of live shows – opening for Wishbone Ash, Vinegar Joe, Stone the Crows, T-Rex and numerous other bands, but we but never got around to recording, mainly because Mick Jacques, who was a virtuoso guitar player, insisted that we were not ready to record. After Cat Iron split up, Kim and I formed the Watt-Roy Turner Band with Garth Watt-Roy of East of Eden. I then got a little disillusion with the music business and spent some time working in the rag trade. I spent a few months playing with a rockabilly band called Rock Island Line before I returned to Torquay in 1976, when I got a call from a friend of mine who had put together a blues/rock band called Electric Harry. I spent a couple of years with them, doing a lot of work in Europe, where we earned good money. By 1982 I'd returned to London where I joined a rhythm and blues band called Laughing Sam's Dice, who also featured rock journalist David Sinclair on drums. In 1987 I got a call from band in Plymouth called Mercedes who had seen me play. They were a three-piece and wanted to add another guitarist. I spent three years with them and consider this the best thing I was ever involved with. We were playing 90% original material and the songs were really strong. Since then I've remained active within music and have played in a number of bands and duos within the Torbay area.

During the weeks following Glenn leaving the band, Steve and I would go over to Miles Copeland's house at 21 Marlborough Place, St. John's Wood, London to chat and have meetings. Generally we saw eye to eye with Miles and felt that we could really go places together. In those early days, Miles was like another member of the band really. He was really keen on concept the original three-piece band, with my brother Glenn in it, and so we set about trying to find a replacement for Glenn. We placed an advert in the 9 August 1969 edition of *Melody Maker* which read: "WANTED - LEAD

GUITARIST: Positive thinking, creative and adaptable, for strongly backed group with great future." Miles picked up the tab for the ad, because we didn't have any money. We were already looking around for guitarists but Miles felt it would speed the process up if we placed that ad. We got a great response and there were a lot of guitarists who came down to audition. I can remember Dave "Clem" Clempson, who went on to join Colosseum and Humble Pie. There was also James Litherland, the guy who Clem eventually replaced in Colosseum, as well as Tony Lander, the guitarist from Episode Six, who had disintegrated shortly after Ian Gillan and Roger Glover left the band to join Deep Purple. We felt some of the guitarists who turned up to play were over-qualified. Dave Clempson, for instance, was a really good player, but we wanted someone that was more at our level. Someone who, like us, was just starting out and didn't have a history. Initially we were looking for just one guitar player to replace Glenn and that person needed to be able to play both lead and rhythm guitar well and also be able to sing. But we weren't totally happy with anyone, individually.

One applicant who impressed us was a young guy from Birmingham called David "Ted" Turner (born 2 August 1950). We really liked Ted as a guy. Instinctively we felt a kinship with him, but at that point he was what you would call a three-chord merchant – he could play a twelve-bar blues in about three different keys. He was a bit of a beginner musically, although he had briefly played in a local blues band called King Biscuit. We certainly didn't feel he could step in and replace my brother, although he did have a great feel and a positive attitude – two factors which, to me, are just as important as technical ability. Ted looks back on his formative musical experiences:

> **TED TURNER:** *I remember the radio as being my early influence - my connection to music. Born in 1950, my access to the arts and entertainment were through this media. TV came about ten years later so I think the value was imagination. My family would all listen to plays, stories, comedy shows,*

etc. I used to enjoy listening to the Top 20 or Pick of the Pops with Alan Freeman. This was the early sixties when The Shadows made a big impression. Their work was well crafted. It introduced me to guitar tone and melody. Hank Marvin was also a big influence. Then Beatlemania came along. These were exciting times for music – everything was new with bands breaking into undiscovered territory. These were the days when British pop music dominated the world. My mates - the local gang - introduced me to the blues. The appeal for me was the honesty of the music. To play a solo in a slow blues format will demonstrate one's ability or lack of the same and allow the listener to penetrate the very soul of any player. At first we were listening to a variety of American blues artists and then the British blues boom arrived. The John Mayall and the Bluesbreakers Beano cover album featuring Eric Clapton, and the album Hard Road featuring Peter Green were a big influence on me. Seeing Peter Green play live for the first time showing his ability to convey such emotion through a single note moved me so deeply that it convinced me that this was something I must do. These now heralded British guitar players including Jeff Beck, Jimmy Page and Pete Townsend were influenced by this simple yet engaging music and later delivered their own style of playing and music never before heard. These were the guitar players I found inspirational and tried to copy, listening to their records time after time. This was how I learned to play guitar. I had no formal training. After about a year I joined the King Biscuit Blues Band - the local street band - and did about twenty shows or so. These shows were full of desire, laughter and adventure. In particular I have a fond memory of playing a gig at my local school. To return to the hall where I had spent all those morning assemblies listening to those "boring old farts" onstage and now to be playing my guitar on the same stage, was an experience I found very rewarding. My life was on the move. Before I answered the ad in the Melody Maker to meet with Martin and Steve I had auditioned for the band that became Colosseum. These were very accomplished musicians. They saw the potential within but, after only eighteen months of playing the guitar, it was an understandable decision for them not to hire me. I appreciated their encouragement, support and kindness and I was invited to appear with them at their shows whenever they came through town, which did happen several times. In later years when Wishbone was a big draw I remember meeting Jon Hiseman backstage at a festival where both bands were appearing and him saying "maybe we should have hired you, Ted", to our mutual amusement.

Another guitar player who attended a later audition was Andy Powell (born 19 February 1950), a more experienced player living in Hemel Hempstead but originally from Stepney, East London. Andy had played in a number of local soul bands such as the Sunsets, the Dekois and the Sugar Band – larger line-ups which incorporated brass sections – as well as smaller blues based bands such as the Ashley Ward Delegation. Again, there was something about his playing we liked. He had his own style, but again we weren't sure that he was the right player to replace my brother. We'd reached the point where we'd auditioned everyone and there was no single one person who we felt was right.

At that point Steve and I had to reconsider things somewhat. I gave it a lot of thought and wondered about bringing on board a keyboard player as well as a guitarist, but I soon got over that and we didn't actually audition any keyboard players. I came to the conclusion that what we needed to do was to get two guitar players and between them they would be able to cover everything my brother used to do. However, we didn't want the classic "I'm the lead guitarist, you're the rhythm guitarist" type situation. We wanted them to both be able to play lead together in harmony. This wasn't a totally original idea – the early Fleetwood Mac had hinted at it, as had a short-lived band featuring Jim Cregan called Blossom Toes. We'd also briefly experimented with harmonies in the Empty Vessels days. So, with the idea of harmony guitars in mind, we thought "Wait a minute, why don't we go back and take a look at all these people we've auditioned already and see if any two of them would work together in a four-piece band." The first two we picked were Ted Turner and Andy Powell. We called them and asked them to come for another audition, with a view to meeting each other and seeing how they would play together. As players, Ted and Andy definitely established a rapport immediately and it was clear that the concept was going to work. Personality-wise, I really liked Ted a lot – there was such warmth between us and I really took to him as a person. Andy was a bit more of an enigma really. Although we were impressed with his playing, I wasn't totally sure about him from some of the things he said. He was very hung up about the fact that he'd joined a few bands before that had never come to anything and he was concerned about the fact that he had been offered a really good job at a leading tailor's. He was very much in two minds and I recall him saying "I don't want to end up joining another band that ends up going nowhere and pass on this job." So, we had to convince him that this was a band that was going somewhere, but would need a professional commitment, which would mean it was not going to work if he was working in a shop all day. He did eventually decide to join the band and our line-up was finalised.

> **TED** TURNER: *Mart and Steve were a great team. They were very together and connected. This is what I remember meeting with the boys. This was evident the first time we played music together. Both had command of their instruments. There was a purpose, as if they were sharing a secret. Personalities? Mart was jovial, gregarious, and talkative. Steve was serious, thoughtful and pensive. Andy played guitar very well in an articulate and clean manner. Conversation between us was*

easy regarding music because essentially we had the same influences. Andy and I were born in the same year and he was exposed to much the same musical styles. This had a natural effect upon the rapport between us as people and as guitar players. Getting to know each other we all would express our likes and dislikes, favourite bands, tasty birds and such. We wanted an identity, to try something new. After all, this was what all the bands we were listening to were doing. The harmony guitar idea was a natural flow out of our mutual appreciation of bands like Blossom Toes and Fleetwood Mac. These bands only scratched the surface compared to what would later develop into the unmistakable Wishbone sound. Musically the Wishbone sound was fresh, interesting, melodic and exciting, and expressed with great passion. The harmony guitars soared. Andy and I were tight. We both knew our strengths and our weaknesses and learned how to play to them. We were a quite a team.

Wishbone Ash – Ted Turner, Steve Upton, Andy Powell, Martin Turner – an early publicity shot, 1970

Ted and Andy joined us to live in Chalk Farm, where we found them a bedsit near to ours, owned by the same landlord. By this time things were getting pretty tough and we were struggling to survive. Ted and Andy's room was above a shop that was also owned by the same landlord and we even used to resort to stealing food from the shop just to stay alive. We felt it was morally justifiable because the landlord was ripping us off left, right and centre for rent, electricity and gas, so if a few boxes of Vesta dehydrated curry went missing then that was his own fault for being a greedy bastard.

We set up base camp at Miles' house in Marlborough Place. We would go there every day and rehearse in his basement studio – jamming and putting together new material and generally knocking the band into shape musically, while Miles worked on agents, promoters, publicity, etc. I spent quite a bit of time teaching Ted everything I knew on guitar, to try to broaden his limited skills. Amazingly he was like blotting paper – he just soaked it up like a sponge. In fact, I'd teach him fairly complicated stuff, he'd go away and learn it and come back to me and play it better than I could. As far as coming up with new material, there was a lot of spontaneity – jamming with tape recorders running. On any day we could find ourselves listening back to maybe half an hour of music that we'd played, most of which was fairly self-indulgent, but out of it would come a minute or two of something that really sounded interesting and was worth pursuing. Sometimes one person would have the germ of an idea. For example, whenever Ted first plugged into his guitar amp, he would always play this lick on his guitar neck – "do-de-do". Then he would twiddle some knobs, come back and play it again – "do-de-do". One day I said to him "Ted, play that lick again", and he played it. Then we just gently knocked it into shape. We organised it and put it over a rhythm and it ended up becoming a sketch of what would become 'Blind Eye'. Songs used to get written in all kinds of different ways. Sometimes I would have a lyrical idea from my poetry book – my jottings. Other times it would be a melodic idea based on a song by someone else that I liked and felt I wanted to do something similar. I was also very good at concocting pseudo-classical melodies which, if sang, sounded somewhat less interesting than if you transposed them onto guitar. That's how a lot of the early twin-guitar parts for the band came about. I would sing a part, one of the guitarists would copy it on guitar, and then we would add a harmony for the other guy to play. It was a bit of a laborious method but it worked very well for us at that point and that's what helped to give the band its sound and identity. If it had been left to a guitar player to construct those melodies from scratch it would tend to be much more angular and less melodic, but because it was originally sung and then transposed to guitar, it sounded melodically richer. I was pretty good at coming up with these pseudo-classical melodies on the spot – to order – having been bombarded with classical music for most of my childhood.

Aside from the band and Miles, another important character in the early days of the band was Mark Emery, a.k.a. "Hobbit". He'd been with me since about 1967 when he got friendly with Glenn and started coming out on gigs with us in the Empty Vessels days, helping with equipment. Mark has his own memories of those times:

> **MARK EMERY:** *I went to see the Empty Vessels at a club called Monroe's in Torquay. I was absolutely blown away with this psychedelic three-piece, especially Martin's unique home-made bass guitar, which had a pencil-thin neck, and Glenn's Marshall stack. I was sixteen and impressionable, and they were great. I went on to become very good friends with Glenn, who introduced me to Martin and Steve. We went up to visit them at their place in North Row, Exeter, which was a groovy little place with all kinds of psychedelic pictures on the wall, most of them drawn by either Steve or Martin. As our friendship grew and I went to a lot of the Empty Vessels gigs, I used to hang out with them and help with their gear. I enjoyed*

the music and Martin's girlfriend Maurn and I used to dance a lot. Martin was very serious about making a career out of music. He was very self-styled, used all his creative powers, whether they be in singing, song-writing, musical choice or art. I thought Martin was a very creative guy and I think he knew what his goals were.

Mark used to hang out with us and came to London around the same time as we did. He helped with recording Wishbone Ash's early jam sessions and eventually, once we got gigging, he came out on the road with us and helped with equipment, eventually becoming our live sound engineer. He went from being a puny little runt to a big, muscular Popeye-type character through schlepping equipment around, which does wonders for your physique at that age.

MARK EMERY: *When the band moved up to London, I went to live in the same block as Glenn at 106 Gloucester Avenue, near Primrose Hill. I was working at an industrial photography company. I also had an interview to be a ships photographer for P&O lines and got the job, but once I started gigging with Wishbone I decided not to take the job but to carry on working with Wishbone as their roadie. I remember the early rehearsals at Marlborough Place when they were coming up with songs for the first album. There was a lot of excitement around. The key point was when the harmony guitar lines began to evolve. This really gave the band an identity and their musical style evolved. Andy was probably the more technically competent guitarist, while Ted had the feel of a blues player, being heavily influenced by Peter Green and people of that ilk. I would record those early rehearsals at Marlborough Place and this continued through the first few albums.*

We started working on the equipment and I remember painting all the speaker cabinets white to try to get some kind of identity on stage and make things look professional. A little later we started using Orange amps, which were new onto the market. Martin had a big 200 watt Orange valve amp. Ted and Andy were using four 4x12 speakers with a couple of 200 watt heads and a reverb unit which I had to run on and offstage to plug in and out for certain songs as the footswitch took away the signal.

There was also a guy called Chris Runciman who worked with us during those early times. He had a mad frizzy hair-do, but was quite civilised as far as roadies go – back in those days they were usually a right bunch of pirates and gipsies. I used to call him the Runcible Spoon. He used to work with Hobbit – they were both capable of schlepping gear and doing sound.

A special mention should also be made of Miles' two younger brothers – Stewart and Ian. Young Stewart, a budding drummer, would come home from school and watch us rehearse at Marlborough Place. I always think of him as being in short trousers. He probably wasn't, but he was very young. He was pretty wide-eyed, taking in everything that was going on. We always got on with Stewart very well. His bedroom was actually in the basement of Miles' house, a few yards away from the soundproof rehearsal room. A little later he got involved in tour managing several of Miles' artists, including Cat Iron – the band that featured my brothers Glenn and Kim. They really were funny. They used to do a skit as part of their stage act where Stewart would come on stage dressed as a policeman to tell the band they had to stop playing because it was too loud and was upsetting the neighbours. Then all of the band would surround Stewart and grab hold of him. They would unzip his trousers and pull out this plastic penis that went on for about eighteen inches. Then Kim would emerge from behind the drum kit with a pair of garden shears and goad the audience – "Shall I?" The penis would then be guillotined with the garden shears before the band carried on with the next song. The audience were quite bemused and didn't always know how to take it. It was actually quite punk-ish, yet this was several years before the punk explosion.

Ian Copeland was the middle Copeland brother. He'd been a tearaway in Beirut in the sixties, hanging out with all the Arab kids on the street with knives and weapons and stuff. His Dad didn't like the way he was shaping up so put him in the American army. Ian ended up getting shipped out to Vietnam in the late sixties. When he came back, a little while after Wishbone Ash had started, he was dressed in military uniform and his hair was about a quarter of an inch long. He'd seen so much destruction out there in the Far East that he just wanted to hitch himself into sex, drugs and rock 'n' roll to the eighth degree, which is exactly what he did. He was a fantastic character – larger than life, noisy, crazy. He was a natural leader and one of the gang. He was thoroughly entertaining and used to keep everyone in fits of laughter. We all loved him.

We'd been rehearsing for several weeks before we decided on a name for the band. We had a big sheet of paper and anyone who had any suggestions for names was at liberty to write them down. There were some pretty stupid things on there. One of the Copelands had written down Martin Mortician and the Coffinettes! Miles' suggestion for the name of the band was Jesus Duck, on the basis of the two most successful people in the history of the world having been Jesus Christ and Donald Duck. We weren't happy with any of these suggestions. I had written "Wishbone" down, which was a name I'd always been fond of. To me "Wishbone" had a kind of magical connotation. Someone had possibly written "Ash", or maybe it was just cigarette ash on the page. Miles came rushing into the rehearsal room one day and said "Mart, I'm on the phone trying to negotiate for you guys and we ain't even got a name for the band yet. We need a name and we need it now." So I replied "Listen Miles, we're trying to rehearse a bloody tune here." I grabbed the piece of paper and said "Okay, here's a name – WISHBONE – ASH. Okay, that's it – Wishbone Ash". Miles said "So the band's called Wishbone Ash now?" And I said "Yes, that's it. That's the name." So off went Miles with a band name and then, after he'd left, everyone turned around to me and said "Uh? Wishbone Ash? Is that gonna be the name of the band? We're not so sure about that", and I replied "That's the name of the band until you come up with something better. If you can suggest a better name, we'll take a look at it." And…what year is it now? 2012? I've waited all this time and no one else has come up with anything better yet…

Wishbone Ash played its first ever gig on 10 November 1969 in front of 500 people at Dunstable Civic Hall, supporting the Aynsley Dunbar Retaliation for which we were paid £5! My recollections of that first gig are almost non-existent, but what I do remember about those days is that, although Steve and I had a wealth of experience, having been playing for quite a few years semi-professionally, we were quite in awe to be in London with all these bands and artists who were already an established

The Copeland Brothers - Ian, Stewart and Miles

part of the music business. Aynsley Dunbar was certainly a known figure on the music scene – he'd played in John Mayall's Bluesbreakers – and we felt quite different to people like that at the time. We felt very young, new and fresh and almost outside the music industry at that point.

> **TED TURNER:** *The band played well in front of 500 screaming, excited people. I remember the guitars sounding really good. Backstage, after the show, the girlfriends and close friends and supporters were there enjoying the moment. These early days were good times for the band. We were all very close, like a family. There was a sense of anticipation. Something was happening.*

Gigs were thin on the ground to start with. In those days we used to invite just about every friend we had, because we were literally an unknown band. We would do whatever it took to secure work and Miles was particularly entrepreneurial. On one occasion he spotted that Colosseum were doing a gig at Bedford College, which was just around the corner from his house. He actually rang up the social secretary and explained that he was the manager of this band called Wishbone Ash. Obviously the guy had never heard of us and so Miles said that we were friends of Colosseum. This was certainly stretching things as our only connections with them were that Ted had previously done an audition for them and that one member of their band, Dave Clempson, had actually auditioned for us. But we certainly didn't consider ourselves friends of theirs. Anyway, Miles told the social secretary that he would really like to get us on the show but the guy said he didn't really need us because he already had a support band. So Miles said "Well, listen, we'll come down anyway". So, we rolled up there and looked around. Colosseum's equipment was already set up on the stage, the support band hadn't arrived yet, the social secretary wasn't there, so Miles said "Okay, get the gear in and set it up". So we literally hi-jacked the stage and set our equipment up in front of Colosseum's. Meanwhile the support band arrived and said "What's going on? We thought there were only two bands on." So we said "No, we've been put on the show, so if you could set up in front of us…" Then the social secretary arrived and said

"What the hell's going on here? I didn't book you guys", and so Miles said "Hi, I'm Miles Copeland, we spoke the other day, let me buy you a drink." So off they went to the bar and Miles, by the end of the evening, had this guy fairly plastered. The support band went on first and played, and then we took the stage and managed to do about forty minutes before Colosseum's road crew intervened and pulled us off. But we played to a hall full of students and after the show Miles told the social secretary that we really needed to contact a lot of the other colleges and asked if he would mind us giving all the other colleges his phone number so they could call him to ask about Wishbone Ash and how good we'd been on the night, which he very kindly agreed to do. Miles may have even oiled his palm through virtue of expenses.

We managed to get quite a few gigs as a result of that one hi-jacked gig and got ourselves onto the London college circuit, usually opening for bands that were considered more established than us at the time. Miles also started a magazine called *College Event,* designed to keep the college circuit informed of which bands were playing. Miles managed to keep his name out of it by using a frontline editor, so that he could write glowing articles about his artists, including Wishbone Ash. The guy who set up the magazine up with Miles was going out with a girl called Lindsay Boyd. She used to come along to our gigs, along with her mother. That was Doreen Boyd, who ended up setting up the Wishbone Ash Fan Club for us in 1972. Doreen did a great job on the original Wishbone club, which everyone remembers with affection, and was involved with the club until 1979. Doreen then spent many years running the Police/Sting fan club. There were a lot of contacts made during these early years. It was very dynamic and one connection would inevitably lead to another.

Imperial College was another great gig. We played there a few times, including one gig with T-Rex, which at that point was pretty much an acoustic duo. We didn't have time to have a real good chin-wag with them. We just spoke to them, said "hi" and exchanged niceties, but I did watch them play. Marc Bolan was very hippie-esque, sitting on the floor, looking like a little pixie playing acoustic guitar. He was a great looking guy – so handsome and oozing star quality – but I can remember thinking "You're going to have to get lucky to become successful doing that, mate". Little did I know what he was going to become when he underwent a complete change of direction a little later. It's often hard to recognise the true potential of someone that early in their career.

We played the famous Marquee Club a number of times in the early days. It was run by Jack Barrie – a fantastic guy who we got on with brilliantly. I used to go there in the sixties when I would come up from the West Country to visit the big metropolis. I saw quite a few bands there. I saw future Rolling Stones guitarist Mick Taylor there, playing his first gig with John Mayall's Bluesbreakers, where he had replaced Peter Green. John McVie, later of Fleetwood Mac, was playing bass. I also saw the Alan Bown Set and Georgie Fame play there. The first time Wishbone Ash played there we supported Slade, who at that point had not become the "glitter" band we all know and love. They were actually bovver-booted, denim-clad skinhead lads who had originally been called Ambrose Slade. I didn't really know what to make of them to look at, but once they got stuck into their set, it was clear they were a really good band. They changed their image a little later and kind of became a caricature of that whole glam-rock period, with their stack-

heels, mad clothes and glitter, as seen in all their appearances on *Top Of the Pops*. If anything they aspired to become everything that we didn't want to be. I think if you choose to go down the hit singles road you do carve yourself a lucrative career for a while but it does tend to burn out quickly and become cliché-ridden.

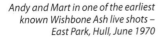

Andy and Mart in one of the earliest known Wishbone Ash live shots – East Park, Hull, June 1970

Another very famous club, close to Oxford Circus, was the Speakeasy. Playing there was like being thrown to the lions because it really was a musician's club and was frequented by a lot of famous people – Jack Bruce, the Beatles, Jimi Hendrix, Eric Clapton, etc. There were we – this scrubbed-clean, tidy little band from the sticks – being thrown onto the stage at the end of the room, much to the amusement of the "serious" musicians in the audience who would be in various states of drunkenness. One night when we were playing there, Keith Moon suddenly appeared in the middle of the stage from nowhere saying "Right lads, let's get this place rocking, shall we?". He wanted to play drums, so we did a couple of tunes with him and he was brilliant. He was an absolute gas – a great guy. I always loved him. He was a hell-raiser for sure, but extremely funny with it. He had a real style about him. Wishbone Ash also supported The Who at Dunstable Civic Hall in July 1970 – almost exactly four years since the Empty Vessels has supported them in Torquay and Barnstaple.

The Roundhouse in Chalk Farm, North London, was another one of those gigs which is chiselled in the stone of London rock 'n' roll history. It was a disused railway shed, a Grade II listing building, within walking

distance of our flat. It was a big gig with a receptive audience, but the air was always thick with marijuana smoke, which was something of a hangover from the sixties. Ian Copeland came down to the Roundhouse with us one night and he tried to score some dope. He spoke to all these hippies and none of them would sell him any. They all thought he must be some kind of undercover narcotics officer because his hair was so short at the time, having just

Ted in another of the earliest known Wishbone Ash live shots – East Park, Hull, June 1970

returned from Vietnam. We got back to Marlborough Place and Ian says "I tell you what – I got it sussed. I'm going to get myself a wig." So he went out and bought this girl's wig and came back with it stuck on his head. We were all falling around laughing, it was so ridiculous. He went straight back down to the Roundhouse the next evening, found some hippie who was selling weed and the guy sold him some immediately because he looked like one of them.

One show we played at the Roundhouse in the very early days was with Supertramp. Years later one of the guys from Supertramp came up to me and started talking to me about some gig that we'd done together and I was a bit taken aback because I didn't even remember that we'd done a gig together. That used to happen a lot, particularly at some of the bigger gigs. Quite often you would get rushed back-stage, have interviews to do in addition to getting ready and you wouldn't always get a chance to check out who else was on the bill.

One band I do remember playing with was Taste, featuring Rory Gallagher. We played with them a few times including Newcastle City Hall. They were a great band and Rory was a lovely guy and a wonderful guitar player. After Taste had played they would break down their gear, and put it all in the back of a Ford Cortina estate car. They got all four of them – the band and Rory's brother, who was their road manager – plus the equipment into the back. I was very impressed with the modest size of their transportation and touring set-up, which was obviously worked out to a tight budget. There we were with our big van thinking "Wow, that's the way to do it."

Most of our early gigs were in and around the London area, but by the Spring of 1970 we were starting to travel further afield. We played The Swan in Yardley, Birmingham, which was Ted's neck of the woods. I can remember going up to Birmingham and meeting Ted's family – his mother, father and sister, who were all lovely people. We also played The Cavern Club, where the Beatles had started, in Liverpool. The place had become quite legendary because of the Beatles, but we arrived there to find this disgusting smelly little hovel of a place. The backstage area was a closet with room for one or two people. The drainage and ventilation were awful. Condensation would run down the walls and the place just stank of mould. It was very unhealthy in a lot of respects, but a great gig nonetheless, despite having clearly been left untouched for so long that it was literally falling apart at the seams. Years later, of course, it was rebuilt very accurately, using many of the bricks from the original building. I heard that the sewage discharged into an open pit at the back, hence the rather unpleasant aroma. When they dredged it all out they even found skeletons which dated back to the fifteenth or sixteenth century – nice job for someone! I went back there recently and thought they'd done a brilliant job and turned it into a really nice gig. It's a lot better than it was originally. Across the road they have a wall of bricks with the names of all the bands that played there. Right in the middle of the wall are the Beatles and just beneath that is Wishbone Ash! What a flattering place to be – right at the centre! Somebody in Liverpool must have been incredibly fond of us to have afforded the band that level of significance. It's quite an honour – thanks Liverpool!

We also supported Free at Lancaster University around the time of 'All Right Now'. They came on after us and we were really expecting to be blown away, but they really struggled to follow us for the first few songs and this was the closest we'd come to blowing the headline band off the stage at this point – Paul Kossoff was having a few drug-related problems, I think. However, as the show went on they got stronger and by the end of the evening they were really rocking. They were a great band. Paul Rodgers is such a great front-man and probably has the greatest ever British bluesy rock 'n' roll voice. Andy Fraser was, for me, inspirational as a bass player. He was so different and had a great sense of rhythm. I got to know him a few years later when my brother Kim played drums in his band. Paul Kossoff was a guy who played so little – he was very economical with his playing – but his feel was just phenomenal. The same applied to Simon Kirke. The drum break that he plays on 'All Right Now', that brings the song back in after the guitar solo, is probably one of the greatest rock 'n' roll drum-breaks ever. It's so predictable, so ordinary, but he plays it superbly with great confidence and it just punctuates a classic song.

We also supported Emerson, Lake and Palmer during their first major UK tour. We'd cross paths with them quite a bit, including on later tours of the States. At the time I can remember thinking they were rather egotistic and quite full of themselves but more recently I've gotten to know Greg Lake socially and he's actually a really nice guy. Just goes to show how it's easy to get the wrong impression of someone. We also played alongside Smile, which featured Brian May and Roger Taylor, later of Queen. Steve and I had met Roger previously, when his earlier band The Reaction had played alongside the Empty Vessels at the Flamingo Ballroom in Redruth, Cornwall.

There were numerous other bands we played with during the first year of Wishbone Ash's existence – Caravan, Van Der Graaf Generator, Heads, Hands and Feet, May Blitz, Heavy Jelly, Stray, Stone the Crows, Brinsley Schwartz, Kevin Ayres, Juicy Lucy, Incredible String Band, Hardin & York, Keef Hartley. The list is endless.

> **TED TURNER:** *We were like the Four Musketeers! Total commitment to our music and all that was required. Our home was a yellow Transit Van. This is where we spent most of our time together driving to the gigs. We had a great work ethic. We applied ourselves hard. This was to our mutual benefit. This all reflected in our music and particularly our live performances. This was the key to our rise in popularity. We would excel in a live situation.*

Andy and Mart - Wishbone Ash live shot - East Park, Hull, June 1970

John Sherry was involved from a fairly early stage as our booking agent. He was introduced to us by Rod Lynton of Rupert's People. Like the rest of us John was just starting out in the industry. He'd worked for one of the bigger agencies but had decided to go out on his own. At the time that we first met him, he'd rented a room in London W1. In fact you couldn't really call it a room – it was more like a closet. But it was a W1 address, which he believed you needed if you wanted to be taken seriously as an agent. He didn't have a desk, didn't have a chair and didn't have a pot to piss in. All he had was a phone which sat on the floor. John worked hard for us in the early days. However it was when Ed Bicknell got involved as a booker for John's agency that things really began to take off. Ed had started out as a drummer in the late sixties. In fact, he'd been in a band called Brotherhood with ex-Colosseum guitarist James Litherland, who had previously auditioned for Wishbone Ash, and bassist/vocalist John Wetton, who would cross paths with Wishbone Ash much later. Brotherhood evolved into Mogul Thrash, another band we used to get billed alongside in the early days. So many coincidental connections! I wasn't that aware of Ed's musical activities back then – we knew him as the social secretary at Hull University, where we had played, and had linked him up with John Sherry. Once Ed got involved the workload increased dramatically – he had us playing all over the place. That was fine by us as it was exactly what we needed to be doing. Ian Copeland later worked for John Sherry and both he and Ed really did a fantastic job for us in the early days. Agents and managers in the music business constantly

get sent tapes that bands have recorded. A few years later John opened a package containing another tape, threw it across the room to Ed, saying "Band needs a manager". Ed listened to the tape later and thought "yep, let's give these guys a shot" and ended up managing Dire Straits – good catch Ed!

Ed Bicknell - worked with our agent John Sherry during Wishbone's early years. Several years later he managed Dire Straits.

CHAPTER FOUR

First Light

WISHBONE ASH made its very first recordings at West of England Sound studios in Torquay on 16/17 March 1970. We went in for a couple of days and laid down some demos. I don't recall the sessions as being particularly great and am not sure if the recordings even still exist. A little later we made another recording at Advision in London with Phil Dunne and future Yes producer Eddy Offord. The pair of them took turns to do sessions with us. They would book us in at ten o'clock at night and we'd be booked in until midnight – just a couple of hours each night, although we generally used to run quite a bit over time. Over a period of a couple of weeks, we managed to record an album's worth of material which we did, at the time, consider a pretty decent recording and something good enough to be released by a record label. It was pretty much the same material which was eventually featured on the first Wishbone Ash album release – songs such as 'Blind Eye', 'Lady Whisky' and 'Queen of Torture' – but obviously this was an earlier recording. Worthy of note are a trio of obscure tracks recorded during these sessions – an early version of 'Alone', a track that would eventually be revamped for our second album *Pilgrimage*; a song called 'Roads of Day to Day', which had been largely written by Andy, plus an untitled jazzy instrumental piece. When we later came to record our first album properly, these songs were shelved in favour of our lengthy stage favourite 'Phoenix', which we didn't have at the time of the Advision sessions. The Advision recordings were considered lost for many years until fairly recently, when a private collector managed to locate an acetate of them, which was used to produce the *First Light* CD in 2007. Listening to these recordings today, the music sounds full of energy and gusto, with the band sounding very young and naïve. The recordings do have a certain charm though, even if vocally we sound like a bunch of choir boys!

Our first experience of playing abroad was a week of shows in Paris during April 1970. This came about when we rolled up to rehearse one day at Miles' house. There was a girl upstairs – a rather attractive young lady who was an old friend of Miles from his Beirut days. Apparently this girl was working in Paris managing a nightclub. So we said "Miles, if she's managing a nightclub, could she not get us a gig there?" And he said "I'm working on it, but it's complicated." We said "What do you mean? How can it be complicated? Can she get us a gig there – yes or no?" It turned out that Miles'"complication" was the fact that she was interested in his body. So, our immediate response was to produce the management contract that he'd signed with us where it said that he would do anything within his power to obtain work for us. We translated and explained that to him along the lines of "If that means a girl wants you to screw her in order to get us a gig, then you are obliged contractually to do it." And so he did! She ended up getting us this week-long residency at a club in Paris called Le Bilbouquet. It turned out to be an Arab club – all red velvet and gold tinsel – and the minute we chimed up all these Arabs began running around like headless chickens. They could not believe how loud it was. To give Miles his due, he got out on the street while we were busy sound-checking and found out where the rock venues in Paris were. One was called Le Gulf Drouot and there was another one called Le Rock 'n' Roll Circus. Miles managed to get us dates at both. They actually needed a band that week, so we actually pulled out of Le Bilbouquet and played the rock venues instead, going down like a house on fire.

Another important stepping stone for Wishbone Ash was when we supported Deep Purple at Dunstable Civic Hall on 18 May 1970. Andy Powell and Deep Purple's guitarist Ritchie Blackmore found themselves onstage together during the sound-check, and spent a few minutes trading licks – talking to each other through their guitars. Ritchie watched us perform that night – I saw him on the side of the stage having a peek at us – and apparently he liked the band, possibly because of the pseudo-classical melodic quality. He didn't say much to us, but he rang Derek Lawrence, who had produced Deep Purple's first three albums, and told him that we were worth checking out. Derek then contacted us and said he was looking for bands to produce and that he would like to come to see us play. We didn't have any gigs lined up, so we invited him to come to a rehearsal. He came down and after hearing us said "I really like the band. I've got a friend in Los Angeles who has just been made head of A&R at MCA in Los Angeles. He's looking to sign bands at the moment and if you guys are willing to pay for an airline ticket for me to go to L.A., I can pretty much guarantee that I will come back with a record deal for you," to which we responded "We haven't got that kind of money – we can't afford it." In the end we agreed to pay half, and Derek flew out and signed us to MCA for a $250,000 advance, with him contracted to producing our first three albums.

Things were certainly looking up for the band with a record deal in place. We were also able to move into more comfortable accommodation. This came about when we played Upstairs at Ronnie Scott's, a venue we were a little apprehensive about playing due to the fact that Ronnie Scott's was a jazz venue, although everyone assured us that Upstairs at Ronnie Scott's

Wishbone Ash - 1970

was a rock venue. We got set up, and then I went out to get a bite to eat. When I came back into the room, right there in front of me was this girl that I'd known from the West Country. Her name was Mona. She was Norwegian and I'd dated her friend Liz for the best part of a year. Mona was a "beatnik" type – educated, opinionated, socialist, anarchic even. She was very punchy, didn't wear a shred of make-up and didn't wash her jeans for a year. Liz and Mona were at Dartington Art College together and I got on with them both really well. They came very much as a package – they were inseparable. If you went out with Liz, you were with Mona as well, and so we became good friends. We'd all gone our separate ways as we moved into the seventies and I hadn't seen Mona for years, so I was really pleased to bump into her in Upstairs at Ronnie Scotts. She was living with a guy called Peter Burden who was a nice chap but a bit of a toff. His Daddy owned a building society so they had been able to get a mortgage. Mona and Peter had bought a house in St. Quintin Avenue, North Kensington. The problem was that Mona was now one of these eternal university students. Her parents were involved in the UN and were intellectual types and they wanted Mona to be as educated as possible, so she was going to be going back to Oslo to go to the university there. Peter was going to be going with her and they were very concerned as to who was going to be looking after the house, so I just said on the spot "I'll take it", because we'd been living in this real hovel of a bedsit in Chalk Farm and various other crash pads. I went over there to take a look pretty soon after that and the place was great with loads of space, and so I moved in together with Maurn, my girlfriend from the West Country who had moved up to London shortly after I had, and a girl called Wendy from Bristol and her boyfriend. The four of us lived on the ground floor and we got Steve and Ted into the flat upstairs. Andy managed to get a place just around the corner. It was a pretty good set-up. They were great days. Lots of great things happened there. We put together a lot material in that flat. We'd go off gigging from there and had lots of parties. We were still very young and none of us were married or had children. We weren't encumbered by mortgages and property and all those materialistic things. We were young and idealistic and free to be creative. The place was decorated by art students – the kitchen was pretty big and had a black and white chequer-board floor. In fact quite a few of the pictures which appeared in various publications and albums sleeves were taken there.

In September 1970 we recorded our first album. Although Derek Lawrence had used the recordings we'd made at Advision to help get us a record deal, he wanted to produce us at De Lane Lea in Kingsway – a studio he was familiar with, having worked there with Deep Purple. So we set about recording the album from scratch. Derek brought with him Deep Purple's engineer Martin Birch, who was a vital part of the team for our first three albums. Martin was a great character who we liked a lot. He was young, full of beans, down to earth and had a good feel for rock music. He was a good engineer. Derek, meanwhile, was very non-technical, very instinctive – what you would call "old school" really. He didn't want to get involved in twiddling knobs and all the technical aspects of recording.

Wishbone Ash - 1970

He was purely instinctive and knew when something sounded good and when it didn't. He was very adept at being able to keep the sessions on track if we were getting silly or over-indulgent. Conversely, if things were getting fraught or frayed he would lighten the atmosphere by telling jokes. He steered the ship very well. His instinct as far as music went was absolutely spot-on.

I can remember walking into the first recording session we did with Derek with my home-made £5 bass guitar. I'd been using it for years and was perfectly happy with it, but Derek took one look at it and said "We need to hire you a proper guitar". I tried various different instruments, none of which I was happy with at all. In fact, that process went on through the first and second album. If I'd been a little more cocksure, I'd have told Derek to sod off and I'd have used my "£5 guitar", but he did encourage me to get confident with a serious instrument. In the end I used a Fender Jazz bass, but it was too "clicky" for me, because I played with a pick. You can hear that clearly on the first album. I tried a six-string bass as well, which I didn't get on with. I don't think I tried a Fender Precision bass at that time although later I ended up using Precision basses in the studio for years. As for the other guys' equipment – Ted had a little Gibson SG Junior fairly early on, while Andy used what we called the Les Powell, which was a copy of a Les Paul which he had made himself. It certainly looked the part, even if it didn't quite have the sound of the "real deal", but obviously he knew how to play it. Andy later progressed to a Gibson Flying V, which became the instrument he would be most associated with.

> **TED TURNER:** *I remember being envious of Andy's guitar. My dream guitar was a Gibson Les Paul but I couldn't afford one. Although this guitar was a copy and was hand made by Andy, I was impressed with this guitar and his ability to make it.*

Around the time that we were recording our first album, we also recorded our first BBC radio session. Over the next couple of years we would record many sessions for the BBC, usually at Maida Vale, for DJ's such as Bob Harris, Pete Drummond, Stuart Henry, and John Peel. Typically we would record three or four songs for each broadcast and the songs would then be slotted into a programme which was broadcast later. These sessions provided new, often unsigned bands and artists with the opportunity to get their music across to a wider audience by means of national radio. In today's more corporate broadcasting industry such opportunities simply don't exist, but in those days the BBC was quite brave in providing air-time to highlight new talent. Having said that the BBC back then still had a kind of clinical, "white coat" vibe and the studios did have that BBC stamp over them – slightly conservative, safe, nothing too radical – but I remember those sessions with fondness. The studios were good facilities with good equipment and plenty of space. The rooms were fairly dead sounding and a bit difficult to play in, but we got some good results nonetheless. The recordings we made there were pretty much done live, although we were given the chance to fix any glaring mistakes. As a band we were pretty well rehearsed and usually got everything done in the allocated time. It was all good experience. Back then, the more you played on stage, the better you got at it, and the more you went into different studios to record, the more you would learn about the trade. Nowadays it's slightly different. Kids go to college to learn the ropes and to me it's all become a bit "production-line" and very much against the spirit of rock 'n' roll. Back then we learned through experience.

Aside from the BBC studio sessions, there were also programmes recorded in front of a live audience for shows such as *John Peel's Sunday Concert, Sounds of the 70's* and *In Concert*. These were usually recorded at the BBC's Paris Theatre in Lower Regent Street (although, as the seventies progressed, and the scale of our touring grew, the BBC would bring its mobile recording truck out to a tour date rather than have the band come into the studios especially). I distinctly recall one *John Peel's Sunday Concert* recorded at the Paris Theatre alongside the Faces. We were still at a point where we were new in the music business, whereas all the guys in the Faces had been around for a long time and had been in successful bands. They were really nice to us. They really liked the band and made us feel part of the music business too. They went on after us and were great. I've never seen a band so drunken in one sense, yet so together in another. For me, fronting that band was Rod Stewart's finest moment – he was brilliant. He was a great rock 'n' roll singer in those days.

Our first album *Wishbone Ash* was released through MCA on 4 December 1970. It basically comprised of the songs which were part of our stage act at that time. The album opened with 'Blind Eye', which as I mentioned earlier evolved from a lick Ted would play when he set up his amp. Ted also wrote the lyric and the song was put together pretty quickly. Although I sang the bulk of the lead vocals on the first album, Ted took lead on 'Blind Eye'. I was always very fond of Ted's voice and always encouraged him to sing. I think in the early days both he and Andy considered themselves primarily guitar players and they were a bit reluctant to sing lead, although they both contributed harmonies.

'Lady Whisky' was pretty much a song that I put together. The lyric was inspired by the flat in Chalk Farm that we lived in when we first moved to London, which was owned by an Irish family who all used to drink heavily and ran a working-men's club in Camden Town. The landlord was always red in the face and smelled of alcohol – a big brute of a man, who reminded me of a bull, his neck being about as thick as his head. One day the landlady came up to our bed sit and took the bottom off the electric meter to retrieve the money and put it back on skew-whiff, leaving it so that you could easily pull it to one side and get the coin out and put it back in again. We spent several weeks recycling the same coin through the meter and saved a fortune! But obviously when she came back to empty it again, there wasn't actually a lot of cash in there. She went into this dramatic rage screaming "Oh Begorra! I've been robbed!" not realising there had been no money in there because of her own stupidity. She ran out of the room and rang her old man. I was dreading him coming home that night. He arrived back at one o'clock in the morning, drunk out of his mind. He was smashing on the door and you could feel it vibrating. It was about to come off its hinges and I'm sat there thinking "If that guy comes through that door he's gonna kill us". We either had to jump out the window and do a runner or pull a knife out the drawer and stop him. Fortunately his wife and daughter, who were downstairs in the basement, heard all the kerfuffle and came up and, between the two of them, they dragged him away. On another occasion he actually knocked his wife through the front door during an argument. She went through the glass, rolled down the steps and into the street. There was blood up the wall. I actually heard him the next morning on the phone trying to find out where she was and it turned out she had actually been taken to hospital when somebody had seen her in the street and called an ambulance. It was pretty low-life stuff. Fortunately we managed to pull out of that place soon after that, but the one thing that did come out of it was that song.

'Errors of My Way' was largely Andy Powell's composition – certainly the original idea was his. When we'd recorded it at Advision, Andy had double tracked the two harmony vocal parts himself, but when we came to re-record it at De Lane Lea we decided to record it with him and I singing harmony vocals together. This particular blend of voices would become an early Wishbone Ash trademark and was probably put to its best effect on our third album *Argus*. In the very early days there really was an atmosphere of everyone pulling together and contributing to the whole, so it's quite hard to break songs down into exactly who did what. But you can usually tell – the individual influences are fairly obvious. Andy, for example, was largely responsible for bringing in the folk influence that can be heard on the early albums. It was something we all liked. We'd been into Bert Jansch, John Renbourne, Pentangle, Fairport Convention, and Andy was particularly good at coming up with ideas in that style.

'Queen of Torture' was about one of Ted's girlfriend's who used to enjoy tying him up. The song basically emerged from the title and it would be pretty hard to state who did what. There was a lot of jamming in those days, with everybody chipping in with ideas. That song actually reminds me somewhat of the kind of stuff Steve and I were doing with The Empty Vessels.

'Handy' had certainly been knocking around since the Empty Vessels days and we'd played it as a three-piece. Steve was very much into jazz in those days and we used to play a lot of tunes from musicians such as John Handy and Jack McDuff, almost as a musical exercise in order to learn a few different licks. Bits and pieces of other songs on the first album also dated back to the three-piece band.

The album's tour-de-force, 'Phoenix', evolved out of jamming and was probably the first of a series of Wishbone Ash long-form pieces where we would have two pieces of music that couldn't really be called "songs", because they didn't really have verse/chorus-type structures. They were really just ideas rather than finished songs, but were in the same key, so we'd experiment and see if we could morph one into the other. I quite liked this and to me it resembled the classical format, where you have different movements moving from something fairly light and pastoral into something more raucous. It would make for a lengthy piece of music which went through various emotional changes and would end on a high – almost a concerto, but not quite. It was a format we returned to again and again. I wrote the lyric to this one, which was inspired by the mythical bird which is said to rise from the ashes.

A little known fact surrounding the first Wishbone Ash album concerns its sleeve design. The design originally intended for the album cover was the picture which eventually turned up on the cover of our second album *Pilgrimage*, designed by Storm Thorgerson and Aubrey (Po) Powell of Hipgnosis. This was originally presented for the first album, but MCA in Los

Angeles didn't like it. They felt that for a band called Wishbone Ash going out with its first album, something more "in your face" was required. So, a record company executive said "What's the band called? Wishbone Ash? OK, let's get a Wishbone, burn it so we got some Ash and take a picture." And that's exactly what they did. We thought the idea sounded a bit crass until we saw it – it looked great!

Our first album peaked at number 34 on the UK album chart. We were all pretty pleased with this level of success, especially for a band that was clearly not aiming at the singles chart or the *Top of the Pops* market. We were basically a live band and live performance was our main strength. We were still pretty young and inexperienced at that point, so it was a level of success we were able to deal with and absorb. We took it in our stride. It wasn't a case of "in at the deep end" in the way it is for many young bands starting out these days when they get a number one album with their first release. We weren't catapulted into the frontline; we were building a career step by step.

As our touring schedule got busier, our road crew expanded. In the very early days, including the trip to France, we had a friend of Andy's by the name of Terry Finn come out and help with equipment. Terry did a very good job back in the days when we were getting going and he had a girlfriend by the name of Rose who was studying at Roehampton. I believe they have stayed with

Rod Lynton - our publicist for many years

each other ever since and raised a family together. Terry has had a few jobs in the studio equipment supply business and is currently working with Affinity Audio.

A little later we were joined by Kevin Harrington, who had previously worked for the Beatles. Kevin was somebody else we'd been introduced to through Rod Lynton, our publicist and a former member of Rupert's People. Rod had been invited to play on a session for John Lennon's *Imagine* album and had been given the task of rounding up a posse of guitarists to play acoustic guitars. Ted and Andy were asked if they wanted to go along. Andy was busy, but Ted went down and played on the track 'Crippled Inside'. I think Andy always regretted not going. So, aside from Ted getting his name on a Beatles solo album, which was quite a feather in his cap, that session also introduced us to Kevin. He used to drive George Harrison's big Mercedes saloon car and would often come to visit us together with George's personal assistant Terry Doran. We'd often go riding in George's car with them for a taste of the big time and what it must be like to be a rock star. They used to hang out at Marlborough Place. They liked the band and were willing to help in any way they could. Eventually Kevin started working for us as our tour manager. He did a great job and he remained with us for many years. There were a host of other people who came on the road with us as the seventies progressed including various tour managers such as Mel Baister and Mal Ross. We also had Mal Craggs join the road crew. Mal was a good guy. He was a Robert Mitchum lookalike – a really good looking guy who had some kind of magical power whereby he could draw any female towards him just by looking at them – he didn't have to say a word. He was from the north east of England and with me coming from the south west, I usually had to have someone translate what he was saying – I've always had a problem understanding accents from that part of the country! Mal went on to have a great career within the music business, eventually tour managing huge tours by bands such as Genesis and Pink Floyd. Later on Mal brought in Alan "Granny" Grange, another north east guy who became part of our team for a number of years.

> **MARK EMERY:** *Mal was a really nice guy to have around – I've never heard a bad work said about Mal Craggs. He later became Phil Collins' tour manager and did the two Live Aid shows with him in London and Philadelphia. Granny Grange was a laugh a minute and an absolute riot to be on the road with. He got up to all kinds of naughtiness with girls in hotel rooms.*

1971 began with us playing a handful of UK dates, including a string of shows opening for Mott The Hoople. They were a fantastic bunch of guys. I got on particularly well with Mick Ralphs and Pete Watts. Ian Hunter was quite shy, and a little bit older. I can remember getting stoned one night when we were supporting them. We were all sat down in the basement having a laugh with the Mott boys, smoking a bit of weed. All of a sudden Kevin Harrington pops his head in the door and says "Guys, you're onstage in ten minutes". So we went off to put our dancing shoes on, get our drinks, set lists and whatever else we needed, and went straight on stage. I'd never been in a habit of doing gigs stoned. Even as a smoker, I was never a huge fan of marijuana, although I did smoke it occasionally in those days – as we all did. You needed

Stoned laughter, 1971

to be reasonably together to do what we were doing. On this occasion I did end up getting stoned and going onstage. I thought the music sounded absolutely fantastic that night. Everything we played sounded totally incredible to me. I came off stage absolutely buzzing thinking how wonderful it had been, but the moment I got back in the dressing room all the guys pitched straight into me telling me how messy and sloppy my bass playing had been. I absolutely loved it and thought it had sounded brilliant, but everyone else gave me a really hard time after the gig for being all over the place. Years later we'd be in rehearsals getting ready to do an album or tour and everyone would be sitting around smoking marijuana, yapping for hours on end and we wouldn't be getting any work done. Marijuana seemed to act as a de-motivator. I knew too many people who spent their whole lives sitting around smoking marijuana, having a great time, but to me they were just on permanent holiday. I didn't want to be doing that – I wanted to go places

A little later, Mick Ralphs invited me down to the studio when Mott were recording *All the Young Dudes* at Trident Studios in London with David Bowie producing. I also remember going to Mick's place for a coffee one day and him telling me that he'd written a song called 'Ready for Love' that Ian Hunter wasn't entirely comfortable singing. Mick felt that it was the best song he'd written and that it was in danger of not going on the album, so he asked me if I thought Wishbone would be interested in recording it. So, I took a recording of it away and played it to the guys, but they pretty much rejected it as an idea. I really felt strongly that we should have done it and I've loved that song ever since. As it turned out, Mott The Hoople did release it, with Mick taking the lead vocal. It was also re-recorded by Mick's next band Bad Company – a great version with a fantastic Paul Rodgers vocal. I eventually did get around to recording a version of it in the eighties, although it remains unreleased.

In February 1971 we undertook our first US tour, flying out on 22 February 1971. I can remember being a little bit apprehensive about going to America so early in our career. I would have preferred we'd done two or three albums and achieved a greater level of success in the UK before going to America. Traditionally that was the way it usually went with most British bands, but in our case we were signed to an American record label based in Los Angeles and we had an American manager in Miles Copeland. So both our record label and manager had their sights set on America pretty early on. What this meant was we had to build a career from the ground up on both sides of the Atlantic. I can remember Miles saying to us "You wait till you get to the States, guys – they've got McDonalds!" I can remember thinking "McDonalds? What is that? Somewhere that sells tartan kilts?" Within twenty-four hours of arriving there, he'd taken us to McDonalds and I can remember sitting there watching all these gross obese people stuffing all this crap down their throats and thinking how obscene it was.

Our first US show was in Austin, Texas on 25 February 1971, opening for the Guess Who. It was a huge gig by our standards, playing in front of 10,000 people. The Guess Who were a great band for sure – the forerunner of Bachman Turner Overdrive, who later had a huge hit with 'You Ain't Seen

Wishbone Ash - 1971

Nothing Yet' – and they pulled a huge crowd. This was a whole new level of existence for us. You could walk around back-stage and stand a good chance of either getting lost or picked up by some 1960's, thirty-something year old groupie. We were terrified of some of those women. They were so experienced at being able to pick up musicians and some of them were old enough to be our mums! I can remember at one gig, one of us asked Miles if he could lock the dressing room door so they couldn't get at us. We were very young and inexperienced. We soon got used to it…

There were obvious cultural differences between the Americans and ourselves. I can remember sitting in a restaurant in Texas and hearing the waitress offer all these different salad dressings – "What would you like on your salad, Sir" – and thinking "What is this?" Then some guy ordered a steak on the next table. The waitress asked "How would you like your steak cooked, Sir?" and this guy – a six foot eight tall dude with a Stetson and cowboy boots – replied "Rip its horns off, wipe its ass and put it on a plate." Being in Texas was like being on another planet. We were fascinated, wide-eyed and took everything in. When we went back to Texas a little later, Henry Withers, the local MCA promotions man, took us to Houston Astrodome to see Johnny Cash and June Carter. The auditorium was massive and there was a thick fog in the air – you could barely see the other side of the stadium. Johnny Cash was driven to the stage in a pick-up truck, waving to the ecstatic audience that consisted of cowgirls and cowboys with their Stetsons, country and western gear and bootlace ties. It was an education.

On that first American tour we had an agent Miles had found called Ron Sunshine. This guy was huge and had clearly eaten a lot of hamburgers, doughnuts and cream cakes. He was fat and sweaty and we weren't keen on him at all. He'd booked us our first American tour, yet when we got out there a lot of the gigs started to evaporate – they didn't exist. You would fly into some town to play a gig and find that the venue had been knocked down the month before. That kind of stuff used to go on a lot in the early days, until we established contacts that were more reliable. When we played a gig with The Who a little later on, they spotted Ron Sunshine with us and said "Is that guy with you? That's Ron Sunshine, isn't it?" and we said "Yeah, it is". Apparently, they had a bone to pick with him as well. Anyway, after we'd played the gig and got back to the hotel, Pete Townshend called up Ron Sunshine and asked him if he had a gun, because Keith Moon was on his way down to see him and he did have a gun. Moon went down there and kicked the door off its hinges! The thought of this large fat guy who looked like a Sumo-wrestler sitting in his underpants and quaking in terror because this nutter and just burst into his room, dressed in Nazi military garb and carrying a sub-machine gun, had us in hysterics. It turned out that Keith's gun was only a replica and didn't fire anything at all, so he was lucky that Ron Sunshine didn't pull out a real gun and shoot him first.

Another key gig on that first American tour was the Whisky-a-Go-Go, in Los Angeles, where we played a three-night stint. Miles announced to us that because this was L.A. and was where our record company was based, we needed to make a big impression. So Miles came up with this idea where he would take a station wagon, drive up into the hills to a farm, and buy a load of chickens to release into the audience during the show. As they were released, we would announce from the stage that the first person up to the stage with a wishbone would get a free copy of our album. Miles said "Everyone will be talking about it – it'll be a sensation!" Our response was "No, Miles. We don't think so." We would have taken a lot of flak for that. It would have been like Ozzy Osbourne biting the head off a bat. It would have attracted a huge amount of publicity, but would have created utter mayhem as well as being rather tasteless. We over-ruled Miles on that one and said "Absolutely no way".

After our first night at the Whisky, Ted got interested in some girl. It turned out she was with this guy who was content to use her as bait to get Ted out partying. He reminded me of Charles Manson. There were some crazy people around L.A. at that time and lots of drinks and drugs going around. That was L.A. in the early seventies – total madness. They all ended up driving up into the hills and taking all kinds of drugs, getting on a hallucinogenic trip and watching the sun come up over the hills. Come day two, Ted didn't arrive at the Whisky and we were seriously worried, particularly given that only a week earlier Jeremy Spencer of Fleetwood Mac had taken a walk in Los Angeles and gone missing, having been recruited by the Children of God. We were about five minutes away from going on stage as a three-piece when Ted walked into the dressing room. I could immediately see what kind of state he was in – he was physically shaking – and everybody started giving him a really hard time. In the end I had to ask everyone to back off. There was a lot of resentment towards him for being so self-indulgent and not putting the band first. We did the gig, but it was pretty messy.

We played Bill Graham's Filmore West in San Francisco alongside Poco – a band which featured future members of the Eagles, although they were more country and less rock than the Eagles later became. They were very mellow and laid back. The bill was a bit of a mismatch. The audience were all stoned and they were laid on the floor ready to listen to this chilled-out mellow music. When we came on and started with 'Blind Eye', it was quite funny to watch them all rise up like mummies in a crypt, as this loud band assaulted their senses. By the end of the set they were with us. We certainly made an impression and we went back to play for Bill Graham a lot at both the Filmore West and also the Filmore East in New York, as well as numerous other venues. We also supported Elton John at the Filmore East during that first American tour. Elton, being quite nervous because it was the first time he'd headlined in New York, came down to our dressing room to see us and brought a bottle of champagne, which was very sweet of him. I don't think he'd developed the superstar, hissy-fit thing that the press always accuses him of at that point. He was really good to us that night. His band were absolutely brilliant – his original three-piece band with Nigel Olsson on drums and Dee Murray on bass. People think of him as a solo artist, but he had a great rapport with his band and he kept that line-up for quite a few years. On that first US tour we also played a couple of shows with Mountain in Detroit. They were a loud, powerful band. They had a brilliant bassist/vocalist, Felix Pappalardi, while their guitarist Leslie West was a huge man and a larger than life character as well as being a great guitarist. They were a great band and our paths would cross on several occasions through the years.

Mark Emery looks back fondly on our first American tour:

> **MARK EMERY:** *For the first year or so, Chris Runciman was the head roadie and sound guy. A little later I took over sound duties. My first gig doing sound was at the Marquee Club. We had two WEM Audiomaster microphone mixers, which were not very elaborate but were the going thing in those days, and we had a terrible incident where someone knocked a drink over from above me and it went all over the mixers – an absolute nightmare. When it came to going to America it had been decided that there wasn't the budget to take a soundman along. I was very disappointed as it looked like the band was going to go and I wasn't going to be going with them. I recall Ted Turner speaking up for me and really holding his ground. He put his foot down and said "We want Hobbit to come". I don't know how, but he did manage to persuade Miles to take me along. I felt very honoured and privileged that the guys, and particularly Ted, had spoken up for me. So I went along on that first American tour. It was awesome, even though we had a few unfortunate cancelations. We ended up in Wildwood, New Jersey where we sat on the dock there for a week between gigs that had been cancelled. It was here that I had my first very bad encounter with a bottle of Bourbon, which I'd never drank before and didn't drink for years after that. I was terribly ill but I did drink a lot of it so probably deserved it.*

Upon returning from the States we played a show at the Lyceum in London, supported by Climax Blues Band – or Climax Chicago as they were known then – and Thin Lizzy. I was very fond of Climax and we ended up getting paired up with them on quite a few occasions, particularly in the States. Peter Haycock was a great player – a beautiful blues guitarist with a wonderful feel. I got on really well with him, as well as Derek Holt, their bass player. Thin Lizzy had just come over from Eire for the first time and this was one of their first English dates. They were a three-piece at this time and had yet to adopt the twin-guitar format which they, like us, became known for. They came to a few of our shows around that time and they obviously watched what we were doing and could see the success we were having with it. Eventually, they decided to revamp their format and add harmony guitars to their sound. They had a great front-man in Phil Lynott and went on to be more commercially successful than we were. All power to them – another great band.

CHAPTER FIVE

Warriors

IN MAY 1971, just five months after the release of our first album, we went back to De Lane Lea studios to start work on our second album, *Pilgrimage*, with Derek Lawrence and Martin Birch at the helm again. We were all a little more confident this time, with the experience of the first album behind us. The band was extremely tight by this stage, having honed our musical skills by playing live and *Pilgrimage* was certainly a technically better recording than the first album. However, one thing I did feel was lacking this time was material. We'd been so busy working live that we hadn't had the time to get into writing. As a result a lot of the material that ended up on *Pilgrimage* was material that we didn't get to use on the first album. There were disparate elements there and it was all very experimental, but it was still early days in our career. I'm not ashamed of *Pilgrimage*. It's a lovely album as far as being a document of where we were at that particular point in time, and obviously each album leads to the next stage.

The album opened with our cover of the old Jack McDuff jazz number 'Vas Dis', which had been part of our stage act for a while. I'd been listening to Jack McDuff's version in the sixties – it was on an album called *Jack McDuff Live* that featured George Benson – and thought it would be interesting to see what a rock band could do with it. It was a tricky number and on the day we recorded it, I'd asked the band to get in early, so we could get some extra rehearsal time in before recording it. So, we all arrived about half an hour before the session was due to begin. We got the amps and guitars fired up and launched into 'Vas Dis'. We ran it through just to make sure it was going to work and that we were all comfortable with the arrangement. We got to the end of playing the tune and I turned around and spotted that, to my surprise, both Derek and Martin were in the control room. I shouted to them "Can we record this tune now? It's sounding really good". Derek came down the intercom and said "You can record it again if you want, but I've already got the take that's going on the album". We had no idea they had been recording us and said "What do you mean? We were just rehearsing". Derek said "You may have been rehearsing, but that's the one that's going on the album." We had a listen to it in the control room and it was clear the recording was as good as we were likely to get. It was so intense, it pinned you to the back wall! So we said "Alright, let's leave it at that – job done". I think we did a really good job of taking something that was out and out jazz and turning it into a rock tune.

I can remember putting 'The Pilgrim' together in my flat. It was in 7/4 timing, which was unusual. I'd seen Soft Machine playing in an odd time signature and this inspired me to try something similar. At first I found it quite difficult. In fact, I can remember at one point I got Maurn to sit beside me and count while I concentrated on playing these bass riffs. Eventually I got the bass-line in the fast section down and managed to build the various different movements. There's one part in there that's a bit like Gustav Holst's *Planets* suite, except instead of using violins we used feedback. For the main part of the fast section, we got Ted to play along with the bass riff, while Andy improvised solos over the top of it. Andy really struggled with it to start with as it's not the kind of thing a rock guitarist would normally be asked to do. To give him his due, he persevered with it and managed to hone down a structure, and it turned out great. The first part of the track – the slow part – is an entirely different piece of music and we managed to put the two together – something we'd done previously on 'Phoenix' and would do on quite a few tunes over the years. In the first part we did the exact opposite to the second part and had Andy playing along with the bass-line and Ted improvising over it. The whole piece is very much based around bass-lines. I put a lot into the backbone of that track – the arrangements, dynamics and different mood-shifts – and I think it ended up being quite a powerful piece of music.

'Jailbait' was cobbled together in ten minutes down in the West Country. Chris Runciman's parents had a pub down in Exeter and we rehearsed in a room there for about a week and set about putting a few tunes together. With a lot of the other tunes we had for the second album being quite musical with a lot of fancy chords and mood changes, we needed some basic rock 'n' roll music to balance things out somewhat. Somebody suggested a shuffle, which was a rhythm we were pretty good at. The thing that I particularly wanted to do was try to hang out on one chord for as long as possible, so that there wasn't a lot of different chords and complex structures. It's a nice way to let your hair down sometimes, where you haven't got to think too hard about what's coming next. That was the concept of the song and it came together pretty quickly through jamming. Then we put in together the arrangement with all its stops and starts. Obviously there's quite a bit of guitar solo work as well as our trademark twin guitar harmonies. We also used some feedback at the start to give it an ethereal quality. All it lacked was a lyric. When you've only got one chord, there's nothing to dictate to you where you should go with the vocal, so it's actually harder than you think to come up with suitable lyrics. Ted and Steve went off to the kitchen to put the lyric together. Ted had a few lines and Steve helped complete the lyric. Then they came back about half an hour later and Ted sang it. The lyric was about a girl Ted had met in the States. I think she was only about fifteen when he met her. She was a stunning girl, but jailbait for sure. Overall 'Jailbait' came together pretty easily.

'Alone' was a song that dated back from the pre-first album days. We'd recorded it at Advision, as can be heard now on the *First Light* album, but when we came to record our first album properly with Derek Lawrence, we decided not to use it. The tune actually goes back to the pre-Wishbone Ash days, as Steve, Glenn and I had kicked it around in one form or another with the Empty Vessels. When we re-recorded 'Alone' at De Lane Lea for *Pilgrimage,* Derek decided he wasn't over keen on the vocal. I think he felt it was a bit too sweet – a bit too choirboy-ish and not rock 'n' roll enough. Derek suggested doing an edit on it, where we cut out the vocal sections and just had it as a little instrumental piece. I agreed to give it a try to see if it worked. Everybody seemed to like it, although I wasn't entirely happy about it and thought it was a bit of a waste. I tend to be quite precious with my songs and my creativity – I'd rather either use it or not use it – but 'Alone' went out on the album as an edit. With hindsight I'd rather have saved 'Alone' as it may have fitted better on our next album, *Argus*. In fact, I think the song may have given Steve the inspiration to write the lyrics to 'Leaf and Stream', which is very similar. Both songs are contemplative and talk about streams and rivers in a somewhat nebulous, airy-fairy, hippie-esque, dreamy fashion. Many years later the full length version of 'Alone' from De Lane Lea was released on the *Distillation* boxed set.

'Lullaby' was another short instrumental. That was something that Ted and Andy worked on quite a bit. It had no drums and I think we even talked about recording it without any bass, although I did put a bass part on. I think it would have worked either way. Ted and Andy put together some really nice, sweet, dreamy guitar parts for that one.

'Valediction' was pretty much Andy's song, although Ted contributed significantly, adding the almost reggae-like section towards the end. It's a fairly sad and melancholy song in the folky vein that Andy was really into at the time. Andy took lead vocal on this one and I added a harmony. It's a nice contemplative song.

'Where Were You Tomorrow' closed the album – a standard rock 'n' roll twelve-bar that we had been playing as the closing number of our live show. It's a boogie-woogie blues and the only thing totally original about it is the lyric, which Miles contributed to – he was itching to be a song-writer as well! I think he also came up with the title, which we liked a lot – it was nice and ridiculous! The song is basically jammed, with everyone contributing. It certainly served a function as our encore for many years. It was basically a live song, which is why the version we used on the album was a live recording, made at De Montfort Hall, Leicester. We had recorded a studio

Andy Powell and Gibson Flying V, 1972

version, which much later appeared on the *Time Was* anthology, but we really weren't very happy with it at the time. The song needed the energy of a live audience.

During June 1971 we undertook our first major nationwide tour, alongside Renaissance and Stackridge. Although we had maintained a busy schedule of gigging, this was by far our most prestigious activity in the live arena to date, as we headlined at major UK venues such as Bristol Colston Hall, Sheffield City Hall and Manchester Free Trade Hall for the first time.

Stackridge, who lived around the Bristol area, were managed by Mike Tobin, who had kindly given Maurn and myself a room at his home when I was between pads, so to speak. Stackridge had rather passionate followers, similar to those of Wishbone, and their brand of quirky music with wonderful Beatle-esque melodies and childlike lyrics gave them an endearing quality, which was quite addictive. Only recently, our one time publicist Rod Lynton took me along to see them perform at the Bull – an intimate little theatre in Barnet, North London. I went along not knowing what to expect, but the years had brought about a maturity and sexiness that the original band lacked helped by a young lady violin player and back up vocalist. The band performed their music with amazing finesse and an absolutely wonderful technicolour soundscape. It was a pleasure to see them perform again after many years and I do hope they achieve the recognition they deserve.

Shortly after the completion of our UK tour, Maurn and I got married at Kensington Town Hall on 2 July 1971. It was something of a last minute arrangement and we phoned all our friends and family about ten days before the wedding was due to take place. After the ceremony we threw a huge part at the house in St. Quintin Avenue.

August/September 1971 saw us undertaking our second US tour – a more substantial helping of dates this time around, including some dates at major venues opening for The Who on their *Who's Next* tour. While on tour in the States, we were told that we had been voted best new band in both *Sounds* and *Melody Maker* reader's polls. We were pleasantly surprised by this, especially given that we were not a "pop" band that had records in the charts every five minutes. We didn't have singles played on daytime radio, although people like John Peel at Radio One, and Kid Jensen at Radio Luxemburg did play our album tracks. The recognition from both the press and the public was very flattering. There were people in the music business in London who couldn't believe how quickly we reached this level of success. Some people believed we'd been hyped by a wealthy American businessman – Miles Copeland. This could not have been further from the truth. We got there through sheer hard work and through playing a huge number of gigs up and down the country.

Our second album *Pilgrimage* was released in September 1971 and reached number 14 on the UK chart, getting some great reviews in the press from writers such as Ray Telford and Roy Hollingworth. We also made an appearance on BBC2 television's *Old Grey Whistle Test* performance playing 'Vas Dis' and 'Jailbait'. The *Old Grey Whistle Test* was a great vehicle for bands like ourselves, who didn't necessarily fit the bill for programmes like *Top of the Pops*. It featured album tracks and the bands generally played live in the studio although, if I remember correctly, our session actually featured us singing live over a specially recorded backing track, due to some strange union regulation at the time. We ended the year of 1971 with a New Year's Eve show at the Marquee Club, and the following day we all attended the wedding of Andy and Pauline Powell in Dunstable.

January/February 1972 saw us undertaking our biggest UK tour to date, this time supported by Scottish band Glencoe. They were a good band. Graham Maitland was their keyboard player and he was to work with us a few years later. Norman Watt-Roy was the bassist and John Turnbull the guitarist. Those two ended up with Ian Dury and the Blockheads. We liked them a lot and enjoyed having them on the road with us. However, I do remember a couple of years later, driving up to Leicester de Montfort Hall where they were supporting Deep Purple, going into the dressing room to say "Hi" and John Turnbull really steaming into me about some gig where we'd both played on a festival together. They had asked if they could use our drum kit and we'd said "no", the reason being that they were on at four in the afternoon while we were on at eleven at night – it just wasn't practical, but John got rather angry with me. I was a bit miffed, having schlepped all the way up there to watch them play, only for this stroppy little man to give me a hard time.

We began recording our third album *Argus* during the tail end of February 1972, following our UK tour. Once again we used the tried and tested team of Derek Lawrence producing and Martin Birch engineering. De Lane Lea had just moved to a new studio in Wembley, located in the shadows of the famous twin-towers of Wembley Stadium, and had upgraded from the eight-track, 1 inch tape that our first two albums had been recorded on, to sixteen-track, 2 inch tape. These gave us much more control over the sounds and separation for each instrument. We spent a week recording and then Derek spent a week mixing. My only regret is that the vocals were a little rushed, recorded in one day in between completing the music and Derek mixing the album.

As for the song material, we'd actually started putting ideas together for the album a few months earlier, pretty much directly after we'd finished *Pilgrimage*. Much of the song-writing took place at 43 St. Quintin Avenue in North Kensington. We were a pretty tight little unit by this stage. With Ted, Steve and myself all living together and Andy just around the corner within walking distance, it was easy to get together to rehearse new material, which we did pretty regularly. We'd rehearse new songs with Andy and Ted playing acoustics and Steve playing a practice kit. I'd be the only one who would use an amplifier, for the bass. In fact, sometimes we didn't even amplify the bass – often I'd just lean the headstock against a hollow door to get a bass sound. We worked the arrangements up acoustically and I can remember it being quite a thrill to hear the material with electric instruments for the first time, because we'd been so used to hearing the songs acoustically.

Ted Turner 1972

Personally I'd spent a lot of time – every minute I could muster – writing most of the lyrics and melodies for the album over a period of about nine months. I wanted to put together an album that was much more defined and integrated than *Pilgrimage* had been and the themes I began writing about were things that had been on my mind for many years. With *Argus* I deliberately set about writing something that I felt dealt with really important themes, one of these being time and the illusion of time. The realm in which we live is restricted by time and space – I much later wrote a song called 'Time and Space'. To some extent I've always felt I could step outside of time by tuning into the psychic world. In the sixties I used to go to a spiritualist church and I've had a variety of psychic experiences myself. Once you get into the psychic realm, there is no time and the past, present and future kind of merge into one. That was one theme I wanted to delve into and 'Time Was' and 'Sometime World' both hint at the struggle to reconcile the restrictions and confines of time.

> **TED TURNER:** *The songs displayed a growing maturity. We were also maturing as a band. Our well oiled machine was a result of constant touring over the previous two years. The music had become more focused. Earlier the band was going in different directions, exploring our interests in musical styles. Individually the music was strong but lacked the cohesion that came together on Argus. The conceptual element within the songs was a first for us and all our efforts resulted in Argus being a "real album".*

'Time Was' and 'Sometime World' were both songs that had two distinct parts – a structure we had used previously on tracks such as 'The Pilgrim' and 'Phoenix'. Ted added the opening acoustic section to 'Time Was'. That was pretty much his song idea and lyrics and I shared harmony vocals with him on that before it gave way to the main body of the song, which had a distinct Who influence, particularly in the rhythm section. I pushed Steve quite hard on that one, trying to get him to play in a style similar to Keith Moon – he did a great job. That was the kind of energy I wanted to create for it.

'Sometime World' was another one of our songs that had slow and fast sections. I'd come up with the melody and lyric. I recall Andy suggesting the rhythm figure for the fast section, although his often quoted claim that he wrote the bass line is utter rubbish. What actually happened there was that I was a bit stuck for a bass part on the fast section. I had a couple of ideas in my head, but was not really happy with anything. I knew I wanted it to be very dynamic because of the pace of the track. At one point, because I hadn't come up with a bass line, Andy suggested that I play a Tamla Motown-type bass line – not a style I would normally play. What I ended up doing was putting a very high bass line together that was not really Tamla Motown, but did have a similar kind of phrasing. It was my intention to only have that high bass line playing as an intro, and to then drop down into a more orthodox bass part. But everyone really liked it being up in the air, dropping down only for the chorus. I put a lot of time into working out all the little runs in it. That bass-line is typical of my pushy style – it's got my paws all over it.

I originally had the idea for 'Blowin' Free' in the sixties, when I'd written the lyric for it. I had a basic sketch of how I wanted the song to sound – like a joyous love anthem – and had been trying to get the song recorded ever since. The lyric is trying to express the youthful buzz of falling in love with someone. In the sixties, I'd got really hooked on this Swedish girl called Annalena Nordstrom. She was completely unlike me. I stayed up at night and played in rock 'n' roll bands, smoked, drank and hung out in smoky bars. She was the daughter of a university professor, educated, liked riding horses and bikes and enjoyed the open air and the countryside. She was very healthy and how I ever got involved with her I don't really know, but we spent some time together over a couple of summers in the sixties. On one occasion I took a drive out to Dartmoor with her in the band's van. It was difficult to communicate – she didn't speak much English and I certainly didn't speak much Swedish – so we'd just hang together, look at each other, make facial expressions, touch, and just generally be loving. Not a lot was said verbally. It was a fascinating relationship. This particular afternoon we were sat on Dartmoor and watched a thunderstorm miles away just rolling across the lowlands below us. It was a fantastic experience.

I asked her if I could kiss her and she managed to cobble together "You can try" – whatever that was supposed to mean. We were both pretty shy and came from different cultural backgrounds, but we were typical teenage kids fumbling around. At the end of her three weeks here she would go back to Sweden and maybe I'd see her the next year, or maybe not, which left me with feelings along the lines of "I thought I had a girlfriend, because I saw her there in front of me. Then she disappeared into the ether, she exists no more. Did that really happen?" I never really felt the band really understood the song and where it was coming from or what it was about, because it pre-dated Wishbone Ash lyrically. It's full of youthful exuberance. Andy Powell turned around to me one day and said "You can't sing that – 'I thought I had a girl, I know because I seen her'". So I said "Why the fuck can't I sing that? That's what I wrote and that's what I'm gonna sing". So he said "Well, it's bad English – you should write it properly." So I said "No, mate. You're missing the point. Okay, it's bad English but that's a different way of saying it's poetic license." When I sing "Her hair was golden brown, blowin' free like the cornfield", I'm talking about her long blonde hair which rippled in the wind in the same way in which the wind brushes over the top of a field of golden wheat and you get a wave effect. To anyone in America "corn" would mean corn on the cob, but we used to call the wheat fields the "cornfields", and corn on the cob was known as "corn in the gob"!

The opening guitar lick on 'Blowin Free' eventually became one of the most common guitar licks, alongside 'Stairway to Heaven' and 'Smoke on the Water', to be played when young guys go into music shops to try out instruments. The way that lick came about was by me asking Andy and Ted if they knew a song by Steve Miller called 'Children of the Future'. They hadn't heard the song, so I tried to describe the guitar part to them, which was a syncopated, hammer-on type of riff. They tried to play it and over a period of time it became a little exercise for them which gradually morphed from this Steve Miller lick into something of its own. I do remember that during the making of the *Argus* album there was quite a bit of debate as to whether or not 'Blowin' Free' belonged on the album, because it had such a different atmosphere and feeling compared to the other tracks, which had a more serious edge. I think the general feeling at the time was that it may be better to keep it for another album. I felt differently – I had this song that I'd been trying to record for years, we now had a decent recording of it and I really wanted it to go on the album. I also felt it acted as a good counter-balance to the more serious nature of the other tunes as it was poppy – for Wishbone Ash, at least – celebratory and upbeat. Maybe this was my Libran attempt to balance things. Looking back I think it was always destined to be on that album. It fits like a glove to me and the album wouldn't be the same without it. I felt we managed to get enough gusto and joyousness in there and everyone did a great job in contributing to the arrangement – Ted's little lick in the quiet section in the middle, Andy's solo work. I really love gusto of the bass sound on that track.

Another factor that played a big part in influencing the direction of *Argus* was my fascination with and enjoyment of religious music. I was a member of the church choir as a young lad and really did get a lot out of my exposure to religious music and its rich melodies and harmonies. It was a fascinating experience and I had the patience and stamina required to stay with it. Having said that, I wasn't that keen on what I was exposed to in terms of orthodox Christian religion. It seemed to be full of contradictions both spiritually and materially and only served to reinforce my perception that religions throughout world history have probably been more responsible for death and destruction than any other thing. For *Argus* I wanted to explore some of the classic Christian religious themes – Jesus Christ, the son of God; his crucifixion and resurrection; paying for our sins; and the eventual end of the world. I attempted to explore these themes through the lyrics of 'The King Will Come'. I have to confess the lyrics to the first verse are lifted pretty much from the Bible, although not in the exact words. Steve Upton helped with the second verse. He'd been reading a book called *The Prophet,* written by a Muslim writer named Khalil Gibran and this inspired some suggestions he came up with lines for verse two. We were clearly on the same wavelength. Musically, although the song was largely my composition, everybody contributed to the arrangement. Andy added the reggae-ish rhythm figure that opens the song, then I suggested a military drum beat to give the impression of an army coming over the hill with their riffles, pipes and big bass drums. Ted contributed the wah-wah guitar to the intro and the subsequent opening guitar licks.

A lot of time and effort went into writing *Argus*. I personally worked very hard on it and it became a discipline, because I could feel that I was starting to grab hold of the pieces and pull them out of the air. To me it was clear that once I'd managed to find all the pieces of the jigsaw and put them together, the project was going to be really strong and would have a real measure of substance. Maybe this was partly my reaction against some of the pop music that was around at the time – 'Chirpy Chirpy Cheep Cheep' and some of the utter crud that was masquerading as music on television. Having said that, music is no different than wallpaper really and if it serves

Steve Upton 1972

as a backdrop to cheer people up as they go about their lives then who am I to be slagging it off? But to me it was very insubstantial.

'Leaf and Stream' was pretty much a band effort, worked on with acoustic guitars. Steve put a lyric together which, initially, was pretty much unsingable. Steve was very cerebral and through talking to him I was able to get at the picture he was trying to paint with his lyrics and the emotions and feelings he was delving into. I managed to knock the lyrics into a form where they became singable and managed to get a very lilting kind of melody going. All of these things inter-react. Andy and Ted were putting a guitar part together and because the song was going to be called 'Leaf and Stream' we wanted the guitar to sound a bit like a bubbling brook. Likewise the melody has got a very dreamy, contemplative quality to it.

Another theme I had been fascinated by was that of war. If you come from a working class background and you want to escape the confines of your little community and make your way in the world, one of the ways you could do this was to join the forces. I did consider that at one time, because it would have given me a way of earning an income and seeing the world. The other way, which became apparent as the sixties wore on, was to put together a rock 'n' roll band. Obviously you had to become a success in order for it to result in you being able to travel around the world, but I did feel that it was a better option than joining the forces, because I wouldn't be asked to shoot people. For me, my love of music was deep within my blood by that point and I chose the rock 'n' roll band option. Many young men, however, don't have such an option. They are young guys, loaded with testosterone, possessing passion galore and boundless physical energy and it's very easy for this energy to be harnessed by governments, dictators and people who want to create conflict and war. Very often young men will sign up to a cause – something they can channel their passion and their energy into – and I was fascinated by this whole syndrome which had existed since the beginning of time and was showing no signs of changing.

That was what the song 'Warrior' was about. I was putting myself in the position of a young man wanting to be involved in a passionate cause. I was a passionate young man myself and had indeed been a teenage street warrior and still have the scars to prove it.

After I'd written 'Warrior', I felt it needed to be counter-balance with an anti-war peace statement. At the time, I'd been reading books like Tolkein's *The Lord of the Rings* trilogy. I loved reading literature and listening to radio plays because they fired my imagination and allowed me the freedom to picture in my head the scenes that are depicted in the stories, rather than it all being done for you in a movie, where you just sit back and eat your popcorn and it all appears in front of your eyes. I really enjoyed the creative aspect of being able to use my imagination and I think it will be a sad day when that eventually is bred out of the species. At the end of 'Warrior', I could picture all this stuff – huge battles, dead guys with spears and busted swords, the smoke in the air, the stench, the whole ugliness of it all. The feeling that, having gone through this whole tribal conflict and having been a warrior, you've been there and done it and now you just want to go home to your wife, your children and your land and live in peace. That theme seemed to me to be the natural follow-on from 'Warrior', so I set about writing 'Throw Down the Sword'. I think clearly in the music that I put together for that song you can hear my religious musical influences. It's very hymn-like. Having put that song together I did feel myself that it had a wonderful sad but uplifting quality about it. Andy added the guitar introduction, which came from a little finger exercise he used to do. We built it into a moody context, put a harmony on top and put a little shift into it. Once again Steve Upton contributed the military snare. 'Warrior' and 'Throw Down the Sword' kind of became the core of the album.

The guitar solo section in 'Throw Down The Sword', which actually features two different Andy Powell guitar solos overlapping in the mix, came about in an unusual way. When we were recording the guitar solos we encouraged Andy to play something with a slightly regal, classical feel, rather than the bluesy solos that guitarists usually come up with. He really got into it and made a few attempts to put the solo down. In these instances the engineer usually keeps each take so we can mix and match later – for example, taking one good bit from one take and putting it together with another good bit from a different take. In this case Martin Birch played the recording back with one of Andy's takes pushed stereo left and another take pushed stereo right, and let them play simultaneously so that we could compare the two. Storm Thorgerson, our album cover designer, was in the control room at the time and when the track had finished playing he said "I really like that". So we said "What do you mean – the two guitars playing at the same time?" He said "Yeah, that sounds great." So we said "Well, actually, that's probably not how it's going to sound when it's mixed. We were just listening to the two at the same time to make a comparison." Storm said "No, I think you should use them like that, with both solos playing together". Everyone thought about it and said "Why not?" and Martin Birch went about mixing the two overlapping solos in a way that they became intertwined. Obviously there were places where they blended well and other points where they clashed and so Martin would push the faders up and down at the appropriate points as he mixed the song in order to get the right mix and match. In the "chorus" part the two solos went magically to the exact same phrase and made it sound very powerful. It was quite an unusual thing to do and we have to give Storm a certain amount of credit for that. Of course, it was totally impossible to reproduce live at that point, as Andy had played both parts and the solo needed a rich chord texture which Ted provided on rhythm guitar, together with John Tout of Renaissance on organ. To have reproduced it live Ted would have needed to have taken on one of the solos, which would have left the music quite bare with no real foundation, because the bass part in the solo section doesn't have me playing root notes.

We went through every single note on *Argus* with a fine tooth comb, prior to recording. I didn't want anyone playing anything that wasn't necessary or required. I seem to remember at one point getting very frustrated with Andy because he was trying to change the chords in the verses of 'Throw Down The Sword', which seemed absolutely pointless to me. Having written the bulk of the material I felt I had every right to be musical director and oversee what was played. Having said that, regardless of who wrote the melodies and lyrics, everyone contributed to the arrangement of the songs and the album, as always, was a team effort. We were pretty well rehearsed this time around and we'd even introduced much of the new material into the live show during our January/February 1972 UK tour. That was common practice in those days – to preview your new material onstage prior to recording a new album. It can, however, be difficult for an audience when presented with unfamiliar material, but in this instance I recall there being a real degree of focus from the audiences and they listened quite intently.

Although we had no idea that we'd created what would later be revered as a "classic album", I knew we had something special with *Argus* from the first time I heard the album played back in the studio from beginning to end, after everything had been mixed and edited. It was a relief to get the album finished and it was also a release for me as a lot of personal energy had gone into it – I was absolutely drained at the end of the sessions. That album was like the male equivalent of giving birth. I found myself sitting in the control room and being gobsmacked by what I was hearing. I was completely overcome with emotion and actually started crying tears of joy. I thought the album sounded absolutely wonderful. It was everything I'd always imagined the band could be.

The distinctive album cover for *Argus* perfectly complimented the music. It was designed by Hipgnosis – Storm Thorgerson and Aubrey "Po" Powell. They had designed the previous cover and we had got along with them really well. Po was a fantastic photographer and he took a lot of great photographs of us in the seventies. Storm was more of a creative powerhouse. He had an artistic pride about him. Whenever we had a meeting with him to discuss ideas for the latest album cover, it would be almost like a session with a psychotherapist. He would get in your face, he would provoke argument, try to find out where you were coming from and where you were headed. I actually enjoyed that part of the process, although he did have a knack of upsetting people on occasion. I distinctly remember a later album session, where the band and Miles had a meeting with Storm, who this time had envisaged a cover design featuring two wild horses that had been running and had steam coming off them and their heads thrown back. This was supposed to be symbolic of the harmony guitars and behind them was to be this really heavy, thundering, stormy sky. As Storm explained his idea, I noticed Miles was getting increasingly uncomfortable. Eventually in typical gung-ho fashion, Miles interrupted, "Wait a minute. Horses? That's country and western. No, no – we cannot have horses". Storm got really irritated by Miles' comment and they ended up having this huge argument. Storm's other idea on that particular session was a picture of two guys embracing each other, displaying genuine love for each other. The English tend to be very uptight about this kind of thing, but it is of course traditionally quite common for men of other nations, such as the French, to embrace each other in this way, or even kiss each other on the cheek – I do it with my mates even when I'm not dressed up as Martina! Again, this was supposed to be symbolic of the harmony guitar factor in the band. Miles absolutely flipped and screamed "God-damn, I'm not having two guys kissing each other on an album cover" and then Storm turned on Miles and said "Oh, do I detect a hint of homophobia?" The album cover design sessions used to be hilarious – they should have been recorded for posterity. There would be everyone screaming and yelling, with Storm conducting the orchestra, cranking everyone up. A certain amount of this was deliberate because the last thing he wanted was for everyone to say "Oh, that very pleasant, let's go with that." His psychology was that you don't get great art unless there is a certain amount of pain involved. Storm's process usually consisted of him finding two disparate elements, putting them together in some contrived but artistic picture – either photography or an original piece of artwork – and the obliqueness of it would be quite arresting. I always enjoyed working with Storm and Po. They were both great at what they did. Storm had a reputation as being very provocative and a bit of a prickly character but I always loved him. Storm by name, Storm by nature!

In the case of the *Argus* album I can quite imagine Storm saying to Po, "Listen, old chap, I really fancy a week in the South of France. Wouldn't that be an ideal location to shoot this *Argus* cover?" So, they agreed a budget with us and off they went on their little adventure to the South of France to capture a moment at dawn when the mist would be hanging in the valley. Either Po or Storm had a friend who had worked on the Ken Russell film *The Devils* and that's where they got the warrior's props from – the cloak, the spear and the shiny helmet. I don't recall who actually wore them for the picture but quite often people come up to me at gigs and say "Who was that on the cover of *Argus?* Was that you, Martin?" I often reply by saying "Yes it was, but you should have seen the shots when I turned around, because I was naked underneath!" That usually gets a laugh or two. One day recently when I came out of my front door, up on a hill in Guildford, I suddenly realised as I looked down the valley at the mist, that I was actually living in the *Argus* album cover – a scary moment, especially when I looked around and saw the flying saucer. My eyes are not so good now – it turned out to be a helicopter.

Hipgnosis went on to have enormous success with their album designs throughout the seventies working with a lot of the top bands such as 10cc, Led Zeppelin, Genesis, ELP, Yes, UFO, Nazareth, Bad Company, Wings, Black Sabbath, Peter Gabriel and Status Quo. They are perhaps best known for their work with Pink Floyd, including the iconic *Dark Side of the Moon* and *Animals* album covers. Po would later diversify into video direction, while Storm continues to this day to design album covers in his own right.

With my Thunderbird bass guitar, acquired from Pete Watts of Mott The Hoople, 1972

Meanwhile, with the recording of *Argus* complete, we continued touring. We played some European dates during March 1972 and it was during a flight back to the UK that my Rickenbacker bass, that I'd been using for less than a year, got broken. By this time we were pretty friendly with Mott The Hoople and so I called up their bass player Pete Watts to see if he had a bass guitar that I could borrow. I went over to see him and he gave me this sunburst Gibson Thunderbird which he'd thrown up in the air on stage and had failed to catch. It had broken into thirteen separate pieces, if I remember rightly, and had been glued back together by the road crew while on tour. It was in a right mess and had become a dog of an instrument to play, although I did fall in love with it. I'd always wanted a Thunderbird ever since I'd seen Johnny Gustafson play one onstage with the Merseybeats and I wanted to get Pete to sell me his. So I rang Pete up and said "This guitar you've lent me is a dog. You've really abused and mistreated this lovely 1960's instrument and what I want to do is buy it off you and get it rebuilt properly by someone who knows what they're doing." He said "No, Martin, I don't want to sell it. I only lent it to you." So I said "That's a pity, because I was just about to drive over to your place with a wad of crispy, spanking new smelling bank notes." There was a little pause and then he said "Why don't you come over anyway and we'll have a cup of tea and chat about it." I ended up paying him £250, which was a bargain, even though it was in a right state. I had it rebuilt by Sam Li. The headstock had been smashed off and it was so bad that it couldn't be repaired properly, so he carved a new headstock and spliced it into the neck. He stamped the original serial number on the back, although I kept the original headstock to prove that it was legit. I've been using that instrument on stage ever since, although it got re-sprayed white around 1975.

As much as I love the Thunderbird, I think I did over react a bit with the broken Rickenbacker. That particular Rickenbacker was a really nice instrument – an early seventies model complete with the chequerboard inlay and "toaster" pick-up that I'd not been using for long. I started playing it around the time of *Pilgrimage* and used it throughout the recording of *Argus*. To this day, many people I assume I played the Thunderbird on *Argus* due to the fact that I am pictured with it on the inner gatefold sleeve. That is because there was a two month gap between the end of the recording of the album in February and its release date of 28 April 1972. During this gap the sleeve was put together and during that time I made the transition from Rickenbacker to Thunderbird. As such it was the Thunderbird I was playing when we were photographed for the live shots which appear on the sleeve. In actual fact I've rarely used the Thunderbird in the studio, even though it is the instrument I am most associated with. On later albums I would tend to use my 1960s Fender Precision basses. I still love the snarling sound of the Rickenbacker on *Argus,* which was used to great effect on 'Blowin' Free'. It sounded wonderful and I was mortally wounded when that guitar got broken. I just placed it back in its case and parked it in Miles Copeland's basement from where it eventually disappeared, probably ending up being used by one of Miles' other acts who stored gear there. At the time I wasn't too bothered and felt that, as I wasn't using it, if somebody else could put it to good use then fine. Years later I ended up really wishing I still had that guitar. I've used various other Rickenbackers since but none have quite had that same "growl".

I acquired a second Thunderbird a little later that year. We were in New York around the time of my birthday and Miles had been down town checking out Manny's guitar shop. He'd seen a Thunderbird bass in the shop window and actually bought it for me as a present. I thought that was a really generous gesture because at the time a guitar like that would have been quite expensive. I was gobsmacked and thought the world of Miles for doing that. It was a beautiful instrument and when I started to play it I could tell from the sweat marks that my fingers left on the fingerboard that it had never been played – it was mint. I handled that guitar very carefully and only used it on important gigs and special occasions. A few years later, when the band based itself in the US for a period in the mid-seventies, it ended up in storage in a warehouse we used in Connecticut, nearby where we were living, where it was eventually stolen by one of our road crew – an American named Tom Hagen, who I had discovered was smuggling drugs inside our equipment. We'd just finished recording *Front Page News* in Miami. I was awake late one night and saw there was a light on at the end of the corridor. I decided to have a look to see who it was only to find that it was Hagen sat there in his underpants spooning cocaine through a vegetable sieve – he had about two kilos of it. I took one look at him and said "A-ha, I think I know where that might be going, Tom?" We were leaving for the UK the next morning. He said saying "Don't tell the band, man". I responded by saying "I think you're overlooking one thing there, Tom – I am actually in the band". A few months later, following a nasty accident at Leicester de Montfort Hall where he ended up getting taken to hospital, we decided he was becoming a liability and he was fired on the spot. We gave him his ticket and he went back to the States. He went up to our warehouse and grabbed my Thunderbird guitar as well a few other bits and pieces. I did eventually track him down and called him in New York. I said "Hi, Mr Hagen," and he said "Mart, how are you doing?" So I replied "I'm doing okay, but I have a little bone to pick with you, my friend. You walked off with one of my instruments and I want it back." He eventually agreed to send the guitar back to me. He called me back with an air waybill number, but it was all bullshit and the guitar never arrived. I was really angry about that. The only thing I can imagine is that, like a lot of guys who are doing drugs heavily, he probably owed someone a lot of money and once he got fired he realised he wasn't going to be able to pay it and they were going to come looking for him. Perhaps selling my guitar stopped him getting killed, but it was a beautiful instrument and, because it had been given to me as a present by Miles, it had sentimental value. I was really upset to lose it.

Speaking of stolen gear, in June 1972 we headed out on our third US tour. It was due to be a six week stint but ran into problems on 19 June when we hit St. Louis. We had played a gig and the band and crew had gone back to our hotel, with our equipment truck parked outside. In the middle of the night Chris Runciman came into my room and woke me up, saying "We've got a problem. Somebody's stolen the van with all the gear in it." We were in a habit of pulling out the guitars and taking them into the hotel with us, just in case we wanted to have a practice or run through anything in our rooms, so I'm pretty sure Andy, Ted and I all had our instruments with us, but the U-Haul truck containing our backline had been taken and it was found empty a few miles away by the police. This was severely depressing, as we now had no gear transportation and indeed no gear to transport. In those days we used to fly our equipment to the States, because freight was relatively cheap. Nowadays, you just rent a whole backline to your specification. Our amplification back then was predominately made by a company called Orange and had a very distinct sound. It would have been almost impossible to rent this equipment in the States. We were a couple of weeks into a six week tour and so, being that it was going to be impossible to get the right equipment in place to complete the tour, we decided to fly back to England immediately and postpone the rest of the tour. We had to put in an insurance claim and get ourselves new equipment. The really ridiculous thing was that on our next tour we got a phone call from someone asking if we would like to buy our equipment back. So we said "No thanks, we've replaced our stolen equipment with lovely new shiny gear, so we don't need the old gear anymore – that's for you now. Thank you for calling – bye." That totally blew their minds. It must have been pretty disheartening for them when they had got the equipment off the van and realised it was all bright Orange, with each piece sprayed on the back with the Wishbone Ash logo. Orange was a pretty small manufacturer and their equipment was fairly obscure. There was only one other major band in the UK that I can think of who used it at the time and that was Fleetwood Mac. In the States it was simply unheard of. The equipment was therefore impossible to sell in the States because everyone would have known where it came from.

St. Louis, which is located right in the centre of the States and often referred to as the gateway to the west, was always a meeting place for hooking up with second hand guitar dealers – people like Paul Hamer and his sidekick Jol Dantzig. They would roll up at shows in a station wagon full of these wonderful 1960s Gibson and Fender guitars. They would bring them into the gig and show them to us and we'd buy the odd instrument or two. Being Americans they would come on with such a hard sell. "Hey guys, you won't believe what these instruments are going to be worth in ten years time. They're just not going to be available anymore." Allowing for the hype, I would usually keep my hand on my wallet, although I did buy one or two. Looking back on it now I wish I had listened to their sales pitch and bought every guitar they ever offered for sale. Eventually Paul and Jol started the Hamer guitar company and asked us if there was anything we needed that they could build for us. I said to them "How about a bass guitar in the shape and style of a Gibson Explorer guitar". So they took some measurements from my Thunderbird bass and I told them I had a pair of pick-ups from the Gibson Kalamazoo factory that we could put on it. They made me a Hamer bass with serial number 0001, which I used for years alternating with my Thunderbird on stage. I used it on and off from around 1975 through to 2006, when I started to fall out of love with it and decided to sell it.

Whenever we were in St. Louis we would often drive down to East St. Louis, which was predominately populated by black folk, to visit the pawn shops, where you could pick up some really great instruments at low prices, although as a bunch of young long-haired white guys, we didn't tend to hang around there for too long, as our presence could attract hostility in those days.

Not long after we got back to the UK following the postponement of the US tour, I found myself being rushed to hospital with acute appendicitis. I was at home at our place in St. Quintin Avenue and had gone to bed quite early – unusual for me. I started to experience pains and thought I had been poisoned. The whole of my gut felt like it had a lead weight in it – I was in agony. A doctor came out to examine me and told me to put a few things together ready to go to hospital straight away. An ambulance rolled up and I was operated on that night. I woke up the next morning and tried to get out of bed and it felt like someone had stitched my knee to my chin. I'd never stayed in hospital overnight in my life and haven't again to this day. On arriving at the hospital I was apprehensive but once they gave me a pre-med and I was wheeled in on a trolley, I saw the operating theatre sign above me and found myself laughing – drugs can be wonderful and I think that the general anaesthetic gave me the best night's sleep I've ever had. The ward contained guys from all over the place. There was a Spanish chef who in the heat of action had walked onto a fridge door that someone had left open and now had one testicle the size of an aubergine. He kept asking us not to make him laugh as it was such a painful experience for him. It kept us amused but we did wince in sympathy on occasion. There was also a Hungarian chap who showed us his collection of machine gun wounds from the Russian occupation in Budapest in 1956. Understandably he became very agitated when a Russian guy was wheeled into the ward in need of a toe amputation. The Hungarian dude swore to kill him unless he was removed immediately. Some of us intervened, alerted the staff, who quietly shunted him elsewhere. Like many people in our wonderful land I was immensely grateful that the NHS a) existed and b) did such a great job on me.

Once I'd recovered from that little ordeal, we set about recording a single featuring a new song called 'No Easy Road' backed with a re-recording of 'Blowin' Free'. We'd never really been a band that concentrated on singles. There was an element within the band, in later years, that was inclined to want to be more commercial in order to achieve greater success, but I certainly didn't write with the commercial market in mind. 'No Easy Road' was considered light enough in mood for a single release and in many ways was a reaction to the weightiness of *Argus*. We'd worked with the same team for the first three albums. Derek Lawrence had been great for us and did a really good job on the first three albums. Likewise, Martin Birch was an immensely talented engineer and eventually became a successful producer in his own right. But at this stage we felt we really needed to try a few new things such as working with different people at different studios in order to avoid the risk of repeating ourselves musically. So we decided to produce ourselves, working with Keith Harwood as engineer, and went to Olympic Studios in Barnes, South West London. Olympic had a long history of British rock music – The Who and the Stones had recorded there. Although it didn't chart at home, 'No Easy Road' was actually a big hit in the southern States, around the New Orleans area. There were a couple of radio stations down south who played the record a lot and really liked it and so it became a big hit in that area. The next time we went to play in New Orleans there was a huge crowd and we were actually greeted at the airport by a New Orleans trad jazz band, complete with a black dude at the front – kind of like a male cheerleader – all done up with diamonds and gold in his teeth, a fancy hairstyle, funky clothes, skulls hanging off him and a bent cane stick – all very "voodoo". They marched us through the airport, with the band playing trad jazz tunes. It was quite a spectacle and very entertaining both for ourselves and everyone else in the airport.

By July 1972 we were back in the States, honouring the commitments that had been postponed following the equipment theft in St. Louis. During this trip we played an intimate radio concert in front of an invited audience at WMC-FM studios in Memphis. An hour's worth of music was broadcast and three songs from the show later surfaced on the *Live From Memphis* promo album, released by MCA/Decca in the US as a promotional aid to help boost our profile. Our record company felt there were areas in the States where we were well known, but other areas where no one had heard of us. The idea behind the promo album was that it was something that could be sent out to radio stations to educate its listeners as to the existence of the band and the quality of our live performances. The show was pretty nerve racking. It was quite a dead sounding room, hot and sweaty with a small crowd crammed in there. We were playing at a much lower level than we normally would on stage. I don't remember the show as being anything special, but the recording came out pretty well and the album has now achieved an almost legendary status amongst our fanbase.

September 1972 saw us back in the UK, playing a handful of gigs. We played quite a few UK festivals during 1972. Earlier in the year we had appeared at the Great Western Express festival in Lincolnshire alongside Nazareth, Rory Gallagher, The Faces, Roxy Music, The Strawbs and Stone the Crows. There was also the Bickershaw festival near Wigan, which was organised by a very young Jeremy Beadle, who later achieved success as the host of UK television's *Game For a Laugh* and *Beadle's About*. On 16 September 1972 we appeared in Buxton alongside Family, Uriah Heep, Roy Wood's Wizzard, Steppenwolf, Glencoe and a host of other bands. The weather was dreadful and Curved Air were also on the bill and due to perform but vocalist Sonja Kristina threw a wobbly and decided she was cold, freezing and hungry and it was too late for her to perform and so she pulled out of the gig and buggered off. I can remember thinking it was most unprofessional and a bit prima donna-esque, but it is tough at these events when the weather's bad and you're hanging around for hours on end waiting to play. That was also the gig where I first met and chatted with

John Wetton, who was playing with Family at the time. We got on great and I thought he was a really talented guy. He was a fantastic bass player and, of course, later would emerge as a vocalist and songwriter in his own right, although at that time Roger Chapman was very much the voice and front-man of Family. I really enjoyed chatting with John, although it was to be many years down the line before I met with him again, as is often the way within the music business. We played very late at Buxton, in the early hours of the morning. It's always difficult on festivals. You have no idea how it sounds out front and you're up there on a big stage feeling a bit remote from people, which takes a bit of getting used to. Having said this, we did generally tend to go down well at festivals, a lot of people got to hear us and this all helped towards building our following.

On 30 September 1972 we appeared at the *Melody Maker* Poll Winners concert held at the Oval cricket ground in London. We were on the bill by virtue of *Argus* having won Best Album category in their poll. Other acts included Focus, Genesis, Argent and Emerson, Lake and Palmer. We had a lot of trouble getting to the Oval and arrived really late. When we finally got there we were told that headliners ELP had already gone on because people had given up all hope of us turning up. I can remember being told that they were really upset because it made it look like they were supporting us because we went on after them. After the show, we got whisked away quite quickly and were not afforded the luxury of being able to hang around afterwards and say hello to a few people. I can't remember exactly why we had to leave straight after the gig but it seemed to upset a few people. Obviously when the press have given you an award, they want to be able to offer you their congratulations. It's basic good manners to at least acknowledge the press and the media at an event like that. But we were not very skilled with that kind of protocol and under estimated how important all that stuff was. In those days we were very green and didn't really understand how the music business worked. Certainly no one was deliberately trying to snub the press.

October 1972 saw us back in the States. As with most of our early US tours there would be a mixture of our own headlining shows as well as dates supporting bigger, more established artists. On this occasion we had the pleasure of playing some shows supporting Alice Cooper. I really liked Alice. He was a great guy – offstage he was cultured and intelligent, yet on stage he played the role of a complete and utter bogeyman. You would be having a conversation with him backstage and he would be completely lucid and together – he was a good communicator. Then the stage manager would come in and call stage time. Alice would leave and five minutes later he would stagger onto the stage holding a whiskey bottle and looking like death warmed up. The whole front five or six rows in the stadium would shrink back in utter horror with girls screaming and nearly wetting themselves at the sight of this madman in front of them. Off stage he wasn't like that at all – he was actually a really nice bloke. The original Alice Cooper band was great. They reminded me of an American version of Mott The Hoople. Aside from Arthur Brown, Alice was one of the first artists I'd seen who introduced theatre into a rock event. At the end of their first set, their drummer would come out playing this marching roll on the snare room, while the rest of the band captured Alice, took him up to the gallows and put a noose around his neck. The whole of the stadium would suddenly go dark, and one super trouper spotlight would hit Alice in the face as he went through the gallows floor with the noose around his neck shuddering to his "death". Then the whole place would go black while they removed him. It was spectacularly vivid and like something from the middle ages. They were very entertaining shows to play on.

During that same US tour we also played in Des Moines, Iowa on 28 October 1972, supported by US bluesman Taj Mahal. If anyone was to ask me what was the worst show we ever played, that would have to be top of the list. At the sound-check there had been a lot of problems with the power supply and the sound-check took forever, resulting in the doors opening really late. Outside it was about minus fifteen degrees – absolutely perishing. When the doors finally opened everybody rushed in from the streets, freezing, and headed for the bar to get some alcohol down their necks and generally get warmed up. Gradually, as the place filled up, it became quite rowdy in there. Then Taj Mahal walked on stage to start his set. He didn't say anything and nobody took a blind bit of notice. No one even knew he was there. We expected him to be playing acoustic guitar, but he actually started his set with a kalimba – a tiny little handheld device with metal keys that is also known as an African thumb piano. He started playing this into the microphone and you could hardly hear it. He went on like this for four or five minutes and then all of a sudden he completely lost it. He grabbed hold of the microphone and started screaming abuse at the audience, calling them "White, mutha-fuckin', honky bastards" in this really loud voice. He threw the microphone to the floor – it sounded like a thunderclap – and marched off the stage. The place went from being really rowdy to deathly quiet, like a doctor's waiting room. Then all of a sudden some joker at the back broke the silence by yelling "Yeeaah! Rock 'n' Roll, maan" and the place erupted again. I went backstage to see what was going on and the promoter came rushing in yelling at Taj asking "What the hell are you playing at?" Then, in a classic example of attack being the best form of defence, Taj pitched into this guy about how the audience didn't show him any respect – "Listen to me, man. I am the last of the line. After me there is no more." He even insisted on being paid. At that point, given the state the audience was in, we thought it would probably be best if we went on to entertain the troops for a while and Taj could go back on later. With that agreed, the promoter gave Taj a fistful of dollars and went back to his duties. We got kitted up ready to go onstage and just as we were about to go on someone asked "Do you know where Taj is?" and one of the road crew said "Oh, I've just seen him getting in his car." He'd grabbed the money and done a runner. Anyway, we went on stage and pitched into 'Time Was'. I don't think I'd even started singing before the power went.

We left the stage and the road crew scurried around trying to sort out the power problem. Then we were assured everything was okay, so we went back on and started the same song again. This time we got about a minute and a half in before the power went again. I was starting to get really pissed off by this time. I can remember coming off stage and saying to the road crew "Look, we can't play a gig without electricity. I don't care what is involved or whatever it takes. If you need to run a power line from the nearest power station, then do it. Just make sure we've got something that works." So they spoke to the promoter and eventually they ran a power line from another building and assured us that this time everything was going to work. So, about thirty minutes later we were ready to go again. Everyone agreed this was to be our last attempt. Off we went again with 'Time Was' and this time we got about two minutes into the song. We came offstage – Miles was there, the promoter was there. By this stage it was getting so late and it was clear that the electricity supply just wasn't up to it, so we told the promoter that somebody was going to have to go onstage and tell the people that the gig was not going to be happening and that they could have their money back. Miles was brave enough to offer to do this and when he announced that the show was over he got bottles thrown at him, there were doors and windows broken and a near riot broke out – but what else could we do? We ended up with an armed cop at the dressing room door because people were trying to get backstage to sort us out. That whole gig from beginning to end was a complete and utter disaster. I'm sure there are people in Des Moines who must hate us to this day for what happened that night, but it really wasn't our fault. If you're going to promote a gig, you do have to be able to cover a few basics.

We closed 1972 with another headlining UK tour, playing the by now traditional circuit of theatres and town halls – venues such as the Rainbow Theatre in London, Colston Hall in Bristol and the Fairfield Halls in Croydon. The tour was organised by a promoter named Peter Bowyer. Working for him on the tour was a lady named Corinne Schwab. I can remember her introducing herself on the first day of the tour and her saying she was going to be on the tour with us. She was a very good looking girl, so I took her into the dressing room to introduce her to the guys. The minute she left, the guys all went "Whooaaa!!" and I thought "Oh no, there's going to be trouble here," and there was when we reached Scotland.

As we were getting in the lift of the hotel in Edinburgh, having travelled from Glasgow, I looked at our road manager Kevin Harrington and could clearly see he was not his usual self. So I said to him "What's the matter, Kev? You don't look very happy, mate." It turned out he had actually lost his bag. He'd left it on the back step of the van, but it had fallen into the road and someone handed it into the police. The bag contained our list of dates and the hotels we were staying in together with a large bag of marijuana. The very next day, just as Steve and I were going out for some Christmas shopping, the cops rolled up at our hotel. Steve had put the key in the ignition and we were about to take off, but one of the cops reached in and pulled the key out. We asked "What's going on?" and then realised we were surrounded by guys in suits, who were local CID. They wanted us to take them up to our hotel rooms. I'd been up there just minutes before. Hobbit and Kevin were up there, and so was Ted and they were all smoking weed in one room. I really didn't want to go back to the room so I tried to bluff the cops by saying that I was sharing with Steve. Then a guy walks over and says "It's okay, I've got the room list" and I thought "Oh, shit, we're done for now." I found myself in the unenviable situation of having to knock on the door and introduce Ted, Hobbit and Kevin to the local CID. Amazingly they'd finished smoking their marijuana and had thrown the joints out the window or something. The cops searched everything and they found some marijuana in the pocket of a jacket which Ted and Corrine had been sharing, having become quite friendly. Corinne decided to claim ownership of said garment, aware of the fact that a band member could have problems getting into the USA with a drug conviction. She therefore got arrested, as did Kevin (they had his bag full of evidence from Glasgow). They were released on bail and Kev was convicted fairly quickly. When Corinne's case came up a few weeks later, by which time we were all back in London, she came to me and said she was seriously concerned about the outcome of the case. She'd had a little fling with Ted but by this time they were no longer seeing each other. She had to go back to Scotland to appear in court, and was now feeling a bit apprehensive and alone in this situation. I discussed it with her and Maurn, and said that I would help her as much as possible. I did also discuss it with the band and was fairly surprised at their reluctance to get further involved. We were gigging on the day of the court appearance and so I asked Maurn if she would travel up to Edinburgh with Corinne, which she did, and I helped out financially with the whole trip which went fairly okay, with no jail sentence - just a fine. Strangely, the whole thing ended up with Maurn and I becoming good friends with Corinne who went on to great things in the music business soon after. She went to work for Mainman, David Bowie's management company and when he partied with Tony DeFries, his manager, Corinne stayed as his personal assistant and has been with Bowie ever since. Maurn invited them along one night when we threw a party and she brought David along. I don't think anyone could really believe that Bowie was there because he'd become quite famous by then. Corinne, or Coco as she became known, was a great lady and Maurn and I later met up with her in Paris and we all went down to stay together in the Dordogne at a house with no electricity that I ended up wanting to buy. Coco brought Jimmy (a.k.a. Iggy Pop) along with her and we all had a good relaxing holiday together, away from the rock 'n' roll madness.

On a subsequent American tour, Kevin Harrington again found himself on the wrong side of the law over drug possession, this time to quite devastating effect for him, as Mark Emery remembers:

> **MARK EMERY:** *We got busted in Nebraska on an early tour when Ted Turner, Kevin Harrington and myself were all at a club on a night off and the place got raided by police looking for under-age drinkers. We didn't have our passports on us and we got taken back to our hotel to get our passports. While we were there the police found a bag of grass in Kevin's boot, which he carried around for the guys to have a smoke after a gig. Because I was sharing a room with Kevin, he and I ended up in jail for the night and because Kevin was in possession he got deported and that was the end of his US touring career, which was very sad indeed. Luckily none of us had any repercussions from that.*

Our November/December 1972 UK tour was a huge success. We were by now firmly established as a full blown concert band and this circuit was ideal for our style of music. We took to playing that kind of venue like a duck to water and for the next few years we had an era of absolutely stonking gigs in these places. At venues such Newcastle City Hall the whole building would quite often be vibrating and throbbing with the sheer energy of the band's music and the audience's reaction.

At The Airport;
On The Plane...

1973 BEGAN with us retreating to a cottage on the island of Anglesey, North Wales, to put together music for our fourth album. Writing in the countryside was pretty much the done thing at the time – bands such as Traffic, Led Zeppelin and Deep Purple had prepared for albums in similar settings. We rented a holiday cottage and because we went there out of season we got it fairly cheap. The weather was brutal, but getting away from our normal everyday routines allowed us to devote twenty four hours a day to our music without any distractions. As usual I came to the project with various ideas for melodies and lyrics. I was the one guy in the band who was fascinated by the process of recording and all the paraphernalia involved and by this time I was beginning to amass my own recording equipment so that I could record sketches of songs at home. Typically these would contain just acoustic guitar, vocals, and bass. Sometimes I would have a few guitar licks already mapped out. This was great for presenting my songs to the band and giving them a snapshot of what I was aiming for. Of course, once we got into rehearsals and worked on the songs as a full band, then everyone would contribute to the arrangements and it would become a group effort.

With the experience of the 'No Easy Road' single behind us we again decided to produce the album ourselves, with Keith Harwood engineering.

We spent the months of February/March 1973 recording the album at Olympic, with some additional work at Apple Studios. I think we felt we'd learned enough to be able to produce ourselves. In retrospect that was maybe a bit naive and I was really disappointed at how the album eventually turned out, mainly because something went seriously wrong at the mastering stage. When we were recording it in the studio it sounded really good, but all the balls and hi-fidelity got lost during the mastering, making it sound very mid-rangey. I don't think enough care was taken over the mastering. Maybe that was down to us and, through inexperience, we under-estimated how important that final stage was. That was one thing Derek Lawrence was very good at. He always used to follow it through until the test pressing was received and if it didn't sound right he'd go back and do it again. I would love to get my hands on the multi-tracks tapes and actually re-mix the album. As yet I have only been able to find one reel. That is a real disappointment because the album really could benefit from being re-mixed.

Upon its release on 11 May 1973, *Wishbone Four* was well and truly slated by the music press, and to a certain degree, an element of our fanbase. I think that was mainly for two reasons. Firstly, it was not what people were expecting to hear after *Argus*. They wanted more of the same and we were quite stubborn in not wanting to do that. We wanted to move in another direction – a more straight forward, mainstream rock approach. Even the cover was kept deliberately simple with a group portrait on the front and some individual shots of us at our place in St. Quintin Avenue in the centre of the gatefold, which I was always quite fond of. Secondly, for the album to have had any chance of acceptance, it needed to have sounded better. I would like to think that the fact that the material went off on a tangent would have been more accepted had the album sounded right. However, I will stand by the quality of the songs, many of which have, with the passing of time, become fan favourites and have found their way back into live shows in recent times.

Wishbone Four cover shoot outtake, 1973

'So Many Things to Say' came from my good self and was inspired by one of my favourite bands, The Who. The lyric finds me venting off about female expectations. I suppose you could say it's quite a bitchy lyric – I don't write many like this. 'So Many Things to Say' was also notable for introducing Ted's lap steel guitar playing. He'd picked up a lap steel somewhere in the States and soon found that it was something he had a natural feel for, although he approached it in quite a unique way. Ted was never a technical guitarist – he was a feel player – but he really got to grips with the steel and we quite liked the idea of having a different guitar sound in there. It's an unusual instrument which you don't see many rock bands using. The first time he took it on the road he had it sat on an ironing board for the first few gigs. How rock 'n' roll is that? Eventually we managed to get a proper stand for it.

'Ballad of the Beacon' was pretty much Andy's idea and featured him on lead vocal. I contributed the lyrics and the melody for the middle bit which

I sang, and Ted also contributed some lovely guitar work. It really does seem to have absorbed a little bit of Wales and I think Andy was expressing his desire for a pastoral life during a period that was hectic and very "city to city" for all of us.

We re-recorded 'No Easy Road', which had originally been released as a single, this time adding piano and brass. Graham Maitland of Glencoe played the piano. We were looking for a traditional rock 'n' roll piano part, along the same lines as Nicky Hopkins – the guy who played on a lot of records by the Stones, the Who and the Kinks in the sixties. Graham did that really well. Andy had worked with a band called the Sugar Band in the sixties, who had a brass section in their line-up. He was keen to try something similar within Wishbone Ash and so we put a brass section on 'No Easy Road'. We all got into the idea but in retrospect I'm not sure of the wisdom of that. Trying something that radical will always take the music off in a different direction and for people who were fans of the first three Wishbone Ash albums, it was maybe a little too different, but it's easy to be wise after the event. The brass section, comprising of Jimmy Helms, Phil Kenzie, Dave Coxhill and Bud Parks, did a really good job and even played with us live on a few special occasions. 'No Easy Road' was very much a band thing and we kicked this one around on numerous jam sessions. The lyric tells of the fairly crazy rock 'n' roll existence we were living as seen through my eyes.

'Everybody Needs a Friend' was a song that I'd written and put in a lot of time into prior to presenting it to the band. It literally started out as me trying to play the second movement of Ravel's G-major piano concerto. I was trying to play it on a guitar – I got close to it but couldn't quite work it out. But what I was playing led to me getting this sequence which became a whole new song. Andy plays what is probably one of his greatest ever guitar solos on this. It sounds improvised but I spent quite a bit of time with him on that, ensuring that it had the right amount of melodic content. Usually both Andy and Ted tended to play bluesy licks, but this one needed something more melodic. There was some pretty original rhythm guitar from Ted, using a twelve string guitar, which gave it a new texture, as did the keyboards which were played by a session player called George Nash. Lyrically, I think it is rather sentimental, but a lot of people seem to relate to this song. You could hardly call the song mainstream rock music. I guess it comes from my sensitive feminine side – just call me Martina.

'Doctor' was pretty much my idea and something I'd had kicking around since the pre-Wishbone Ash days. Musically, it was another one of our songs that was quite Who-influenced. The lyric was written about Susie Turner, my brother Glenn's girlfriend back in the sixties. She was very beautiful and had been a very successful model in London at the age of sixteen but she'd developed a drug problem and had come home to the West Country. As stated earlier, she was a state registered heroin addict and was on a mission to get the whole world hooked. She blazed a trail and I think she made it to her thirties, but she's been a long time gone now. Thanks for the song babe.

'Sorrel' is very typical of me. That was a song I'd written about a flower that I'd left at home. It was just a little weed with a flower that I'd fished out from between some paving slabs and potted in a plant pot. It was my first attempt at gardening and it was doing really well. I asked my missus to look after it while I was away on tour, but when I got back home it had died. I was a bit bummed out about it so I wrote a song about it and called it 'Sorrel'. The plant actually wasn't sorrel at all. I looked it up in a book and it was something completely different. But I liked the word 'Sorrel' so, for the sake of poetic license, I kept the title. In the song it's personified – it sounds like I'm singing about somebody.

'Sing Out The Song' was one we all contributed to. My lyric was about a pub we used to hang out at in the sixties. I had in mind us young lads drinking cider, singing songs and generally getting fairly drunk and disorderly. I was never that happy with the recording of this one. It should have been looser but everyone did their best with it at the time.

Steve's lyric to 'Rock 'n' Roll Widow' was about an event that happened at an open air gig in Austin, Texas during 1971, where a hot dog salesman was shot very close to the stage we were performing on. It was generally understood by locals we spoke with that he had been having a liaison with someone else's wife. Presumably the angry husband had arrived with a weapon. The shooting took place as we were playing. We were aware of a bit of a scurry going on while we were performing, but as the song goes "the band played on" and it was not until we came off that we were told that someone had been shot. Everyone contributed to this one musically, particularly Ted who shines on the lap steel and lead vocal.

We went back on the road immediately after we had finished recording *Wishbone Four* and debuted our new material at a couple of shows at London's Marquee Club on 17/18 March 1973, before embarking on another lengthy US tour throughout the Spring, which saw us teamed up with Vinegar Joe and the Climax Blues Band. They were both great bands to work with. We were very fond of Climax and had played with them before. Vinegar Joe were a good band as well, fronted by future solo stars Elkie Brooks and Robert Palmer. At one show we did in one of the southern States, we were sat outside the venue with Elkie. It was hot and dusty. Suddenly this guy came cruising up on his Harley Davidson – a leather-clad, midnight cowboy type. Elkie got up and started chatting to him and he said "Wanna go for a ride, baby?" So she jumped on the back of this bike and didn't come back for an hour and a half. When we went back inside her husband Pete Gage – the band's guitarist and bandleader – asked "Has anyone seen Elkie?" So we all said "Err, no, we're not sure where she is." She did come back eventually. I was amazed when Elkie reinvented herself a few years later and popped up on television one night singing that 'Lilac Wine' ballad complete with a whole new set of teeth. She looked great, but completely different to the way I remembered her. Robert Palmer was a fantastic looking guy with a great voice, but he seemed to lack a bit of confidence in those days. I always used to say to him "Robert, just get up the front there and push her out of the way, grab the microphone and go for it." He just needed the encouragement to be able to put in a stronger performance. Elkie kept him somewhat in check and considered herself "the" lead singer and front-person – bless her. Robert certainly got it together eventually and I went to his first solo gig in L.A. a few years later.

Three-band line-ups were commonplace around that time. In fact, we even did a few shows with four bands on the bill. On one of the three-band tours we got a call from our US agent saying "Guys, I want you to do us a favour. Joe Walsh has got a record going out, it's looking good and we want to add him to the tour." We weren't initially keen on having a fourth act on the bill but we agreed to let Joe come out and join the show. Joe's record 'Rocky Mountain Way' was out and it was rocketing up the charts. As it got higher and higher in the charts, he gradually got bumped further up the bill. At one gig we were getting out of the limousine as they were playing 'Rocky Mountain Way' on the radio – it had just got to number one on the American charts. We walked into the gig and Joe was on stage playing the song. It was an amazing moment and things were going really well for him. In fact, if the tour had gone on much longer we would have ended up supporting him. Joe had a great band at the time – we'd played with him years before when he was with the James Gang, but at the time of 'Rocky Mountain Way' he had a band called Barnstorm featuring Joe Vitale on drums and Kenny Passarelli on bass.

Another band that used to support us on shows was ZZ Top, especially when we played in the southern States. The first time I ever heard them was in a field when we were doing an open air gig. When we arrived at the show I could hear this band playing and remember thinking "Wow, that sounds good. Must check that out". I went out onto the side of the stage and couldn't believe there were just three guys making this huge sound. I became an instant fan. I loved Billy Gibbons' guitar playing and voice, which was so low that he sounded almost like a black man. Dusty Hill, the bass player, was great and always used to play an early Fender Precision.

Wishbone Ash and winged critter, 1973

Their drummer Frank Beard was really solid and played straight down the line. They were real authentic Texan guys and always dressed in cowboy boots and hats – this was a few years before their trademark long beards appeared. They were a great band, even then, and worked really hard for years before finally achieving a higher level of success. They have that rare quality where they are able to make totally uncompromising rock music, yet at the same time they have also been able to have hit singles. They've also managed to keep the same line-up throughout their career, which is incredible, especially for a three-piece band. Generally throughout rock history, three-piece bands tend to burn out fairly quickly – take Cream or The Police, for example – because it's difficult to keep it fresh. There are always limitations as to what you can do with three people, but ZZ Top seem to be able to hang in there forever. I take my hat off to them – and my beard too!

Those early US tours were a pretty intense experience. We'd be out there for six weeks or more at a time, playing in a different town or city each night. Looking back on it now, the sheer amount of ground we covered is quite staggering. We would do a gig and have to be up early in the morning to fly to the next show. The road crew would take the gear by road and often had to leave straight after the load-out. Then there was the partying. In pretty much every town you went to there would be a bunch of crazy rock 'n' rollers that would want to get together, meet you and have a party after the gig. You would often end up with a large group of people in somebody's room back at the hotel. We wouldn't get to bed until three or four in the morning, and then we would have to be up early to catch a flight to take us to the next show. Of course, once we'd left town the locals could get some early nights in, whereas we would have to do it all over again in the next town. It wasn't all partying though. As young men we certainly took to the lifestyle, but the main focus with Wishbone Ash was always the music and our performances.

I just mentioned the aeroplane flights. There were a number of flights that I found particularly alarming – particularly when you've been up half the night and only had a few hours sleep. You would get onto some plane in Texas and before you'd even got off the runway there would be some gung-ho Texan pilot coming on the intercom saying "Hi there all you good folks. We're a little bit late today, we're about to take off and we're going to be headed for Atlanta like a bunch of ding-bats." I'd find myself thinking "Oh my God, who is this dude? Is he late to meet his chick for a date or something?" There were certainly some scary flights. We were coming into Atlanta one day – a perfectly normal landing, gradually going down. We must have been a hundred feet off the ground when all of a sudden the plane just shot back up into the air – the G-force was colossal. The pilot came on the intercom and said that something had come on the runway and he'd had to take avoiding action and go for a second attempt. We landed okay second time around but it certainly was a nervy landing.

On another occasion, we were coming into New York. Ian Copeland was just across the aisle from me, pouring a coca-cola into a plastic cup. All of a sudden there was a colossal bang and the plane dropped for what seemed like a couple of thousand feet before the pilot got it back under control. We were coming into heavy clouds and it was getting darker and darker. People were screaming. Ian's coca-cola just shot up into the air and absolutely drenched this business man sat in front of him. People were freaking out but I had actually seen what happened. A thunderbolt had hit the plane and a huge ball of flame shot off the wing. When we eventually landed, the pilot apologised and said there had been a big thunderstorm in the area and that he had asked for permission to fly around it, but because we were so close to the airport and there was so much traffic in the air, he had been told to stay on course.

We had a similar case in Miami one night, when heading out onto the end of the runway. The pilot made an attempt to take off and then had to abort, because the rain was so torrential – it was a tropical rainstorm. So we went back to the airport and waited twenty minutes before trying again. There was a lot of thunder going off around us but we took off and this time didn't get hit. But, boy, that was a bumpy ride.

Later on we were travelling to one of the northern States on a plane that was like a bus, stopping off at various places en route. This time the captain didn't come on the intercom, but actually came into the cabin and said "The airport we're flying to has just been closed because it's snowing heavily and there's snow on the runway. I've asked them for permission to land and because this is a four engine turbo-prop plane, I think I can land it." This sounded like the "latest adventure", so we ordered gin and tonics all round to relax a bit. As we flew into the airport it was getting darker. As we got nearer the ground you could see total white-out – snow everywhere. Approaching the runway we could see clearly that the runway was going left to right and we were going from right to left, so I guess the pilot couldn't see the lights. So he went round and tried again to line up with the runway. We touched down and for a moment it was all looking good. Then gradually the plane just started sliding sideways down the runway. As I'm thinking "Ah, great, we're going to be in a plane wreck now, but I'm sure we'll be cool – we'll get out," the pilot revved up as hard as he could and the plane lifted into the air and straightened up. On the intercom the pilot apologised profusely and said that after a couple of attempts to land it was too dangerous and he was going to have to take a diversion and land at another airport a few hundred miles away where there was less snow on the ground. So we flew off to this place, got out and rented a car and pitched into driving through the storm to make it to the gig. It was an exciting journey, with plenty of skidding and sliding, but eventually we got there ravenously hungry, and in desperate need of a sprinkle. We burst in through the back door and some guy was straight in our faces yelling "Where have you guys been, you were supposed to be onstage ten minutes ago?" What can you say other than "Fuck off, man" – if only he had known what we'd been through to get to that gig! We made it, though, and everyone had a good time.

There was another flight where there was hardly anyone else on the plane – just us and a few other people. There were a couple of black girls who were singers in Patti Labelle's band. I got chatting with one of them and then the plane started pitching about all over the place. Now, as a consequence of the previous night's generous alcohol and drugs consumption I was now getting pretty twitchy / paranoid. In fact, I was still so high I could have flown to the gig myself without a plane. The only good thing about thinking one is finally going to perish, is that it usually guarantees increased album sales. Anyway, I was grateful to the lady who held my hand and talked me down – she was an angel.

Bloody plane rides. It got so bad for me that I ended up feeling "I'm not sure I can hack this anymore." Flying became a serious issue for me in that I found it hard to handle every day when my nerves were frayed from the intense work / partying schedule. Sensitive little soul that I am, I also developed a fear of dentistry, which stemmed from having been traumatised in my late teens when I'd gone to the dentist in Exeter. My usual dentist had been away on holiday and an assistant had put a filling into one of my teeth that had an abscess underneath it. That weekend I was literally crawling up the wall – the pain was unbelievable. I even went out and bought a bottle of whisky and drank until I was comatose to block out the pain. I went back to him on the Monday and he apologised and fixed the problem, but for me that whole experience was so traumatic that I couldn't face walking into a dentist for many years. When I finally did go back to a dental surgery, the smell as I walked in the door, and the sound of the drill, was enough to cause palpitations – my body was very disturbed and I just wanted to run out of the door as fast as I could. I asked the dentist if there was anything that could be done to help me address my fear of dentists. He said I needed a prescription for Librium or Valium – years later they would give you Temazepam. You pop one of those down your

1973

neck and you don't have a care in the world – you just completely relax. Now, that enabled me to get over my fear of dental treatment, and it also allowed me to get over my fear of flying. I'd pop one of these tablets every time I had to get on the plane and everything would be alright. I managed to recondition myself using pharmaceutical drugs. Nowadays I don't have that problem at all and haven't had to take tablets for many years. In fact, I'll fall asleep before the plane has even taken off.

It wasn't just plane journeys that could be problematic – there could also be problems when travelling by road. Fairly early on in the band's career we'd done some gigs in France and Germany. In those pre-EU days you could either get a green card from your vehicle insurer or you could purchase insurance at the border. On one occasion we had elected to buy insurance at the border of each country we entered, as it was generally cheaper. We had done that successfully in France and Germany. Then we rolled up at the Italian border and Steve Upton, with his managerial head on, jumped out of the wagon with his clipboard and pieces of paper and marched over to this uniformed Italian immigrations officer who couldn't speak a word of English. Doing the usual hand gesticulation, Steve said "Hello, we want to buy insurance for Italy". The guy looked at Steve's documents and said "No green card – No Italia". So Steve said "No, we don't have a green card. We want to buy insurance here" and started to get money out, waving it in front of the officer to demonstrate his ability to pay. This guy clearly didn't realise you could buy insurance at the border and came straight back "No green card – No Italia." So Steve said again, "No, you don't understand. We want to purchase insurance to go into Italy". The guy looked over at us and then snatched all this paper that Steve was holding straight out of his hand, and proceeded to screw it all up in a ball in front of his face, still screaming "No green card – No Italia!" The look on Steve's face was priceless and he was totally mortified that he couldn't make this guy understand that he wanted to buy insurance. We were all sitting in the van rolling around with laughter. Of course we now had to figure how we were going to get into Italy. We followed the maps and went to another town about fifty miles away and tried at another border crossing. Of course, there were absolutely no problems. The guy there spoke a little bit of English and understood what we wanted to do immediately and we got in. All this meant we were a little late getting to the gig. When we got there we opened the back of the van ready to get our gear out. The people at the venue stood there looking and said "No, no, no, no, no – come". So we followed them into the gig. They pointed at this crappy little set-up on the stage which consisted of some little tiny amps and a cheap drum kit. "Use this – for you", they said. Realising they wanted us to use their gear we said "No, that's okay. We'll bring our own gear in." So we all marched out to the back of the van and started getting our equipment off. Then one of the guys at the venue came after us and shouted "No, no, no – use this" and pulled this gun out from under his jacket. At this point we realised it could well be in our best interests if we did the gig using their equipment and so we said "Oh, okay, no problem". We'd had a few situations like that in the States where the local sheriff wasn't happy with where we were parked. You would try to explain and negotiate and then out would come the shooter. We didn't expect that in Italy though.

June 1973 saw us back on the road in the UK, taking the Rolling Stones mobile recording truck out to a number of shows to compile material for a live album. We'd always considered ourselves essentially a live band. We were arguably at our best on stage and we'd spent a number of years developing our stage show. By this time we were playing quite a wide range of material on stage, selected from the four albums we'd recorded up to that point, and we really wanted to put out a document of how the band sounded on stage. We broke off briefly from the UK tour for a trip over to Holland for an appearance at the prestigious Pink Pop Festival on 11 June. Then, following the UK shows, it was back to the States for another couple of months touring throughout August/September 1973 – the band's schedule really was quite intense around this time.

We returned home to mix the live album at Olympic Studios and play a handful of UK shows during October 1973, supported by a band called

Receiving BPI awards from Janet Webb, Dec 1973

Home, who we really liked. They were a bit quirky and had their own style. Their main songwriter and lead vocalist was a guy called Mick Stubbs and they also had future AC/DC bassist Cliff Williams in their line-up, as well as an impressive young guitar player called Laurie Wisefield, who stood out immediately on stage – we all thought he was a little star. Another US tour followed and took us through to December 1973, a month that saw the release of our double live album *Live Dates* as well as a short European tour. We rounded off the year with a pre-Christmas show at Alexandra Palace on 22 December, headlining above Al Stewart, Vinegar Joe and Renaissance. This was a pretty prestigious show. In addition to being joined by Graham Maitland on piano as well as the brass section for the encore of 'No Easy Road', we were also presented with BPI awards for *Argus* and *Wishbone Four* by Janet Webb of the *Morcombe and Wise Show* fame.

Shortly after we had recorded *Wishbone Four,* I bought a house at the end of Meredyth Road, Barnes. I took out a huge bank loan because I couldn't get a mortgage and I paid this back over a few years. So, for a while I was sitting pretty because I owned the house outright, while everyone else would eventually have huge mortgages. Now, once Maurn and I had got our house together, I thought that it would be really rather cool if I invited the parents to come and stay with us at Christmas, which they were very happy to do. I had a good friend Hilary (married Tony Self, one of our soundmen, years later) who was working in catering, so I asked her to capture a rib of beef on the bone for us. She did so about ten days before the celebratory day. I figured it would be fine in the fridge for that amount of time, well matured even! As is the custom, we had all had a bit to drink on Christmas Eve and, when I emerged the next morning in search of a much needed cup of PG tips, I discovered to my horror that some pissed plonker had left the fridge door open all night and the beef, which was already looking very dark, had been subjected to gas central heating all night and had partially slow cooked to almost black in places

With Ted Turner, Alexandra Palace Dec 1973. Ted and I always enjoyed a warm relationship and I regard him as a truly great guitar player.

and had now acquired an extremely unhealthy looking green fungus over various parts. So, in utter panic I was headed for the door to plonk it in the bin or feed to some poor malnourished passing critter – not that there were many wolves or hyenas in SW13 in the 1970s – whilst at the same time pondering the embarrassment of trying to find a pizza joint or curry house that was open on Christmas day....ughh! My Dad (Ed) was coming downstairs and spotted me with the beef – "What are you doing with that?" he asked. "I'm going to bin it," I replied. "I've seen better looking road-kill – its 'orrible." "No, no, give that to me" said Ed. I watched as he sharpened a knife and with experience gained by living through the war, I guess, he set about slicing off the entire surface of the beef and then rubbed it all over with salt, onion, vinegar and mustard. It went in the oven early and spent hours cooking slowly and when it emerged I swear it was the best piece of beef I had ever tasted and a memorable meal was enjoyed by all!

To continue the Turner household hilarities I thought I might recount to you some of the conversation that took place over Christmas dinner. Some male person – probably me – had mentioned oral sex.

Eileen (my mother): *"What is aural sex, dear? Is that talking about it?"*

Martin: *"No Mum – I don't think it's right for me to explain that to you. Why don't you ask Ed?"*

Ed whispers in her ear, to which Mum gasps and utters:

Eileen: *"But only a street girl would do that"*

Martin: *"Mum, are you calling my wife a whore?"*

Eileen: *"Maurn would never do something like that"*

The whole table of inebriated family members collapsed in fits of giggles and raucous laughter. It is revealing to look back on those times when we had three channels on the TV and nobody had even conceived of anything like the internet. Very sweet!

A little rhyme I wrote about this:

When its wine that we drink
We begin to think
In a slightly more relaxed way
When we've cooked the goose *
And the tongue is loose
It's amazing what people will say.

*or beef in this case!

On the subject of Barnes SW13, which I discovered whilst working at the old Olympic Studios, and became very fond of, I discovered that I was not the only musician who had made the decision to live there. I used to regularly see fellow members of the rock fraternity driving by, and later found out that they lived locally also – Roger Chapman, Greg Lake, and Paul Rodgers all lived there at around that time, as did Roger Taylor who I got together with a few times. Barnes was such an eclectic place to live then with a real mix of residents and many small businesses. We bought a lot of our furniture from our friends business, Remember When. The cafés were artisan – now it's all Starbucks and bankers. I guess you could say it changed from wankers to bankers – if that is a change?

1974 began with us playing another US tour – our eighth within the space of less than three years. We had then planned to take some time out to write material for our fifth studio album, for which plans were afoot for us to record in the States. After playing a live set for BBC Radio 1's *In Concert* programme at the Paris Theatre in Lower Regent Street, London on 21 February 1974, we began writing and rehearsing for the new album at Miles Copeland's basement. We'd had not got very far at all when on 2 May 1974, Ted Turner, one half of our twin-guitar frontline, called a meeting at Miles' house and announced to us that he wanted to leave the band – it also happened to be Miles' birthday.

By this stage the band had been together for just over four years. We'd reached a level of success where there was now such a huge demand for live performances and recordings that we could all see our lives mapped out for months on end – jump through this hoop, jump through that hoop. Generally there was an air of tiredness and frustration around that time. We had reached a point where we were all really fatigued and we all desperately needed a month off, for the sake of our own sanity, if nothing else. We just needed to refresh our heads. Ted was the youngest member of the band and, unlike Steve or myself, he had never worked at this level before. Steve and I had both done a six year apprenticeship, playing in semi-pro bands prior to Wishbone Ash, whereas Ted had come straight out of school, joined our band and was launched into stardom within a year. I think he found that hard to handle and I don't think he was really ready for the intensity of being in a major league rock band. He used to get burned out quite badly. On stage he used to sweat profusely – you could see it squirting out of his pores when he was playing – and he would get dehydrated. We even had to rush him to hospital on a couple of occasions. Having said all this, it is inevitable in the life of a band that things can become stale and jaded and the exit of one band member and introduction of a fresh face can provide the dynamics to rejuvenate things. In that sense a change can be as good as a rest.

TED TURNER: *My decision was based upon artistic needs. Our personal worlds were changing. I was listening to Stevie Wonder (Talking Book era) and I was attracted to the strong rhythmic groove in his music and many others during this time. Being able to dance to music seemed to me to be essential to constructing music. This is a different thought pattern than I had been used to but a direction in which I wanted to go and this led to a general dissatisfaction to continue playing music which my heart was no longer into. I could have stayed with the band and made much money over the next decade, enjoying the success we had generated.*

I think few would have argued that I had earned this, but as a musician to stand on stage and fake it was a situation that I could not contemplate or tolerate. I was also burnt out. The rigors of constant touring and incessant demands of the crazy world of rock 'n' roll took its toll on a young man still only twenty-three years old. There had to be more to life than this.

I did question Ted's decision, but his mind was made up. He'd met a girl in New Orleans called Anastascia and between the two of them they had decided that they wanted to do some travelling. So they bought a couple of donkeys and set off for the mountains of Peru. We didn't hear from them for about six months. Ted's Mum even called me up and said "I'm really worried about our David." I think they did run into a few problems and I believe they were even attacked by bandits at one point. I'm sure Ted could write a whole book on that trip alone. Ted moved to the States when he returned from Peru and ended up living in Los Angeles, near the Sunset Strip, where we used to play at the Whisky-a-Go-Go in the early days. A little later he moved up into the hills and lived in Buckminster Fuller's geodesic dome overlooking L.A. Ted provides his own recollections of his spiritual and musical journey during the mid seventies:

TED TURNER: *Personal growth had been my quest for quite some time. Some of my choices gave amusement to some. However, inner peace and spirituality were of significant importance for me to attain. This yearning led me to R. Buckminster Fuller, who became my mentor – my greatest teacher. His always comprehensive vision, love and compassion for our world touched me deeply. He presented information and knowledge in a manner that was unbiased, logical and factual. It was great science. He allowed me to understand how the Universe always incorporates all in such an elegant manner. He changed how I view the world and my place in it. He is the best human being I have ever met.*

Michael Mitchell is a student of Bucky and followed him around the world on his lecture tours gaining deep insight and giving valuable support in return. I first met Michael in New Orleans. He was introduced to me by Brian Glynn – a mutual friend who was a co-partner in Beaver Productions, the agency that promoted all the Wishbone shows and many other bands around the southern states. Michael was looking for a rock star. Brian had direct access to the rock star store. Years of experience gained working with the agency enabled this. Conversations between them, fueled by their mutual appreciation for Bucky, led them to me. Michael asked Brian which rock star he would choose to front this band. So, after careful consideration, with all that he knew, who do you think became the candidate for the job? I had just returned from Peru, after reading one of Bucky's books supplied by Brian. He mentioned Michael to me and his idea, so I requested an opportunity to meet with him. The idea was seeing that music transcends the borders of countries on our planet, and being one of the most effective, powerful ways of communicating to people – particularly to the young – what about trying to put Bucky's information to music – a radical notion, even then. To serve humanity and the attempt to bring the tribes of all our races together through music was the challenge. This was a noble cause and a cause worth pursuing. This is how the World Man Band came into being. Remember this was way before Live Aid and the eco songs and movement of the eighties.

We packed our bags and equipment and moved to Los Angeles, set up a studio on top of a mountain in Topanga Canyon, with views to the Pacific Ocean, in a geodesic dome overlooking Malibu Beach. We worked for about a year producing songs, ideas and then moved north along the coast to Carmel Bay. Michael had friends in the area who owned the Mr. Natural fruit juice company. They supplied us with a studio in the local redwood forest, where music could be played any time of day with no interruption. Mike on drums, me on guitar – hours and hours were spent playing together developing ideas. I remember Ian Copeland stopping by and playing bass in between his travels and brother Stewart calling informing me that he had just formed a band called The Police (strange name I thought – little did I know). During this period a local band The Misfits would allow me to step in and jam with them. It was all good fun. I learned how to surf and how to ski in this beautiful area of central California.

Distractions were many. I was a young man enjoying life. This led to failure – failure to bring this great intent to the world. But it was the foundation for me as a songwriter. Many songs were developed for the World Man Band project – some incarnations made it to later recordings. For example 'Why Don't We' on Here To Hear and 'Something Between' and 'Time Will Call' on Ecklektic Value are World Man Band songs in spirit. Perhaps in the future this music may come to light.

Last US tour with Ted Turner – January 1974.

CHAPTER SEVEN

Tonight I Saw The Magic In Your Eyes

REGARDLESS OF Ted's decision to leave Wishbone Ash, Steve, Andy and I remained totally locked on to what we were doing and were determined to continue. We weren't crazy about going the route of advertising for a replacement for Ted, so we made some phone calls to people we knew. We had a few people in mind, including Mick Ralphs of Mott The Hoople. I was quite friendly with Mick around that period and would see him from time to time and remember asking him if he would be interested in joining Wishbone Ash. In fact, I was cruising through Shepherd's Bush in my Daimler coupe when I saw him pushing his car. I slowed down and adopted a mock classic rock star pose and shouted out of the window "Hey, man, do you need a hand pushing that piece of shit?" We both had a laugh at the situation and I gave him a hand to push-start his car and then we went back to his place for a coffee. He was actually quite enthusiastic about the idea of joining Wishbone Ash, but he had already signed a contract to form Bad Company with Paul Rodgers and Simon Kirke of Free and Boz Burrell of King Crimson. Since they were managed by Led Zeppelin's manager Peter Grant – who did have a bit of reputation – Mick didn't feel it would be a very good idea not to fulfil his agreement. But he did come down to a rehearsal and had a play with us. However, when we started to play together, I started to doubt whether he would have fitted. The Wishbone Ash guitar style is so precise

– it's almost like being part of an orchestra – whereas Mick has a more orthodox rock 'n' roll style. Mick's a great player, but as much as I loved him as a guy and thought he was a great guitarist, I'm not sure that he would have been right for us. Certainly if he had joined the band it would have changed us into something quite different. One name that kept coming up amid suggestions was Laurie Wisefield, the then twenty year old guitar player from the band Home. Here Laurie fills us in on his background:

LAURIE WISEFIELD: *I got my first acoustic guitar at age eight – it had a very high action and was very difficult to play, as a lot of cheap acoustics were back in the day. My dear Grandfather bought it for me. My main early influences were Elvis and Scotty Moore, Cliff and the Shadows and tunes like 'Shaking All Over' by Johnny Kidd and the Pirates, with those amazing electric guitar riffs that made the hairs on the back of your neck stand up. When you heard that stuff coming out of a jukebox, the sound was electrifying and, at the risk of sounding like a grumpy, better dare I say than MP3 files. I really loved Hank Marvin's playing and still do – lovely touch, very elegant and melodic. There was also a band I saw when I went to Butlins holiday camp as a kid called Dave Curtis and the Tremors. They played some Eddie Cochran stuff, early R&B and I remember they did an instrumental version of 'Hall Of The Mountain King', also with Shadows kind of moves, which was great. That also made a big impression. I guess I was around eleven years old then. I was mostly self-taught although I did have a few lessons learning some scales and basic stuff. There were quite a few school bands – The Inquests and the Four Fables come to mind. The latter appeared on Stubby Kaye's Silver Star Show on TV. I was singing and playing guitar. I was around thirteen years old at that time I think, but my first pro band was called Dave Andrews and the Sugar which later became just the*

> *Sugar. It was a five piece band made up of my oldest pal Cliff Williams, who went on to join me in Home and has been with AC/DC now for many years, Dave Wheelock on drums/vocals, Malcolm Weyman on Hammond organ, as well as a few lead singers whose names I can't remember.*

We'd been impressed by Laurie when Home had toured with us. We liked him as a guy, his playing was excellent and he had a certain charisma. By this time Home were beginning to fall apart. They had split with their songwriter Mick Stubbs and were out in the States backing Al Stewart. We had links with Al Stewart through his manager Luke O'Riley. In fact, Luke had previously been a radio presenter in the States and we were instrumental in getting him into the management side of the business. Luke had done an interview with Wishbone Ash during which one of us had sworn on air, not realising he had gone live with the microphone, and he had got fired over it. We had felt really bad about this and so Miles said to him "Luke, get yourself on a plane and get over to London and I'll get you a job in the music business." Miles was true to his word and that was the start of Luke's career in management.

LAURIE WISEFIELD: *I don't remember there being a massive bonding between Wishbone Ash and Home at the time we toured together – just a mutual appreciation really and maybe a drink or two. I do remember thinking how interesting and unusual Steve Upton's style of drumming was as he played open handed hi-hat with his right hand and left footed bass drum which was pretty unique to me. I hadn't seen anyone play that way before and I haven't since. I remember seeing Wishbone Ash once before that tour at the Zoom Club which was a pretty dodgy little place in Frankfurt where Home used to play fairly regularly. The owner of the place was a guy named Cookie who was a big Home fan and he helped us along in the early days but the place was always getting raided by the Polizei! Of course the way Wishbone*

Ash gelled together was really nice – how the three guitar players played together. I say three guitars as Martin's bass was also playing harmony lead lines at times. We really enjoyed them. The sound of the band was really clean and the folky-rock thing was pretty prevalent at that time, which was refreshing.

The break-up of Home was a difficult time. In retrospect I think we were all fairly exhausted but especially Mick Stubbs who was the main writer in the band and a family man with a wife and children. Our third album The Alchemist took a lot out of us all, followed by a lot of touring, constantly up and down motorways, moving around Europe – the usual stuff that you do. We would play pretty much anywhere and anytime. Then there was the partying that needed to be done, which is another story! I think if we could have taken a break and recharged our batteries maybe we could have stayed the course a little longer. Anyway it wasn't to be and Mick Stubbs left and so Cliff Williams, Mick Cook and I started auditioning for another singer, but hadn't yet settled on anyone. Ian Copeland was a bit of a party animal and a friend and so Cliff and I would go and hang out over at his flat – or should I say den of iniquity – in Hampstead along with a whole load of people depending on who was in town. Ted, I seem to remember, would also frequent at times. Another regular there was a chap named Luke O'Reily who at the time managed Al Stewart. So there's the connection – Al and Luke loved the band and asked us if we would be interested in being Al's backing band for a tour of America along with a keyboard player called Francis Monkman (ex-Curved Air). Home had been offered a tour in America but it had never come to fruition for one reason or another and so we jumped at the chance of going to the USA for some excitement and adventures.

With Laurie being top of our list of potential replacements, we decided the best course of action would be for one of us to go to see him in the States. Andy had already agreed to play a couple of shows with Renaissance at the Academy of Music and so was well positioned to catch up with Laurie and have a chat with him about him joining the band. This made sense because obviously it was him who was going to have to play alongside Laurie.

LAURIE WISEFIELD: *Andy turned up. We were just chatting, being social and I asked him what he was up to? He said he was guesting on a couple of shows with Renaissance as he'd played on their album. He also told me that Ted had quit the band and that I was his first choice to join Wishbone Ash and replace Ted, and asked how did I feel about it? I was quite taken back that Ted had quit the band but also very chuffed that Andy was excited about us playing together. I told Andy I was sorry to hear it hadn't worked out with Ted, but I knew from my experience with Home how things can get. I said "Yes, I would love to get together with everyone, have a play, see how we get on and take it from there." I did the remaining shows with Al and then went back to England where we all got together at Miles' house in St. John's Wood for our first musical encounter that led to many years of playing together. It was all very informal and it seemed from Andy and Steve that the decision had already been made. Martin, I think, may have had some reservations because I was quite different to Ted, whereas Andy and Steve seemed to embrace the change. I think Mart was a little slower in coming to terms with it. Anyway from my standpoint I knew it may take some time to integrate my style musically but it was a no brainer really so I just threw myself in the deep end, as you do.*

I don't think Laurie took much persuading and by July 1974 we had a new line-up in place and were busy writing and rehearsing for our next album.

> **LAURIE WISEFIELD:** *My initial feeling with the guys was very positive. I think everyone seemed to get on pretty well. Steve was great, pretty easy going and just loved to be playing and jamming. Andy seemed to be very enthusiastic and was very open to any suggestions guitar-wise, encouraging any different styles that I was into like finger-picking techniques and any melodic ideas. He was very keen on opening new avenues that had not been explored in the band before and anything that could be a bit hip. Martin was cool and open to suggestions also, but as I said before seemed to have a few more reservations in the early stages, maybe understandably, as I was probably throwing a lot of stuff in the hat stylistically – perhaps quite different at times from what they had done in the past, but to let creativity flow you need to be open and get everything out as much as possible. Some of it sticks to the wall and some of it doesn't. Martin had a very strong sense of melody which I believe was a huge part of the band's strength.*

Obviously when a new player comes into a band, there is always an influx

of new influences and fresh ideas. Laurie was very self-assured and very confident, which is a quality I like, and he truly was a fabulous musician. However, when Laurie first joined the band he was really into speedy, finger-picking, very much along the lines of Albert Lee and certainly very different to what Ted brought to the table. That influence is certainly evident on the work he did with Home, as well as in Laurie's

Laurie Wisefield, USA 1974 - his technical ability made everyone step up a notch

early work with Wishbone Ash – it was an almost country-style technique. Both Laurie and the band had to modify their styles a little in order to absorb these different influences and as time went on Laurie's style became more rock-based, but I think Laurie really got into the spirit of what we were about. Obviously on stage he had to play a lot of Ted Turner's licks, which were probably a million miles away from what would come naturally for him, and he did a great job on that front. He was able to put his own stamp on the music without losing too much of the original feel. He also made his influence strongly felt on the new music we were putting together and it was great having a new guy on board who could offer something different. Laurie was such a good musician technically that I think it made everyone step up a notch.

Laurie joining Wishbone Ash also resulted in a change of dynamics within the lead guitar department in particular. The relationship of the original harmony twins had been that Ted was the slow, bluesy, laid back, feel player, whereas Andy was the faster, flashier, more technical player and more of a performer on stage. The two sides married together very well and there was a common ground in the middle. It worked beautifully. The rapport musically between Andy and Laurie was completely different and initially it appeared to me as though Andy was somewhat intimidated by the fact that there was now such a technically proficient guitar player in the band. Steve and I recognised Andy's need to adjust, but also advised him to just do what he did so well naturally. I think Andy did feel at the time that he needed to improve to attain Laurie's technical agility. Laurie's addition to the band certainly inspired Andy to concentrate on his technique and over the course of a year or so he spent a lot of time practicing in order to match Laurie's technique. Arguably this made Andy a better musician and no longer intimidated by the Speedy Gonzales alongside him. Personally I've always thought that music is not purely about being able to play at lightning speed. When you get hung up on being the fastest guitar player in the west, there is invariably someone who comes along ten minutes later who is faster. To me, the feel and the creative aspects are far more important than technical ability. Mark "Hobbit" Emery remembers the changes within the band at this point.

> **MARK EMERY:** *I never got involved in the inner dealings within the band. I always kept myself respectfully private on that and I respected their privacy and their business with each other. I always minded my own business as far as who was or wasn't getting on in the band. There were times when Ted was the outsider and, of course, he did become the outsider voluntarily after he got into Buckminster Fuller and geodesic domes in L.A. and got influenced by a few people who led him down the road of dispossessing the need to be a rock star anymore. Laurie had no such doubts about his ambitions. Laurie was good fun to work with – a brilliant guitarist who had a very professional approach to the band. I remember anytime Laurie made a mistake in the studio he would say "Just Testing" – for some reason that sticks with me.*

We spent the months of August/September 1974 at Criteria Studios in Miami, recording *There's The Rub* with producer Bill Szymczyk. This would be our first experience of working at an America studio with an American producer. Likewise it would be Bill Szymczyk's first experience of recording a British band. Bill had worked with a host of US artists – Joe Walsh, The James Gang, Eagles, J.Geils Band, etc – but was looking to record with a British band. He wanted to record with The Who. They were on the top of his list, but weren't ready to record at that point. We were also on his list and were contacted via Miles Copeland. I think Bill was intrigued to find out how British guitar bands went about recording guitars. Likewise, we were just as keen to experience working in a top American studio with a successful American producer. It was an equal trade-off.

When we first arrived in Miami, Bill was a bit taken aback to find that the line-up had changed. Bill was expecting Ted to be with us and was a little surprised when we turned up with this new chap. But everyone got to know each other and everything went pretty well. We respected Bill's experience and the success he had achieved and were keen to learn from him. There were, however, occasional differences of opinion, particularly between Bill and myself as to how my bass should sound. He wanted something that was much more orthodox – like the Eagles. My reaction to that was "No, mate, that's not what I do. I play my bass guitar through a guitar amp – it distorts, growls and sounds generally nasty." Bill was fairly amused at my concept of a bass sound, but we worked together and agreed on a sound we were both happy with.

Not all of Bill's recording preferences and techniques were what we would have called orthodox, however. For example, we'd been lugging around tons of equipment for years and during the course of a recording session we'd experiment with different amps in order to get the sound we were looking for. At Criteria there were walls of amplifiers in the studio – 4 x 10 Fenders, Fenders Twins, Marshalls, Orange, you name it. On one occasion Laurie was trying to get a certain guitar sound and said to Bill "What I'm after Bill, is the kind of guitar sound you got with Joe Walsh on 'Rocky Mountain Way'" Bill replied, "Oh, you want that guitar sound, huh? Give me two minutes." Bill disappeared from the studio and a few minutes later came back with a Pignose amp – a tiny portable amplifier with a 5" speaker. Everyone laughed and said "You've got to be joking, right?" and Bill replied "No, that is the actual amplifier we used to record Joe's guitar." We plugged it in and fired it up and said "Wow". It was a whole new world – take a tiny little amplifier, stick a microphone on it and it sounds massive. I was so impressed that I asked the crew to go out and find me a bass version. They came back with a Dwarf amp, made by a company in California, which worked on the same principle as the Pignose. That became my recording amplifier for the rest of the seventies. In fact I still get a good sound out of it today. That was a major breakthrough for us – it was like walking into a session with your handbag instead of tons of gear.

Bill did actually try to get Joe Walsh involved with us at one point. Joe was on holiday in the Bahamas and he stopped off at the studio in Miami on his way back. Joe was having a hard time with the loss of his daughter in a road accident and the break-up of his marriage and Bill thought it would

Andy Powell, USA 1974

be a good idea to get him involved with another band. At the time we were still adapting to having Laurie in the band and we felt the last thing we needed was a third guitar player. Much as we liked Joe – we'd toured with him in the States both with the James Gang and his own band Barnstorm and thought he was a brilliant player and a great guy – we just couldn't see it working. Towards the end of the *There's The Rub* sessions, the Eagles came to town, ready to record their next album, *One Of These Nights,* and we would often all go out for dinner together. Bill always used to say "If I could get the guitars out of Wishbone Ash and the vocals from the Eagles, I could make the best hit record ever." That's exactly what he did a couple of years later with *Hotel California,* Joe Walsh's first album with the Eagles. When I listen to that album I can hear the room at Criteria as well as the tricks Bill learned from us about recording guitars. We used to put a lot of time into the guitar parts – we would try out different instruments, different amplifiers and different sounds, even changing them during a solo, so as to add variety. That way you can have prolonged instrumental guitar sections without it ever getting boring. You can hear that right across the 'Hotel California' title track in particular.

Just as Bill picked up a few things from us about recording guitars, I equally learned a great deal from him about recording techniques. At that stage I'd become totally fascinated by the whole process of recording and wanted to learn as much as I could about production. What better person to learn from than Bill Szymczyk? I was constantly asking him questions about equipment, effects and the desk. I learned a hell of a lot from him and I was really impressed by both his craft and his skill.

LAURIE WISEFIELD: *From when I was involved and we started writing and recording together, it all moved very quickly. I felt accepted as an integral member of the band, I think mainly because we had come up with a newer sound on There's The Rub which was a different sound and direction from anything the band had come up with in the past. Some of the fast, flashier guitar parts and layered parts were quite different and a lot of that stuff came from my style and input. Also a lot of credit should go to Bill Szymczyk and Alan Blazek who were at the helm as producer/engineer. There were some skeleton ideas that the guys had – I remember the early bit of 'F.U.B.B.' which got developed into a bit of an epic. Also the opening riff of 'Hometown' was there. 'Don't Come Back' was started but very basic – the flashy harmony guitar stuff at the beginning and end was my input and fairly obvious to hear really. 'Silver Shoes', 'Persephone' and 'Lady Jay' I think we put together pretty much from scratch together. I'm sure everyone will have a different slant on what was there and what wasn't. I can remember most of it vividly as it was an exciting time for me. Pretty much everything on that album was written from a musical standpoint first and the lyrics came later. You can hear the difference in styles on that record. You can pick out who's playing what most of the time and it blends nicely between us, I think – partly because the styles hadn't had much time to come together yet. As Andy and I played together over the years, we influenced each other a lot and our styles became much closer. That is he may do something that would be very much the kind of thing I would do and vice versa.*

During the course of the recording sessions for *There's the Rub*, we reached a point where the album was taking shape and we were on schedule, so Bill Szymczyk decided we could afford ourselves the luxury of a night off and kindly invited us all over to his place for a barbecue. We met his wife and kids and enjoyed his lovely home with a dip in the pool and a fabulous meal, accompanied by the usual consumption of alcohol and weed. Fairly late in the evening we discovered a mutual liking for the card game of poker and, after midnight, Laurie and Andy, having little interest in the game, took our car and went off back to our temporary home whilst Bill, Alan Blazek, Steve Upton and myself settled in to do battle at the card table – with a fist full of dollars each, of course. We moved on to the serious stuff at this point – Scotch whisky. I just have to add that of the many varied inventions to come from Scotland this must surely rank as one of the greatest in my humble opinion. So, the hours went by with all of us engrossed in our pursuit. There was Bill – wise, intelligent, older and a much respected producer; his sidekick, Alan – a young, gung-ho, tough guy with a dash of redneck on board; and then Steve and myself – both of us deceivingly good poker players for young dudes. By about 4.30–5am we had utterly fleeced the pair of them – I don't think they had a dollar left between them. Our next problem was to find a way of getting back across town, the harmony twins having taken our wheels. Bill kindly called up a cab company or two but did not have great success – they were all quoting 40 minutes or so. He suggested that we take his car and that Alan would pick him up for the studio the next morning. This was clearly a generous gesture on his part but he did add that the car was low on gas and we would need to stop at a service station. "OK, no problem Bill," I said and, knowing that he had no more cash, I added "So, have you got some money for the fuel?" while holding out my hand. He looked incredulously at me and said: "I don't believe you guys – you lounge around my place all evening, swim in my pool, eat all my food, drink me dry, empty my wallet, then take my car and you want money for gas! Do you want to get in bed with my wife before you leave?" We did have a great laugh that night and I became immensely fond of Bill.

One evening during the *There's The Rub* recordings we went out to Tony Roma's restaurant for a meal. We were all eating at the table when this huge Mafioso-type dude walked in with his entourage and a dynamite-looking woman strolling along behind him, just oozing sexuality and dressed like some movie starlet. I don't think there were too many folks in the place unaware of their entrance. This guy was a massive, mean looking son-of-a-bitch, which was, of course, exactly the impression he wanted to give. Miami is a place where narcotics from South America enter the USA and enormous sums of money are made and lost when it gets ugly, as it so easily can, and this guy looked like the type who was probably in the thick of it. So anyway, Bill casually leaned over to Laurie – as one Jewish guy to another – and said "Laurie, I'll give you a hundred dollars if you go over to that guy who just walked in and say "Could I screw your wife for you, Sir?" The thought of little Lol doing such a thing was totally mind boggling and extremely funny – he is not exactly a huge guy and guns would probably have appeared within seconds. It had our whole table in stitches. Laurie, of course, politely declined Bill's generous offer.

There's the Rub was released in November 1974. It attracted pretty respectable reviews from the music press, which was encouraging given the negative comments that had been made about *Wishbone Four*. However, I was never really affected by the press reviews. What was more important to me is what the people buying the albums thought. For Wishbone Ash fans at the time *There's the Rub* was fresh, new and interesting. It had a different sound to previous albums. Laurie's input was very exciting, and the American era of Wishbone Ash had begun. Most of the press feedback we received at the time was very positive and to this day many fans consider it one of our strongest albums.

The album's opening track, 'Silver Shoes' was pretty much a band effort, featuring a lyric written by Steve. It had a fairly "up" vibe to it and Laurie did a great job on the guitar solo, which has a sound that almost talks. I threw in some pretty mad ideas as well, such as the scat singing – a throwback to some of our earlier piece such as 'Vas Dis' and 'Sometime World'. Laurie's influence can be felt quite strongly on this one. He was new to the band and very keen to contribute and was throwing ideas in all the time. I do think he was a little bemused by the fact that I would throw ideas at the guitarists for them to play as harmony guitar. I don't think he was used to having a bass player as the musical director and he'd probably always assumed that all the harmony guitar parts had been written by the guys that were playing them. From this point on, more so than with the original band, the guitarists started to come up with more of the guitar parts themselves, which gave some of the harmonies a quite different quality.

'Don't Come Back' was another song that came mainly from me – certainly the lyric and melody – but to which everyone contributed. It's quite a bitchy lyric. That mind-boggling fast guitar lick came mainly from Laurie, although both he and Andy played it.

'Persephone' was another one where I had written the basic "song" element, but we did throw that one around quite a lot in rehearsals and so, again, everyone contributed to the final arrangement. Laurie's rhythm guitar on that song is quite distinctive and a very important part of the tune, and both Laurie and Andy also did quite blistering guitar solos – Laurie's is spectacular, and the one from Andy that follows is nice and moody as well – a beautiful piece of playing. Part of Andy's solo actually came about through a mistake. He had recorded a couple of guitar solos for the song, from which Bill Szymczyk was going to make a composite – i.e. he would take the best parts from the two solos. As he was putting it together, bouncing between the two solos, Bill made a mistake. He said "Guys, I've screwed that up. Let me go back and do that again," but we really liked what we heard and said "No, play that again, Bill. That sounded really interesting". We listened again and it was clear that, totally by accident, Bill had created from Andy's playing something that sounded brilliant. Of course Andy said "No, you can't use that. It's not the way I would play it. I'm the guy who's going to have to play it on stage every night and I don't even know if I'd be able to play that." So Andy went off to check that he would actually be able to play it. Fortunately he could and so we kept it in. I was really pleased with the guitar elements on 'Persephone', and the vocal had a nice mood to it as well. Andy also added some mandolin, while Criteria studio musician Albhy Galuten played keyboard. We were always keen to try out different instruments and this all added extra colour to the music.

Crazy Mart, USA 1974

The lyric to 'Persephone' was for me about the emotions that I felt over Ted Turner leaving the band, although it's not very literal. I was quite upset about Ted leaving, because I was very close to the guy and felt that it shouldn't have happened. I'd hoped that after he left the band Ted wouldn't blow it but would go on to do something great with his talent. The lyric, which is written in feminine terms, is just me fantasising about that. 'Persephone' was a title that Steve had, around which I wrote this story. Although in the song it's written as though it's about a female artist, I'm basically talking about my feelings about Ted.

'Hometown' was a song that I'd written on an acoustic guitar, although Laurie contributed the middle-eight, as well as providing some great guitar playing. At the end, where it starts to get a little bit funky, he plays some guitar licks that are very much in the style of a guitar player called Buzzy Feiten, who we were all into at the time. Again it's quite an upbeat song and not a million miles from 'Blowin' Free' in mood. Lyrically, it's about those trips that we did in the early seventies where we would be away for several weeks or months at a time, then every now and again there would be a couple of days when I would get an opportunity to go back to my home town of Torquay to see family and friends. Those moments were few and far between and 'Hometown' was me writing about the emotion you feel when you go home after a long period away.

'Lady Jay' was, as the album sleeve stated, inspired by a Dartmoor folk legend that I had remembered. My brother Glenn and I were always interested in paranormal and psychic stuff – in the sixties we used to go to a spiritualist church in Paignton. We had heard this legend about a girl in the late 18th century named Kitty Jay, who'd had an affair with the son of the local lord of the manor. She had become pregnant by him but they were not allowed to marry and so she committed suicide. As those who took their own lives were not allowed to be buried in hallowed consecrated ground, she was buried at the side of the road on Dartmoor. The legend went that her lover used to lay fresh flowers on the grave every day and that after he died the flowers continued to appear, even to this day. I was fascinated by this and one night on the way back from a gig in the sixties, we decided to stop off to have a look. It took a while to find the grave – it's high up on the moor in the middle of nowhere. We eventually found it, parked the van and walked back up the road to visit the grave, which is just a small mound of earth at the side of the road. And sure enough there were the flowers! We didn't stick around long – it was two o'clock in the morning and a little scary being stood by this grave in deepest, darkest, chilly Dartmoor, but I was always fascinated by that story. I thought it was tragic yet very romantic. Musically, 'Lady Jay' had a folky feel that was similar to some of the things we'd done in the past. I think we all contributed to this one. Andy added some banjo, which again added an interesting texture to the music.

The final track of the album evolved out of jamming. We had this long piece of music that Steve had written a lyric for, based on the four horsemen of the apocalypse. It was a bit "the end of the world is nigh" and I just couldn't get my head around it. I couldn't identify with the sentiment behind it – I couldn't feel it and couldn't sing it. I tried it about two of three times before I said "Look, guys, I'm really sorry but I just cannot feel this lyric. It's pointless me trying to sing it." So we had a problem in that we were in danger of losing a very long piece. Then Bill popped up and said "You know what? I've got an idea. I think I could edit this piece of music and take out the section of music that the vocal appears on". We were recording on 2 inch tape on 24 tracks and I had never seen anyone edit 2 inch tape in my life, but Bill thought he could do it. We got on with other stuff and agreed to look at it the next day. The next day Bill turned up with some really strong marijuana, which was duly passed around. It was pretty punchy stuff which made you feel like you were strapped to the nose of Concorde as it was taking off. We were all in the control room, high as kites, when Bill did the edit. I was absolutely fascinated to watch someone slash up a reel of 2 inch tape. He cut the vocal section out and when we heard it played through it just sounded like it was meant to be. It just sounded so right as a piece of music and what we ended up with was a very long instrumental, which became known as "F.U.B.B." – or "Fucked Up Beyond Belief", which accurately described the state we were in when we listened to it in its finished form.

Just prior to the release of *There's the Rub* we embarked on our first world tour – a six month long period of touring that would take us across the UK, Europe and the USA as well as to places we hadn't visited before such as Japan and Australia. We were by now a full scale concert band, known for our ability to recreate the intricacies of our studio recordings on the live stage. A lot of work went into our live production and we paid great attention to ensuring we were able to deliver a quality live sound. Mark Emery was heavily involved in helping us get this together.

MARK EMERY: *We were quite innovative as far as front of house equipment went. We started using Evantide Clockwork Digital Delay units and P.A. systems that had stereo features so that we could set up delays to ping-pong left and right and also deliver automatic double tracking – at that time that was pretty groundbreaking stuff. We always insisted on working with a full stereo discreet system and we had a fairly complex monitoring system that evolved over the years from a small system we bought from Martin Audio. We even used to take our own monitors to the States, which you wouldn't have to do now, but back then you couldn't rely on there being good monitors or good front of house systems. We used some pretty unique systems in the States. We toured with a Showco crew who provided big Altec and JBL systems which were great in a way but were not very modern. We then hooked up with a company from Ann Arbor, whose systems were miniaturised but were super hi-fi quality, using EV equipment and a small 24-track desk with tiny knobs on – the sound was brilliant. One of the most memorable gigs I remember doing with that was at the Warehouse in New Orleans – it was a packed gig, really hot with no air-conditioning. We used that equipment for several tours and we took their monitor guy with us when we went to Japan for the first time. We used to take our own equipment wherever possible, which these days would be unnecessary. I don't know how we used to get away with flying all this stuff around – we used to tip baggage handlers and freight guys to get it on and there were all kind of underhand deals made in order to get the equipment from one place to another.*

Martin was always the most technically enthusiastic of the band members and we would work closely together on producing sounds. He was very innovative and I learned a lot from him and hopefully was a good working partner with him. Wishbone Ash, although being a guitar rock band, were never a blast-your-ears-off heavy rock noise – they were subtle and dynamic and with this you needed a quality sound. We used quite a lot of special effects, such as phasing on drums, delays on vocals – things you wouldn't have heard if it was just a bash of loud guitars and noise. The guitar sounds were well controlled yet still had an edge. This is something that Martin has retained to this day – I was at a recent show in Paignton and the guys were doing a great job with the guitar sounds.

We kicked off our world tour with fifteen dates in the UK, with Laurie making his stage debut with us on 2 October 1974 at Plymouth Guildhall. Our audience in the UK was pretty established by then. Obviously there was a little apprehension from people regarding the change within the band, but once we hit the stage the enthusiasm for the new line-up was palpable. On the surface, I don't think we'd actually changed that much. Although Laurie obviously brought his personal style to the band, our mode of operation was still pretty much the same. It still sounded like Wishbone Ash and we still played a lot of material from *Argus*. Having said that, we were also very keen to move forwards, as displayed by our decision to play the entire new album on stage. This was the first time since the first album that we'd included a whole album in our set list – even *Argus* was not played in its entirety at the time of its release. Ted came down to the London Rainbow Theatre gig and it was great to see him again. It was a bit weird for everyone, but we were all relieved to see that he'd made it back to the UK after his experiences in Peru.

After the UK we played a series of dates throughout Europe - Switzerland, France, Belgium, Holland, Germany, Denmark – before we embarked on a lengthy US leg that ran from November 1974 through to February 1975. We spent Christmas away from home for the first time, aboard a yacht on the sunny Florida coast.

Steve Upton, USA 1974

We were supported on most of the US shows by Camel. However, I do recall one show towards the end of the US tour where we were joined on the bill by an up and coming US band called Kiss. By that time we'd probably been on the road a little too long - we were tired, homesick, the equipment was starting to fall apart and we were getting very road weary and needed a break. There were a few dates left and Kiss were added to the bill at Longbeach Arena, Los Angeles. Although they were a new band they had a fantastic following and were taking off like a rocket. They emerged in full war-paint, with platform shoes and a really explosive show. Then we went on and did what was probably not one of our better performances – nobody was very happy with the show. We had a reputation for not doing many duff gigs at all, but this gig was not a good one. We came off and went back into the dressing room and were really depressed about our performance and the state of our equipment. Somebody had arranged to bring down all the people from MCA in Los Angeles to meet Wishbone Ash that night but we didn't really feel like socialising at all and got whisked away fairly quickly after saying a quick "Hi" to a few people. The people from the record company thought we were being jumped-up assholes who didn't want to talk to them, but it was a really bad occasion for us.

> **LAURIE WISEFIELD:** *All the record company guys were there. We were the headliners and I remember hearing this amazingly loud racket coming from the stage, so I went out to see what was happening only to find the support band was a band called Kiss (no offense about the racket, chaps!). Well, we had never heard of them at the time and they were spitting blood with the larger than life costumes and the fireworks. The crowd loved it and when we went on everything just seemed to go wrong – the equipment kept going down and everything was just awful. Anyway I remember in the morning having breakfast at the Hyatt on Sunset (The Riot House) and Gene Simmons comes and sits next to me and starts a conversation. The words he said stuck in my head "There's a lot of money to be made in this business and I'm gonna make me some." I think at that time a lot of changes in the business were happening – the start of serious merchandising and all the other stuff that makes this the wonderful world of showbiz.*

Japan was very different. We were with a different record company over there, as MCA had negotiated a licensing deal with RCA-Victor and they promoted the band very much as a "pop" group, which of course we weren't. All the advertising was very much along those lines. They even re-touched photographs of us so that we had slightly slanted eyes, so that the Japanese would relate to us. I seem to remember being really taken aback when we were told that the shows would start at 6.30pm. This was because there was a curfew in Japan for anyone over sixteen. They had to be off the streets by 9.00pm. I didn't imagine that affecting one of our shows too much as we didn't really attract a teenage audience, but once we started playing the shows we were all really surprised to find that most of the audience were teenage girls. They used to shout "Lolly" at our new guitarist! When we came out of the shows to get in the limousine there would be girls in the street chasing after the car – it was like Wishbonemania! I remember getting stopped by a couple of girls outside a hotel. They asked if I would sign autographs, so I said "Sure" and stopped to sign their stuff. Then suddenly about two or three dozen girls just appeared out of nowhere and I was literally surrounded. They were pushing towards me and I just couldn't get out. I realised I was pushed up against this huge plate glass window and I could feel it buckling and I was going "Whoa, gently!" Luckily Miles Copeland spotted what was going on and came and rescued me. A smashing time – almost.

After Japan we flew to Australia and that was a complete culture shock. In Japan everything is so formal, polite and gentlemanly. Everyone bows and shows great respect. When we arrived in Australia some guy walked straight up to me and said "Hi Martin, my name's Bruce. I'm from your record company. Is this your old lady? Nice pair of tits. Fancy a beer?" All without a breath – it was so in-your-face. I was absolutely mind-blown. New Zealand was strange too. The wildlife there was unlike anything I'd seen in my life. It was fascinating to travel to all these places, especially for someone like me who'd come from another planet – a council estate in Torquay.

Towards the end of the Australian leg of the tour, I started to get really poorly. I would be doing some minor thing such as moving across the room to turn the television on and I would just break out into a sweat. I was really lacking energy and my urine had turned dark brown, like the colour of tea that's been stewing in a tea pot. So I went along to see a doctor in Australia and he said to me "Well, it's quite simple, mate. You're going down with hepatitis." He figured that I'd probably picked it up in Japan through eating raw fish. In addition we were all pretty ensconced in the rock 'n' roll lifestyle by this time. My alcohol consumption had by stages reached severe proportions and I was not eating properly. There was also a fair amount of cocaine around by this time – something we had been introduced to by engineer Keith Harwood during the *Wishbone Four* sessions. The doctor told me that if I stopped drinking, stopped drugging, started to get to bed early and started to eat properly and took 5000 milligrams of vitamin C per day, I may be able to shake it off before I went down with hepatitis C. I took his advice and I did manage to shake it off. Fortunately a few days later the tour was over and we travelled back to England and I was able to rest up. This was a close call and I was lucky to have escaped a serious illness.

We closed our exhausting World Tour with a show at Western Springs Stadium, Auckland, New Zealand on 15 March 1975. A long established feature of our show had been the emergence of Steve Upton from behind his drum kit mid-way through the set to introduce the band. Steve would usually introduce the members of the band to the audience and say a few words about the next song. On this particular tour, Steve had been introducing our instrumental 'F.U.B.B.', revealing the acronym as standing for 'Fucked Up Beyond Belief'. He'd done that pretty much every night and usually the audience would just laugh or titter – certainly there had been no major repercussions. However, New Zealand at that time was a very "straight" country and apparently it was an offense to swear in public. We were playing at an open-air event. Behind the Stadium were a bunch of homes where a woman who was having a barbeque with her family heard this English bloke come out with the F-word and didn't take kindly to it. She rang up her friend – the Mayor of Auckland – and insisted that this person be arrested. So, the Mayor had to do something about it and sent the cops down there. The cops arrived while we were still performing and said "Sorry, mate, but we're gonna have to arrest the guy that said "fuck"." Our tour manager Mel Baister said "Come on guys, you can't arrest him now", to which they replied "Why not?" So Mel said "Well, the guy's performing. There will be a riot if you try to drag him off stage and take him away". In the end they were at least sensible enough to wait until we had finished performing, at which point they arrested Steve as he came down the steps from the stage. It was ridiculous. I think they thought he was going to do a runner – as if Steve would do that! Steve took it totally in his stride, "Okay, righty-ho, so be it. Do you want to put handcuffs on me?" They kept him in jail overnight and he was whisked to court the next morning, because we were leaving later that day to return to England.

He received a rap across the knuckles over it from the judge and had to pay a $30 fine. We thought that was the end of it but it actually made the front page of the national daily news papers. We were back in England by this point and so didn't even know about it, but about a week to ten days later all these bulletins started coming through from N.Z. telling us that it had been on the front pages and consequently our album had shot up the charts, all thanks to the exposure we'd received, proving there's no such thing as bad publicity.

Wishbone Ash Mk.2 – Mart, Laurie, Andy, Steve, USA 1974

CHAPTER EIGHT

In New England

WE HAD just a month's break following the completion of our 1974/75 world tour before we were back on the road again, with more shows in the States during the Spring of 1975. By now we were spending so much time touring the States that a group decision had been made to relocate and set up base over there. We had a good agent, a decent publicist, our record company was based there and we had been touring the States for years. But there were also other considerations; one being that all was not well with our management in London. Basically, Miles Copeland had over extended himself. He was managing way too many bands. He'd set up a huge office that was employing all kinds of people. He'd grown too big too fast and eventually his empire fell apart and things got very ugly indeed with law suits going on left right and centre. Miles' business operations were always a bit slap-dash. He was great at going into a major record company and walking out with a million dollar advance, but I felt his day to day running of the band and its finances was very untogether at times. Going to America was to some extent running away from all of this. There were also discussions about taxation and it was felt that we would be better off in the USA. Inevitably when you move abroad the press assume you are doing it for tax reasons and you get branded a "tax exile". It seems to me that it is easy to think that "the grass is greener" because income tax is lower in the U.S., but when you take into account property tax and pay all the lawyers and accountants you end up with much the same whichever side of the pond you live on.

I personally disagreed with the decision of going to America. I just didn't see the point and felt there was a danger of the band losing its British identity. Because the USA has such an overwhelming culture, I felt the musical influences would be so great that we would start to lose our English-ness, which I wasn't happy about. When it came to matters that were strictly of a musical nature, I was very forthright with my opinions. Certainly in the early days I regarded myself as the musical leader of the band. I was the main creative force and people were usually willing to listen to me when it came to the music itself. However, when it came to business matters and matters other than music there was a general modus operandi whereby we would take a democratic vote. In this case, three of the band – Steve, Laurie and Andy – wanted to go to live in the States, whereas I didn't. I told the guys that I didn't think it was a good idea. I told them that just because the democratic vote was three against one, it didn't necessarily mean it was the right decision. Obviously it caused a certain amount of upheaval for all of us personally. I had to pull my wife Maurn out of a really good job – she was working as the Beatles' publicist Derek Taylor's assistant at Warner Bros. In addition, some of us by this point had bought houses.

Once the decision had been made to move to the States, the question arose as to where. We spent the first few weeks in the States either on tour or living out of a New York hotel. Now, I assumed everyone would be happy to live in New York, which I considered only place to be. We already knew a lot of people in New York. Roy Hollingworth was there, as the US correspondent for *Melody Maker* - he had been hugely supportive of Wishbone Ash during our early years. David Bowie was moving to New York at the same time as us, with Coco, who Maurn and I were friendly with – we used to call them Coco and Bobo. Coco showed us around some property in New York. The other guys, however, had been checking out a small town up the coast called Westport, Connecticut. We went for a drive to take a look and as we hit the main street, I questioned whether the other guys really wanted to live there, because to me it resembled Hemel Hempstead High Street. I thought that Andy at least wanted to escape from that but actually he really liked it and so did Steve and Laurie. Once again, a democratic decision had been made that I was not entirely happy with. So, we ended up renting several houses within the area. I had trouble finding a suitable pad but eventually we found Laureledge, Weston, which was bigger than I needed but we agreed to use upstairs as a hotel for anyone visiting us on band business. We used the basement as a studio and everyone had use of the swimming pool.

By this time, Russell Sidelsky had joined our team. We had met Russell in London in 1975 and he came to live and work in the USA with us. He had grown up in Zimbabwe, although he had a South African passport. Russell's job was to assist Steve in the day to day business of running the band, which he became accomplished at during our three years together. He lived with me at Laureledge at first and then eventually moved to his own pad just down the road. He came out on the road as part of the team during those years when we operated from Connecticut. We filed with US immigration for resident's permits – green cards – and Russell was included in this. When we decided to return to the UK three years later, he expressed a wish to stay in the

USA, so we asked our New York Lawyer Allan Grubman to find him a new job if possible. Allan had a new act that he was representing and offered Russell a gig as their personal manager. The act was Village People and I'm sure that Russ had a busy few years ahead of him there. When we left the States he kindly sorted out an outstanding tax bill for me and I gave him my Mercedes 230SL sports car which had just been resprayed.

Maurn would often get homesick while we were living in the States and, whenever she did, she would go straight back to London, so I found myself spending quite a lot of time alone there. In the winter when there was fourteen inches of snow on the ground and the power had gone out for two days, I lived in the lounge and kitchen with a live fire to keep warm and cook on. Hurricane Belle came up the Eastern seaboard in 1976, clipped the end of Long Island and slammed straight into Westport and Weston. Many trees came down and a house a few hundred yards down the road was completely demolished and ended up as matchwood. On another occasion I got up at two o'clock in the morning, dressed only in my underpants, to go and see off a racoon that was raiding the bin in the garage. I arrived a few feet from him and growled at him to frighten him

Maurn and Mart, 1975

away. He stood his ground and bared his fangs and growled back at me, which was a bit of a surprise, never having met one before. I resorted to brandishing a large lump of wood in his direction and that did encourage the little bleeder to go find dinner elsewhere. Whilst living at Laureledge, I learned to swim, then nearly drowned in the deep end, did a bit of growing plants, developed an ability to drive on snow and ice, and also became friends with my landlord Lee Shoenberg. It was a new and fascinating time in many respects.

LAURIE WISEFIELD: *I was up for anything really being young free and single. We were touring a lot of the time in the US so the idea was to relocate there and set up a base so that we wouldn't be going backwards and forwards all the time. The choice was to move to somewhere near to either New York City or Los Angeles, as that's where the biz was. We didn't want to dive straight into city life so Mel Baister who worked for us at the time suggested this quiet area an hour north of New York City called Westport, Connecticut, which was supposedly very nice. Steve and I had three different places together – the first was a log cabin, the second a very modern glass fronted house in Georgetown and the third was a house on the water back in Westport. Martin had a large house in Weston, just up the road, called Laureledge, with a pool and that's where we put the studio in the basement. Andy had a very straight-ish family kind of residence, then there was Hobbit our sound man and "fifth member", I would say, who had a place and Russell Sidelsky also had a place. All the houses were lovely and a great time was had by Steve and I for sure. We went to the local car dealer on Main Street who must have really seen us coming. We walked in there in our flared jeans and platform shoes saying we wanted five or six cars. "Sure, come this way, boys, I've got just what you're looking for at a very good deal."*

> **MARK EMERY:** *Martin's house Laureledge was a great centre where the whole band could meet – we could eat there, swim in the pool, hang out as well as get down to work in the studio.*

We undertook a short US tour in the Spring of 1975, including a series of shows alongside rising US stars Aerosmith, the arrangement for which was that they would support us in the towns where we were the most successful and we would support them in the towns where they were more popular. It was early days for them, although they had already made a huge impression with 'Dream On' and 'Walk This Way'. We used to travel together and got on great with them. Steven Tyler was a great front-man. I also liked Joe Perry as a guitar player. Although technically he wasn't anywhere near the level of Andy and Laurie, he was very creative and I think he did some really great stuff through the years. I also remember rolling up at

a sound-check one day and noticed that their bass player Tom Hamilton – who always used a Fender Precision bass – was up there on the stage with a Thunderbird bass like mine. So I walked on stage and said "Oi, what the fuck's this then?" He replied "Whoa, man, you always seem to get a pretty good sound, so I thought I'd better check one out." They were a great band and a great bunch of guys. I always thought of Steven Tyler and Joe Perry as the American version of Mick Jagger and Keith Richards.

If I really was Martina, I might be able to fly on this broomstick - Laureledge, 1975

I saw a programme on MTV a while ago about the Top Ten "wildest rock bands". Aerosmith were number one. I thought "Wait a minute, we helped teach them all that!" Back then though they were a regular rock 'n' roll band – young guys, just starting out, and it was clear they were going places.

Aerosmith's managers at that time were Steve Leiber and David Krebs – a pair of New York lawyers. They were doing a fantastic job of managing Aerosmith and seemed really together. They told us that they had wanted to get involved in managing Wishbone Ash for America right from when we first started and asked us "Did you never receive our offer?" They had contacted Miles Copeland and asked if they could represent us in the USA. Of course, Miles had refused because he didn't want to give anyone else a slice of the action and had never even mentioned it to us, so we were fairly surprised. They said that offer still stood and they wanted to sit with us and thrash out a management deal. Steve was nominated as band representative and he went into town with Mel Baister to meet with them. They came back from the meeting and were fairly annoyed that Leiber and Krebs had offered to manage the band on the basis of them receiving fifty per cent of everything, including back catalogue sales. That was a bit of a sticking point. Everyone was outraged that they should offer such a heavy deal but Leiber and Krebs had said "The reason we offer such a deal is because we don't want to do what so many other managers do, which is end up managing eighteen different artists and not doing a very good job for any of them. We want to manage Aerosmith and one other band. We will do a fantastic job for you and in a couple of years you guys will be millionaires." But everyone was pretty upset about it and was not even prepared to talk to them about this deal. Again, I found myself in a minority and remember saying to the guys "Wait a minute. You were the ones who wanted to come and be in America, it being the place where the big money can be made. So, we get this massive offer for management from two of the best people in the business and you guys want to pass on it. It doesn't make sense – we've got a great New York lawyer in Allan Grubman, so let's put him in a room with Leiber and Krebs and tell him to thrash out a better deal." I knew that if we'd put Allan in a room with them he would probably have chiselled their cut down to forty per cent and re-negotiated on the back catalogue, but the other guys in the band wouldn't even agree to that – it was just dismissed out of hand. I thought that this amounted to shooting ourselves in the foot. At that point I began to question the wisdom of my fellow band members and whether they wanted to make it really big within the business or if they were merely content to continue working at the same level. I couldn't figure out where they were coming from. Leiber and Krebs went straight out and signed up Ted Nugent – an unusual and interesting character - and even managed to make him into a huge star. I have no doubt at all that they could have made Wishbone Ash's career blossom in the USA if we had come to some agreement.

In the Summer of 1975 we took part in the *Startruckin'* tour. Miles wanted to be the first manager to put on a package tour that went all over Europe, playing major festivals and stadiums. We were to be headlining and then there was to be a full supporting cast of bands such as Lou Reed, John McLaughlin's Mahavishnu Orchestra, Renaissance, Climax Blues Band, and Caravan. The *Startruckin'* tour was conceived as a vehicle to help Miles get out of the financial hole he found himself in. Because we knew he was in a mess financially, we asked for half our money upfront the week before the tour started. The money never arrived, and so we told him we weren't going to do the tour. He actually flew out to America and came to my house and virtually got on his knees and begged us to do it. He said "If you guys don't come out to Europe and do this tour, then I will be finished in the music business." We went back a long way with Miles – we started out as friends in the music business together and didn't want to see him go under financially, and so we agreed to do the tour. The financial climate at the time was very difficult as there had been a recession and everybody involved wanted their money upfront – PA companies, road crew, etc. Nobody wanted to do the tour unless they could be sure they were going to be paid. We had three days rehearsal time booked in England before the tour started and Steve spent most of that time running around drawing money out of our bank account to pay people to get them to go on the road to do the tour.

The first of a series of setbacks on this tour came when Lou Reed pulled out at the last minute, giving promoters an excuse to not pay out the contracted fees. The next problem was with the plane Miles had rented to carry all the bands and their equipment. It looked like a jumbo jet, but it was actually a turbo-prop. It was a big passenger plane with a large freight compartment. The airline company had asked for accurate weight measurements on all of the equipment. Of course, when we all arrived at the airport the weight of the gear was so far over the figures that had been submitted that it was a wonder how the plane managed to get up into the air. The pilot was not happy about it at all and, in fact, a few shows into the tour when we were in Europe, he just refused point blank to take us any further. By this time the equipment had got even heavier, because we'd picked up another band along the way. We were going off to play in Orange, France and were flying into Marseille from Stuttgart. We arrived at the airport in Stuttgart early in the morning and the pilot said "You cannot take all this equipment and all these people." So, we let the first bunch of bands go, and there was us and one other band who were left to get to Orange under our own steam. We all went back to the hotel and tried to organise alternative transport. Of course, as the morning went on, the options lessened. We could have rented a couple of people carriers and got there in time, provided we'd done it by 10.00am, but it got to noon and still nothing had been organised – it was getting to be really tight on time. So the next option was to get a plane. We tried all over the place to get a plane that could carry two bands and their equipment and in the end they had to fly a plane down from Amsterdam. We went back out to Stuttgart airport with all the goings-ons being witnessed by Chris Welch, who was on the road with us reporting for *Melody Maker*, watching this make-it-up-as-you-go-along tour. We eventually got on the plane, which was a large lear-jet capable of carrying about thirty people. There were half a dozen stewardesses all dressed up to the nines and you could tell it was going to cost someone a small fortune. I looked nervously at Steve and said "Who the hell's paying for this? Not us, I hope!"

So, we flew into Marseille and then boarded a coach to take us to Orange, where we were playing at a three-day festival in a Roman amphitheatre. We were headlining on the very last day of the festival – Bad Company had headlined the night before. The show was fraught with various behind the scenes problems. The French promoter had phoned up the French customs office and told them that Ike and Tina Turner, who were joining the tour for a few shows, had drugs hidden inside their equipment. Consequently Ike and Tina and their crew were detained and searched when they came into the country. There were no drugs found, but because of the delay they failed to arrive at the gig and the French promoter refused to pay Miles the full performance fees due – it was a set-up and things got really ugly. There were punches thrown and at one point one of the French promoter's henchmen pulled a knife – it got rather heavy for a while.

The show in Orange was also running badly behind schedule. John McLaughlin was on before us and he didn't get on stage until midnight. In addition, I'd gone down with food poisoning and had gone to sleep in the lion's den in the amphitheatre. There was nothing to lie on, so I think I ended up lying on some amplifier covers – it was desperate. Kevin Harrington woke me up at about 2.30am telling me we were about to go on stage. There was nothing I would have liked less at that point than to have gone on stage to perform, but I did. We went on stage and the sound in the Roman amphitheatre was amazing. It remains one of the best sounding gigs I've taken part in. The audience were very attentive but obviously tired – a lot of them had been there three days - and at the end of our set, we finished with 'Phoenix' and as we did so the sun rose above the amphitheatre wall and shone directly at the stage. There followed a standing ovation - it was absolutely magical. That show was spoken about in France for many years in much revered terms. Those clever Romans knew how to build a gig! As we walked back to the coach, a lovely young lady from Paris appeared by my side for a chat and I ended up inviting her for breakfast back at the hotel. It was a memorable gig!

The *Startruckin'* tour included a date at the Reading Festival – our only UK appearance of 1975. We had actually played the very first Reading Festival back in 1971, but this time around we were headlining, closing the Sunday night (Hawkwind and Yes headlined the Friday and Saturday nights respectively). Our set was plagued with technical problems. All our backline equipment operated on Variac transformers, which could be changed to whatever output voltage you required. On this occasion we'd been playing in Europe and our road crew had left them on the wrong voltage, forgetting to change them back to 240V. As a result, during our set the power blew and Steve Upton just carried on playing for a few minutes while everyone scurried around trying to get the mains up and running again. That was a bit naff for a major festival, but the crowd seemed to enjoy it.

At the end of the *Startruckin'* tour, in a hotel room they were counting all the monies from the tour, all in different currencies – Deutschmarks, French Francs, Swiss Francs, Spanish Pesetas, you name it. Steve had arranged to pick up our money at the hotel after the last show before we returned to England, but Miles and his people persuaded him that there was a limit to the amount of cash he was allowed to carry and that if he got caught with the money, customs could end up confiscating the whole lot. They persuaded Steve that it would be better for the money to be put into the bank, so that's what was arranged. The money got as far as Amsterdam but never made it to London and we never got to see a penny of it. In order to get the tour on the road, Miles' accountant in Amsterdam had taken out a bank loan, for which he had put up his house as security. Because he was an accountant he was in a position to see that the tour was going to lose a lot of money. So he grabbed the funds to pay back the bank loan rather than risk losing his house. We were supposed to have been paid about £50,000 for that tour – a hell of a lot of money in those days. That really poisoned the relationship between Miles and ourselves. Miles also fell out big time with our agent John Sherry, which put us all in an awkward position.

With Miles facing bankruptcy, a decision was made by the band that we should part company with our manager. This was not an easy decision to make. We'd started out in the business together and by this stage had a six year working relationship. Miles had done a lot of great things for the band and had played a huge part in the band's success, but things had gotten pretty ugly and there were writs flying every which way. We didn't want to get bogged down with all of that and rather than sue for the money we were owed, we decided to chalk it up as experience and write it off. That whole situation virtually put us out of business as well. It was a really difficult blow for us to recover from. With hindsight we perhaps should have been more loyal to Miles and stuck with him, but that certainly wasn't the majority view at the time. The band was so traumatised by the experience that everyone refused to even contemplate having a manager again. The word "manager" had become something of a dirty word and the majority decision was that Steve Upton should take on the day to day management duties. We announced our decision to Miles at a meeting with him on 19 September 1975.

> **LAURIE WISEFIELD:** *A lot of work went into the Startruckin' tour, so we were pretty pissed off when we didn't get paid for it and Miles was going bankrupt. We just carried on as we always did and got on with writing/touring. Although we were living very well, because we had a good record deal and used to work a lot, I don't think any of us were particularly motivated by the money at all. It was always the music.*

Regardless of the problems behind the scenes, it was business as usual for Wishbone Ash on a musical basis, as we prepared to record our sixth studio album *Locked In* at Atlantic Studios in New York with producer Tom Dowd. This was an arrangement that had been negotiated prior to us parting company with Miles and had come about through Miles managing the Average White Band. They'd had a huge hit with 'Pick Up The Pieces' on Atlantic Records and Miles had been very impressed with Atlantic Records in New York. They were considered much hipper than our record company MCA and so Miles had negotiated for us to be released to Atlantic, solely for the American market, for two albums. With Atlantic Records came their in-house producer Tom Dowd. He was hugely respected and had produced a lot of successful records dating back to Aretha Franklin. He'd also worked with Lynyrd Skynyrd, Rod Stewart, Eric Clapton, The Allman Brothers, and a host of really successful artists, and at that point he was considered to be one of the best producers in the world. We met with Tom at his office in New York, prior to commencing recording in November 1975. He was very nice – a real gentleman. We really liked him but he dictated the recording process completely. As we were getting up to leave the office, he casually slipped in that when we went into the studio he did not want any of us to use any alcohol or drugs. We all just stood there with dropped jaws. None of the guys in Wishbone were particularly heavy users of anything, but we did like to indulge on occasion. Generally we were all fairly sensible, well-balanced chaps. However, we were gobsmacked at the thought of doing an album stone cold sober. It was certainly going to be a new experience, but Tom had clearly had some bad times with Eric Clapton and Lynyrd Skynyrd and their indulgences in various substances, so we agreed to do it his way. Tom also wanted us to set up in a semi-circle, with little tiny amplifiers and play live with a keyboard player Peter Wood added to the line-up. Peter was a very accomplished musician and a good bloke – he'd played on a lot of successful records, including Al Stewart's 'Year of the Cat', and later worked extensively with Roger Waters and Cyndi Lauper. I was saddened to hear that many years later he took his own life. We also had a trio of black female backing vocalists singing on a couple of tracks, fronted by Cissy Houston – the mother of Whitney Houston and aunt of Dionne Warwick. Cissy was a well known session singer with a fantastic voice. She came into the studio with these really fit looking black girls behind her. It was like mother duck with little ducklings – they walked in a line behind her. The young Whitney was one of those girls, getting an early glimpse of life in the recording studio, no doubt. All the additional musicians did a good job, but to me it didn't really seem to have much to do with what I thought Wishbone Ash was about. However, we tried to be positive and trusted Tom's expertise and were willing to compromise and adapt.

Within hours of going into the studio with Tom Dowd, it was clear that he had some pretty serious personal problems. He was getting phone calls, with someone screaming abuse at him down the phone, and it soon became apparent that he was embroiled in a divorce. I do know how much that can affect a man – I went through it myself a few years later and also witnessed it with several close friends. Tom looked like a wizened old man / mad professor, virtually bent double over the troubles he was experiencing at this point in his life – he was not in great shape at all. By contrast, I saw him a year later at Criteria – he had a lovely looking lady on his arm, was wearing great clothes and had clearly reinvented himself and had become a tall handsome guy. He was a lovely man and we got on great with him, but I have to say that, while his concept had worked fine for Eric Clapton and Rod Stewart, I don't think it was right for Wishbone Ash.

In addition to the problems with Tom Dowd, I experienced vocal problems in the studio. I'd gone in to record one particularly belting vocal and when I started singing Tom stopped the recording. He didn't even speak to me on the intercom – he came into the studio with his crossed arms up in the air, signalling "Stop". He informed me that I was not allowed to sing anymore and that I had nodules on my vocal cords. I said "You what?" I didn't even know what nodules were. He gave me the name of a doctor in New York – a little character called Dr. Friedrich Brodnintz. I went arrived at his office where he put me through this question and answer session.

Dr. Friedrich: "So, you sing in a rock 'n' roll band, huh?"
Martin: "Yeah, I do."
Dr. Friedrich: "Real loud is it?"
Martin: "Yeah, the band is loud and I have to sing loud as well."

Dr. Friedrich: "D'ya drink alcohol?"

Martin: "Yeah."

Dr. Friedrich: "What kind of alcohol? Beer?"

Martin: "I do drink beer but I usually drink scotch and cola."

Dr. Friedrich : "D'ya smoke cigarettes?"

Martin: "Yeah."

Dr. Friedrich: "What about marijuana?"

Martin: "Well, on occasion, but I'm not that big on it."

Dr. Friedrich: "You snort cocaine?"

Martin: "Er, yes."

He chalked all this up before concluding:

"Look. I get friggin' guys like you come in here every day of the week. You're young guys, you're rock 'n' roll musicians, you chuck all this shit down your neck and then you end up with a problem. What the fuck do you expect?"

It was so funny – I wish it had been filmed. I thought he was going to ask me to bend over while he thrashed me with a big stick. In actual fact what he ordered me to do was to visit a singing teacher to learn how to sing without straining my voice. One of the occupational hazards of singing in a rock band is that when you've got a bunch of guys behind you pumping out 130 decibels, the only way you can hear yourself is to resort to shouting. Your vocal cords take the most unbelievable punishment and end up with calluses on them, which turn into nodules and can ultimately become cancerous. I had to go through a process of re-learning to sing so that I wasn't forcing my voice. I must admit after a while I probably reached a point where I was singing the best I'd ever sung, but on the *Locked In* album I was pretty lame – I was basically told that I couldn't sing. Although I insisted on singing some of the tunes, Laurie ended up singing a lot of the songs instead of me. As Laurie is keen to point out, though, this was certainly not a case of Laurie trying to take over the lead vocalist slot:

> **LAURIE WISEFIELD:** *I was quite happy playing the guitar. I guess it just evolved as I came up with some song ideas and Martin had a few problems.*

Locked In was one problem after another. In addition, we were staying in the Holiday Inn in uptown New York. The hotel was a funky little pit, with hookers everywhere. The whole experience was pretty awful and by the end of the album I felt miserable. When they played the album back to us at the end of the recording, I felt it sounded a million miles away from my vision of what the band should be. I can remember lying in a foetal position in the corner of the control room and I just started crying. I was not happy with what I was hearing. The engineer picked up on how I was feeling. He put his arm around me and said "Martin, listen man, this is just a bad time for you – you gotta keep going, man. I've seen a lot of dudes go through the same thing. You'll come out the other end and look back on it all."

Locked In should have been great. We were with a great record company, recording an album in a very famous recording studio just a short walk from Times Square where everyone had recorded going right back to Frank Sinatra, and had the services of one of the world's greatest producers. It just wasn't right though – as a band, we had moved to the USA and were unsettled as yet. For me personally, it seemed we were being forced to be something that we weren't – more American, more commercial, and it was like trying to make a silk purse out of a sow's ear.

> **LAURIE WISEFIELD:** *I haven't heard the album for a long time now. My recollections though are not bad. I remember some of the beginnings and jams of things like 'Rest in Peace', 'Half Past Lovin' and they were just storming. I liked 'Say Goodbye' as a song. I think there were some good ideas but the end result didn't come out right at all. The experience of recording the album was not bad at all for me. In fact quite enjoyable as it was great spending some time with Tom Dowd at the helm, who'd produced so many great artists and was such a*

nice bloke. But it was a very American R&B approach and didn't really suit us as it was quite combo-like instead of the big British, yet subtly more bombastic approach and sound. The mix was also very dry which didn't help.

One good thing that did come out of *Locked In* was that, for the first time, the individual songwriters were credited. I'd been banging on about this since 1971 and finally we felt confident enough for the writer of the song to have credit for what he'd created. Hallelujah!

Locked In contained a mixture of songs written by individual members of the band as well as some songs which had evolved out of jamming and were more of a collaborative effort. Album opener 'Rest in Peace' fell into the latter category, although I wrote the main body of the lyric, and was probably one of the more successful tracks on the album. We'd already played it on stage during the *Startruckin'* tour, it was a pretty good tune and it at least sounded like a rock band.

Laurie's 'No Water in the Well' is one that's been heavily criticised over the years, but I actually think it's a pretty good song. Obviously it's a ballad, but it's got some pretty interesting musical shifts in it. I think Laurie struggled to sing it and it was a bit beyond his range. Under normal circumstances I would have probably ended up singing it, but I was under a singing ban to a certain extent.

'Moonshine' unbelievably went on to become a huge hit in Japan. Its such a wacky tune, most of which came from Laurie, and it's clearly us trying to be funky, which was not really our forte at all. Although Laurie sang lead we all got involved in the vocal harmonies. In fact there's one harmony on there which, to me, sounded wrong – it was a discord, a clash note, but Tom Dowd insisted on leaving it on. Maybe he felt it summed up the state of his life at that point in time – discordant.

'She Was My Best Friend' was a ballad that I had written. My first wife Maurn's mother had died unexpectedly, very young, and that's basically what the song was about. Maurn had been very close to her mother and I tried to write that song from Maurn's perspective, although because it was so personal, I made it sound more like a standard love song. Vocally it was a little over ambitious for me. I like to sing within the limits of my natural vocal range. I don't like to be pushing beyond that and reaching for notes that are a struggle. This one was a bit of a stretch for me. This was recorded after I'd started visiting the vocal tutor and so I was starting to get in pretty good shape vocally by then. Initially I thought I wasn't going to be allowed to sing on this album at all, so I was pleased that we were eventually able to get my voice onto a few of the songs.

'It Started In Heaven' was a song that Laurie and Steve put together. As with much of the material on the album, it was an attempt at being commercial and poppy. It's sometimes nice to have something on an album that has an upbeat, joyous feel – like 'Blowin' Free' on *Argus* – but it's a long way from the creative output that I felt constituted Wishbone Ash music. It was an attempt at the kind of music that would put you in the singles market.

'Half Past Loving' was another song we had already played onstage and could best be described as another of our attempts at being funky. When you go to live in America you become totally immersed in the country's overwhelming culture and inevitably some of that influences the music. That was one of the reasons why I was against going to live in the States. 'Half Past Loving' is a good example of that. It finds us trying to play American music which was some way out of our area of expertise. I didn't feel it suited the band. The song evolved out of a jam session and I contributed the lyric, which has references to time – a recurring theme in my lyrics.

'Trust in You' was a band composition, sung by Laurie. There was quite a lot of input from everyone on this one, although I don't think it's a particularly memorable track.

The album's final track 'Say Goodbye' was written by Laurie and I – the only time we shared a co-writing credit on an album as a duo. Despite being a fairly mellow tune, it was more in the realm of what we normally do and I felt that it fit like a well worn shoe. I've revisited the song for live shows more recently and it feels right. Unlike much of this album, 'Say Goodbye' feels like putting on clothes that are mine.

Locked In was released on 12 March 1976 and I think it would be fair to say that it was panned by critics, and also by our normally loyal fan-base. We embarked on a US tour in support of the album, playing some of the country's major venues including New York's Madison Square Garden. In fact, we were probably at our peak as a US concert attraction around this period. Having said this, playing venues of this size didn't feel at all alien, as they were not a lot different in size to venues we had played earlier as a support act for bands like the Who. The new material sounded a lot stronger on stage and we had Graham Maitland with us on keyboards for these shows – he had played with us before both on record and on the occasional live show and was a great guy and a great player. I love the sound of the Hammond organ and it was great having one onstage with us. It was an interesting experiment but, ultimately, it still felt like a departure too far and we had to adapt our style of play to fit in around the keyboards. It didn't feel like Wishbone Ash anymore to me.

Supporting us on some of the US shows were Status Quo. They had achieved a great deal of success in the UK and Europe by this time, with both album and singles success, but their brand of denim-clad boogie rock had failed to make an impression in America. Possibly this was because America already had a number of bands doing a similar thing and it was almost like taking coals to Newcastle. They had a very hard time trying to crack the States and they rarely went back there again. There are a lot of people who didn't make it in America - Cliff Richard is probably the earliest example of a successful British artist who is unknown in the States. On one of the gigs Status Quo did with us, their guitarists Francis Rossi and Rick

Parfitt had come from the dressing room up to the stage ready to play. Then their bassist Alan Lancaster and drummer John Coghlan came walking through to go to the stage and suddenly the pair of them started fighting. They were smacking the shit out of each other, having this full-on bundle, just a few yards away from me. I went over to them and grabbed them and said "Guys, for fuck's sake, your guitar players are up there onstage. You've got a show to do – why don't you just postpone your little brawl until after the show." They were clearly not happy, but they went on and did the show. Years later Status Quo memorably opened the *Live Aid* event and were seen by millions as they performed 'Rockin' All Over the World'. What a great way to open that show.

There was no UK or European tour to promote *Locked In*, although we did manage a trio of German festival appearances in June 1976. These were our final outstanding commitment to Miles Copeland and we headlined a bill that also featured Bob Marley and the Wailers, the Kinks, Van der Graaf Generator, War (with Eric Burden) and Man. Stephen Stills was supposed to be on the bill, but he didn't make it. One of the shows was running late and Bob Marley and his band were up there in a stoned stupor, just

Locked In tour with Graham Maitland (keyboards), USA 1976

jamming away forever. They sounded really good, but Miles had decided that they'd gone well over the time they had been allotted and went up to the stage and told them to get off. When they didn't respond, he pulled the power on them. Bob Marley just walked off and went back to the dressing room but some of his henchmen were leaping all over the place, screaming abuse at Miles. The Kinks actually got bottled off at one of the festivals. I couldn't believe that. They were a great band, although

they were perhaps a bit stuck in the sixties – for example, they all still wore matching suits. The audience hated them and threw bottles and cans at the stage and booed them – eventually the Kinks had to come off. I actually shared a car with Ray Davies back to the hotel and we chatted. I felt really sorry for him – he is a great songwriter, but at that stage the Kinks were viewed as some kind of pop group from the previous decade that nobody wanted to know about. Of course, with the passage of time, they've been afforded the acclaim and appreciation they deserve and Ray Davis is rightfully revered as one of the quintessential English songwriters of our generation. Every time I walk across Waterloo bridge on my way to the train station, I find myself looking down the Thames in the direction of Parliament / Big Ben, thinking to myself what a great city London is, whilst singing 'Waterloo Sunset'.

During the Summer/Autumn of 1976 we returned to our base in Connecticut and directed all our energy into writing and recording our next album. By this time we'd put together a pretty decent rehearsal studio in the basement of Laureledge, where the walls, floors and ceiling were covered in carpet underlay. We built a little control room for Hobbit, where he had an eight-track Teac tape machine that I had purchased and which we used to record our rehearsals onto multi-track for the first time. We really enjoyed working in that room. When it came time to record the next album, everyone was against the idea of paying to go into a recording studio with a producer and maybe ending up unhappy with the result again. In the same way that we had been traumatised by our manager going bankrupt on us, we had also been traumatised by working with a producer – Tom Dowd – who had such a good reputation, but obviously wasn't pushing on full throttle at the time we were working with him. We were therefore adamant that the next album had to be done under our terms. By this time we felt we were experienced enough that we could handle our own production and have a little more control over how our records were made. I suggested that we record our albums in our rehearsal room, in my basement. I felt we should take the plunge and purchase professional recording equipment in the form of a 24-track tape machine and a decent sized desk to accommodate all the channels. MCI manufactured both and we had successfully used their equipment at Criteria. In fact Criteria had told us that if ever we wanted to buy recording equipment to let them know as they had a very good relationship with MCI, who were just up the river from them in Florida. We could have bought a set-up for about $20,000 - $30,000 at the time. Since we were getting a pretty hefty advance from the record company, I tried to persuade the band in this direction and Hobbit supported me, but in true conservative manner the band vetoed the idea. They were concerned that after spending a substantial amount on equipment, the recordings may still not turn out professional enough and we'd have to go into a recording studio and spend more money. I felt this displayed a lack of faith in my judgement and ability, as well as that of Hobbit – it was a disappointment, but we eventually settled on the idea of bringing a mobile recording studio to Laureledge – the kind of unit we would normally use to record a live show. We parked the mobile outside my house and recorded in the basement. Producers Ron and Howie Albert became involved at that point and they were up for recording in this way. The Albert brothers were house producers at Criteria studios and we had met them previously. They were great guys, two brothers – a fat bloke and a thin bloke – who had set up a production company called Fat Albert Productions. They liked working in tandem because all too often when bands really get into recording they want to continue for long periods of time. When you find yourself working fourteen-hour sessions, it's a challenge to maintain concentration, and obviously with two of them they could work in shifts and we could keep going. Once we'd got the basic tracks down we took the recordings down to Criteria in Miami where we recorded vocals and mixed the album. The set-up worked well and I really enjoyed recording in the basement, but part of me still wishes we'd been brave enough as a band to buy our own recording equipment. I think we could have made some really good recordings over the course of the next few albums. Having said that, it was fairly radical in those days to set up

Laurie and Steve in our basement studio at Laureledge with Mark "Hobbit" Emery, 1976

your own studio and it would have been a fairly dynamic move on our part. Nowadays it's totally different – everyone and their brother has got their own recording studio.

Musically there was a conscious decision not to go outside of our realm this time. With *Locked In* we had tried to do something that wasn't natural to us. When you have someone as respected as Tom Dowd telling you what to do, you are obviously swayed by that and are prepared to give anything he suggests a try. Once we'd been through that, our attitude was "Fuck that for a game of soldiers, let's do it our way now". So, with the *New England* album we decided to just do what came naturally. The whole period spent writing and recording *New England* was a very positive and productive time for the band.

There was a lot of jamming involved with *New England*. Obviously when you have your own rehearsal facility you can afford yourself the luxury of kicking ideas around for hours on end. During rehearsals we would try songs in different ways, experimenting with different feels and tempos just to get a different slant on things. This was probably the first time since the early days of the band that we'd had the luxury of being able to spend so much time, day after day in a studio environment writing, rehearsing and recording. As such there was a lot of group collaboration, both on the music and the lyrics, and all the songs were jointly credited – justifiably so in this instance.

> **LAURIE WISEFIELD:** *It was much easier for us as we were down there jamming every day so we were very comfortable with our own casual environment. It wasn't as stuffy with less pressure than being in a "proper" studio. Hobbit used to record nearly everything on a Teac 8-track. An American named Tom Hagan who was our guitar tech at the time used to keep us amused as he was quite a comedian. I remember*

coming into the studio one day and on both sides of the studio there were these massive posters he'd had made up of a Japanese audience facing me (or where I would always stand in front of my amps), as I was very popular with the Japanese fans and facing Andy was an American audience as he was more popular there – it was quite hilarious. Also on tour if someone was a bit low or gaining a lot of popularity for some reason, he would get t-shirts made up saying "The Laurie Wisefield Band", "The Andy Powell Band", "The Steve Upton Band" or "The Martin Turner Band" and would be wearing one for our sound check depending on what was going on at the time. Tom was a real character and deserves a mention. We nicknamed him Bunter. I'm not sure he ever knew who Bunter was though. Then there was Mal Craggs and Granny who also worked for us – a couple of English guys who are a book unto themselves.

MARK EMERY: *When it came to New England, we built the studio in the basement and did all the pre-production recording there. We built a soundproofed area using underlay from the carpet store and loads of hardboard and made a control room area for the Teac desk and tape machine to go in. We made some great recordings and I think Martin still has them. We worked long hours and had some very funny sessions there – it was very successful and the band really enjoyed themselves. I was heavily involved with the pre-studio work although when it came to the actual studio work, obviously there would be a producer who would have his own engineers. I wouldn't undermine what they were doing and would take a back seat, although if I was ever asked to offer an opinion on things then I would and I think I was always respected for that.*

Album opener 'Mother of Pearl' started with a Laurie guitar riff that sounds like a chicken. That song was very typical of the four of us knocking up a song together, as was quite common on this particular album. Laurie, Steve and myself collaborated on the lyric, although when the song was recorded I wasn't totally happy with the vocal. It was fairly improvised and I hadn't really burned it in.

'(In All Of My Dreams) You Rescue Me' was another one where everyone made a substantial contribution, particularly Laurie. I wrote most of the verses, although everyone chipped in with lines here and there, including Pauline Powell, who is credited with assisting with the lyrics on this song on the album credits, and Laurie, who came up with the chorus lyrics and song title. '(In All Of My Dreams) You Rescue Me' has some wonderful rhythm work from Andy, the bass is quite intricate and is hopping around all over the place, which made it very difficult to sing and play live. There are also some really unusual harmony guitar lines in there as well – quite wacky things that you only really get when you're together in a rehearsal situation and everyone's smoking marijuana – something which everyone used to do around that time. Everyone would come over to my place to rehearse at about eleven in the morning. It would be a nice sunny day and we'd all end up in our shorts out on the lawn, dipping in and out of the pool, drinking gin and tonics and smoking spliffs. Then about three o'clock in the afternoon we'd get down to some work, often playing music until late in the evening or into the early hours. This was pretty commonplace for rock bands recording in America in the mid-seventies.

> **LAURIE WISEFIELD:** *I had the chorus melody and the chorus lyric first. The lyric came from my girlfriend at the time who wrote "In all of my dreams you rescue me" on a Christmas card that she sent to me – Aahh, that was sweet! Well, l I thought so and that kicked off the song. Everybody chipped into that song though and I think it's a great blend of all of*

us. Martin wrote most of the verse idea, with some help from Andy with the chords, which worked well with the chorus. Some of the guitar stuff on that I am most proud of as I think it was pretty original.

'Runaway' was an odd little tune that I wrote the lyric for, ironically about something that would happen to me about a year later. That was very odd indeed. Musically it's got Laurie's stamp all over it, but having said that most of what we put together on this album evolved out of jamming, with everyone contributing. In fact it would probably be fair to say that out of all the Wishbone Ash albums, *New England* is the one which can most truly be described as being very much co-written by all four members of the band. As such everyone was credited as co-writers on all songs on this album. I would have to say though, that there was a lot of musical input from Laurie on this particular album.

> LAURIE WISEFIELD: *'Runaway' started from a jam. The main verse riff was my lick and the strange accents at the end were where it started from. Martin came up with the chorus riff, which is blinding and complimented it great. Martin wrote the lyric on that one. Andy played some really stinging lead licks on 'Runaway' too. That was one of my first attempts at playing slide with Wishbone.*

'Lorelei' came from an idea Steve had, inspired by the German folk legend about a female water spirit who would lure you onto the rocks on the banks of the Rhine. Steve and I collaborated on the lyrics. I think Steve's initial idea was to get more into the actual legend in a literal sense, but although I loved the title I kind of pulled it away from the legend a little and took it into a different area. Musically Laurie really shines on this one with some lovely guitar lines that run all the way through the tune. Andy contributed some nice rhythm work as well.

> **LAURIE WISEFIELD:** *Steve came up with a lot of lyrics on many of the albums and was great at taking away a jam and coming up with a vibe for a lyric.*

'Outward Bound' was a total jam session. There was never any thought of it becoming a song with lyrics – it was always destined to be an instrumental piece and a pretty fast paced one at that. It's got all the elements that Wishbone Ash is known for – the twin lead guitar harmonies, busy bass lines, and a driving rhythm. There's even what sounds like a guitar solo during the middle section that was actually played by me on the bass – that was totally impossible to reproduce live, and one of the guitarists would take that line when we played the song in concert. There is also another trick we used where we got Laurie to play scales up and down his guitar neck. We speeded it up considerably and dropped it into the song as an effect during the middle section, where it actually sounds like a synthesiser – but that is actually Laurie playing scales. I do remember one particular funny moment while we were recording 'Outward Bound'. Our publicist Rod Lynton was staying with us at Laureledge. He was in the studio with us when one of the Albert brothers said "I think this tune

Wishbone Ash Mk.2 treading the boards, 1976

could do with a tambourine to emphasise the rhythm. Does anyone play tambourine?" We all looked at each other and said "At that speed? No." Now, Rod is one of those guys who is always itching to get into a recording studio and do anything he could – be it vocals, guitar or even tambourine. So he put his hand up and said "I'll play it". So we put him in there, and Rod soon found out that it was totally impossible. To keep that rhythm going right the way through the song was a very tall order indeed. He made a couple of attempts, ended up sweating profusely and eventually gave up, although I think we did use some of it in places.

'Prelude' was a short little instrumental piece that again evolved out of jamming. It had an almost medieval feel, a little reminiscent of some of the stuff on *Argus* with that marching feel which conjures up images of an army marching towards you. It was something which could have been developed into a song in its own right, had we put a little more time into it, but in the end we decided to use it as it was, and it served as a prelude to 'When You Know Love'. There was always a question mark as to whether that worked.

> **LAURIE WISEFIELD:** *'Prelude' was my style of finger-picking coming to the fore a bit there, I think. That was the kind of thing I was doing with Home, but it was just a short piece of music really.*

'When You Know Love' was one that I wrote the lyric for and one of those songs that never got played live. We spent quite a lot of time working on that one and it was quite a stretch vocally for me. I'm not sure why it got overlooked. It's actually a pretty decent tune with a lot of emotion that I know a lot people are quite fond of.

'Lonely Island' is a song that goes back to the sixties, which I wrote way before Wishbone Ash even started. I think we'd attempted to record this one quite early on, but it never really worked. It's very mellow and moody and, as such, it could quite easily end up sounding like a right dirge, but by the time of *New England* we decided to give it another go and I think the band really got into it and interpreted it very well and it had a lot of vitality. Laurie, in particular, did a great job recording the lead guitar lines. Andy was also really good at constructing some very evolved rhythm parts and there's a lot of that in there as well.

'Candlelight' was actually written by Ted and Andy. It was a mellow little acoustic guitar piece and something they used to play in rehearsals when Ted was still in the band, but had never been recorded or worked into a song. Fast forward to the *New England* sessions and I seem to remember Andy was playing it one day and Laurie joined in. They developed the idea a little, but I think initially the feeling was "We can't really use that, because it's one of Ted's pieces." In the end we decided we would like to use it and so we contacted Ted and asked if he would mind us including it on the album. He was happy with that and we gave him a credit on that track. It was almost as a goodbye or salutation to Ted and we all felt it was a nice move to include a piece of music that echoed back to his time in the band.

> **LAURIE WISEFIELD:** *We all agreed it was a nice melody and a tipping of the hat to Ted. I played Ted's melody line.*

New England saw the return of Hipgnosis for the album cover design, following a break for the *Locked In* album. As usual they came over and we threw ideas back and forth. They liked the 'Outward Bound' theme and from that they decided on the imagery of young guys together, out in the wild, surviving on their own – a bit like a rock 'n' roll band, really. Although we thought it was a bit homo-erotic – naked bodies, fit young lads sharpening a stick, almost like a penis substitute – it was certainly different and we all went with it, although we could have been setting ourselves up for some criticism. Thankfully nobody responded to it in that way when the album was released. For the inner sleeve pictures, Storm has us cavorting about in a stream in Connecticut. It was absolutely perishing and Storm asked us "Can you guys get in and paddle around up to your waists?" and us replying "Sod off, have you felt how cold it is?" It was unbelievably cold.

We debuted the *New England* material on a tour of Japan during October 1976, ahead of the album's release. This was the most extensive of all our excursions there and we played a total of ten shows, taking multiple nights in the obvious strongholds such as Tokyo and Osaka, as well as shows in some of the smaller cities. Japan was always fabulous – we used to have some great times there. Our promoters out there were Udo Artists and Mr. Udo was a truly lovely man – he is still promoting today. He was very fond of us and very good to us. On one occasion he actually took us to a geisha house. He'd booked this but didn't know we were bringing out our wives for the tour. He said to me, "Martin, this is a difficult situation. I have booked the geisha house and now you are here with wives." So we said "Well, that's okay. We'll straighten it out with them." So we told them we were going to a geisha house. They said "What's a geisha house?" So we said "Oh, it's just a place with girlies, where you get a massage, a wash and a scrub. Here's some money, why don't you go out shopping that day." It was all part of experiencing traditional Japanese culture, although Mr. Udo was quite amazed that the wives were happy about us going. Travelling on the bullet train, past Mount Fuji, was another wonderful experience. I fell in love with the country and really became immersed in soaking up Japanese culture – I even started reading Japanese literature. I was amazed at Japanese language and the way they constantly make reference to nature. I was also fascinated by the way the language is written – the calligraphy and the artistic sweep of the letters really is something of immaculate taste. The Japanese also have an amazing sense of aesthetics. When we visited a traditional Japanese restaurant, there was nothing in the room whatsoever. No table, no chairs, just a white room with one object of art – a wooded stand, with a vase on top of it containing a twig with cherry blossom. It was arranged to be aesthetically exquisite. Of course, there was a table, but it was on the floor – everyone would sit cross-legged while these little ladies in traditional Japanese dress served the most wonderfully presented food such as raw fish and kobe beef. Japanese food, for me, is incredible, with a bias towards fish rather than the dairy products which seem to dominate the typical Western diet. I once joked with a Japanese girl, telling her she smelled of fish – when one consumes so much fish, it comes out through the pores as one perspires. In return she said that they all thought Westerners smelled of cheese because we eat so much dairy food! We had a great laugh about it.

The Japanese are wonderful people – they are polite, cultured, very civilised and have a great sense of honour. Japan has so many parallels with the U.K. in that it is an island just off the coast of a mainland, it used to have an empire, and the people are very independent and industrious. The difference over there though is that, in typically Eastern Buddhist fashion, the centre of the universe is not "me". Instead, they have the ability to think in terms of the welfare of the collective. As a result they are much better organised when it comes to working as a team. Our road crew couldn't believe the way the Japanese stage hands broke the stage down. They would go in there mob handed – about ten of them – and each guy had a diagram and a list of specific tasks he had to perform. We'd never seen a stage broken down so quickly and it was quite a shock for our road crew, who thought they were pretty good – such organisation was unheard of within British or American crews at that time.

Our road crew actually got thrown out of one hotel, the Tokyo Prince. They were bringing up girls into the rooms and the management of the hotel were not very happy about it. They put a guy, dressed in a uniform with braid on his shoulders, down on the ground floor by the lift to stop the girls going up. So the road crew started bringing them up the fire escape. The management could see what was going on because each time the fire escape was opened it set off an emergency light in reception. When the management figured out what was happening they sent a team up to our floor and told our crew that it had to stop. So then our crew hot-wired the alarm system on the fire escape door so it wouldn't show up on reception. The hotel found out about it – they were incensed and ordered us all out of the hotel. We managed to negotiate it down to just the road crew – the sinners who had been involved.

Meeting Japanese fans, 1976. I have always felt a strong connection with the Japanese people and their beautiful country

We had all agreed that we would not take drugs into Japan. It was just too much of a risk. It was a very "straight" country and there were very heavy penalties for those who got caught. At the last minute, however, I decided to take my stash of white powder along. At one of the Tokyo gigs an old girlfriend of mine called Sally Ower turned up. I hadn't seen her since the late sixties. She was a model and she was out there with a group of models from all across Europe – London, Paris, Milan. They were all working in Tokyo and it was great to see her. After the show she said "We're going out to a club afterwards, do you want to come along? There'll be a load of models there." I told her that I had to wash my socks back at the hotel. In reality Laurie and I went straight to the club – a wacky, crazy place with a lot of freaky folks rocking away. There were about a dozen of us Westerners. One of the models was going back to Paris the next day and she went out into the street with a drink in her hand, which was strictly forbidden in Japan. The cops were out there – they hated this establishment and as far as they were concerned it was full of drug-ridden deviants. They wanted to shut it down and put everyone in jail. So they grabbed this model and asked to look at her papers. She was a day or two over on her visa and so they arrested her and took her to jail. Sally also went outside and, even though her papers were in order, they gave her a hard time as well. Meanwhile this club was rocking with about 300 people inside. Gradually word got around that the cops were outside the door hassling people and looking to make arrests. With some gusto, the Japanese fraternity in the club – all acting en masse, as they do – just vaporised. They disappeared in about five minutes flat, leaving us twelve Westerners in there all on our own. Somewhat alarmingly, I remembered a dream that I'd had a week before in England where I'd been trapped in a room with a cop outside who was going to bust me. Back in Tokyo, as I came around the corner of the club, I caught sight of this little cop with a droopy bottom lip and a funny shaped nose, wearing military style clothes with a steel helmet and kicking boots. He was wielding a large cudgel that he was itching to crack someone around the head with. I thought to myself "Whoops - this is my dream from a week ago." I never imagined in a million years that it would actually be happening to me in Japan. Now, it was looking like we could get hassled by the law the minute we tried to depart this establishment and Japan would not be a good place to be caught with anything illegal, so, checking my pockets, low and behold I discovered some white powder which I decided to jettison without further deliberation. An American girl and I scanned the club trying to look for an alternative way out. We found a restaurant that was locked and we persuaded the guy who ran the place to open the door again so we could access their fire escape, still not knowing whether there would be cops outside. As it happened we burst out through the fire doors and within ten seconds we were in a cab and headed up the road. The next day when I stopped to think about what had happened to me, I started cracking up. I'd been taking that rubbish every day for quite a while and I got very angry with myself for having let my guard down. One of the tricks of that drug is that you become deluded. You think you're on top of everything, but actually you're not – it gets a grip on you and I had a rude awakening there. I realised I was in a real mess and had to straighten my act up. Fate had contrived a situation where I was forced to confront my little problem.

Of course all this needs to be set in the context of the times and the traditional rock 'n' roll lifestyle of the day. This kind of behaviour was par for the course if you were in a successful rock band in the seventies, to the point of being considered almost the norm for both the bands and their crews. We were young guys travelling the world and pretty much anything we wanted was available to us. Musicians and creative people, by nature, tend to be quite vulnerable at the best of times and almost everyone on the scene who we knew was doing the same – or worse – and so it was very easy to fall into the trap. In fact our band's activities in that department were quite modest compared to some in our industry. Thankfully we all managed to escape the drugs trap largely unscathed. As the years went on we all matured in our behaviour somewhat and none of us became rock 'n' roll casualties, thankfully. Sadly many of our contemporaries in the business were not so fortunate.

We followed the Japanese shows with an extensive UK tour – our first in two years. By this time the album had been released and had attracted much publicity and some great reviews. This was, of course, a great relief for the band after *Locked In,* and we were very proud of *New England*. We had produced an album that we were pleased with. Working in an environment in which we were comfortable and with people who understood what we were trying to achieve, we delivered an album that had the vitality of our live performances and epitomised everything that Wishbone Ash was about. The rock 'n' roll rollercoaster seemed to be on an upswing.

The original Wishbone Ash - l-r Steve Upton, Martin Turner, Andy Powell and (seated) Ted Turner

Clockwise from top - Martin, Ted, Steve and Andy on stage 1973/74

Top: Colonel Upton in flight, 1973

Bottom: Onstage towards the end of the Mk. 1 band, 1973

Wishbone Ash Mk. 2, Japan 1976

From top - Martin, Steve, Andy and Laurie

Laurie Wisefield, World Tour 1974

Martin onstage during final Mk. 2 tour, Bracknell 1980

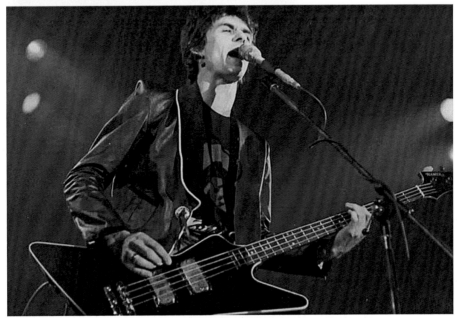

*Top: Back together
- the original
Wishbone Ash,
1988*

*Bottom: Here to
Hear tour, 1989*

The reunion years

Top: with Andy Powell, 1988
Bottom: The Harmony Twins - Andy and Ted, 1989

Martin and Susie - backstage at the Town & Country Club, London March 1990

Top: Athens, 1990

Bottom: Martin, Ted, Andy, and Ray Weston - Japan 1991

Martin Turner's Wishbone Ash, first line-up - October 2005
Clockwise from top: Martin Turner, Keith Buck, Ray Hatfield, Rob Hewins

Current MTWA line-up - with Dave Wagstaffe and Danny Willson, Wolverhampton 2011

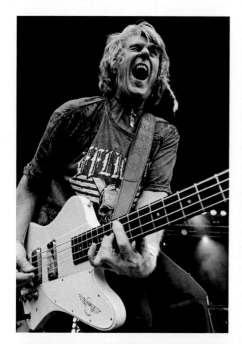

Reunited with Ted Turner - High Voltage festival, London 2010

Classic members of Wishbone Ash reunited - Liscombe Park 31 August 2012

Past and Present - Assorted Wishbone Ash and MTWA alumni - Liscombe Park 31 August 2012

Ted Turner can still play... golf! He hasn't lost his touch on guitar either.

Steve Upton graces the MTWA Garden Party with his presence
- his first public appearance in 22 years

Above: Laurie Wisefield joins MTWA on stage at Liscombe Park

Left: Book signing at QEDG Management offices for first edition of No Easy Road - Liscombe Park, July 2012

CHAPTER NINE

Carry Me a Little
Closer Home

WE ENJOYED the *New England* experience so much that we retained the services of the Albert Brothers for our next album *Front Page News*. Once again a lot of the material was co-written by the band as a unit and rehearsed in my basement in Connecticut, although this time there were also quite a sizeable helping of individually written songs, coming mainly from Laurie and myself. By this time we had gained enough confidence to contemplate recording in a professional recording studio again and decided to record the whole album at Criteria. As such *Front Page News* ended up bearing the hallmark of a studio-type album – a direct contrast to the raw live feel of *New England*. We stayed at Barry Gibb's house while we were recording the album. The Bee Gees had also recorded at Criteria and had based themselves in Miami. We would see them from time to time as they were always cruising around on boats on the inter-coastal waterway. Barry's house was a Spanish villa right on the edge of the water and it was absolutely beautiful down there at certain times of day, such as sunset. The house had about eight bedrooms, so was able to accommodate the band and crew as well as anyone who came to visit us. We had a bearded pirate-come-yachtsman dude, whose name I can't recall, who was a fisherman and a smuggler, who used to go over to the Bahamas. When he was on land he would come to the house early in the morning with a big bag of oranges. He would cut them all up, squash them in a machine, out of which would come fresh, warm, mellow orange juice. He would wake us up by putting a glass of it next to our beds. Then he would go downstairs and cook fresh fish for breakfast. It was a wonderful way to start the day. We loved staying there and it was a better deal than staying in hotels.

I'm quite fond of *Front Page News*. The album captures a certain atmosphere and, like all our albums, is a "record" of where we were at a particular time – in this case finding us towards the end of our period of living in the States. Even the cover quite accurately captures the vibe at the time, with the band, wives and crew acting out various scenarios. Even Mark Emery and Tom Hagen are pictured down the end of an alleyway doing a "drug deal"!

The title-track 'Front Page News' was a song we'd knocked about a great deal in our rehearsal room. I really liked its moody feel and ambience and felt it was really well constructed. Steve was heavily involved in the writing of the lyrics, which were partly inspired by the incident where he had been arrested in New Zealand a couple of years earlier – in particular the publicity that it had generated, which was out of all proportion to the event. Everyone contributed and the guitar players did a great job on the vocal harmonies. 'Midnight Dancer' was put together in pretty much the same way, by the four of us thrashing it out at Laureledge.

'Goodbye Baby Hello Friend' was one of Laurie's songs and was chosen as the single from the album. It had a nice feel and I was a little disappointed it didn't meet with more success.

> **LAURIE WISEFIELD:** *'Goodbye Baby Hello Friend' came very quickly, in about half an hour. It was written about the same girl who wrote me the Christmas card with '(In All of My Dreams) You Rescue Me' on. Unfortunately it didn't work out, partly through moving our base back to the UK.*

'Surface to Air' was one of my songs. That was written in Miami and is probably the fastest writing/recording of a Wishbone Ash song ever – the process was over in 24 hours. I had a little tape recorder set up in a room in the house we were staying in. One evening I went in there about eleven o'clock and stayed there until about three in the morning. I put together a sketch of the song and played it to the guys the next morning. We went into the studio and recorded it the same day. The lyric deals with the surface-to-air principle, which is based on something going off on a random journey and finding out where it needs to go, based on knowing where it doesn't need to go – just like life really! There was quite a lot of hilarity attached to some of the lyrics – everyone thought they were ridiculous. Ron and Howie Albert questioned some of the words – for example, when I was singing "eagle", it was sung in such a way that you couldn't quite tell whether I was singing "eagle" or "ego". That was deliberate – I wanted it to be neither one nor the other, so you could read into it what you like. It's poetic license. "Eagle" is a much more magnificent word to use in the context of a song – it basically meant "ego" but was sung as "eagle". The song is fairly unusual and not a typical Wishbone Ash song by any means, but I'm quite fond of it.

The instrumental '714' was Laurie's composition. When we finished recording it, the auto locator on the tape machine was parked at that number – 714. We were wondering what to call the piece and somebody pointed at the auto locator and said "How about that?" '714' was also the number printed on Quaaludes – American tranquilisers that were quite a popular recreational drug around the time. Because the track had a very relaxed feel, it was deemed to be an appropriate title. '714' was one of two tracks on the album to feature strings – our first experience of orchestration. There was a small orchestra in Miami that Ron and Howie knew of and they suggested we give them a try. Sometimes it's nice to use guitar harmonics and effects to provide a hint of "strings" on a song, but I wasn't too sure about the idea of using real strings. Although I love orchestral music, I personally find that quite often when you graft strings onto a rock song it ends up sounding a little disparate, but we agreed to try it. The orchestra came in and recorded both tracks and everyone agreed it sounded good, so we went with it.

> **LAURIE WISEFIELD:** *'714' was an instrumental idea I wrote, but I would like to give a mention and tip of the hat to an old friend of mine and Steve's who was our next door neighbour in Georgetown, Connecticut. He was a very talented guitar player chap called Brian Keane – more of a jazzer really, he used to come over to party and jam some nights. He inspired me to write that as he showed me the minor ninth chord, I think it is, that runs through that piece of music. It's more like a piece from a film really – not sure how it ended up on a Wishbone Ash album, but everyone liked it and the orchestra arrangement was fab.*

'Come In From the Rain' and 'Right or Wrong' were both my songs – up-tempo bluesy rock tracks in the middle of what was overall quite a mellow album. There was no conscious decision to make a mellow album – it just turned out that way, possible influenced somewhat by the Miami scene.

'Heartbeat' was another of my songs, a mellow track about relationship troubles in my life and one I would love to have a go at playing onstage one day.

'The Day I Found Your Love' was a group composition and the album's big ballad. It had some wacky key changes and I found it quite challenging to sing. It was quite difficult for someone with my rock vocal style to get my head around performing that. It's got some nice stuff on there – guitar harmonies, etc – but personally I found the song very schmaltzy and, for me, the whole production with strings and saxophone was too far off on a tangent from Wishbone Ash's style.

I'm immensely fond of the album's final track 'Diamond Jack', another one we all contributed to. It was a very easy process putting that one together – it flows beautifully. We all put time in on the lyrics, which have a kind of philosophical but light-hearted touch. The whole song is a very efficient use of the band's energy and the song has a nice structure. It's us cruising along playing Wishbone Ash music. I thoroughly enjoyed singing it and I think Andy and Laurie did a great job on the vocal harmonies. We'd all been having singing lessons for a couple of years. When I'd hit my vocal problems around the *Locked In* period, I went to singing lessons with an opera singer in New York called David Sorin Collyer and Laurie and Andy started coming along with me as well. We all noticed the improvement.

Touring to support *Front Page News* saw us at probably our peak as a European crowd draw. We headlined the Pinkpop Festival in Geleen, Holland during the Summer of 1977, playing in front of 45,000 people – the largest audience we played to as a headline act – on a bill that also included The Kinks, Manfred Mann's Earth Band, Tom Petty, Nils Lofgren and Golden Earring. We then undertook a lengthy European tour taking in all the major sports arenas, as well as a string of UK dates culminating with a sold out show at the 10,000-capacity Wembley Empire Pool, or Wembley Arena as it is now known, on 31 October 1977. The band was doing excellent business on the live circuit.

We slotted in an intimate gig at London's Marquee Club a couple of days before the Wembley show. It had been a long time since we'd played a club gig and we thought it would be nice to do a special one-off small gig for the fans. We always loved the original Marquee Club, even though the dressing room was a nightmare because it was so small. Although it was only announced through our fan club at the last minute, word got around

1977

that Wishbone Ash were playing the Marquee Club for the first time since 1973, and an insane number of people turned up. They ended up letting in double the capacity. The place was jam-packed and consequently a lot of people started passing out in the heat. There were girls fainting near the front of the stage and the only way to get them out was over the stage – it was a crazy gig. It was so hot in there and we had a lot of problems with guitars going out of tune due to the heat. They certainly let too many people into the building. There must have been 1200 people crammed into a room that was only intended to hold 600. One of us mentioned this when a journalist brought it up in an interview a couple of weeks later and, as a result, the Marquee Club got a visit from the London fire brigade, who wanted to close them down. This was the early days of Health and Safety – or Elf and Safety as we like to call it! We could have been responsible for getting the Marquee Club shut down, but fortunately it didn't come to that.

By this time we'd got into a routine of recording quite a few shows to multi-track, starting with dates on the *New England* tour, in order to gather material for our next live album. The Marquee gig was one that was recorded, although very little of it ever got used. I really wanted to use it – it had a really rough and ready, raw feel, which I liked. When you've got that many people crammed into a small room, the vibe gets really intense with a massive amount of energy focussed, and that really came through on the recording, even though it was a little messy. When we got around to putting *Live Dates Volume II* together a few years later, most of the Marquee recording just didn't fit together with the other shows we had. When you're recording at venues such as Bristol Colston Hall, Sheffield City Hall and other larger halls that were recorded at that time, you tend to get a far more controlled and civilised atmosphere and sound and a similar acoustic quality from the room. This makes it relatively easy to piece together an album from different shows. The Marquee recordings, however, sounded quite different – they are absolutely raw. I personally think that if the multi-track tapes of that recording, which I still have, are intact enough we could possibly release an album of that show at some point. Watch this space...

The Wembley gig took things from one extreme to the other. The Marquee had a tiny dressing room just a few feet away from the stage, acoustics that were dry as a bone and there was the added craziness of people getting carried out through heat exhaustion. Two days later we were in this bloody huge barn at Wembley, where the sound tends to wallow around a fair bit. At the Marquee, most of what people were hearing in the audience was coming off the stage, whereas at Wembley what people tend to hear mainly is the PA. These venues are not my favourite place to play acoustically but, having said that, I'm actually quite fond of Wembley Arena and I've seen some great gigs there over the years. It's a big London venue and it was nice to have headlined there. It was a high profile show, promoted by Harvey Goldsmith, and illustrated just how successful and popular Wishbone Ash was at this time.

Although Wembley was our first arena show in the UK, playing large sports arenas was by no means a new concept for Wishbone Ash. We'd played venues of this size and bigger in the States, dating back to our early shows supporting The Who, as well as similar venues across Europe. In fact the European tour for *Front Page News* that had preceded the UK dates was almost like an entire tour of Wembley Arenas. We followed the European and UK dates with a tour of the States alongside Robin Trower.

The experience of living in America had an impact on everyone's lives. As I stated earlier, I had persuaded Maurn to accompany me to the States somewhat against her own will, because it would have been unworkable with the two of us living on opposite sides of the Atlantic. Andy and Pauline Powell seemed to really take to America and years later went back there to live permanently. Steve met an American girl called Nancy out there, who he ended up marrying. Laurie's personal relationships seemed to be fractured by both leaving the UK and, again, leaving the USA, but he seemed to take it in his stride and a couple of good songs came out of it. Personally, although it was an interesting experience, I didn't care too much for being stuck out in the backwoods of Connecticut. I was an urban animal at that time and wanted to be in a big city. There were various anomalies between the four of us that meant we reacted to America in different ways.

By the time of *Front Page News* I had decided that I really wanted to go back to the UK. The American experiment was originally intended to be for one year – we ended up staying there nearly three years. During the time we had been in the States, the band had passed on some really good deals and in addition I felt the band was losing its musical identity and becoming more and more Americanised, which I didn't think was the way to go. So, towards the end of the album sessions, I said to the band, "After we've finished this album, I'm going back to the UK. We belong in our country of origin. I want to return and re-establish contact with my roots and I think we should do it as a band." I didn't think the other guys would go back – in which case we really would have had a problem – but with our agent John Sherry also recommending this as being best for our career, they did all end up coming back to the UK, albeit a little reluctantly. The move back to the UK was not particularly easy. There was a lot of upheaval getting all our stuff shipped back, but I felt it was necessary for the band if it was to survive. Possibly there was a little resentment towards me from the others for pushing them into coming back. No one has ever said as such, so I'm only guessing here.

> **LAURIE WISEFIELD:** *Living and working in the States was an adventure in all senses. When you go to another country you can be whatever you want to be as nobody really knows you. You discover all sorts of new things and your horizons broaden. That's a book in itself. Musically, it was a journey of discovery, professionally not so much. Returning to the UK was mostly Martin and John Sherry's idea. I didn't really mind too much where we were as there were pluses and minuses to both. I had family and friends in England and we were going to be concentrating more on working in*

*Europe, so that was quite appealing. On the other hand I had
a relationship which was quite serious at the time in the US,
so that was a little difficult to keep going, and it didn't.*

Once back in the UK, we all had to find places to live. Maurn and I had by this time outgrown our house in Barnes. Our personal relationship had also suffered as a result of living in the States and the whole experience had really taken its toll. A year earlier I'd also been guilty of having an affair with a girl I'd known in the sixties who was by now married. Sue and I had been in love back then and we'd been torn apart by circumstances, specifically her Dad sending her away because he didn't want her getting tangled up with a rock musician. It was an unresolved relationship and so when, in 1976, I walked into Bristol Colston Hall and saw her stood right in front of me after all those years, I was overcome with emotion. One thing led to another and my life got really messy for a while. Maurn and I were still recovering from this when we came back to live in the UK again and coming back to our little house in Barnes made me realise that it was not somewhere I wanted to stay. I wanted a fresh start and to move on and so we moved up the road

to East Sheen, SW14. We sold the house in Meredyth Road, Barnes to a lady who had put a note through the door a year before, expressing interest in the place. Lucia Chilcott was a real character – we became good friends and she once told me of an encounter on Barnes towpath towards Hammersmith Bridge where some scruffy oik had come up to her as she was walking and said: "Oi love, do you fancy a fuck?". Lucia turned to him and responded in her cut glass English:

Photo by Phil Matthews

Laurie Wisefield - Cardiff, 1977.

"No thank you, I've just had one" and walked off leaving this guy with his jaw dropped. We moved to a bigger place in East Sheen Avenue – the 'Broken Down House', as it would be referred to in a later song – which gave me more space to set up a studio to record in. It was a wacky old place that I think had been a rectory at some point – it was a higgledy-piggledy corner house, right opposite the church.

It was around this time we officially appointed John Sherry – our agent since the very early days – as our manager. I'd always been very friendly with John. We used to go to motor racing meetings together – we'd go to the Grand Prix every year, back in the James Hunt days. He lived quite close to me and it was easy to get together – we used to enjoy each other's company a lot. He'd always given us sound advice over the years, going way beyond his duties as agent to the point where he was in reality managing the band's affairs.

The band at this stage was still very "anti-manager", after the experience with Miles following the *Startruckin'* tour and were at first reluctant to

Laurie Wisefield with our "Godfather" manager John Sherry, Japan 1978

allow John to take over as our official manager, even though in reality he had been involved in a managerial capacity while we were still living in the States. In John we had a guy who we trusted and was able to do a decent job for us. By 1978 things had improved sufficiently that we began formally crediting John as our manager. He was strongly behind us returning to the UK and helped us get a game-plan together for future recording and touring commitments worldwide, as well as restructuring some of the recording and publishing deals.

Our first recording project after returning to the UK was the *No Smoke Without Fire* album. Having already made the decision to go back to our roots and try to capture some of the English feel that the band was known for during its earlier years, we decided to record at the old De Lane Lea studios in Wembley (which by this stage had become CTS), where we had last worked during the *Argus* sessions in 1972. We also hooked up with our original producer Derek Lawrence again. It was a bit like going back to visit an old school and De Lane Lea studios hadn't changed a bit, even though the whole music industry had moved on considerably. It was certainly a little strange after having been in America for three years.

No Smoke Without Fire was forged in the shadow of the twin towers of the old and much loved Wembley Stadium. I felt Laurie was particularly inspired on this album and by this stage had started to put together some really good songs.

LAURIE WISEFIELD: *We made a conscious decision to get back to a more English rock sound and vibe, with a bit of the old folky Argus-period influence, initiated by John Sherry partly. I remember Derek Lawrence used to tell a lot of jokes, was very down to earth and very English. We had a plan of which way we needed to go and I think he perpetuated that at the time. John Sherry asked me one day if I could write some material that leaned more towards the old style. He got me quite motivated in that direction, so that's the way I was* *thinking and approaching the writing. I demoed the songs that I'd written for No Smoke on a Revox 2-track machine, so for me that was really the beginning of home recording, which enabled me to actually put the songs down myself with harmony guitars and all, so they were pretty complete. Lyrically it was just stuff that I'd draw on from experiences, films, and stuff that was going on in friends lives – anywhere really. I was just letting it flow.*

The album's opener and single release 'You See Red' was one of Laurie's finest songs to date and had everything the band was known for – guitar harmonies and solos, tight three-part vocal harmonies. As always, although the song had come from one member of the band, everyone contributed to the arrangement. 'You See Red' was probably one of the more commercial tunes the band had recorded and it became a favourite onstage, where lighting engineers would get busy with red lights coming up from behind the band, which was quite effective. Laurie was quite good at writing commercial songs, whereas my ideas tend to be a little more instinctive and obscure. I thought this one worked very well – it had a very "up" vibe to it, even though it's about anger.

'Baby The Angels Are Here' was one of my songs. This one came out of the affair I had with Sue after we had met up again after all those years. By then she was married and so was I, and she also had a couple of children. It was a pretty crazy time for everyone and, realising that this was not to be and that we both had to move on with our lives, I asked her to go back to her family. We'd created a very difficult situation between us and, realising how many other people's lives were being affected, I got quite depressed about the whole thing. At one point I ended up staying at a friend's house. He had a case full of shotguns and for one minute I did wonder if it might be better if I just ended it all. His wife had some books there, one of which was the Bible and so feeling quite manic, I picked it up and read some stuff which somehow got me through, hence the line "Brought me a bible and a gun". Another highly emotional song for me.

Laurie's 'Ships in the Sky' was an unusual and quite magical piece of music, with a unique feel. It's very moody and atmospheric, with a lyric about flying saucers, which was quite different for Laurie. We jokingly used to refer to it as 'Chips and a Pie'!

'Stand and Deliver' was another of Laurie's songs. It had some really nice stuff musically, which I'd contributed to helping with guitar harmonies and arrangements as usual, but I strongly disliked the lyric. It sounded to me like it was about "rape" and I really couldn't sing it with any feeling. I felt it hard to relate to the sentiment expressed in the lyric and, as the singer, I did not want to be accused of being distasteful. My reticence was outweighed by everyone else's enthusiasm for the song, which was certainly very good musically. If one thinks of this tune as something that was depicted in a movie from the 15th or 16th century, then arguably the sexual politics involved do not constitute quite such a hot potato.

Steve Upton, 1977

'Anger in Harmony' came from my pen, with some help from Andy and Steve. The lyric explores the friction that occurs between band members from time to time. Often when disagreements occur, people can get polarised. Once they adopt a stance they don't want to give ground on principal and you end up with what is commonly referred to as a frank exchange of views. I think it's the same with most bands. There are always moments of disagreement, although most of the time you get on fine. At that point in time there were some fairly major differences of opinion and yet we all managed to hold the band together and make harmony guitar music. That song was an attempt to also look at myself somewhat. I've always been capable of blowing a fuse and putting my views across in colourful terms, for want of a better description. I've always been a punchy little sod, although I'm a little older and mellower these days.

'Like a Child' was another of my songs that was born of a personal entanglement. I had got to know Sue's children well and it made me realise for the first time in my life that I loved kids. Before that I'd had a typical rock-star, self-involved attitude which kids did not really fit into. I learned a lesson there and suddenly started to really begin thinking about children and enjoying their company. 'Like a Child' was an attempt to re-establish contact with the innocence that children have. They are so naive, yet at the same time see things so clearly sometimes. It would appear that my paternal instincts were beginning to surface at this point in my life.

The album's final track 'The Way of the World' was another one of our two-part extended songs, this time written by Laurie. As always with those long songs, everyone contributed to the arrangements, guitar parts, and vocals. We'd done a lot of tracks of this kind over the years – 'Phoenix', 'Sometime World', 'The Pilgrim', 'FUBB', etc – and this one was one of my particular favourites. It had a nice moody vocal and was full of interesting riffs, bass lines and guitar melodies, together with a really good energy.

The whole period following our return to the UK was very productive from a song-writing standpoint, for Laurie and myself in particular, and for both this album and the one that followed, we found ourselves with much more material than was needed for the album – remember we are talking pre-CD days when the average vinyl album lasted around 40 minutes. Inevitably this meant that some material got left off – in the case of *No Smoke Without Fire,* this included two of my songs, 'Fire Sign' and 'Time and Space' and a beautiful ballad of Laurie's called 'Hard On You'. All of these would see the light of day many years later, either as bonus tracks on CD re-issues or as part of archival collections.

'Fire Sign' is actually a song that had been put forward for previous albums, but we were never really happy with the way it sounded – a bit like 'Blowin' Free', really. It was a song about reincarnation and the idea that if you can't get together with someone in this lifetime, maybe the next lifetime will do. Steve Upton used to nearly fall off his drum stool with laughter every time I sang the line "I hope I'm not a dog or maybe a monkey". Steve always used to see people as animal characters. Sometimes when you look at people's faces you can see an animal. Ted could well have been a lion, and Andy must have been a turtle – his nickname was Snap back in the early seventies. I've always had an affinity with the heron or a wolf. I also remember Steve describing Annie Haslam of Renaissance as a canary – she certainly sang like one! She was living with Miles for a while and when Miles came home she would fly down and land on his perch. That struck me as an extremely funny image at the time. Speaking of reincarnation, Sarah – my Miami psychic friend – once told me that I was a pirate in a previous life and had got thrown off a ship in the Caribbean, when it was captured by government soldiers. I drowned – what a total bummer. "What did you do in your last life?" "Oh, I just robbed and raped and pillaged, but I ended up being a sharks breakfast." Strangely, I have always had a severe fear of water and didn't even learn to swim until I was about thirty. As a kid, whenever I drew a picture, it almost always was of a pirate ship complete with skull and crossbones. I suppose pirates and rock musicians are not a million miles apart in lifestyle. Take Lemmy – does he look like a pirate from three hundred years ago?

'Time and Space' had a very similar melodic quality to 'Like a Child' and both songs explore my usual preoccupation with time and also space. Everyone felt there was too much of a similarity between those two songs and that we didn't need them both. There was also a bit of a concern about the reference to "nuclear bombs" in the lyric, as although we had touched on war as a theme on the *Argus* album, Wishbone Ash was not really a band that mixed politics and music. The recorded quality of 'Fire Sign' and 'Time and Space' was not quite up to the standard of the other material, but I really liked both songs and I've revisited them both with my band in quite recent times and they've both sat well as part of our live show.

I personally thought 'Hard On You' was one of the best songs Laurie had ever written. Quite often at that time, both Andy or Laurie would write a song and then struggle to sing it in the studio and I think in this case we probably weren't quite certain that Laurie had nailed the vocal, although listening to it now he actually did quite a good job and it's a really nice song.

Japan 1978

No Smoke Without Fire was released in October 1978 and came packaged complete with a bonus live single, featuring two songs recorded during our previous two tours and gathered from material we had recorded with a future live album in mind. MCA also released 'You See Red' as a single from the album, with a live recording of our traditional encore number 'Bad Weather Blues' on the b-side. This was a song that only really worked as a live performance, with crowd response, and we never felt the need to attempt to put it on a studio album. It's a standard twelve-bar, boogie-woogie blues, sung by Andy, and was a good vehicle for audience participation. Having said that, I do think we overplayed it somewhat through the years.

Although *No Smoke Without Fire* was received well by our audience, the UK media by this time was firmly focussed on the punk/new wave explosion that had been sweeping the UK for the past couple of years and it had become quite fashionable for the press to dismiss anything put out by the established bands who had stayed the course since the late sixties or early seventies. We all had mixed feelings about the punk phenomenon. It was great as a street level reawakening of the spirit of rock 'n' roll music, just like The Who had been in the sixties, and it was more about the energy rather than the musicianship. To a certain extent I do subscribe to that, but I think punk very quickly got hijacked and became quite negative. I think there was a lot of hype there, particularly with regard to the contempt that was supposedly being directed at the older bands. Years later it became known that people like John Lydon actually liked Wishbone Ash. In fact John ended up married to a lady named Nora, who was a former girlfriend of Ted's and had been instrumental in getting us out to Germany in the early days. In reality, the punk explosion shook things up for a couple of years and passed almost as quickly as it arrived. There were, however, some great bands that did emerge during the punk era. The Police for example were brilliant musicians and wrote great songs. Although you could never really call a band like The Police a punk band, they certainly had a punky energy and their career was very much launched off the back of the punk scene, although they soon developed their own sound. Our audiences remained loyal to Wishbone Ash and its music and we came through that shift in musical trends reasonably intact.

Touring for *No Smoke Without Fire* was relatively brief. We undertook a major tour of the UK, with sell out shows at theatres across the country, before making a return visit to Japan, where we recorded the live album *Live in Tokyo*. This was at the instigation of the Japanese record label, MCA-Victor, who requested something unique for the Japanese market. We were happy to allow this, but we did insist on taking the tapes back to London to mix the album ourselves and I took on the task of producing and mixing the recordings. The eventual album featured five tracks, including stage favourites 'F.U.B.B.' and 'The Way of the World'. The inclusion of live versions of our more recent material obviously attracted interest from our fan-base outside of Japan and the album soon began to make its way into the import racks throughout the world at rather high prices.

Although *Live in Tokyo* marked my first production credit on a Wishbone Ash album, record production was something I had always been interested in. Even in the very early days of Wishbone Ash, I was the one who had a Revox tape recorder which we used to record the early jam sessions with Andy and Ted. Just before we left for America I'd got myself a Teac 4-track tape machine with Simul-Sync. On the basis of that I eventually bought a Tascam 8-track machine, which I ordered in advance before they had even reached the market. I actually suggested that the band should buy it, but they said "no", but we did use it to record all our rehearsals at Laureledge. That got me into the mechanics of production. I also learned a lot from working with Bill Szymczyk, who was very much a "hands-on" producer, unlike Derek Lawrence who was great in his own way but liked to steer clear of the technology in order to leave himself free to visualise and rely on his musical instincts. I started collecting recording equipment in the seventies and have been doing so ever since. I'm probably not the most commercially-minded producer, but I've got a certain style which tends to be slow and fastidious. I tend to take a long time getting guitar sounds and effects just right. That's just the way I am, but I enjoy recording a lot. I always know what I'm after and I recognise it when I get there. I have a passion for the recording process and the gear involved, especially "old" stuff with valves on board.

Still doing good business in 1978
– sell out concerts at Hammersmith Odeon

CHAPTER TEN

Outward Bound

ALTHOUGH I had found the experience of working in the UK again for the recording of *No Smoke Without Fire* very positive, I would have to say that, with the benefit of hindsight, I'm not so sure that going back to the old De Lane Lea studio with Derek Lawrence producing was such a good idea. Although we worked well with Derek, what we probably needed was some fresh dynamic energy. In retrospect, working with Derek at Wembley was a bit of safe haven – we probably needed to be a bit braver, but with *No Smoke* we were still finding our feet, having been out of the country for three years. When you are looking to record, you don't just go through the phone book – it has to be on the basis of a personal recommendation or a studio you've been impressed by. This was the case with Surrey Sound studios, which I had heard about through my brother Kim, who was now working alongside Miles Copeland managing The Police. I attended a couple of their sessions there and got to know its owner, Nigel Gray. Nigel was actually a doctor by profession, but he had a keen interest in recording and had assembled a studio in a converted village hall in Leatherhead, Surrey. We began recording our tenth studio album *Just Testing* there in March 1979.

The recording process for *Just Testing* was fairly long, taking about six months – by far the longest amount of time we had ever spent on an album. The album credits would eventually read "Produced by Martin

Turner, John Sherry and Wishbone Ash" – a ridiculous credit. John was "executive producer" really, and oversaw the whole process and made some valid suggestions, but I was the one very much in the producer's seat and leading the way creatively. By this time, I had a studio at my home in East Sheen, where I would write and record music, and I was getting some pretty good results and had come in with quite a few really good tunes and so I was feeling very positive about the upcoming album – I must have been because it requires a lot of energy to write, play, sing and produce, all of which I felt very confident enough at this stage to take on, although it did prove to be very hard work requiring much stamina – I once described it as being akin to pushing a truck up a hill!

Things were changing for us as a band and as people around this time. Back in the early days we had all lived very close together and could dedicate twenty four hours a day to the band, but by now things had become a little more fragmented and everyone was laying down roots and making babies. That's all part of human progression and I'm in no way saying that was a bad thing, but it did certainly affect the group dynamic. It did seem at this time that there was a bit of weariness and lack of motivation in certain quarters, which bugged me a bit because we were being advanced a substantial sum of money to make this record and I felt that we should have been more aware of what a privileged position we were in. I did express this to my fellow band members at the time.

Laurie was living in Essex at the time and would come to stay at my place in Sheen and so I would drive him down to the studio. Steve was living in Surrey and would make his own way there. For Andy, things were a bit more involved. He was living way north of London, near Hemel Hempstead, and it was a longer journey for him. In addition he and his wife Pauline had just had their first child – he was the first member of the band to have children – and there were a lot of times when he would find it quite difficult to get to the studio or get too involved, because his time and energy were needed elsewhere. Therefore quite a bit of time at Surrey Sound there would be just Steve, Laurie and myself in the studio.

Despite the workload, I really enjoyed making *Just Testing* and I was really getting into a flow with song-writing. I have read Andy Powell claim that this flow was at the expense of the group spirit of old. Frankly that sounds a little sad to me. The fact is that I was writing songs, as I had done fairly consistently throughout the seventies, but I think there was a spirit in the camp where they would like me to have been writing something more along the lines of *Argus*, or something more commercial. The latter had, by that point in time, become a pressure from within the band, but the fact of the matter is that I don't write songs from that standpoint, and I think that did frustrate the other guys somewhat. I write from my heart and soul and if it turns out to be commercially successful, then great. Some people are very good at writing commercial songs to order, but that is not what I do. With *Just Testing* I think we did something that was new, fresh and creative, yet still had a very distinctive Wishbone Ash sound. We started to take some chances, in the guitar sounds department especially, and I felt we should have continued down that road. It gave the band a sense of direction for the eighties, which were now approaching. Although some of the album could be seen as un-commercial, I think *Just Testing* contained a solid balance of material and set us off in a positive fresh direction as we prepared to enter a new decade.

LAURIE WISEFIELD: *I enjoyed most of those sessions up at Surrey Sound Studios. I seem to have always taken something of a positive experience from all of the albums we made together, although maybe some of the outcomes were more successful than others, looking back on it. Andy was having a tough time on that album for some reason – maybe a personal thing, lacking a bit of confidence, I think, and maybe not so in tune with what was going on musically. His writing contribution on that album was just 'Master of Disguise', but he did pull some nice licks out of the bag as usual on 'Lifeline', 'New Rising Star', and 'Insomnia', using some quite synth-like guitar sounds.*

The album's opening track and single release 'Living Proof' was written by Laurie, together with Claire Hamill, who also sang backing vocals on the album. On this album I had found it quite hard to get the guitar players to play with the same excitement, passion and enthusiasm with which they played when on stage in front of live audience. At one point I even considered getting a picture of a live audience and putting it on the studio wall to try to get them to play with more passion – that was a constant frustration of mine throughout those sessions.

Around this time John Sherry had undertaken to represent Claire Hamill and one day he brought her down to the studio to show her around and let her see how we worked. John took her into the control room – we could see her through the glass, bopping away as we were playing. It was fascinating to see the guitar players begin to start strutting around and starting to play with some passion and energy, once there was a female presence in the studio. They were clearly checking Claire out and it certainly made me laugh. Later on that day, I said to John Sherry "Did you notice the difference in the guitar playing today?" He said "Yes, I did. What was that all about? There seemed to be a whole different atmosphere. They seemed to actually start performing a bit today." So I said "That was because you brought Claire down to the studio – bring her down tomorrow, and the next day and as many times as you want to." So he said "Okay, I will." So Claire started coming down all the time. I think one night she and Laurie drove home and started working together and also got "quite friendly", as the saying goes. They wrote 'Living Proof' together, which turned out to be one of our most enduring songs from this period. We then got Claire singing on a couple of tunes and even recorded some of her songs including 'Haunted House'. It was a pleasure to have her on board and her contribution to the album was most welcome.

> **LAURIE WISEFIELD:** *John Sherry brought Claire down one day and she did some backing vocals for us and we reciprocated by recording some of her songs with her singing, which was a lot of fun as they were very different from any Wishbone Ash*

songs and it brought out a lot in us all as we weren't tied to "does this sound like Wishbone Ash material?" – we could be free to do whatever came naturally, which is usually the best way to go. There was a song of hers called 'Intoxicating' which I really loved. Claire and I kind of hit it off on a personal level also and we had a little fling for a bit – I don't think she would mind me mentioning that. Anyway she came over to a cottage in Steeple Bumpstead where I was living at the time and I played her a revox recording of the backing track to what was 'Living Proof,' a bit slower originally and a bit more Stones-y, I had some of the chorus idea so we knocked it into shape there and then and she pretty much wrote most of the lyrics on the spot, perhaps tweaked a little later. Claire's a great talent and I love her to bits. We keep threatening to write together again sometime and I hope we do.

One morning I'd driven Laurie to the studio, where he sat down, rolled a joint and had a little smoke, before falling asleep in the corner. I was recording 'Haunting Me' – I'd got my bass and Steve's drums down and had played rhythm guitar myself and put down a rough vocal, but I needed some input from a guitar player. Being that there was only one of them around, I gave Laurie a little prod, which woke him up, and said "Laurie, have a listen to this tune and tell me what you think it needs next. I've run out of ideas and need some input from someone else?" So, we had a listen to it, as Laurie rubbed his eyes trying to stay awake. Afterwards, Laurie said "It sounds like a pile of shit to me". I went absolutely berserk and took this as a personal affront and an insult. I said to Laurie "Listen mate, your job is making music, not reviewing it. There are guys out there who would give their eye teeth to be in the position you are in right now, so get off your scrawny little arse and contribute something instead of telling me my songs are crap." I removed myself from the studio completely and went up the road to get some cigarettes and burn off the adrenalin rush. I went back to the studio about twenty minutes later and as I walked down the corridor to the control room, I heard this music, which was the instrumental middle section in 'Haunting Me', over which I could hear Laurie playing some solos. I thought "Wow, that sounds good – I must have pushed the right buttons there!" I walked into the control room very quietly and listened to what he was playing and when he finished I said "Laurie, mate – that sounds great! Well done – brilliant". Working in a band you do get these little volcanoes that go off from time to time and I've been guilty of mouthing off at times, but I would have to say that Laurie's playing on that track is probably just about as good as it gets. I don't want to make it sound as though Laurie was lazy all the time, because he most certainly wasn't. Laurie did a lot of work with the the guitars generally on that album, partly because he was having to make up for Andy not being around much of the time, and I do believe *Just Testing* contains some of his finest performances ever. He really had developed into a top class player.

LAURIE WISEFIELD: *I think the main thing that developed at that time for me was my forethought, which I think is a very important part in creating and crafting music. If I can elaborate, sometimes things come in a very organic way without too much thinking – just instinctively and sometimes it helps if you can envisage what you want to hear (or see, if you are painting). You know instinctively when something excites you and then you need the technical know-how to be able to put it onto a recording or a canvas. I use that analogy as it's much the same to my way of thinking. I think it was Derek Lawrence that implanted a seed for me in saying that "the next step for you is thinking about what you want to say" and I remembered that and some years later I understood what he was talking about. Both sides to the equation are vital and getting the balance right is often when you come up with the best stuff, for me anyway. So it's a juggling act so to speak. The biggest problem for the band on any album we did* *except perhaps New England in my opinion was the time it took recording in a studio and getting the backing track down and in the pocket. When it takes too long all the life and fire can get knocked out of it, whereas sometimes it doesn't need to be perfect, just to feel good. I remember some absolutely killer jams that would just happen but could not be recreated.*

On *Just Testing* we had a young engineer called Martin Moss – I used to call him Goldilocks, because he had a big mass of blonde curly hair. One day we'd started a jam in the studio – we were just playing spontaneously and it was sounding really good. Nigel told Martin Moss to grab a tape and start recording, which he did. We captured a jam session that had some good bits in it, but he managed to record over the top of another song that was virtually finished – we'd lost a whole song! Nigel Gray was going to sack him on the spot, but I begged him not to do that. Anyone can make a mistake – I've done it myself.

'Insomnia' had a really distinct mood. It was a shuffle – a rhythm that we were well versed in. I pushed Andy to get a very original guitar sound there, for which we used octave dividers and lots of compression. Andy responded to these effects excellently and played some very original parts with that set-up – it sounded like a synthesiser but was all done on guitar. Lyrically it's me talking from the heart about real life experience – I've always suffered from insomnia and, in fact, a lot of my creative work has been done late at night and into the early hours of the morning.

'Helpless' was a song suggested by John Sherry and written by a writer named P.Kendrick. It was a blatant attempt to record a commercial song in an attempt to have a hit single and I personally had my doubts. I thought it was trying too hard and was too conservative and safe, whereas most really good hit singles are successful because they are different. I don't believe you can contrive commercial success – you either make commercial music or you don't. Unlike the other tracks on the album, which were all recorded at Surrey Sound, 'Helpless' was recorded at the original De Lane Lea studio,

Laurie Wisefield – Just Testing, Surrey Sound, 1979

where our first two albums had been recorded, and which was by now owned by Ian Gillan and known as Kingsway Recorders. We actually passed on an offer to buy into the studio with Ian at one point, mainly because although we remembered the place with great affection, we were no longer keen on its central London location.

'Pay The Price' was another of my songs and had a mid-tempo, scruffy, rock 'n' roll edge to it which I was quite fond of. There were people who were critical of the opening riff and claimed it sounded like Deep Purple's 'Smoke On the Water'. I guess it is similar, but I certainly wasn't trying to play 'Smoke On the Water'. The lyric is a bit barmy and sounds like I am writing about a hooker, but it wasn't about that at all. It was about what a relationship with a punchy chick full of attitude can cost you emotionally. It was never meant to be taken too seriously.

'New Rising Star' was a total contrast musically and lyrically and was a nice moody piece. It was written about a girl who Maurn and I met after we'd bought our first house. Her name was Karen – she was originally from Ashington, near Newcastle, and she ran an antique pine shop in Barnes called Remember When. I went in there one day to buy some furniture for our new home and she got a bit stroppy because I'd interrupted her listening to a play on Radio 4 – it was clearly a bit of a nuisance that a customer had come into the shop at that particular time. I was quite intrigued by her and her accent and over a period of time I went in the shop on a few occasions and gradually got to know her – she became good friends with Maurn and myself. Her partner at the time was a bit of a rogue – he was a drinker who would get into trouble with the law. When we went off to live in America in 1975, I asked Karen if she wanted to move into our house, which she did. Maurn and I would stay at the house whenever we came back to the UK and on one particular occasion we came back to find that Karen's bloke had been physically violent towards her. Maurn and I had a real heart to heart with Karen and encouraged her to dump this guy because he was clearly a bad apple. She ended up living with us for a few years – even after we'd bought the new house in East Sheen Avenue. Initially she was very shy and unsure of herself, but gradually over the years she emerged like a butterfly from a cocoon and developed a real confidence and sense of beauty. I never had a relationship with her – she was just a friend. In fact I saw her recently when my band played in Ashington and it was a gas to spend time together again.

'Master of Disguise' was a song that Andy wrote. I think he originally wanted to sing it and I believe we did try to get his vocal on there, but it was quite ambitious and wasn't quite getting there, so I offered to sing it to see how my voice suited the song. For me the vocal came together really easily and we also had Claire Hamill sing some

Andy Powell – Just Resting,
Surrey Sound, 1979

backing vocals as well as some harmonies with Laurie, Andy and myself. I've always been very fond of that song and would have to say that, for me, it's the best song Andy ever wrote. It seemed to me he was writing about the juxtaposition between his private life and how people saw him as a rock personality, although I don't like to interpret other people's lyrics or indeed review music, as I seem to be doing in this book, but hopefully my observations will supply the reader with some insight into where the music cometh from! The fact is that people will invariably relate to good songs and read into the lyric whatever they want to, and that is how it should be.

'Lifeline' was another one of our two-part "epic" tracks with a moody slow part at the start followed by an uptempo section which built to a crescendo. The bass part is unorthodox, loud and pushy – a bit like me I suppose. You would never believe that I'm actually a shy chap would you? I was always particularly fond of 'Lifeline', which evolved pretty much out of a jam session between Laurie, Steve and myself. As the piece began to come together Laurie said to me "Mart, sing something over this", but I didn't have anything prepared. Back then I would carry around with me a notebook in which I used to jot down rough ideas for lyrics, and so Laurie said "Get your little notebook out and sing something". So I got my book and opened it up at a page which contained some stuff that I'd written about my Grandmother (my father's mother) dying. She and I were really close – she had a wicked sense of humour that I loved. She was really fond of me and I loved her as well. She was a piano player, was always up to mischief and used to keep a bottle of gin in her room upstairs. She had always said that when she died she would "visit" those she loved. I was asleep in London one night – it was about half past one in the morning – when suddenly I sat bolt upright in bed, wide awake and I could feel her in the room within a foot of the bed. I could almost see her in a ghostly way. I could hear a wind rushing, even though there was no air movement as such, and I got this really sickly sweet taste in my mouth. I could feel this really intense feeling of love coming from her. Then all of a sudden her "form" rose up into the air and shot straight through the top of the room with a sound a bit like an elastic band snapping. This was a pretty freaky psychic experience I was having and it was almost as though she put her hand down on my chest and said "Go to sleep, darling", which is exactly what I did. The next morning I woke up and thought "Did I dream that?" I rang my mother and sure enough she told me that my Grandmother had died during the night. Anyway, I had written some stuff down about this in my notebook and when Laurie asked me to get my book, I opened it at this page. I thought "Oh no, I can't sing all this stuff about my Grandmother dying," but I sang it pretty much as it was written down and strangely it did fit like a glove. Whether you call the events that gave rise to this song psychic or spiritual is unimportant, but I do seem to be open to a lot of this kind of occurrence and I do not find it threatening or scary – in fact, quite the reverse – but I do notice that some folks find it hard to accept. It can be incongruous with male cerebral energy, but female finds it easier to handle, so I guess you'll have to call me Martina once again here!

As recording for *Just Testing* had dragged on somewhat, our record company were keen to get some product out to maintain interest. We had a couple of songs that, due to the time restraints of the vinyl record, were not going to fit on the album, and so MCA released 'Come On' (our cover of the Chuck Berry song) and 'Fast Johnny' as a single during the Summer of 1979. 'Fast Johnny' was probably our hardest rock track up to that point, with a lyric by me about a car chase. I was always really fond of our version of 'Come On'. A lot of people had already done that song, the most famous being the Rolling Stones, but I do believe we gave it quite a unique treatment and we felt it stood a good chance of doing well as a single, although it didn't actually make much of a dent on the charts.

As with the previous album, we had quite a few songs left on the cutting room floor after the completion of *Just Testing* – songs left in various stages of completion that had not made the final running order. These included songs written by Laurie ('The Bells Chime'), Andy ('Out On a Limb') and myself ('Is Justice Done', 'Where You Been?' and 'Football and Boxing'). These recordings would surface many years later on the *Lost Pearls* collection.

We didn't tour during 1979, the year being spent making music and making babies. On 28 August Maurn gave birth to our first child Jessica. This was truly a life-changing experience for me – as it is for most first-time parents. I was up a ladder painting a ceiling and cornice in wacky colours when Maurn came to me to say that the dam had burst, so to speak. It was gone midnight and she wanted to sleep. I had plans on getting my room painted but we got into the car and went to St Mary's hospital in Roehampton – we were there all night. I left for a while once Jessica was born and on the way home I drove through Richmond Park laughing and crying at the same time – it was a magical moment. I was very proud, yet also emotionally frail, having been up all night and about to embark on this whole new chapter in my life. John Sherry phoned just after I arrived home and he was the first with congratulations. I was completely overwhelmed by the whole experience and I remember it as being a happy time, although both Maurn and I struggled somewhat to adjust to the new role. I've got an inkling that the little spirits are floating around up there, see us making love and they actually choose us as parents because it is all bound up with the spiritual process of learning for both parents and offspring. I don't think it all just happens by coincidence, randomly. Also they have the right name for themselves – it's just down to the parents to be able to find it, which does not always occur and inevitably they often end up adopting a name or nickname that better fits their personality, rather than some awkward name that was given them and doesn't really belong. What parent cannot be moved by their baby's first smile and attempts to speak to them? I found the whole process of seeing the world afresh through my children's eyes to be a very rejuvenating experience. The refocusing on what was really important was well overdue in my case, me thinketh.

Our only live performance of the year was at the televised UNICEF *Year of the Child* charity concert at Wembley Empire Pool on 22 November alongside Gary Numan, David Essex, Cat Stevens, Sky and The Real Thing. We played a short set which included a couple of songs from the new album and, because this was the only show we were doing this year, we invited lots of people to the show – friends, relatives and associates. Our slot in the show was really early in the evening and once we came off stage our dressing room quickly filled up with all our friends – it was packed in there! Everyone was getting quite excited and passionate and lots of drinks were being consumed. I'd had quite a bit to drink after our set and I'd not had much in the way of food before we'd gone on stage. Later in the evening we all decamped across to the Hilton hotel where Gary Numan had laid on a drinks party and things got even crazier – at the end of the evening I was as pissed as a rat! I had to go back to Wembley Empire Pool to get my car – a rather powerful Jaguar with a V12 engine – and there was no way I was going to be able to drive home in that state. I actually had my first wife Maurn with me, as well as Susie, who was a good friend and would later become my second wife, and between them they drove me home. On the way home, on Barnes Common, a car pulled up alongside ours and the driver, who had obviously seen the state I was in, leaned out the window and shouted "'Ere darling, you wanna kick him out. He's not gonna be much use tonight!" I laughed about it the next day but at the time I wasn't very happy.

1980 kicked off with the release of *Just Testing* and an extensive 59-date UK and European tour to support the album. We really were a tight unit onstage by this point, as displayed by BBC Radio 1's live *In Concert* programme recording of one of the Hammersmith shows from that tour. We played like a well-oiled machine – the culmination of a decade of experience treading the stages of the world. The tour was billed as our tenth anniversary tour and I personally was delighted that ten years into our career we could still attract capacity crowds at top concert venues both in the UK and in Europe.

As with any tour, there were various incidents along the road and one particular memory of this tour was when we travelled to Yugoslavia. We'd been in Italy and we'd all had a fair bit to drink the night before, having gone out for a "real" Italian meal – as you do. I'd gone to sleep in the hotel room fairly blotto and had slept on one of those chopped foam rubber pillows, which I really don't like. I woke up in the morning with the pillow having been despatched across the room. My head was also out of the side of the mattress hanging down and the weight of my head had pulled my neck out of shape. I had a problem – my neck was in a right ol' mess and we had a gig that night. I was not in good shape at all and couldn't turn my neck to one side. We got on board the coach, drove up to Yugoslavia and arrived at the gig. Penny Gibbons, our PR assistant, was travelling with us and I said to her "I've got a real problem – I don't know how I'm going to play tonight," so she said "Let me try to do something". She massaged my neck and back to try to free it up a bit. It didn't really have much effect so she said "I'm not really strong enough to really pummel it. I can feel how knotted up it is but it really needs more pressure than I can apply. If you can lie down on the floor, let me try walking on your shoulders and back – that will put more pressure on it". So there we were – me lying on the floor, half naked and Penny walking on my back – when in pops this little Yugoslavian chap with a tray of things for the dressing room. He saw us on the floor and his eyes filled with total horror. He said "Ah, sorry", and immediately backed out of the room, thinking he'd walked in on some English deviant sexual behaviour. It was a funny moment.

We did a lot of live recording during the *Just Testing* tour, as well as on a shorter UK tour we undertook in May/June 1980. Titled the *Blowin' Free* tour (coinciding with our live double a-side single release featuring 'Blowin' Free' and 'Helpless'), this trek saw us playing smaller venues in some of the towns of the UK that we hadn't reached on the tour earlier in the year. The tour opened at Bracknell Sports Centre on 24 May. This was Steve's birthday and appropriately the venue was just up the road from where he was living at the time. We changed the set a little for these shows and even included two brand new songs that I had written – 'I Need People' and 'Lookin' For a Reason'. This was a whole new experience for us as it had been a long time since we had played material on stage that had not yet been recorded. We tried these songs out on stage in an attempt to get them to bed down. With hindsight, it was a little self indulgent to throw a couple of as yet unrecorded songs into the show like that, and they really needed more work. They had the energy and gusto but they were a little rough around the edges. By playing them on stage we thought they would begin to take form, but it didn't really happen as we didn't get the opportunity to play them enough.

We spent the Summer months mixing recordings for a new live album. It had been seven years since *Live Dates* and there was a lot of demand from our fans for a follow-up. We'd recorded a lot of shows over the course of the past four years and there were a lot of songs that were appropriate for inclusion. I took on the hands-on production task and had the responsibility of wading through the material and finding the best versions of each song we wanted to use. That was a monumental task and I distinctly remember going into the studio the first day and seeing mountains of multi-track tapes stacked up. It took about ten days just to listen to everything – it was a real challenge. In between mixing, we had a series of festival commitments. These included the Loch Lomond festival in Scotland, followed by a huge show in a bull ring in Santander, Spain as well as a pair of German festivals in Nuremburg and Loreley. Our touring for the year was rounded off with a final festival date in Colmar, France on 20 September 1980. Little did I know at the time, this would be the last time that our Mk.2 line-up would appear on stage.

It was not long after we'd come off the road in September 1980 and right on the eve of the release of our *Live Dates Volume II* album that Steve Upton called me up and said "We want to have a meeting to have a chat about a few things". So I said "Okay, fair enough" and so the guys all came over to my place in East Sheen. They expressed to me that they felt the band could be doing better commercially and that, in their opinion, the way to achieve this was through hit singles. In order to achieve this, the guys felt the band needed to bring in a lead singer / front-man to give the band a "focal point". My response was that they were creating a problem that did not actually exist and then coming up with some half-assed idea to fix it. I added: "So, you wanna be on *Top of the Pops*?" to which they replied "Yes". So I said "Well, I don't see us as that sort of band and, in any case, what is this alleged singer going to be doing when we're on stage performing the *Argus* material? Are we not going to play that material anymore? Is he going to sing it for me, or am I going to sing it while he's stood on the side of the stage with a pint of beer?" Their response was "That's not really the issue. We're thinking about the future and we want to get someone in who will help us achieve more commercial success." I completely disagreed with their suggestion. Here we were in 1980 having just undertaken a highly

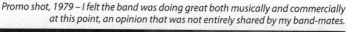

Promo shot, 1979 – I felt the band was doing great both musically and commercially at this point, an opinion that was not entirely shared by my band-mates.

Photo by Aubrey Powell

successful tour and having been advanced a quarter of a million dollars to go into a studio and make an album – not bad for a band that peaked in 1973, I would have thought. We were also earning good money for live appearances, one of the recent gigs being in a Spanish bullring for £8000. As far as I was concerned the band was in great shape both musically and commercially. I had been really pleased with our last album *Just Testing,* which I felt charted a course for the future and gave us a good direction for the eighties. The band had a good balance as the four of us and to introduce someone new – great voice or not – the guy was never really going to be 100% part of Wishbone Ash and its ten year history. Clearly, however, the guys had their own perspective of things, which differed hugely from mine.

> **LAURIE WISEFIELD:** *I think everything just reached a head and we were not all moving in the same direction. Martin could be very difficult – well, I guess we all could – but there was a lot of friction and something had to give. It wasn't a pleasant meeting, let's just say. At that time we had just reached the point of no return, so it was inevitable. Perhaps if we would have taken a very long break it may have helped the situation but everyone needed to just move on and develop. It was unworkable as it was.*

There was always an understanding within the band that when it came to business decisions, we would act as democracy and take a vote. For example, when everyone else said they wanted to go to live in America, I didn't agree but accepted the democratic decision and went with the majority. When it was a musical or artistic decision, however, things were different. Democracy with art doesn't work and, as the main writer, I always had a lot to say about the musical direction of the band, particularly with regard to the songs I had written. Likewise, if someone else had written a song, then that was their right to convey their vision to everyone else as to how it should be recorded and how it should sound. The "front-man" issue to me was very much about the music and I felt that it should not be treated as a business decision and put to a democratic vote. It needed more careful consideration and you don't mess with the chemistry of a band with a history like ours – everyone in Wishbone Ash contributed something significant and the whole was always greater than the sum of its parts. I was strongly opposed to the idea of bringing in a front-man and made my thoughts known to the band in no uncertain terms. They turned round to me and said "We all knew that's what you were going to say, so we've decided between us that we are going to get in a front-man, and if we have to get a new bass player as well then we will." At this point it became clear that this was not a dialogue or exchange of views – this was a conspiracy. To say that I was angry is an understatement – I had steam coming out of my ears and I feared that if they didn't leave immediately things were likely to become very ugly. I was absolutely furious and told them in quite colourful terms to get the hell out of my house there and then – "There's the door – go forth and multiply". For me there was never going to be any compromise. The idea was a non-starter and the guys should not have been bitching about a lack of commercial success. The band was doing very good business, thank you very much, and I've still got bank statements to back that up. It was a really stupid decision and I thought that, once we'd managed to talk it over with John Sherry and bounce it off a few people, everyone would start to see sense. I expected to get a phone call within a few days, once things had died down and I thought that things would get straightened out and this would all blow over, but it didn't. The next thing I heard from John Sherry was that the guys had decided they were definitely going to get a singer and a new bass player and in fact had already gone into a studio to arrange this. I was gobsmacked and very upset indeed. I can, however, categorically state that – contrary to reports – I did not leave Wishbone Ash. The decision to make changes was completely of the other guys making and I was simply put in a situation where my position became untenable. I was forced out – I believe the correct term is "constructive dismissal". It was an absolutely stupid decision and shooting themselves in the foot is the way in which I would describe it. And did they ever get a front-man? I don't remember seeing one – do you?

LAURIE WISEFIELD: *It just didn't happen. We didn't find the right person.*

With the band's decision made, John Sherry and I discussed my severance terms. I was informed that the band's accountant would put together the figures and that I would receive a share of the money that was sitting in the band's bank account, in respect of performances and projects that I had been part of. I was strung along for a couple of years by everyone associated with the band, before eventually being told that all the accounts had been lost on a train, which sounded like bullshit to me. I never got a penny of the money that was sitting in the bank. In retrospect I should have had the band's bank account frozen until the promised quarter share of the six figure sum it contained was forthcoming, but we can all be wise after the event. I felt very aggrieved – it was a very shoddy way to be treated.

My alleged leaving of Wishbone Ash was announced as a "press release" and the matter was neatly tossed aside to the music press and the band's fan club newsletter saying that I had left the band due to a desire on my part to pursue a career in record production! As would often be the case with Wishbone Ash press releases over the years, this was being a little economical with the truth to say the least. Sure, I had always been interested in record production and was eager to get more involved in this, but it need not have been at the expense of Wishbone Ash, which had always remained my priority. How could it be otherwise when so many of its songs were part of the fabric of my life? I was totally committed to continuing following *Just Testing* but the band's alternative recipe for success put paid to that. Excuse me for labouring over this issue but I felt a sense of high injustice over this somewhat seismic event in the band's history and appreciate this opportunity to discuss what really happened. For me, to reveal the truth on this matter is cathartic, particularly given that the ramifications for all concerned were pretty dire as the eighties wore on.

I say all this merely wishing to point out what an ill-considered mess the whole affair was.

The band never carried out their plan to recruit a front-man, but instead began rehearsing with bassist/vocalist John Wetton, formerly of Family, King Crimson and Uriah Heep, on 16 October 1980, four days prior to the release of the band's *Live Dates Volume II* album, which featured recordings from the Mk.2 line-up of Wishbone Ash. It was some time before the news of the personnel change reached the press. As such fans bought the new live album blissfully unaware of the fact that the line-up that played on it was no more.

When I heard that John Wetton was getting involved I went from being really disgusted with my mates treatment of me, to being quite excited for them. I had the utmost admiration for John – he is a great singer and bass player and would later prove to be a hit songwriter. I felt that maybe he would be able to help them achieve the commercial success they were looking for, but before they'd even finished making their next album at Criteria Studios in Miami, I heard through the jungle drums that John was unhappy with the way things were going. In fact, John's wife had spoken to my wife at some gathering and she had said that John had come home not very happy with the way things were going in the studio and that his songs were being rejected and he wasn't being allowed to sing lead vocals. He had said that he didn't really like the situation within the band and was a bit puzzled as to how the band got anywhere in the first place, coming to the conclusion that it must have had something to do with me, being that I was the only one not there anymore. I took that as a huge compliment from John. This was yet another example of how badly things were handled around that period. They didn't only shoot themselves in the foot once – they did it twice! They got a guy into the band who could have given them everything they wanted, yet they alienated him so badly that he left the band once the *Number the Brave* album was recorded. John, of course, went on to have huge success with Asia – the biggest selling debut album of 1982, enormous American success and numerous hit singles. Ironically, everything that my former colleagues in Wishbone Ash had craved.

JOHN WETTON: *I did become a Martin Turner sympathiser. I probably always had been one, but my stint at Criteria confirmed it. Every band has its Zeitgeist and, for me, the band flounders without his presence. I write on a piano keyboard, so all of my stuff that was to surface a year later with Asia was anathema to them. I'd written 'Here Comes the Feeling' and presented it, but it just drew a blank completely. I also had 'Ride Easy.' I wrote that very late at night at the grand piano in Criteria, when everyone was back at the house. What did appear was the only song I wrote on the guitar at that time, 'That's That,' which was written specifically for them. I always imagined them playing that song live. It is ironic that the success they craved was sitting right within those four people at that time, but ego and management decreed that it would not be."*

Following the release of *Number the Brave*, Wishbone Ash got dropped by MCA and, following John Wetton's brief stint, continued with a succession of different bass players – Trevor Bolder, Mervyn Spence, Andy Pyle. By December 1985, Laurie Wisefield had decided to leave the band.

LAURIE WISEFIELD: *It had been building up for a while and it was just before New Year. I had no plans at all, but although I didn't know what I was going to do, I knew that I couldn't give any more to the band at that time and could not face another year without trying something else to rejuvenate and stimulate myself. We all had an influence on each other which creates its own chemistry and dynamics within a band, musically and personally. Over those years we all did a lot of growing up together, experiencing a lot of life together, which I am truly grateful for and treasure the memories. I think a sense of humour was a big plus!*

Despite me no longer being involved in the band's musical activities, there remained shared business interests between myself and my former band members. As such I remained a director of Wishbone Ash Ltd until 1983, when I received a call from John Sherry informing me that he was about to resign his directorship and advised me to do the same. I said "Is this you telling me that the band is in financial trouble and is about to go bust or something?" He replied "Yes, I have advised them to go bankrupt." Within just a few years of the monumental decision being made that resulted in me no longer being in the band, they had gone from being signed to one of the world's biggest record companies, who had advanced large sums of money to make albums, to being without a major record label and verging on bankruptcy. Without the backing of a huge record company such as MCA, they found themselves in a position of recording in professional studios with no record company funding. With the band now having to fund recording costs itself, it was no wonder they were on the verge of bankruptcy. In actual fact they didn't go bankrupt. Steve in particular was far too proud to allow that to happen and they worked very hard on the live circuit to pay off their debts over the next few years. I took John Sherry's advice and resigned as director, as I had no desire to get bogged down further with the band's problems, which were largely of their own making. I should, however, add that while I resigned my directorship, I at no point sold, signed away or otherwise relinquished or forfeited my shares or rights in the band name, which was a separate issue for which no verbal or written agreement was ever made – rights therefore remaining with all core equity members.

The whole business concerning the split with Wishbone Ash and the way it was handled left me feeling very frustrated, disappointed, upset and bruised. I felt it was an unwarranted betrayal at the time, given the amount of input I had made from before day one of the band's existence.

CHAPTER ELEVEN

In The Skin

IT TOOK a while to adjust to life without Wishbone Ash. I am a natural leader – I had played in a band since 1963 but now I found myself on my own. Although this was initially depressing and disappointing, at the same time it was very exciting in that I could now do anything I wanted. I continued to write and record songs in my studio and began to work with other artists in a production capacity. Things started happening quite quickly and before long I had all kinds of people wanting to work with me in my studio at my house in East Sheen Avenue. During the early to mid eighties I worked with quite a variety of artists. It was a huge learning curve for me, from which I learned a great deal about recording and about different styles of music and different grooves.

Shortly after the split with Wishbone Ash, I began working with my friend Roy Hollingworth – a *Melody Maker* journalist who had been posted to New York but had come back to London and wanted to record some of his own music. When Wishbone Ash had played the Loch Lomond festival in the Summer of 1980, our publicist Rod Lynton had suggested that I listen to some of Roy's stuff. I had a listen and it stopped me in my tracks. I thought it was absolutely brilliant – great music, great lyrics, a sense of humour and a really cool rock 'n' roll feel – and I got involved in recording with Roy soon after my split with Wishbone Ash. Unfortunately, we tried to get a deal for the material but nobody wanted to know. It kind of struck me as something of a paradox that here was a guy with all these great songs, full of energy and enthusiasm, yet he couldn't get a deal, whereas on the other hand, Wishbone Ash had been fortunate enough to have had a very lucrative deal with MCA where it was advanced huge sums of money to record albums, yet the band had been so difficult to motivate during the *Just Testing* sessions. We would revisit Roy's material many years later and eventually the album got the release it deserved.

The eighties were a period of musical development as well as emotional turmoil. In December 1980 my daughter Jessica became very ill with an infection in her facial bones. She was in hospital for a very upsetting week and Christmas that year was a time of quiet recovery and introspection.

In the spring of 1981 my brother Kim married Kathy Bacigalupo in New York and Maurn and I, together with my parents, grandmother, Glenn and his wife Lisa, travelled to the wedding and then took a much needed break in Florida. That was the summer of the Royal Wedding and I fell very much in love with the lady who would eventually become my second wife, Susie. We had been friends for a number of years but the chemistry changed dramatically and there was no turning back. With the benefit of hindsight, I think the loss of my band, coupled with the change of dynamic between Maurn and myself that can accompany the arrival of a child in a long established relationship, left me feeling cut adrift. I found the distraction and attention I sought elsewhere and for a while I indulged in the escapism of a cliché situation. Both Susie and I realised I had to try and save my marriage – we were both parents of much loved daughters and the price of our relationship was simply too high.

Kim, sensing the tensions and anxious to support everyone concerned, introduced Susie to the newly separated Andy Summers, guitarist with The Police, who he was co-managing. To my immense surprise and ill-concealed discomfort they immediately hit it off and before I could say "Don't Stand So Close to Him" she had moved into his new home in Putney!

With Andy Summers and my brother Kim –
Stewart Copeland and Sonja Kristina's wedding, Buckinghamshire 1982

By spring 1982 Susie was expecting his baby and he was in America. The Police were really happening at this time and Andy clearly didn't want another child at that point, but for Susie the baby was non-negotiable and they actually split up over this. I saw Andy at Stewart Copeland's wedding to Sonja Kristina in the summer of 1982 and we had to "agree to differ" over his behaviour towards Susie. Later in the evening we ended up onstage playing together with my brother Kim on drums, knocking out a few Elvis songs. I still have a photo of the three of us onstage that night on the wall in my house.

SUSIE TURNER: *A grammar school girl from Surrey, I was fatally attracted to "bad boys" following my early, innocent, teenage acquaintance with the Rolling Stones. In Martin I recognised the same Jagger-swagger, acquired estuary English, in Martin's case with a transatlantic twang, and a patina of urban street cool concealing a sharp intelligence and* *respectable upbringing. For the first few years we were both married and there was no question that we were anything but friends. In 1981 this all changed overnight. For me it was a coup de foudre and my already troubled marriage ended. Martin had his young daughter Jessica to consider and his long relationship with Maurn which had survived the usual rock'n'roll dalliances. They had created a beautiful home to which he was very attached – there was so much to lose.*

I was proud and independent and changed direction, albeit with a heavy heart. I fell in love with Andy on the rebound – he seemed like a knight in shining armour who appeared at the very moment I needed him. He had just come out of a long relationship with his wife, Kate – also with a young daughter, the light of his life. As I soon found out, he was still deeply attached to Kate and later they remarried and had twin sons. I gave birth to Andrew in September 1982 and Martin and Maurn were very supportive friends throughout. Jessica knew "baby Andrew" from birth and has always been close to him. It was to be another five years, bringing Martin a second daughter, Grace, before he and I bowed to the inevitable and were reunited as lovers, our son Tom was born the following summer and we have been together ever since.

I continued to write and record my own music at my home studio. At first I would demo material, playing all the instruments myself, but by 1982 I had started to get other musicians involved in the recordings and was thinking about playing live again. This all started one morning with a knock on the door from my milkman, Nigel Greenway, to collect his money. He said "I know you, don't I? You're Martin from Wishbone Ash, aren't you?" He told me that he had a friend who wrote really good songs and that I should have a listen. I thought "Yeah, yeah, heard it all before", but I said that if he dropped a cassette in, I would at least give it a listen. I listened to this stuff a couple of weeks later and I thought it sounded really good and agreed to do some recording with Nigel and his friend Nick Hadley. That was a bit of an experience, not least due to the fact that Nick was always on a mission to get everyone trashed with various substances before a session would get underway in a rather hap-hazard fashion. You didn't even have to take anything – just being in the room with them smoking copious amounts of marijuana would get you stoned. The results were not that great, but I was fairly impressed with Nigel's guitar playing. Nigel and I then recorded some of my material together and even co-wrote a song. Eventually we decided to put a band together to play live and I asked John Sherry to arrange some gigs for us. We got an Irishman called Al to play drums – he was a local guy based in south west London. I was also keen to incorporate keyboards into the band, as this was the early eighties and there was quite a technological revolution happening within music at the time with synthesizers, drum machines and computerised music. I found all this very interesting and learned as much as I could. We began working with Eryl Price-Davies – a classically trained keyboard player.

> **ERYL PRICE-DAVIES:** *I'd been in a band called The Look who'd had a hit single with 'I Am the Beat.' We'd done a couple of British tours, including one with the Climax Blues Band, who had been signed to MCA, as had Wishbone Ash, and it was through the connection with them that I got word that Martin Turner was looking for a keyboard player. I wasn't actually that aware of Wishbone Ash, but I went down to his house in East Sheen where he had a sixteen-track studio set up and we had a play together. We did some studio work and a few gigs around London, but it was very much an ad-hoc band.*

We only did a handful of shows with the line-up of Eryl, Nigel, Al and myself. It really was just dipping my toe in the water after a period of not playing live. However, John Sherry came to see us one night at the Rock Garden in London and was not impressed. He told me that if I was serious about moving forwards with a new band then I really needed to be working with professional musicians. I always respected John's opinion and in this instance he was right. I wanted to continue working with Eryl, but we had to find a new drummer and guitarist. Through another session, I had been introduced to Ray Weston, a Scottish drummer who was breaking into the London session scene.

RAY WESTON: *I'd relocated to London at age 21. In Scotland I was playing with a big band (with horn section, etc) at a top Glasgow night spot. I was making money and working but keen on moving to London. I auditioned for a London based band while they were playing in town. I was offered the gig and got the train with my drums almost immediately. The band didn't last too long but it had got me to the big city with somewhere to live. From there it was playing at weekends, making money while answering ads in Melody Maker. I joined a band called Drill who were signed to RCA and produced by Chas Chandler. That lasted about a couple of years. We toured with Slade and Chris De Burgh. I was also getting confident in studios at this time which resulted in freelance session work. I met Martin Turner through my friend Phil Brown. He mentioned Martin Turner from Wishbone Ash was putting something together and that I should call. Phil was sound-man for Alternative TV, who I was playing with. His wife Anne Freeman was Miles Copeland's secretary and Alternative TV were managed by Miles. I played drums on their Strange Kicks record on the IRS label. I knew of Wishbone Ash, but not the personnel, so I was not aware of Martin or his role in the band. Interestingly when ATV rehearsed in the basement of Miles' St John's Wood mansion, there were flight cases everywhere with Wishbone*

Ash stenciled. A friend of mine in Glasgow was an Ash fan – he played Pilgrimage to death. The first time I met Martin was at his home. He was carrying a laundry basket from his laundry room. I've never forgotten that! Martin likes to talk and get to know people, so we're in the kitchen drinking tea, chatting. He showed me his studio. Kim, his brother, had left his Ludwig drum set conveniently, so I started playing. We jammed a little, talked, jammed. He played me some things he'd recorded – some covers, originals. He was committed to music and it was easy to connect with him.

Ray got involved and brought in another Scottish musician, guitarist Stewart MacKenzie. I got on really well with both of them. I really liked Ray's drumming a lot – an excellent player. Stewart was great as well, although his style was a little unusual in that he wasn't into playing high bendy notes, or Wishbone Ash-style solo work. His style was a little more spacey and I liked his creativity and originality.

RAY WESTON: *I met Eryl at the first rehearsal. He was a lovely man with a great sense of humour and wicked marijuana. I remember we were auditioning guitar players. Martin put an ad in Melody Maker but nobody seemed to fit the bill. My flatmate in London was Stewart MacKenzie. I mentioned to my fellow Scot and dry humoured friend that we were looking for a guitarist. Eventually he came along for the audition. Martin was knocked out, so Stew was in. Eryl and Stewart have kept up a long friendship, I believe.*

We did quite a bit of recording with the line-up of Ray, Eryl, Stewart and myself, re-recording the songs which I had already demoed – tracks such as 'Kelly's Away With The Fairies', 'The Naked Truth' (aka 'In The Skin'), and 'You'. We also revamped the Wishbone Ash rarity 'Fire Sign', giving the song a quite different feel complete with the synthesiser sounds of the day. Most of our time with this line-up was spent recording, with us only playing one gig in Islington, North London.

> **RAY WESTON:** *I only played one show with the band, in Islington. Friends and family members turned up and gave support. The crowd loved it and the new songs went down well.*

> **ERYL PRICE-DAVIES:** *We did a lot of recording during that time at Martin's home studio. Some weeks we would be there four to five days a week. It was very creative period. Martin would turn up with lyrics, melodies or chord sequences and we would all chip in. He was very receptive to our input. Martin and I wrote some things together, including 'Strangers.' For us, it was great to be working with someone who had a lot more experience of the recording studio than we had. Also, because we were working in Martin's studio, there wasn't the kind of pressure that you're under when you're paying for studio time. We were free to experiment. We experimented a lot in the studio with different sounds. I was working with a Moog Prodigy synthesiser which created an odd sound. Martin also virtually built a pedal board for Stewart. We would also feed a synth through a small Pignose amp, which gave it a strange growling sound. Martin was, at that time, quite keen to move away from the Wishbone Ash twin-guitar format and do something fresh. I think he saw it as a new break for him.*

> **RAY WESTON:** *I instantly heard the difference compared to Wishbone Ash. Rebelling after a lengthy time with duelling guitars maybe? It was something Martin wanted to do. I thought keyboards suited the songs and the times. Mart was listening to Thomas Dolby, Bowie and other early eighties pioneers. He was looking for a new sound – courageous in retrospect. Working the studio with Martin was fun and was*

what he enjoyed most back then. He had his own studio so there were no excessive studio costs, enabling us to search for sounds, parts, ideas as well as rehearsing in a leisurely fashion. He was learning about his recording equipment and working up engineering skills, producing, playing bass, and singing. Everybody had room to come up with their own ideas. Everybody got on very well – no out of control egos, lots of joking around.

We were a fairly solid unit, although Ray Weston was eventually replaced by Tim Broughton – or Brown Rice Tim as he became known – who brought with him a stainless steel drum kit which weighed a ton.

RAY WESTON: *As much as I enjoyed the band I was getting restless with the lack of activity. We had a meeting with John Sherry, but there seemed to be no clear plan. I was asked to join the Heartbeats fronted by John Wilson who was Mari Wilson's brother. The band were signed to RCA and had things going on – gigs, releasing records and a retainer. Unfortunately with bills to be paid I had to move on. The Heartbeats took up about two years of live work and recording. We played the London rock circuit, building up a strong fan base. We were eventually dropped by our record company resulting in the breakup. Later I joined The Armoury Show made up of ex-members from the Skids and Siouxie and the Banshees. We were signed to EMI America and managed by Peter Mensch and Cliff Burnstein, who also managed Def Leppard and Metalica. But Richard Jobson the singer decided he wanted to be a television presenter instead. I joined Fire Next Time, signed to Polydor, who toured and made one album. Another band was A Bigger Splash, signed to A&M. Sting produced our first single which charted. I played other sessions and gigs in between. Good times!*

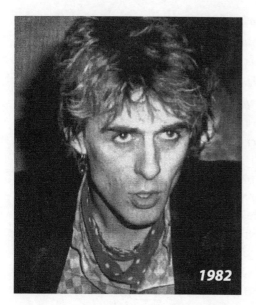

1982

With the line-up of Eryl, Stewart, Tim and myself we did quite a few gigs in and around the London area and anywhere else that would have us. The band went through a variety of names – initially we were called Stolen Face, before changing to Bamboo and finally the Wolf Gang. I tend to always remember the band as the Wolf Gang. I liked the name a lot – it had a very Germanic sound to it as well as being the Christian name of Mozart, one of the greatest composers ever. In addition to the live work we continued recording material at my studio, adding new songs such as 'Hot Surrender', 'Passion' and 'Strangers'.

While this was a very productive time and we all enjoyed the creativity of the studio, the live shows could be difficult at times. To a large extent we were trading off my former glory, yet at the same time we were trying to do something that was fresh and original. Although we were not by any means billing ourselves as Wishbone Ash, my association with the band would understandably always be mentioned by promoters as part of the publicity for our shows in order to get as many people through the door as possible. Overall people enjoyed the shows and were very supportive, but no doubt a few people left disappointed as they had been expecting twin guitars and Wishbone Ash songs but instead there was me with a keyboard player and a different style of guitar playing. At one show in Wales one pissed idiot threw a beer can at the stage. Fair enough – that's one way to express your dissatisfaction! I Eryl, in particular, was absolutely mortified although it didn't bother me too much – mainly because it missed!

> **ERYL PRICE-DAVIES:** *I felt we were a really good live band. The kind of audiences we were attracting varied, depending on the gig. In London, we had really started to build our own following, whereas when we went to other places, it was more of a hardcore Wishbone Ash following that wanted to hear Wishbone Ash songs. I remember one show in Whitehaven where the DJ did nothing but play Wishbone Ash records before we came on. This didn't help, as Martin was trying to do something fresh and wanted to make a clean break. Eventually we did put a couple of Wishbone Ash songs into the set as well as a few covers. I remember us doing 'Pretty Woman' and 'Ready For Love.'*

I sat down with John Sherry one day to review things and he said "Look, Martin, I don't think this band is going to fly. People who come along to your gigs are going to want to see two guitars up there, doing harmonies and solos and, if not doing Wishbone Ash songs, then at least playing something that's pretty similar. That's what you are known for, but you are going off in a much more modern direction, which is kind of alienating for people who were fans of Wishbone Ash. On the other hand there aren't enough people from the new generation of the eighties who are catching onto what you are doing. It's a tricky one and it's hard for me to sell it." This came as a great disappointment as I felt the Wolf Gang was a really good band that was doing something very worthwhile musically. However, without any management or agent backing, it was going to be difficult to take the project forwards and gradually I drifted back into full time production work.

> **ERYL PRICE-DAVIES:** *There was a bit of frustration over which way the band was going. We never really split the band, it just kind of fizzled out and Stewart, Tim and I had all started playing with other bands. I think it's a shame we didn't put an album out during that time. Martin's main business*

contact was John Sherry and, in some ways, I think that was a problem for the band. We did talk about going further afield to try to get interest from record companies, but Martin was very loyal to John and was adamant that we should stick with John and that any work should come through him. I think John would have preferred Martin to play Wishbone Ash songs, whereas I felt Martin had a lot of other creative possibilities besides playing Wishbone Ash music. I really enjoyed the time we spent working together. We all benefitted from Martin's experience and likewise I think he enjoyed and benefitted from working with different people. I'm glad Martin is still playing and would only wish him the best.

Irrespective of the fact that the band didn't take off in the way we all would have liked, I really enjoyed working with the Wolf Gang and we had a very productive couple of years. It was very refreshing for me to be playing with guys who were into totally different stuff. It really did a lot for my confidence

Below and opposite: The Wolfgang – promo shots, 1984. I enjoyed the opportunity to explore different areas of music with this line-up.

to step totally away from Wishbone Ash and try something different – probably a bit too different with hindsight – and I am really proud of the material we recorded around that time. I think the material was strong and, although different to Wishbone Ash in terms of instrumentation, it was in the same ballpark melodically. I was also getting great results from my studio and was very pleased with the technical quality of the recordings we made. Some of these recordings evolved into Wishbone Ash songs when the original band reunited in 1987, while others were revisited many years later for my solo album *Walking The Reeperbahn*. Such was the wealth of material being recorded at the time that I have still not exhausted all the songs from that period – there are further tracks that remain in my bank of unreleased songs and may one day see the light of day on a future album project, although I would probably want to re-record them from scratch.

On a sadder note, all did not end well for Nigel Greenway, the guy who had helped get me back into playing in a band situation again. He packed in his job as a milkman and announced to me that he was joining a

The Wolfgang – Tim Broughton, Martin Turner, Stewart MacKenzie, Eryl Price-Davies

"syndicate" based in Leamington Spa, where he originally came from, and that he was going to be running drugs from India. He would board a plane with 10 kilos of hashish bound for Amsterdam, where the weed laws are fairly relaxed, via Paris. Basically he was just tired of working his guts out and never having any money and he wanted to buy a Jaguar, like the one I drove around in at the time. I cautioned him and asked him "Are you sure you're going to be able to cope with going to jail?" This was a guy who had been to public school and was well educated but he was determined to do it. He made a lot of money over a period of about eighteen months and even bought himself the Jaguar he'd desperately wanted, but then he started doing runs for himself, rather than the syndicate. One day he came to me and said "If you give me £3000, then one month later I'll give you £6000". He was basically asking me to buy into his "business", which as far as I was concerned was a slippery slope. So I declined. On his next trip, the syndicate found out that he'd been doing runs for himself and they called up the guy in India and put a lot of pressure on him to phone the airline and inform them that there was a guy on the plane carrying drugs. Nigel used to fly into Paris and then switch to a morning commuter flight to Amsterdam. He never expected to get caught in Paris because he never cleared French immigrations and was just there in transit, but the French cops grabbed him as he got off the plane, beat him up, and threw him in jail. He was tried, found guilty and went down for eighteen months, although he got out after about a year. However, after he returned to the UK it transpired that the French police had passed on information about him to the British police, who then went through his file and found that there were a series of other flights he had been on where he was clearly moving drugs from India to Europe. As a result he ended up going back in jail in the UK for another year. After he got out he set up a CD shop on the south coast – an enterprise that failed within a year. He then took to selling CD cases to radio stations and disc jockeys. He was doing a lot of travelling all over the country and one afternoon he fell asleep at the wheel and had a head-on collision with a British Oxygen lorry. His car was flat underneath this truck and the medics thought he was dead. Eventually when they pulled the wreckage out from under the lorry, one of them thought they heard a sound coming from inside. Realising he still had a pulse they got him to hospital quickly, but his injuries were horrific – the bottom of his legs and his ankles were shattered. They managed to reconstruct him, but he was never able to walk properly again. I never saw him again after that accident, although I spoke to him a couple of times on the phone. He was understandably very depressed about it. He had a girlfriend and a little baby, but he was at home, in constant pain and unable to do anything. He would take his frustrations out on his girlfriend and eventually he ended up living alone in a bedsit, which is where he eventual committed suicide and was found hanging. This is a rather morbid story, but it illustrates one thing for me – that is that taking the kind of risks that Nigel took is basically a loser's game. I went to his funeral and it was very heavy indeed. I was so glad that I hadn't given him that money all those years earlier, as I really would have helped put him in the ground. It was a very sad end. Although he was not perfect I was always quite fond of Nigel and for that reason alone I would like to attempt to record the song we wrote together – a track called 'Lovers' that has never been released – on my next album.

I have great memories of working in my studio at my home in East Sheen Avenue with all kinds of wonderful people. Aside from the music recorded with my band, there were lots of production projects around this time. Back then there were not that many independent producers with studios. With the computer based recording technology available these days it's possible for anyone to set up a recording studio in their bedroom and produce music without massive investment. Once word got out that I had a pretty decent set-up, I had a whole array of people wanting to record with me. I really enjoyed indulging myself in the art of recording and subjected myself to as many different musical influences as I could.

I did a lot of work with a black guy called Dennis Bovell, who was also a producer in his own right and worked with Linton Kwesi Johnson. He was a great guy and we got on really well. I learned a lot from him about recording different grooves. He was a very creative musician who could play anything. I also recorded Edwin Starr. Then there were Richard and Fred Fairbrass – I worked with them in various early band line-ups before they became famous as Right Said Fred. I recorded some early sessions for A Flock of Seagulls, a band that was quite big for a while in the early eighties. I also worked with the Fabulous Wealthy Tarts, who were Paul Young's female backing vocalists. John Sherry got me to record a three-piece heavy metal band called Mad Dog that he was managing. I think he was looking for the next Saxon or something – it wasn't totally my cup of tea but I did the session as a favour to John. I also did some recording with Gene October of the band Chelsea. I produced a single for him called 'Suffering in the Land' (a cover of the Jimmy Cliff song). I also did sessions with Gene that also featured Stewart Copeland on drums, Jools Holland on piano, Brian James of the Damned on guitar, as well as Ted Turner, who had briefly returned to the UK.

> **TED TURNER:** *This was a one off session – just some ideas Miles wanted to try. The Copelands were riding high, mainly due to the success of the Police. I remember really enjoying this combination of players. It all came together very quickly. Playing with Martin was easy and comfortable.*

East Sheen Avenue is located between the Upper Richmond Road and Richmond Park. Quite often I would finish sessions at four in the morning and wouldn't feel like going to bed. I would look out the window and dawn would just be breaking and so I would go for a walk towards Richmond Park, where even though they shut the main gates at night, you could still get in through the pedestrian entrance – you could even get a bike in through there. Sometimes I would go for an early morning bike ride through the park and I found that really fascinating. It was like being in the countryside and you could get close to all kinds of wildlife – birds, deer, foxes. One morning I had a fox stroll past me, about eight feet away. I had been watching some rabbits at the bottom of a hill in a hollow. The fox was watching them as well but he hadn't seen me because I was standing dead still. I got up to about twenty minutes of standing still, which is a very difficult thing to do. I found that by doing that the critters didn't take any notice of you – they would think you were a tree. I even had birds land on my shoulder. This fox came right past me – I caught him out of the corner of my eye. Sure enough he went straight into the hollow after the rabbits,

Young Jessica "recording with Dada" in my studio at East Sheen Avenue

although he didn't catch any. Another summer's morning I was riding through the park on my bike and I came across a couple of human critters on the grass – they'd obviously just come from a party – and there they were going away at the old original push-ups! So, I just went cruising by on this little path on my bike – "Good Morning!"

By 1984 I had moved from the "broken down house" in East Sheen Avenue to another house in Palewell Park nearby. At the same time I moved my studio equipment into the basement of Miles Copeland's offices in Notting Hill. I did a deal with Miles where I got a great rate on the room in return for giving him first choice on the studio as and when he needed it. Running a studio as a commercial operation was hard work, but I worked with some great people there. These included Chris Difford and Glenn Tilbrook of Squeeze, who were putting some music together for an animated film called *Where The Wind Blows*.

I loved working in Notting Hill. It's a very buzzy neck of the woods with a lot going on. We were one block west of Portobello Road and located right next door to the famous 192 restaurant, which was a popular celebrity hangout at the time. We would often go there after a session and there were always famous faces in there. Even Princess Diana came in there one night.

The early to mid eighties were a fairly turbulent time for me. Aside from the obvious changes in my musical career, I also went through a fairly major upheaval in my personal life, as mentioned earlier. I was actually forewarned of this when Maurn did a course in astrology. She came home one night from her class and said "As part of my course, I've got to draw up someone's chart, so I thought maybe I could do yours." Months later when she'd finished she said "You really ought to have a look at your astrological chart. It would seem that in your mid-life, everything is going to crash around your ears and will be laid to waste." I said "Really? That doesn't sound like me", but that was precisely what happened in the late eighties.

My life was about to change in a big way. And who should come out of the woodwork during this period of reinvention but my old band...

CHAPTER TWELVE

Broken Wings Can Heal
and Mend Again

IT WAS one day early in 1987 that Miles Copeland came down to my studio in the basement of his IRS building and said "Mart, I've got a proposition to put to you." So I said "Let me guess, Miles – Wishbone Ash Mark 2?" He replied "Wrong – Wishbone Ash Mark 1" and continued by saying "I'm starting a new record label and I want you guys to reform the original Wishbone Ash to make an instrumental album". He approached all of us independently with a view to us recording an album of new instrumental material as part of a series of albums for No Speak, a subsidiary of his IRS label. Steve Upton and Andy Powell were receptive to the idea. I too agreed to get involved in principle, but only on two conditions, those being a) that it was the full original band, and b) that I be allowed to produce the album.

I had not really been in regular contact with any of the band, although I had seen them all at various times during the eighties. Steve and I had maintained a friendship and our families were quite close. I'd also worked with Ted on a couple of studio projects when he returned to the UK briefly in the early eighties. Of all of us Ted was probably the most difficult to convince. He was living in Los Angeles and in the process of moving to Chicago and so Andy agreed to fly out there to discuss the offer with him. Like myself, Ted was busy getting on with his life and probably hadn't expected Wishbone Ash to come back to him at that time, but Andy helped convince him that it was a worthwhile project.

> **TED TURNER:** *I received a call from Andy. He came to visit. We discussed the idea and agreed to meet up in London. Enough time had passed to return to work with the original guys. It felt like a good time and I looked forward to recording with them again.*

For me personally, I felt there had been enough water under the bridge since my split with the band in 1980 and I was more than happy to contemplate working with my former band-mates again. We were all a little older and wiser and I think we all recognised the unique chemistry that existed between the four of us. The fact that the album was to be an instrumental album, while restricting in some ways, was also part of the appeal for us all in that it was a fresh challenge and we had an opportunity to do something new and exciting within the framework of Wishbone Ash. "Forget about having to come up with a single," said Miles, "don't worry about your image, and don't be concerned with lyrics. Just play your instruments, unencumbered by restraints." We were more than happy to be working with Miles again, although our relationship was now different in that in the seventies he had been our manager, whereas in the late eighties he was running a record label. Although we'd had a bit of a bad break-up with him over financial matters back in 1975, we still considered him a personal friend as we'd started out together in the music business all those years earlier. We all agreed to take part in the project and booked time at my studio beginning in May 1987.

It was a little strange coming back together again, but we were all grown men and felt able to discuss things and air any grievances. Musically we had all absorbed new individual experiences and had a lot of fresh input and ideas to contribute. We started work on the album on 11 May 1987. Initially it was just Steve, Andy and myself working on the music, as Ted had been taken seriously ill with shellfish poisoning and ended up in hospital, just prior to when he was due to fly to London. This didn't really give us the opportunity to work with Ted in a true creative sense. All we could do was begin to compile the music and then put Ted on top of it when he eventually joined us.

> **TED TURNER:** *My role was to support the band and embellish the music already recorded in any way I could. It was like returning home after a long journey and, like my own family, after a couple of days catching up you remember the things that irritate you and the things you adore. Basically people are who they are. Being in a band is a marriage. Playing together was a bit tentative, learning about each other again, checking each other out. A few pints were swallowed, laughter prevailed. There were a few more wrinkles.*

Most of the material on the album was written by Andy and myself. Each track was slightly different in the way it was conceived and constructed. Some pieces came predominately from one writer, whereas others were a true collaboration. Both Andy and I came to the project with a stockpile of material. Andy had a lot of instrumental pieces that had not yet found a home – tunes like 'Real Guitars Have Wings', 'The Spirit Flies Free' and 'A Rose is a Rose'. In fact the latter had actually first been knocked around in rehearsals during the tail end of the Wishbone Ash Mk.2 period. My input was slightly different in that most of the tunes I brought to the table were essentially finished songs, including lyrics, which we re-worked into the instrumental format. Because the melodic content of my material was pretty strong, the songs worked equally well as instrumentals. Examples of this would be 'Something's Happening in Room 602' and 'Flags of Convenience', which started life as songs entitled 'Kelly's Away With The Fairies' and 'The Golden One' respectively - the former eventually appeared in its original form on my solo album *Walking The Reeperbahn*, while the latter is a song that was never released. In fact, I would like to revisit it one day and record it in the way it was originally conceived, with lyrics.

'In The Skin' was a good example of mutually complimentary creativity coming from two different people. I'd written a song called 'In The Skin' a few years earlier. Ironically it had been the first song I'd written after parting company with Wishbone Ash in 1980 and had actually been written about finding myself with no band – I even managed to turn that little crock of shit into a song! The version that appeared on *Nouveau Calls* retained the main riff and melody from my song, but added some guitar parts that Andy had for the chorus section, making for a true two-way collaboration. Ted put the icing on the cake with his lap steel guitar playing, which he would turn into quite a showpiece when we played the song on stage. Incidentally, during the recording of the album all of the tunes had working titles, but these were eventually re-titled by Miles. I did, however, insist on keeping 'In The Skin' as the title for this piece. This is something I came to regret a few years later when I included my original recording of the song, with lyrics, on my solo album. As we had already used 'In The Skin' as a title for the Wishbone track, it would have been confusing to have two tracks with the same title, and so we decided to change the title of my solo version to 'The Naked Truth', taken from the opening lyric of the original song. Other tracks such as 'Tangible Evidence', 'Clousseau', 'Johnny Left Home Without It' and 'From Soho To Sunset' were also very much a team effort between Andy and myself.

'Arabesque' came about quite differently. Miles told me one night about a girl he was living with. He was going to put her in a movie in which there was going to be a belly dancing sequence. He asked me to come up with a piece of music that was Middle Eastern in feel. Of course, I didn't know the first thing about bloody belly dancing, but I offered to give it a try and came up with 'Arabesque'. It's probably not ideal for doing the dance to, but as a piece of slightly Eastern-sounding music, I thought it worked reasonably well. That was mainly put together by Steve and myself. I had the music and ideas and the only person available to work on it was Steve. Then I got Andy to come in and play some guitar parts, although a lot of what you hear that sounds like guitar on that track is actually me playing guitar samples on a keyboard.

Recording an instrumental album with just the basic guitar, bass and drums format for each track could have resulted in an album with little variety between each track. For this reason we were keen to incorporate a lot of different sounds into the music – be it acoustic guitars, lap steel guitar from Ted or mandolin from Andy. My additional contribution was keyboards. I had dabbled with synthesizers throughout the eighties and I liked the additional textures they added. I've got an unorthodox bass playing style, but my keyboard style is even stranger – I break all the rules. When we later came to tour the material on the album, we toyed with the idea of having a keyboard player on stage with us to reproduce the sound accurately. I did actually get together with a keyboard player with a view to him playing with the band. This guy came very highly recommended but he couldn't get close to what I'd played on the record, simply because the parts I played were so unorthodox.

With hindsight the synthesizer sounds do "date" the album somewhat, but it was a new technological world back then and we were all experimenting with it. On a couple of tracks – 'Flags of Convenience' and 'Arabesque' – I also managed to sneak in some subtle, wordless backing vocals. It was just another texture and it worked great. At least nobody has yet asked why there are "vocals" on what was supposed to be an instrumental album. All these additional contributions gave the band a new and fresh sound, rather than us just trying to recreate what we did in the seventies. It was a very exciting time and we all thoroughly enjoyed the process.

There was, however, one setback. My brother Kim, who had worked with The Police and Sting as tour manager and sound engineer, was going to co-produce the album with me. He came down to some of the early album sessions at my studio and put quite a bit of input into how the material should sound. It was great working with him, until Andy Summers decided he was going out on the road and insisted that Kim go with him, leaving us without a co-producer. Everybody felt that there should be someone else involved to work alongside me and Miles suggested William Orbit. I agreed to that on a co-production basis.

Although we had already recorded versions of most of the material at my studio, William was keen to re-record it at Beethoven studios and his own Guerrilla studio. We agreed to this, but we were utterly astonished when William told us it would take too long to record with Steve Upton playing the drums and that he wanted to record the material with a drum machine. Our natural response was "No way, that's not going to work for us", but William assured us that he would listen to the tracks we'd recorded at my studio, program the drum parts so it sounded just like Steve and all we had to do was run the drum machine and play the other instruments. To him, this made the recording process a lot more straight forward and was the way in which he was used to recording, his background being in electronic based dance music. Personally I felt the end result lacked the organic interplay between the musicians which is the essence of a band such as Wishbone Ash. William's manager also pulled a stunt on me where he later insisted that William receive the sole production credit on the album, to which I replied "Absolutely no way". Before William had come on board I had done a lot of production work to steer this album in the right direction and I threatened to take the tapes and mix them at my studio. In the end we negotiated an arrangement whereby William got the main production credit for most of the album, while I got a co-producers credit and the main credit on the four songs for which we used the original recordings from my studio. I wanted to get those tracks onto the album so at least there was something on there with Steve playing live drums. In many ways I actually preferred the recordings made at my studio to a lot of the tracks which made the final album. They were not as squeaky clean, but they had a lot more feel and were more "organic".

Despite a few differences of opinion, I really enjoyed working with William. He is a good man and I really don't want to slag him off, but he came from a completely different background and his way of working was too technological, particularly using programmed drums. He did a fantastic job with the programming and it sounded exactly the same as Steve playing, but it was still a machine. Looking back on it we should have said "William, instead of us learning from you about how records should be made, why don't you learn from us what we know about making records." In particular we were more experienced at the process of recording guitars. Looking back, I should have been more insistent but as always there are time constraints. I don't want to say William did a bad job on the album, because he didn't. Some of the drum and percussion parts he did sounded really good – the rhythms and the grooves – but the guitars suffered a bit and could have been a lot better recorded. If anything it was a mismatch of styles, but I do have the greatest respect for William as a producer – you only have to look at the stuff he has done since to see what he is capable of.

Nouveau Calls was released on the IRS No Speak label in December 1987. We were delighted with some of the feedback the album received both from fans as well as the music press. Our label boss was also pleased with the album. "When I commissioned this album I knew it would be great," said Miles. "I am proud to have this album on my label and be associated again with the first group I ever managed." The general feeling was that many people thought it was really good to see the original Wishbone Ash back together in a completely different way. Although we were initially only getting back together for this one project, the experience of recording the instrumental album had been very positive. We all agreed we wanted to work together beyond the recording project and it seemed only natural to take the music on the road and so on 27 February 1988, the original line-up of Wishbone Ash took the stage for the first time in fourteen years at the Leas Cliff Hall, Folkestone – the start of a major UK tour to promote the *Nouveau Calls* album.

Back onstage with Wishbone Ash, 1988

It took little effort for the four of us to adapt to performing together again. The chemistry in the original band was so strong that it really was like putting on a well worn glove. Steve and I had always locked together well as a rhythm section and the twin guitars of Ted and Andy slotted together as though they'd never been apart. The inclusion of some of the tracks from *Nouveau Calls,* which used keyboard backing tracks to allow us to reproduce the album sound faithfully, gave the show a slightly different feel to our performances of the seventies, but overall the blend of old songs such as 'The King Will Come', 'Throw Down The Sword', 'Blowin' Free', 'Jailbait' and 'Phoenix', together with the new instrumental tracks, went down really well with our fans who seemed delighted to see the four of us back together on stage. There was an overall positive feeling surrounding the shows and we were pleased to have our old friend Peter Haycock, formerly of the Climax Blues Band, along as the support act for many of the shows, promoting *Guitar and Son* – his own album for the IRS No Speak label.

The tour did not totally go totally without difficulties. Due to immigration problems Ted had been late arriving for rehearsals and had only had a chance to rehearse the older music that he knew inside out, so for the first few shows of the tour we had another guitar player – Jamie Crompton, who Steve and Andy had worked with – playing with us for the first few songs, after which Ted would appear, to rapturous applause, midway through the show.

TED TURNER: *I have always been surprised by the impact music has on people – the depths that can be reached. Combine this with the passage of time, nostalgia and sentimental feelings. This is a powerful concoction supported by the popularity of older bands reforming and performing to the delight of their fans. Wishbone always had a loyal following. Even now the band is much loved and held in high regard. This tour made me aware of how the band had changed as players – still kicking, but now with added maturity. Anyone who witnessed these shows I am sure would agree the band was in great form.*

Backstage at hometown concert with our old friend Mark "Hobbit" Emery – Torquay 1988

By the time we were midway through the UK tour, Ted was playing the full show with band and I felt we were in really good shape. The UK tour had many highlights – in particular a triumphant London show at the Hammersmith Odeon which was broadcast by the BBC as well as filmed for a promo video to support the single release of 'In The Skin'. The show at the Riviera Centre in Torquay was also an important one for me as lots of friends and family who had not had a chance to see me performing with the band in many years came along. The show was promoted by our old friend Mark "Hobbit" Emery and my brother Glenn was also there, playing with his band Mercedes, who supported us that night. I'd done quite a bit of studio work with them, trying to help them get off the ground. Following the UK shows we undertook a month-long European tour throughout April/May 1988, including a couple of arena shows in Germany as special guests of Rush.

There had been a very warm feeling surrounding the *Nouveau Calls* album and tour and as a band we were quite eager to take the rapport that we had re-established and move on from there as quickly as possible. Ted and I in particular had a lot of songs that we wanted to record and almost directly after the tour we went back in the studio to record *Here To Hear*.

Here To Hear was recorded at various London studios – Beethoven, Terminal and Beat Factory – during the Summer/Autumn of 1988. I produced the album, with co-producer/engineer Adam Fuest, and this time we insisted that Steve be allowed to play live drums. I thought there were some really good things on *Here to Hear*. The band was working very efficiently at the time – it was a nice recording and everyone contributed positively. My personal life around this time, however, was in complete turmoil.

Throughout the eighties I had struggled with balancing marriage and music. The years in the US had taken their toll on my relationship with Maurn, yet I was devoted to Jessica and her baby sister, Grace, born on 16th July 1986. However, I simply found it impossible to continue to deny my feelings for Susie. Eventually we got together again around the time that the original Wishbone Ash reformed, and this inevitably led to Maurn and I splitting up. I was an emotional mess as I tried desperately hard to cling on to everything I had built together with Maurn, yet at the same time I knew I was going to have to confront the reality of divorce. I ended up going to see a Jung analyst for a period of about two years and he helped me and advised me. As a young man I had been pretty rough on women emotionally and I needed to change my ways. Eventually I managed to get to grips with it, but it took a long time to sort myself out and reinvent myself. I'd led Maurn on a pretty bumpy but exciting ride through the seventies, which she'd taken in her stride and our relationship was very loving and easy, until we hit my mid life crisis! Even through the tempest that our lives became, I continued to think the world of her, and still do to this day.

Susie and I eventually settled down to a new life in Southfields, south west London. We had a baby boy, Tom, born on 2 August 1988 and I also became adoptive father to Andrew, Susie's son by Andy Summers, raising him as though he was my own. Andrew finally met his father when he was sixteen years old, but he calls me "Dad" to this day.

Now, there is a particularly sensitive Irishman by the name of George O'Gorman who runs an acting school in Kentish Town to whom I have turned for help and advice during difficult times in my life, and whilst I was in the midst of my divorce and feeling very low, he managed to open my eyes to something I had virtually no access to. During my marriage to Maurn I'd discerned that she was not over enthusiastic in relation to babies. That is not to say she wasn't a good mother because she certainly was, but since she was petite, carrying those babies was hard for her. During the early days of infancy, I think it's fair to say that she struggled with it all and declared after our second daughter Grace was born, that our family was complete. George pointed out that deep inside me was this huge desire to have a son. Now, I did not feel that emotion particularly, but as he was talking to me I felt a resonance way down in my soul and it opened my eyes to what this stage in my life was all about. The idea that I had dismissed my first wife and chosen another who I knew would bear me a son seemed so hard and calculating. Of course, this was not about a thought process, this was about a deep primeval urge that I was not even aware of until George took me there. I was so grateful for his insight and support through this period, during which I was lost and bewildered. I was able to slowly forge a healing process and it took many years of understanding and commitment to engender a renewal in our extended tribe. Now I can honestly say we are a large and happy, if slightly wacky, family.

I composed most of my songs on the *Here To Hear* album around the time that my marriage was crumbling, and for me the writing and recording of those tracks was a very emotional and cathartic experience. 'Cosmic Jazz' was one of those songs and I refer to it as a "musical exorcism". In the lyric I'm requesting a mischievous Hindu spirit called Kali to leave me alone. The Jung analyst I mentioned earlier ended up performing a magic ceremony at my request, because I had dreamed that this was needed to save me from running headlong into my own destruction.

I'd already made a pretty decent recording of 'Cosmic Jazz', playing everything myself, which I used to present the song to the band. The melodic content already existed and the guitar parts were already there. When it came to recording it with the band, everyone played the parts almost exactly as they were on my demo. Obviously there were a few little embellishments, but in the main it was pretty accurate – in the case of the drums, possibly a little too accurate. I had cut the demo to a drum machine and Steve played it in that vein, giving the song quite a mechanical feel, whereas I'd have preferred it if he'd got a bit looser. But overall I was pleased with the way that track came out – my brother Kim co-produced that track with me. We released 'Cosmic Jazz' as a single (backed with a non-album instrumental, 'T-Bone Shuffle', that had been recorded during the *Nouveau Calls* sessions, and on the 12" another new song 'Bolan's Monument' that did not appear on the new album). I always thought 'Cosmic Jazz' had a good chance as a single. It was commercial enough, yet didn't compromise what Wishbone Ash was all about in any way. The song was loaded with psychic energy and it would have been ideal for a music video, but Wishbone Ash never really got in a position to do that.

'Keeper of the Light', a collaboration between Ted and Steve, contained a really nice lyric from Steve and I always thought it was a really sweet idea to honour the woman's role in things.

'Mental Radio' was one of Ted's songs, featuring his lap steel playing. We needed some high parts on the vocal harmonies and we got a girl singer called Angie Giles to put a backing vocal on it.

'Walk On Water' was a song that I had previously recorded with the Wolf Gang. Originally it had a lot more keyboards on it, but when we came to record it with Wishbone, Andy supplied some guitar work that changed the feel a little bit, but it was still very close to the original. Ted wanted it to stay that way because he felt the song was good as it stood.

My brother Kim Turner during Here To Hear sessions
– we always enjoyed a close relationship

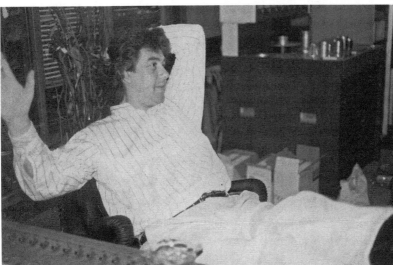

Photo by Susie Turner

'Witness to Wonder' was written by Ted with a little help in the lyrics department from Chris Difford of Squeeze. Sometimes Ted's lyrics can be a little idealistic, mystical and hard to understand, as was the case here – it was quite hard to get hold of what he was trying to say. Miles Copeland suggested Ted get together with Chris to make it a little more coherent and cohesive.

I wrote a lot of my songs on *Here To Hear* in a tiny little room near where my oldest daughter Jessica was sleeping. 'Lost Cause in Paradise' was one of those songs and is about my world crashing down. My marriage was on the rocks and I was bracing myself for what was about to happen. In particular it deals with my concern for my two little daughters, who I was very loath to leave. I used to keep Jessica awake at night, because I'd be in there trying to be as quiet as I could, but you can't help making a noise when you're tapping your foot on the floor or singing. So she got to know those songs quite well. I put in quite a lot of pre-production work into 'Lost Cause in Paradise' and presented it to the band as a fairly complete demo. I had programmed two keyboard parts, which run all the way through the song, and had mapped out the guitar parts thoroughly. As always, once we started recording the song with the band, other members put their own stamp on the music. In this case, Ted double tracked the guitar parts on left and right stereo and played a fantastic bluesy guitar solo at the end. For me the song contains a lot of personal emotion and I was very grateful to Ted that he was able to pick this up and help interpret the song so beautifully. Andy was not involved in the recording of this song.

'Why Don't We' was one of Ted's finest songs ever, I would say. We all loved the song and it had a great feel and a really positive energy. It was a song that had been with Ted for some time, but I felt we all managed to put our own stamp on it. For example, I managed to get a bass solo in the middle, after which there is also a really strong guitar solo from Andy. Ted's guitar and vocals really shine on this track, which is him at his very best.

'In The Case' was an instrumental that Ted contributed and is probably Wishbone about as funky as we ever got. It's not our natural forte, but I think we did a decent job on it. Some of the guitar parts from both Ted and Andy are pretty cool.

'Hole In My Heart' was another one of our epic two-part long pieces, with a moody vocal part at the start, featuring me singing my soul out about what was going on in my life at the time, before giving way to an extended instrumental section. The song grew out of a bass riff that I had. We had a bit of trouble getting to grips with the timing at first, because it was quite loose. I would come in almost anywhere with the bass riff, sometimes in the wrong place of a bar, and this gave it a really spontaneous feel. The fast section was a little more constructed and features some particularly dynamic guitar parts from Ted. It didn't quite turn out to be another 'Phoenix' or 'Lifeline', but I thought it was a still worthwhile attempt to do another song in that format.

Here To Hear promo shot 1989 – a highly productive era in the band's career

The whole period surrounding *Here To Hear* was very creative and we actually ended up with more than enough material for the album. Quite often it's easy to hear why certain tracks didn't make the running order on a particular album but in the case of *Here To Hear*, I'm actually quite fond of the pieces that were left over – tracks that eventually surfaced either as single b-sides or bonus tracks on the CD reissue of the album. These were 'Heaven Is' – basically a studio jam session between Steve, Andy and myself; 'Duffle Shuffle', a very upbeat instrumental piece that Ted and I in particular put a lot of time and energy into; and 'Bolan's Monument' – a song which evolved in quite an unusual way and was another example of how two people's creative ideas could be fused together. I had written the lyric to 'Bolan's Monument', purely as a piece of prose. Meanwhile, we had an unfinished backing track we had recorded, based around a rhythm figure that Andy had put down. I went home from the recording sessions one night and decided to put this lyric on top of the track and try to complete the song. The lyric dealt with my impending divorce and the way I was feeling somewhat suicidal over the whole thing. When you cannot sleep at night through knowing that your whole life is about to come crashing down, you can easily slip into that state, which often seems to be the easy way out. I was not in a good frame of mind with the anguish of my family breakdown.

Marc Bolan was an amazing guy and had quite an impression on the UK music scene. He was also quite an innovator and was one of the few rock musicians to have his own television show. Everything had been looking so great for him at the time he died in a car smash in Barnes, on 16 September 1977. That night I had driven past the scene of the crash at about four in the morning and could see there had been an accident, as there was a lot of debris in the road. I never gave a thought as to who was involved until I heard the next day that it was Marc Bolan. It was tragic. David Bowie had just done an appearance on Marc's television show and had flown back to his home in Switzerland. Then he got a phone call and had to return to the UK for the funeral. He was totally cut up about it and didn't want to come back to London and stay in a hotel, where he would have been harassed by the press, so he came to stay at our house in Barnes. I wasn't actually there because by that time we were out in Europe on the *Front Page News* tour, but I do remember that David got totally engrossed in a couple of my old books – Rappin's history of England, detailing all the Kings of England going back to the six or seventh century. A little later, around the time that Wishbone Ash had returned to the UK after living in the States, I actually made an appointment to view a house – the address being 142 Upper Richmond Road. Right at the last minute I discovered it was Marc Bolan's house and I cancelled the appointment immediately. I just didn't want to go there. Coincidentally Keith Harwood, the engineer on the *Wishbone Four* album, also died in a car accident, a couple of weeks before Marc Bolan. At the time back in 1977, Keith, Marc and myself all had houses in this little triangle. Now, back then I was a bit of a lunatic driver and everyone told me that I would be next. I must have had a guardian angel watching over me because I managed to survive that period.

Anyway, going back to the events surrounding the writing of 'Bolan's Monument', one night around the time that my marriage was breaking down, I just couldn't sleep and I got up about four o'clock in the morning, very unhappy and beside myself with angst. I went for a drive towards Putney and parked up and took a walk down by the river, where I was visited by my old friend the heron, who always seems to appear every time my life is at a crossroads. On this occasion the Heron rose up very gracefully from a pool – the "stagnant pool" as it says in the song. On the way back to Sheen I stopped off at the tree where Marc Bolan had died. I'd driven past there regularly and had always wanted to take a look, but never got around to it, so I decided to spend a quiet moment at the tree. There were always messages on there as well as cards, gifts and flowers, and on this occasion someone had written the words "Marc – Why did you leave us?"

That sign hit me like a thunderbolt. The problem with creative people is that when they do get on a bummer and their lives are troubled, because they have such active imaginations it's easy for them to go on a journey which I refer to as the "spiral of doom". I've seen it with lots of other people involved in music and it's so easy to slip into a state of complete despair where you feel you've had enough. I was definitely at that stage, but when I saw that sign on Marc Bolan's tree it reminded me that I had two little daughters at that point. I considered the fact that if I did go up to the big gig in the sky, then my two daughters would be left without a father and would probably be saying that to me – "Why did you leave us?" Seeing that sign certainly knocked me in the right direction and the song 'Bolan's Monument' is an attempt to grapple with my intense and erratic emotions and then move on, and so I finished the song, putting down the half-spoken vocal and completing the music. I think Andy was in two minds about the whole thing. It's possible that he wanted to develop his idea a bit more and pursue another direction with the piece – which he later did on the song 'Another Time' from his *Illuminations* album.

In between Wishbone Ash commitments, Ted and Andy also took part in the *Night of the Guitar* concert tour. This was a Miles Copeland concept designed to further promote his No Speak series of albums and consisted of a string of shows across the UK and Europe featuring a line-up of nine guitarists – Peter Haycock (Climax Blues Band), Steve Hunter (Lou Reed/ Alice Cooper), Randy California (Spirit), Robby Krieger (Doors), Leslie West (Mountain), Steve Howe (Yes/Asia), Alvin Lee (Ten Years After) as well as Andy and Ted. Each guitarist would play a short set of both new and classic material, and then at the end everyone would appear on stage together. I was asked by Miles to produce the live album and video soundtrack of the tour. We recorded a couple of shows – one at Manchester Apollo and another at Hammersmith Odeon. We ended up using the Hammersmith show, which sounded great, mainly because of the acoustics in the hall.

With that number of guitarists sharing the stage, one could have expected an enormous clash of egos, but everyone got on really well. Randy California emerged as the leader of the pack, in a hippy-ish kind of way. He was very good at interacting with everyone and helped co-ordinate the whole thing. He had a great vibe about him and I thought his renditions of the Jimi Hendrix songs were really outstanding. It's very difficult to take songs from someone with as much individual style and charisma as Hendrix and make them belong to you, but Randy did this fantastically well. His playing was superb and I was very sad to hear that he died a few years ago, drowning while rescuing his son from a rip current.

Leslie West was a massive character. His guitar sound was so unbelievably loud on the stage, even when he was playing on his own. Alvin Lee was absolutely fantastic. When I went to mix the recordings, I had to do quite a bit of work on every guitarist's recorded sound with the exception of Alvin's. He played a Gibson 335 through an old Marshall 50 watt amp. The moment I pushed the fader up I thought "Wow, what a fantastic sound!" I did have a little twiddle with it to see if it could be improved but in the end I thought "No, this instrument does not need a thing, let me leave it exactly as it is because it sounds beautiful."

At this time I didn't really have a studio situation available, as I had just moved out of Miles' basement due to him relocating his offices to Bugle House in Noel Street, W1, so we needed to find a studio to work in. My brother Kim was working with Sting at that point and they had booked a couple of weeks at Air studios in London to mix some live recordings. At the last minute, Sting cancelled the sessions due to other commitments. They were faced with paying for studio time they were not going to use and so Kim offered me the opportunity to mix at Air on a very good deal. I used the first week or so to mix *Here to Hear*, before starting work on *Night of the Guitars* immediately after. I had about four days to mix over two hours of concert material and the process was fraught with difficulties. After spending two days programming the computer for the automated mixing, I noticed that the computer time-code was not reading correctly. It was slipping against what I had programmed for the automation. I knew I was going to get in a right pickle there, so we got in a totally independent clock to check the time-code, both on the computer and what was coming off the tape. We couldn't get to the bottom of what was causing the malfunction and by this time we only had two days left to mix the recordings. The recording studio were adamant that it was not their computer that was misbehaving and that it was a fault with our time-code – possibly some weird drop frame rate from the film crew who had made the video recordings – and so Air London were not prepared to give us any extra time. I sat with my head in my hands thinking "What the hell do I do with this?" The options were limited. All I could basically do was mix it manually which, given the number of songs involved, left me with about an hour in which to mix each song. That is very tight indeed. You have movements on vocals, overheads, tom-toms to push up and down, vocals that needed fixing – all kind of things that needed attention. Basically all you can do in that time is a "rough" mix – put the faders up and get a balance. That is exactly what I did. There was no favouritism towards the Wishbone Ash material and I gave each artist equal attention. I got the concert mixed in two days and that is the mix which went out on the video. After the video had gone out, Miles came back to me and said "Mart, listen, about these mixes..." So I said "Are you not happy with the sound?" He said "Yeah, it sounds great, but the bass drum sounds a bit ambient – the sound of the room is there." Now, one of the tricks in the trade when asked to mix something that quickly, is to push up the audience faders, which gives the sound as it was in the room. That quickly provides the atmosphere of the gig. It enhances the guitars and vocals, but does tend to have a detrimental effect on the bass drum. I don't know if Clive Mayuyu, the drummer, had maybe had a word in Miles' ear about the bass drum sound, but Miles asked me if I could do the mix again, this time with the bass drum sound dry. So I said "Yes, Miles, I can, but I can't do it in one hour per song." Eventually I did do it again at my place which was now back up and running, because we could not repeat the Air London deal and this was the mix that went out on the live album. Personally I prefer the first mix that went out on the video.

One other memory I have from the mixing of *Night Of The Guitars* was Robby Krieger asking if I could send out a tape of his performance so that he could look at his vocals – usually that means re-recording them. Now, sending original 2 inch 24-track masters across the Atlantic is always a bit dangerous so I asked Air studios if they could do a 24-track copy, which they did. We sent Robby his songs and about a week later he phoned to find out where they were as they should have arrived the next day. A little later a secretary at IRS in London phoned me and said "Did you have anything on Pan Am Flight 103, last Wednesday?" I said "Yes, the tapes for Robby Krieger." The secretary said "That was the plane that was blown up over Lockerbie." The thought that I had been holding those tapes a few days before they hit the floor doing 500mph really sent a shiver up my spine. I told the girl on the phone "Whatever you do, don't go and tell Robby Krieger what happened to his tapes – it would probably do his head in." This mix down session eventually became known as the "Nightmare of the Guitars" owing to the technical difficulties, request for remixing and the Lockerbie outrage.

During the Summer of 1989 Wishbone Ash played a short tour of the USA to promote *Here to Hear,* which was released to coincide. It was brilliant going back to the States after all that time – I'd not played there since 1977. Although we were only playing small theatres and clubs, the band was playing really well and we had revamped our live show to include material from the new album. Ahead of the US shows we played a couple of dates in Brazil – shows in Rio de Janeiro and Sao Paulo alongside Leslie West and Spirit. Brazil was quite some experience, with the air pollution in Sao Paulo being really bad. There was also quite a lot of partying going on into

Here To Hear tour, 1989

the early hours of the morning. I took a sleeping pill before getting on the plane to go to L.A., which is surprisingly quite a long flight. When I woke up I said to Steve "How long until we get to L.A.?" He said "Forty five minutes". So I said "That can't be right. We have to land in Peru first for refuelling." Steve replied "We've already done that – you slept right through." Aah-ha – pharma drugs again!

I remember the whole period surrounding *Here To Hear* as being a very happy time for the band. We were all very much enjoying working together

Ted Turner in Philadelphia on his birthday, 1989

again – making new music and playing to very appreciative audiences at our concerts. We undertook a nationwide UK tour during September 1989 which included some very memorable shows, including a filmed concert for Central Television at Bristol Colston Hall and another fantastic concert at the Hammersmith Odeon. I felt the band was playing as well as it ever had. We also had our IRS label mates Spirit opening at several of the shows. This was an extremely busy time – we played six weeks of European dates throughout October/November 1989 and touring continued well into 1990 with another short UK tour. This included our first Marquee Club show since 1977, although the new venue in Charing Cross Road somewhat failed to recapture the atmosphere of the original Wardour Street club. We played the *East Meets West* concert in Berlin in March 1990, not long after the barriers at the Berlin wall had been opened. Although much of the wall itself was still standing, the atmosphere there was fantastic, with a great feeling of anticipation amongst the people there. It was a real pleasure and honour to have been invited there to help mark such a momentous event. We also had our concert at London's Town and Country Club filmed by Thames television. The original Wishbone Ash was truly firing on all cylinders and I was very optimistic about the band's future. It really did seem as though we were back for the long haul. Little did we know, however, that our appearance at the Heineken Big Top festival in Swansea on 7 July 1990 would be the very last time all four original members of Wishbone Ash would appear on stage together.

Martin and Susie - party time!

CHAPTER THIRTEEN

This Strange Affair

WE DECIDED to record our next album *Strange Affair* at Andy Powell's house in Great Brickhill, near Milton Keynes. This stemmed from an idea I'd originally had in the mid-seventies, when we were preparing to record *New England* in the wake of the disastrous *Locked In* experience. Back then I'd proposed that the band use its record company advance to buy some recording equipment and record at the basement at my place, Laureledge in Connecticut. I'd put it to the band at that time but everyone was too afraid to splash out on a recording machine and desk. For me, I thought it was a way of beating the system in that you could record an album for the same amount of money as you would spend on professional studio time, yet at the end of the recording, you still had the equipment to record the next album, and the next one after that, meaning that more of the advance for each album would end up in the band's pockets. Finally, some fourteen years later, I got my way – albeit using equipment that I had invested in.

By this time I had a pretty decent studio installed at my home in south west London. It was of a highly professional standard and I was adding new equipment all the time. Andy, meanwhile, was by now spending most of his time at his home in the States, but he still had a house in Buckinghamshire that he would rent out as and when he wasn't using it. At this particular time he was having difficulty getting anyone to rent it and so – perhaps remembering my idea from all those years previous – suggested that the band rent his house and I bring in my recording studio. We were basically pooling our resources and I felt it would be an interesting project from a creative standpoint. So I took my studio up there, which was a fairly heavy undertaking, moving lots of heavy equipment around, and got it up and running in a day. We had a series of bedrooms at the house which we would use to record in and then there was a barn about thirty or forty feet away, which we wanted to use for recording drums. It was a stone barn with a corrugated tin roof. We set Steve's drums up in there and the sound was incredible, but Andy started to get a bit twitchy because a few hundred yards away lived the local Lord of the Manor type, who Andy thought may complain about the sound, some of which would obviously escape. Andy was insistent that we sectioned an area off and soundproofed it. Our former publicist Rod Lynton was working in the barn and he helped us put together a soundproof room. This was fine until we started recording the drums and discovered that the incredible sound we had going before had gone. We paid an acoustics expert to come in and analyse the room and tell us what tweaks we had to make to get the room sounding good. We had to build a bunch of boxes to soak out the mid-range in the room and once we'd done that it started to sound good, although nowhere near as it was originally.

So there we were at Ivy Lane Farm – Steve stuck in the barn on his own with his drums, me in the control room playing bass, and Ted and Andy in the bedroom playing guitars through amps. We had not been going at it long before we discovered that Steve was not functioning well at all. He was not playing like the Steve Upton we all knew and loved. We all tried hard to get it happening for him but after a while Ted and Andy gave up and it was left to me to help get him playing in the way we were used to. Whether it was down to the monitoring, or the sound of the drums, I had to work with him to get him happy so that he could play properly. What soon emerged was that Steve was actually in the midst of a marriage breakdown, just as I had been during the *Here to Hear* sessions. He was obviously upset and was finding it difficult to play. I managed to talk him up and coax him along and after a few days of working with him I thought he was sounding okay. I went to chat to Ted and Andy about it, quite excited by the fact that Steve appeared to be getting it together, but they were adamant that it still wasn't going to be good enough. They would say, "Mart, because you've been in there with him for days on end, you've lost sight of the fact that when you first started it was truly awful. Although it's better than it was, it's still not of the standard we need for a professional album". I argued the toss with them to a point, but clearly their objectivity was better than mine, because I'd been working so closely with Steve trying to get him in the zone. Steve was obviously conscious of the fact that he wasn't functioning correctly and that he needed to sort his life out – he'd practically been kicked out of his home and had lost his family. We talked about this as a band – all four of us – and eventually Steve just said "I think I should go and let you guys make other arrangements". I thought at first he was just being a bit dramatic and so I couldn't believe it when he got up from the table, went to his room and packed his bags – ten minutes later he was gone. Even then I thought he was going to spend some time with his family to try to sort things out and that he would be back in a few days, but Steve was never to return.

I felt the whole situation concerning Steve's departure was handled very badly. Steve had been with me since 1966 and was the backbone of Wishbone Ash. The band was not going to function as well without him, particularly on the business side of things where he was the key man. As mates we really should have stood by him more at that difficult time in his personal life, but we were pre-occupied with trying to get the job done. As far as I was concerned the door should have been left open for Steve to return once he had sorted his life out. I did feel that Andy, in particular, tended to come at things with a very hard-nosed, somewhat American view point – the "shit or get off the pot" kind of psychology, which is not very soulful. Once Steve was no longer involved, it was never going to be the same again for me. When Steve walked, part of the spirit went with him. He was an important part in the relationship between the four of us and without him it was never going to work in the long term. Even though Andy was happy to assume business duties, Steve was the only guy who was capable of running the business side of Wishbone Ash in a fair way. Fortunately, Miles Copeland offered him sanctuary working down in France and Steve went on to enjoy a new lease of life managing Miles' chateau in the Dordogne.

> **TED TURNER:** *Steve's decision to leave the band initially was a surprise that left us in shock. He was going through some tough personal issues and I sensed much stress with him. It must have been difficult to focus on music, drums being the most physically demanding task in the band. His influence in the day to day running of the band was a big loss. Since day one Steve (the Colonel) had always maintained the books. He took pride in this work especially in the early days, presenting our accountant with the annual reports in his own exquisitely written work, done by hand with a calligraphy pen. He was missed by all. His laughter would fill a room. Sometimes you don't realize what you have until it's gone.*

With Steve out of the album sessions, we continued recording the music using a drum machine. This was not ideal for a rock band, but we managed to build the tracks up. Once we knew that Steve was not going to be returning and we were going to have to bring in another drummer, I told Ted and Andy that I knew the perfect man for the job – Ray Weston, who had played in my band a few years earlier. I tried to track him down but he was working in Germany at the time and wasn't immediately available and so instead we got involved with Robbie France, which I think was a Miles Copeland suggestion. When we auditioned Robbie it was obvious that he was mind-bogglingly good, as well as being a very nice chap – friendly, amusing, funny, very likeable and easy to work with. In the studio,

Guildford, 1990.

Robbie was a dream to play with and took us in some exciting directions rhythmically. He was a great player technically, but also had wonderful feel – a balance that is not easy to achieve. However, I could sense that Robbie was not really a mainstream rock drummer, even though he'd played in heavy rock bands like UFO and Diamond Head. Robbie's style was much jazzier – more along the lines of Vinnie Colaiuta – and although he did a great job recording some of the songs on *Strange Affair*, problems soon became apparent when we took time out from the recording sessions to go out on the road for a previously booked UK tour during August/ September 1990. In particular I was not totally happy with Robbie's treatment of the classic Wishbone Ash songs or the way he and I gelled as a rhythm section. Steve Upton had been a straight down the line player and virtually everything he played was with the kick drum playing straight regular downbeats. Robbie would play it any way other than straight. This made things very hard for me as a bass player, as I no longer had anything to anchor to. I had to simplify my playing in order to hold the beat down. We were also finding that the tempos were all over the place and the songs were really racing. Then one night Ted walked into the dressing room and caught Robbie shoving Bolivian marching powder up his nose, which could well explain why he was playing everything so fast. Ted, who had fought his own battle with the fast white stuff and had managed to stay away from it for some time, simply didn't want to be around this kind of activity. I was actually willing to work at knocking Robbie into shape both musically and personally, but Ted was unequivocal and insisted that we start looking for another drummer. It was a shame, but as much as we loved Robbie as a person and appreciated his technical ability, this was just never going to work. Robbie was a very impressive drummer, but didn't really fuse with what we were doing. Perhaps if we had just been playing the new music that we had been working on with Robbie, then things could have worked, but the style of drumming required on Wishbone classics such as 'The King Will Come' and 'Throw Down The Sword', which were still a big part of our live show, was a million miles from the way Robbie played. Robbie was a brilliant drummer, but in my opinion was not a great fit for Wishbone Ash. However, as always, it was certainly a valid experiment and I was extremely sorry to hear, shortly before the publication of this book, that Robbie had passed away.

We considered options and eventually I managed to get Ray Weston involved in completing the recording of the album – he ended up playing on six of the album's ten tracks. Everything Ray played was to replace a drum machine. By this stage everything else had been recorded and Ray had to play his parts as an overdub. With hindsight I would have preferred it for Ray to have actually played together with the band in the studio, but the time was not there. It's not always easy for a drummer to play on top of an existing track but I felt Ray did an excellent job. We kept Robbie's drum tracks for three songs, which we felt his style was suited to, and mixed one track with the original drum machine, partly because we felt it would be an unusual experiment to have that kind of song with a drum machine and partly because we ran out of time.

RAY WESTON: *Martin called me to ask if I was interested playing on some Wishbone Ash tracks. He explained what was going on. I was stoked he'd kept me in mind. The guys were recording at Andy's place in the country. Martin had moved his entire studio there from his home. The drums were recorded in a small barn detached from the rest of the house across a hilly field, so I would have to walk across the field to get back into the control room that was in the main room of the house to listen to playbacks. I wore wellington boots every time and carried an umbrella – seriously! Steve left in the initial recording stages so they decided to use drum loops to play to in order to get the framework of the songs down before tracking drums. Personally I find this process easier to work with rather than having everyone playing together at the same time. Saying that, when it's a jam band like Wishbone Ash, that element of risk and 'moment' can create magic when everyone is playing together. The unexpected can happen with that interaction. I found it relatively easy to get the drums down after familiarising myself with the arrangements and dynamics. The challenge drummers face in this situation is playing with a metronome or 'click track' as it's referred to. Every pro drummer needs to have this down or it won't work out. I learned to keep my metronome with me always after a Mickie Most session in '78. For most part Andy, Ted and Martin were there, although Martin and I were on our own when Andy and Ted went back to the States. Andy was selling his house so pressure was on to get the album finished and get out.*

Overall I thought the album came out sounding really good, although it possibly lacks the consistency and continuity that *Here to Hear* had, with a lot of different styles being attempted to varying degrees of success. In particular there was a bluesier feel on the songs that Andy had written, as he does have a naturally bluesy edge both vocally and guitar-wise. Sometimes I do feel Andy's material benefits from another singer taking lead vocal. Take for example on the *Just Testing* album, where we recorded Andy's song 'Master of Disguise'. That was quite a bluesy track in feel, but once I took over the vocal I was able to put a bit of melodic content into it that prevented it from sounding derivative and took it away from being just another bluesy rock track. Overall there was arguably a little too much boogie-woogie on *Strange Affair* at the expense of the more melodic side of the band.

The title track 'Strange Affair', which Andy Powell co-wrote with Andy Pyle, was one that I put a lot into the production of. We were experimenting with modern technology and adding samples and keyboard sounds, and you can hear a lot of that on that particular track. I persuaded Andy to let me put in the main riff as a sample, which I popped in from one particular sample all the way through. We also got a very compressed sound on the rhythm guitar – Andy was starting to use a guitar with a Piezo pick-up that reacted really well to compression, and we used that effect on a couple of different tunes. As a naked idea, 'Strange Affair' was fairly orthodox blues-boogie, but by employing various production techniques, I felt I managed to bring it into the 21st century by sculpting a more contemporary soundscape. We also experimented with adding a brass section to this track, as well as 'Dream Train' and 'Rollin' – an idea that Andy wanted to try. We all thought it sounded good and I put some mixes together, but when Miles heard about it he said "Wishbone Ash with brass? No, we don't want that!" and so I had to mix those songs again without the brass.

'Wings of Desire', written by Andy with Rod Lynton, had a very melodic flavour and was quite a commercial sounding song. I loved the title, taken from a Wim Wender film. I mixed a couple of versions of it, one with Andy singing and another with Ted taking lead and me singing the middle eight. We all decided the latter worked best and suited the song's melodic style. I always felt it would have been a good choice for a single. It had that upbeat, pop/rock aspect to it – something we didn't do too often. 'Wings of Desire' was also at one point considered as the title of the album.

Andy Powell, Guildford 1990.

'Renegade' was one of Andy's songs. Stylistically it has a very bluesy groove, somewhat in the style of American bands like Little Feat. Andy has a very good feel for that kind of music, but it can be difficult sometimes preventing these kind of songs from sounding clichéd and old-fashioned. In the case of this one, I think we succeeded in crafting something that sounded modern, even though it's quite derivative stylistically. In the bass department, I got away from my normal style. It sounds quite "slappy" with me hitting the strings with my hands rather than a pick.

'Dream Train' was probably my favourite of Andy's songs on the album. For Andy the vocal was a bit ambitious, but overall I think he did a good job and nailed it. I think the guitars sound really good and the song had a great groove and a really strong band feel.

'Some Conversation' was a song written by Matt Irving from Paul Young's band that was suggested by Miles Copeland. I wasn't too sure about it at first but everyone said that it really suited my voice. It was quite different for Wishbone Ash, being a piano-based song, but it was interesting to do and is a recording I'm quite fond of. I think the band got a really good feel out of it – Andy and Ted added some beautiful twin lead guitar at the end, putting a Wishbone Ash stamp on it. One thing you have to give the original band credit for is its instinctive ability to make a song feel right. That is not something you learn at Rock School. It's nothing to do with technique – just sheer instinct. A lot of people commented on how good my voice sounded on that track, yet when I recorded it I actually had a cold!

'Say You Will' is Ted stretching his wings. It's quite mellow and a bit different with lot of unusual chord changes. It doesn't really sound like anything else – it's simply Ted. As I have said before, sometimes Ted's lyrics can be a little difficult to totally understand the flow of, but they sound lovely and they have a certain poetic lilt to them, regardless of whether they make total sense. It's not everyone's cup of tea, but I kind of like that. I felt the band managed to interpret Ted's idea very well and, again, we got a good feel.

'Rollin' is another of Ted's songs – a fairly standard 12-bar blues – and was one that we'd already played live as an encore number. This is one of the songs on the album that I do have a bit of regret about, particularly the fact that we settled for the drum machine on the finished recording. This took it a long way from how it sounded as a live track. Looking back I was probably conscious of the fact that it was a fairly standard blues. There were already a few of them on this album and I was trying to give it something a little more modern in the production area – again, to stop it sounding derivative.

'You' was my sole composition on the album. I've always got the impression that this song was not liked too much by our audience. Certainly I've never had anyone come up and say "Martin, that song 'You' is brilliant" – something which happens with a lot of the other Wishbone songs, to different degrees. That was a bit disappointing because at that time I considered it to be probably the best song I'd ever written – in terms of its pace, the arrangement, and the emotional content. I'd originally recorded it with my band in the early eighties and the lyric was written about Susie and the affair we'd had at that time. The lyric is written in a very bitchy, jealous lover's kind of way. In one way I'm deriding her for going off with Andy Summers, yet I conclude the song by saying "Don't get me wrong, just stay the way you are." In actual fact, I really admired the dignity and resolve with which Susie handled that whole situation. When the story about her and Andy got out, she had the press / paparazzi camped outside her door offering her huge sums of money to spill the beans on Andy Summers' "love child". To her credit, she didn't do any "kiss and tell" in the national media and I really respected her for that. Musically, I thought we did a good job of interpreting the original song. Andy Powell constructed a really nice guitar figure throughout that had quite a Celtic feel to it, which the keyboards had always hinted at – Andy was always extremely good at being able to construct interesting rhythm parts. The song is quite heavy on the keyboards and there's a lot going on in the production. Possibly the song is a bit too different from what Wishbone Ash fans were used to and the lyrics too personal for people to get to grips with. It was a modern sounding track and far removed from *Argus,* which is generally considered the best music I've written in terms of commercial success and acclaim and its songs contain general lyrical themes that have a wider appeal. But for me, as a writer, 'You' was the composition I was the most happy with whilst recording *Strange Affair.*

'Hard Times' was another Andy Powell song and one that he'd been playing with line-ups of Wishbone Ash prior to the reunion of the original band. I think Andy was quite proud of the lyric, which dealt with the recession. We used to play it on stage where it worked in the same way that 'Bad Weather Blues' had years earlier – Andy's take on twelve-bar blues and another "Do ya wanna rock 'n' roll?" moment from him. Personally I thought the song was rather cheesy and contrived and I was never in love with it. Arguably it has a certain energy and jogs along nicely, but it doesn't do a lot for me personally.

'Standing in the Rain' was the album's closing track and Ted's big number on the album. Personally speaking I would have to say that I think this is one of Ted's finest compositions ever. It's an absolute work of art. I love the song's subject matter – the airport scenario and Ted's real-life problems with immigration. I also love the sheer relentless energy of the rhythm guitar and the beat – it just doesn't let up for a second. Ted's lead playing at the end is just magnificent – it flies like an eagle. Ted has got that magic touch when he's improvising. He knocks out licks played with such incredible feel – his playing can send shivers up your spine. That's what makes him a great guitar player. His style is very distinctive and personal to him and his playing comes loaded with emotional energy. Rather than playing the bass line on a bass guitar, I actually used a programmed bass part, to give it the relentless, machine-like quality that the tune needed. When we came to play it live I really struggled to reproduce it on the bass guitar with the same level of intensity!

'Standing in the Rain' was one of the final songs to be completed for the album. At this point Ted had gone back to the States, intending to come back again to finish the album off. As the album neared completion, Ted called me and said "I don't think I'm going to get back and I don't need to as you've got everything from me that you need". In fact, the only vocal I had from Ted for 'Standing in the Rain' was a rough take, which he'd intended to re-record later. There were a few timing and pitching issues and in those days there was no Auto-tune – you had to do pitch correction manually which could be very tedious. With Ted not around to re-record the vocal, the easiest thing for me to do was to try singing it myself, which I did, to see how my voice suited the song. I nailed it and we were happy with it, so I called up Ted and said "Your vocal on 'Standing in the Rain' was pretty loose, both in terms of pitching and timing, so as an experiment I've taken the liberty of putting my voice on there and everyone thinks it sounds really good. Are you going to be happy with that?" He was unequivocal and said "No, no, Mart, I've got to sing that song. It has to be my voice". I could understand that totally. It was Ted's creative work to which he was emotionally attached and it was part of his life experience. I managed to fix Ted's vocal through various wizardry means – changing the pitch and timing where needed, moving bits of vocal around from one part in the song to another. It was a real labour of love, but I straightened it out and it sounded decent. I am sure if Ted had come back to sing it again, he could have sung it perfectly in half the time it took me to straighten it out, but that was not to be. Sometimes you have to use the tools available in order to get the job done. The track went out and got very good feedback from our fans and so all's well that ends well. The version with my vocal would eventually appear on the *Distillation* 4CD box set collection.

There was one further song recorded for *Strange Affair*. 'Chimes of Freedom' was a tune that Andy wrote and I sang, but we never got around to finishing it properly – we simply ran out of time and this one remains in the vaults.

There have been several occasions in Wishbone Ash's history where you can look back afterwards and realise that never has an album been more aptly titled – like *Locked In*. The exact same could be said of *Strange Affair*. It really was a strange period in the band's career, as we began to adjust to life without Steve Upton at the helm. There were a lot of strange pressures in the background during the making of *Strange Affair*. Andy was at a point in his life where he wasn't sure which way to go – whether or not to sell his house and live in the States full time, which he did shortly after. Throughout the course of making *Strange Affair*, both Ted and Andy had to make trips back to the States, which affected the flow of the recording. Everything was moving in different directions for each person at that time and I think it was a very aptly titled album – it really was a strange affair. Ray Weston recalls the atmosphere at the time.

RAY WESTON: *The mood was pensive. There were always money issues going down. Ted was friendly but edgy. Andy was getting business stuff in order, while Martin was concentrating on the recording and to get the record finished as quickly as possible. I felt for Steve Upton who I never met. His whole world was turned upside down with a pending divorce. Everything he'd built in his life and career being dismantled, consumed with upset and self doubt.*

Photo by Gary Carter

Ted Turner, Marquee Club, 1991.

Andy Powell has been quoted as saying that I was at an all time creative low on this album, given that I was only responsible for writing one song. My reaction to that would be pretty much the same as my reaction to a lot of things that Andy Powell says and that is quite simply – "utter crap". I was always only too happy when somebody else comes up with a song – be it Andy, Ted or Laurie – to put my creative energy into it and help make it a really good track. I certainly did that with some of the songs on *Strange Affair*. I made a lot of creative contributions to some of Andy's tracks on the album, like 'Dream Train' and the title track, and helped steer them in a particular direction, for better or for worse. Those tracks certainly wouldn't have sounded the same without my input in the production area. If you look back over Wishbone Ash's albums, you will note that different writers have come to the fore on different albums. For example *No Smoke Without Fire* was mainly Laurie Wisefield and myself, *Just Testing* had a lot from me, while *Here to Hear* featured songs from Ted and myself. On *Strange Affair* it was Ted and Andy who came to the fore as writers, while my main creative input was in the production and engineering of the album, rather than song-writing. I had no real problem with that since by this time Andy and Ted were quite experienced at putting songs together. I was happy to do whatever I could to support them. For the record I did, as always, have song material available that could have been recorded – songs that would eventually end up on my solo album – but the other guys were not over keen on working on them, largely I think because they had been written and demoed with keyboards and they felt that Wishbone Ash should remain very much a "guitar" band. That needn't have been a problem and to me it doesn't matter on which instrument a song is conceived, as once the band starts knocking it around, the instrumentation changes and it inevitably ends up sounding like Wishbone Ash. Looking back it would probably have been better to have gone into an existing studio and for me to have put my creative energy into writing, rather than getting so involved with the production and mechanics of recording that album. However, overall I think we ended up with a decent sounding album, with some interesting production ideas and I do believe everyone contributed positively towards delivering the best album we could, given the disruption and the restraints placed upon us.

We took to the road to promote *Strange Affair* during the Spring of 1991 with a series of shows in Spain, Switzerland, the UK, Japan and Germany, with Ray Weston joining us on drums. I am immensely fond of Ray and felt he was a positive addition to the band. While we all missed Steve, there is no question that Ray was a solid replacement, arguably with a more modern playing style, and I thought we played some very good shows around this time.

> **RAY WESTON:** *Andy called me and asked if I would like to tour the UK, Japan and Germany. I was sent a cassette of live shows Robbie France had played as well as a couple of recent CDs. I learned a lot of songs and then we chose what was working best. I was stoked to be asked in. I more or less*

stayed with the drum parts already down. As gigs passed I got more relaxed and confident. After that I'd find natural adjustments, bringing more of my personality into the groove. We got on well I believe. I was the new guy feeling things out, listening to their suggestions, making everyone happy with the drumming.

One highlight of our UK tour was the show at Walthamstow Assembly Hall in East London on 16 May 1991, where Laurie Wisefield joined the band on stage to play 'Living Proof' and 'Jailbait'. It was quite an unusual experience having both Ted and Laurie on stage together, as they are as different as chalk and cheese as guitar players. I always thought that it would have been great to have done a tour with the original band with Ted for the first set, and then Laurie replacing Ted for the Mk.2 line-up for the second set, and then some encores at the end with everyone on stage, but that is something we never got around to. It was also great to revisit Japan – a truly wonderful country.

Our touring for *Strange Affair* culminated with a show in Hamburg on 10 June 1991. We all went our separate ways for the Summer, with plans afoot for more UK and European touring later in the year. Then, completely out of the blue, Andy Powell called me up on 1 October 1991 – my 44th birthday, no less. I thought "How sweet of Andy to call me from the States to say "Happy Birthday Mart". Actually what he was calling me for was to inform me that my services were no longer required. I had not really seen this coming. However, I had not been too happy about Andy getting control of the cheque book after Steve had left the band and Andy probably knew that, but I was as usual absolutely committed to carrying Wishbone Ash forwards and had been mapping out my entire life around the next period of touring. However, when I asked Andy if we had any shows confirmed, his reply was "Yes, but you won't be playing them"! I thought it was in particular bad taste of Andy to attempt to take control of the situation, given the amount of collective work we had all put in during the reunion period – efforts which had helped restore the public's faith in Wishbone Ash through a series of decent quality albums and solid concert performances by the original band. However, it seemed blatantly obvious to me that what mattered to Andy more than anything was the financial aspect and he said as much to me on this occasion, stating that now that he and Ted were both in the States, he was going to look at alternative arrangements that made "more financial sense" to him. He told me that he had decided he could "make more money running things from the States" and that I would be "better off" running my studio, doing "all that modern music that you're into". He produced all kinds of excuses but basically I think he simply didn't want to work with me anymore and I think he saw this as an opportunity to take control for himself. Andy appeared to me to be quite determined to establish himself as the leader of the band and, in particular, seemed very eager to take over Steve's role as the business manager. After Steve left the band, we had got involved briefly with a manager named Hana Cunningham (nee Pevny) – a Czech-American lady, who was hard working and very pleasant to deal with. I felt that if the band had stayed together under Hana's management we could have been a very good unit. All the elements were there for a good working relationship and a good business relationship, but with neither Steve nor Hana involved, I was very nervous as to how the business side of the band was going to be handled, particularly given that it appeared to me that Andy wanted to get his hands on the purse strings. I have the utmost respect and admiration for Andy's guitar playing throughout the course of Wishbone Ash's career, but in my dealings with him I've found him to be very driven by money and not the sort of person I would choose to have in charge of financial matters. My opinion is he's as tricky as a barrel-load of monkeys, whereas the other guys in the band – Steve, Ted and Laurie – were, in my opinion, always more sincere and had more integrity. The rapport between Andy and I was, at best, congenial. At times we worked well together, but there was always something about the man that I personally found difficult to trust.

I think Andy felt his position would be stronger if the band was rounded out by "sidemen" – hired hands who would be paid a session fee on the same basis as which Robbie France and Ray Weston had been enlisted, rather than being equity partners in the band's business. It was on this session basis that I was replaced in Wishbone Ash by Andy Pyle, who had previously played with Andy and Steve in the band during 1986/87, immediately prior to the reunion of the original line-up. Andy Pyle is a very gentlemanly, polite, well-behaved bass player – perfect for Andy Powell, who had been used to having to deal with a feisty, intense, creative type like me. I think Andy Powell's idea of a bass player is someone who just plonks away at the back and supplies some low end, leaving him free to front the band and carry the vocals. I don't wish to be rude to Andy Pyle. I have met him quite recently, at Liscombe Park studios, and he is a very nice chap, but he doesn't strike me as being a particularly effervescent kind of character. He's very easy going and his style of bass playing is very orthodox – the exact opposite to what I am. That probably suited Andy Powell to the ground after years of having to deal with me, but to a lot of our fans this was at the expense of what most people recognise as the definitive Wishbone Ash sound, of which my unusual style of bass playing, in addition to my voice, was obviously a very big part. As with my first split with the band in 1980, various "official" reasons for my departure were given to our fan-base by Andy Powell's publicity machine, usually claiming that I had "left" the band due to a desire on my part to return to studio work and spend time with my family. All of this was totally untrue and I did not "leave" Wishbone Ash in 1991. I was simply excluded, against my will once again, from further involvement in the band.

> **TED TURNER:** *Martin is the heart of Wishbone Ash. I knew my own days would be numbered upon his departure. I always held a deep respect and connection for Mart – my mate, my brother. His intuition brought me into the band. For this I will always be grateful. This was the start of Andy wanting to gain control. I didn't like it.*

RAY WESTON: *I don't know exactly why Andy decided to replace Martin. They had a tempestuous relationship, but on a creative level they worked well together, especially in the studio. The road was different. There's a lot of hanging out with a small proportion spent on stage. Andy had already worked with Andy Pyle and I believe he wanted to work with him again. Losing Martin and his unique style obviously changed things dramatically. He has his own sound and technique that cemented both guitars, giving Wishbone their personality. Dynamics change when you replace anyone from a four piece band. Martin was the original guy. He is Martin Turner of Wishbone Ash – always will be! He fronted and gave the band its identity, alongside the others.*

Strange Affair tour, Japan 1991, with Ray Weston

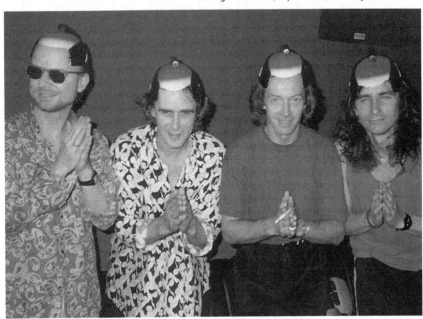

Despite my disappointment at the way the reunion of the original band ended, I have fond memories of our work together during 1987-91 and am very proud of the music we made during that period. I believe we managed to reinvent ourselves, updating the Wishbone Ash sound without ever losing track of what made the band special in the first place. We also gave something back to the fans who had supported the band over the years, by giving them the chance to see the original members together on stage once more. For the most part, the reunion was a highly pleasurable experience and I am very glad we had that second chance to work together. If there were any frustrations shared by us all around that time it was probably largely down to the fact that we would all like to have been working at a slightly higher level. There is no doubt that the band's status was somewhat reduced by this point, when compared to what it had been in the seventies. I personally believe that what the band was doing during my time away in the early eighties, prior to the reunion, did little to help maintain the band's musical style and identity. Those albums don't sound like Wishbone Ash albums to me and I know I am not alone in that opinion – a lot of people share that viewpoint, including a large proportion of our fan-base. Disappointing product always damages the brand and once you lose the support of the fans it's very hard to get it back as people move on and get into different things. I honestly believe that a break may have done the band good at some point and that if the original band had come back after a few years of no Wishbone Ash activity at all, then we could have gone back in at a pretty decent level and with a higher profile.

There were of course other factors. We no longer had the backing of a huge record company such as MCA as we'd had in the seventies. For all Miles' good intentions, IRS was a much smaller label and did have its limitations in terms of advertising and promotional budget. It is also quite possible that the time period in which we put the original band back together was not necessarily the best time to be doing so. The music scene in the UK in the late eighties to early nineties was not a healthy one as far as rock music was concerned. Tastes had changed and there is no doubt that synthesisers, drum machines and computerised music were dictating the general trend at that time. Personally I did I enjoy a lot of the music of the eighties – I think Boy George had a great voice and I loved artists like Thomas Dolby, Freur and the Comsat Angels, for example – but music had veered off in another direction, which was not necessarily about the organic interplay between musicians, which was always one of our great strengths. Bands like Wishbone Ash were not what the UK music press were into at the time and our reunion received very little coverage or support from the media. As such, it was quite difficult to get the word out that the original band was back in action – do remember this was long before the internet, the emergence of which proved to be a revolution in terms of the way information is communicated. I do believe if the reunion had taken place a decade later, by which time people had started to rediscover real instruments and organic playing, then it may have attracted a lot more interest, helped by the obvious advances in communications via the internet. As always it's easy to talk with hindsight. Looking back, the original band was presented with an excellent opportunity by Miles Copeland and we produced three albums which I believe re-established the true essence of what Wishbone Ash was about and were responsible for helping restore the band's reputation. I think it is clear that during the reunion period we managed to record some of the best music Wishbone Ash has ever produced.

CHAPTER FOURTEEN

The Sky is Changing

WITH MY involvement in Wishbone Ash's touring and recording activities having been so abruptly terminated, I was left high and dry, and had to re-think my career in music. I decided to focus on production work again. At that particular time I was very happy living in Southfields with Susie and we were surrounded by young children. My youngest child Melody-Rose (Mimi) was born on 28 August 1991 – coincidentally the same date as my first-born daughter Jessica, years before, proving what a creature of habit I must be. When Mimi was eleven months old, Susie was offered a job she couldn't refuse and I took on the role of being Mimi's daytime carer. This was something I needed to do, having been somewhat absent when my previous children were young. So, at this stage I became one of the few guys to push a pram around the park. You see guys pushing buggies, but I used to go down to Wimbledon Park in all weathers with a bloody great Silver Cross pram – that thing was like a chariot!

> **SUSIE TURNER:** *During the Southfields years I worked part time, cooking directors' lunches for my brother's media company. I would leave home on the morning school run and return in time to pick up from school, an ideal occupation which left Martin in charge of the family from 9 until 3 on weekdays. Weekends and school holidays were wonderful crazy family*

> *times with our bunch of five kids on trips to parks, Wisley, Frensham Ponds, football matches, train spotting, stock car racing, big family meals and many birthday parties over the years as we attempted to give our merged family a happy and balanced upbringing.*

Susie's folks, although British, had retired to live in Sarasota, Florida and eventually she took me out there, having been going herself for some years. Sarasota is a fabulous town and Siesta Key, the beach village, is a wonderful place which gave us an oasis of calm and rejuvenation. We had many wonderful holidays there with the little people and Susie's folks were very supportive and generous. On one visit we started chatting about getting hooked up. We had just been living together and the whole marriage thing was still a bit raw and there were also the feelings of my children and Maurn to be considered – it all seemed to be a tricky equation. However, it came up in conversation that Susie's uncle was a notary public, therefore empowered to conduct a marriage ceremony, so we spontaneously took him up on it and got married one weekend when he came over to the house. It was all conducted in the sun on the Lanai on 17 April 1993.

Martin, Susie and Grace in the "Breadcorn Field" at Bushey Leaze, two weeks before Melody's arrival, August 1991

Photo by Nicholas Lyne

SUSIE TURNER: *Our marriage was glorious. Mimi was an adorable nineteen month old flower girl, Tom an angelic almost five year old and Andrew, a pensive ten year old, a little reluctant to "give his mummy away", despite his great love for Martin. My first born daughter Annalise organised the children all day, an early glimpse of the wonderful mother she was going to become herself. I was just sad that Jess and Grace weren't there as well, as I so enjoyed our complete family whenever it was possible to be together.*

On the subject of marriage as an institution created by religion and states, which does vary hugely from culture to culture, I can understand the reason for it and that it gives security for the family unit and for society as a whole. Of course, when it does go wrong it is a bitch and can cause massive stress and unfairness despite the legal system's involvement. I can think of huge injustices for both males and females that I know. People vary in their emotional/material balance, which I guess causes this unfairness. My own personal experience has been that marriage can produce complacency and I have to admit I am a wee bit wary knowing that although there can be great joy and happiness there can also be the spiral of doom to contend with when things go pear shaped. I do think that the spiritual commitment is vital but when even that fails, people do need to be able to change their lives and that's when the system isn't too kind – "The strong

Getting married in Florida, 1993

give up and move on, the weak give up and stay". For me conversely, once I do give my heart to someone I cannot take it back, so I do have quite a few "loves" out there. Still, better that way because people seem to think that love and hate are opposites, whereas I would suggest that they are right next to each other on a circle, but that hate is "inverted" love and can give rise to extremely negative energy that will even produce the conditions for illnesses like cancer. To put the thing in a long term human context, average life expectancy was about 35 years up until a couple of hundred years ago. People live to a ripe old age in our modern society and it is easy for fatigue to set in when you exhaust the freshness of a relationship over thirty or fifty years, which I would suggest gives rise to a kind of serial monogamy syndrome nowadays. Obviously there are exceptions and extremes – King Henry VIII, five hundred-odd years ago for instance – and we still to this day are living with his legacy in the UK, in my humble opinion.

Obviously it can be hard to hold down a stable relationship within the music business since musicians and artistic / creative types are by nature on the fringe of society, observing and feeding back what they see. We live a pirate-come-vagabond kind of existence at times where

Family time, 1991 – with Susie, Tom, Andrew and Melody

Photo by Ed Turner

decisions have to be made spontaneously in some corner of the world where we happen to find ourselves. It is an adventure but for me I have always thrived on the life style – living dangerously at times, close to the edge, but always coming into contact with new people and places, which is clearly what I need – inspiration, learning, making contact, new ideas, etc. There are times when we all need sustenance, be it food, drink, some place to lay down or just the human touch. Through all the travels and travails we also do enjoy to go home again to our loved ones and there are times when we need to be generous, understanding and big hearted. I have always said that we are born alone and we die alone. The bit in between, however, we try to be perfect, but it is pretty near impossible, so we do the best we can. Nobody in this world really belongs to anyone else exclusively. Susie has been married twice before and she also was with Andy Summers for a while. I know she loved the men she was with at the time, so it's no skin off my nose. I do not feel jealous or resentful about her other loves – rather respect. We all have our passions and callings in life, mine is music. It is easy to be generous with your heart I think, and it should be unconditional – too many people in this world need some love that they are not getting. Enough philosophical thoughts for now methinks, except to say "Life is like a carrot – one minute it tastes so sweet, next minute somebody shoves it up your arse" a saying I picked up from our wonderful old friend, the late Ian Copeland.

While family matters took priority for a few years, I kept my hand in with recording and production, and was able to operate from my home studio, working on various projects. Not long after parting with Wishbone Ash in 1991 I began working with Roy Hollingworth again, re-recording some of the songs I had worked with him on in the early eighties. We got a Dutch guitar player called Robin Berlin involved and finally we got an album release for Roy's material. Although the album *In The Flesh* is quite removed from Wishbone Ash in style, I was heavily involved creatively. As well as producing the album, I also played bass, keyboards, guitar and programmed drums on the album as well as contributing backing vocals. I also worked with a band called Huge Big Thing, which featured Simon Townshend, younger brother of Pete. I liked Simon a lot – a great guy and very talented. I also recorded some songs with Minnie Driver, an emerging actress who had at the time had a role in a television drama that everyone said was going to make her into a star. Her management wanted to capitalise on this success by getting a record out, to prove that she could sing as well. She had a really good voice, but I was not impressed with the songs they chose for me to work on with her. I felt they were too poppy and cheesy and I think Minnie felt the same too. I also did a really interesting album project with a guy called Michael Tyack. He came to me with an album's worth of material that was medieval in style, but with a sixties psychedelic dressing. It was recorded mainly with medieval instruments such as dulcimer, zither and lute and I really enjoyed the challenge of recording those instruments. There was even one song on the album written by Henry VIII, who was someone I'd always been interested in, particularly his impact on the psyche of our nation and his role in moulding the shape of Britain.

Our former manager John Sherry had set up a great studio on a boathouse on an island in the Thames, near Hampton Court. He asked me to get involved in producing material with him there for a greatest hits album he was compiling for the Flying Pickets – the a cappella vocal group he had managed, who had scored a Christmas number one hit in 1983 with their version of Yazoo's 'Only You'. This was another big challenge as producer – recording music without instruments. Unfortunately during these sessions it became clear that John Sherry was not at all well and everyone was worried about him. He'd been suffering with a bad back, had a nasty cough and he generally seemed to age quite badly within a matter of a few months. One night before Christmas 1993 I came out of the studio with him late at night after a session with the Pickets. It was about 11.30pm and was bucketing down with rain – a really nasty storm was coming down the river. By this stage John was very frail and was walking with a stick. He said to me, "Mart, it's going to take ages for us to walk across to my car. Why don't you go on ahead or else you're going to get soaked". There was no way I was going to leave him as if he'd fallen over he would have been in big trouble. So I said "No, John, I'll walk with you." It took about ten minutes to make our way back over the bridge to our cars. I was freezing cold and soaked to the skin, but I managed to get John to his car safely. I was so glad I did that because that was the last time I ever saw John, although I did speak to him once on the phone after that. His wife Nina insisted he go to the hospital to get a diagnosis immediately after Christmas, which is when it was discovered that he was riddled with cancer. The prognosis was not good and he only lasted a few months into the spring. It was desperately sad and I think it would be fair to say that everyone associated with Wishbone Ash was very upset about it. I had a lot of respect for John and thought the world of him. He'd been like the Godfather of our little corner of the music business, and together with his lovely wife Nina and his lads James and Jody we all became good friends.

There was a lot of sadness around the Wishbone Ash fraternity during 1994 and the loss of John Sherry was not the only tragedy that year. In May 1994, my brother Glenn called me up and said that my Dad (Ed) had been involved in a serious motor accident and was in intensive care. I called my little brother Kim and we went down to Torquay in his Jaguar. Kim drove the whole journey at 120mph and it was not the place to be if you were a nervous passenger! Ed had gone to Exeter to pick up his new Mitsubishi car, which Kim had bought for him. He was driving home to Torquay when he crashed. That was the only information we had at that point. When we got down there we started talking with the hospital and the police, who managed to put us in contact with a witness – a nurse who had seen Ed weaving about in the road. She thought he was asleep at the wheel and so followed him to try to attract his attention. When she pulled alongside him she could see that he was clearly not well – his head was jerked back and his mouth was wide open. What we managed to deduce was that he'd had a massive stroke, which had caused the accident – not the other way round as had been suspected. My brother Kim was totally beside himself. Because Ed was such a good driver, Kim was absolutely convinced that the brakes on the car he had bought him were faulty and this had caused the accident. We all tried to convince him otherwise, but Kim clearly felt responsible. In the end we had to get special permission from the police to go back to the crashed car, where we sat Kim in the driver's seat and tried the brakes while Glenn and I attempted to push it – the brakes worked fine. The doctors told us that Ed was being kept alive with a ventilator, without which he would die immediately. He had suffered a massive stroke and they could see from the scans that if he was to recover he would be desperately brain damaged and unable to do anything. I spoke to my mother and as far as we were both concerned he was gone. There was no alternative but to shut the support system down and that is what was advised by the hospital staff. It took my brother Kim about three days to get his head around that. At one point we were all around the bed and Kim was talking to Ed, trying to get his attention. All of a sudden Kim said "Look – he responded!". What he was actually referring to was his big toe moving. Then Glenn said "Talk to him again". We ended up with all of us – three grown men and our elderly mother – clustered around this big toe waiting for it to respond, in the desperate hope that it was going to give us a sign. It was a surreal moment – funny even – in the midst of our tragedy. Eventually we had to accept that this really was the end. The hospital staff were fantastic and very sensitive and didn't put pressure on anyone at all. My two brothers and Susie chose to be in the room with Ed as he left. I chose to wait outside with my mother, who did not want to be there at the moment he died. We said goodbye to Ed and made our way home. Everyone jumped in cars but I decided to walk totally on my own in the gentle sunlight. I cried most of the way home. It was an incredible shock and something that none of us had seen coming.

That evening we all went over to Kim's house and we knocked up a great meal of pasta, pine nuts and pesto. We were all sitting around the table eating when suddenly my Mum started choking on a pine nut. Everyone started to panic and got up to help her. In the end Susie realised Mum didn't want to spit the food out, but once Susie held a napkin to Mum's mouth, she did. When we eventually got sat back around the table I said "Mum, do you realise what was going through my head then? I had visions of calling up the undertakers in the morning to get a discount on a two-for-one deal for the pair of you!" We all ended up having a right laugh, which was just as Ed would have wanted, because he had a pretty sick sense of humour. I was elected to speak at the funeral – something I'd never done before. There was quite a gathering as Ed was much loved. He had been a fireman all his working life and a lot of the firemen came to the funeral. Sting and Trudie were also there. The morning of the funeral I'd woken up with this dream that I'd had during the night going around in my head and I told it at the funeral. Ed was in heaven and was driving around in his fire engine. Eventually this angel came out and stopped him and said "What are you doing?" He said "I'm trying to find the fire". The angel replied "No, no, no – if you want to find the fire you have to go down there!" It's always difficult telling jokes at a funeral, but it got a few laughs and everyone told me I did a good job with the eulogy.

Losing my father was a very heavy emotional experience. Because Ed had introduced me to classical music as a small child, I could not bring myself to listen to classical music for some time after he died. I just couldn't deal with it for about a year until one day some classical music came on the car radio unexpectedly. I saw Susie reach across to turn it off, and I grabbed her hand and said "No, leave it." Then I just started crying for about half an hour. I think it's the English way with grief – it sometimes takes a long time to come out, even though you think you've dealt with it. Ed also loved opera, but I never got the feel for it until after he died, when suddenly I began to understand opera. It was as though he had passed on the baton. Opera is for the most part about tragedy and maybe I had to experience real tragedy first hand to truly appreciate opera. Popular songs such as 'The

Living Years' by Mike and The Mechanics and 'Dance With My Father' by Luther Vandross became songs that could reduce me to tears. Certainly losing my father was the most tragic thing I had experienced in my life at that time.

They say bad luck always comes in threes and the year of 1994 was no exception. What happened to my dear friend Ted Turner that year is something no parent should have to go through, when he witnessed his young son Kip killed by a drunk driver in a hit and run incident, while staying with Ted to celebrate his eleventh birthday. No one can even begin to imagine the impact of what that must do to a parent. Kip was a lovely lad and I have fond memories of the original band spending some time with him in Los Angeles during the summer of 1989 when we were staying at Miles Copeland's place. We had to guard him from Miles' bull-mastiffs which were pacing the garden all the time and staring at him. We had to stay between them and Kip at all times. The loss of Kip in such tragic circumstances was extremely sad and I really felt terrible for both Ted and Kip's mother Debbie. It's the law of nature that at some point we will lose our parents, but no parent should ever have to go to their child's funeral.

I continued my career in music throughout the early nineties, working on production projects from my home studio in south west London. As always I enjoyed working with other artists, expanding my knowledge of production techniques and music in general in the process. This also slotted in well with my personal life at the time and I thoroughly enjoyed having the opportunity to be a hands-on Dad and spend maximum time with my young family. I had also made tentative steps towards a solo album, which would present an opportunity to take another look some of the unreleased songs I had in my archive as well as a chance to get creative with some new material. There was always part of me, however, that missed performing the music of Wishbone Ash.

During the late summer of 1995 I witnessed the "flight of the heron" once again and I sensed that a change of some sort was on the horizon, although

I did not know exactly what. I had a conversation with my brother Kim shortly after. Sting had been taking a break and Kim was keen on getting back into drumming. He suggested putting a band together with my younger brother Glenn, himself and me. That would have been interesting as there have been few times when the three of us have played together. Kim said "Call up Laurie Wisefield and we could go out as Wishbone Ash – right?" I went away and thought about it but we didn't take it any further. It would certainly have been an interesting configuration.

Shortly after that, I received a call from Andy Powell – the first time we had spoken in quite a while. Initially he wanted to talk to me about an upcoming 4CD Wishbone Ash collection that was being put out by Repertoire Records of Germany. This was to be a career retrospective and they were looking for rare live and studio material in order to make the package appealing to ardent fans of the band. Andy was aware that I had a stash of multi-track tapes and would be able to provide what was needed. I agreed to get involved in principle, although as Andy had cut a deal with the record company, I was quite insistent that I be allowed to speak to them directly. By this stage Andy had already been involved in a couple of business deals involving past Wishbone Ash material that had been conducted without the consultation of any of the other original members of the band. I refer to the *From The Archives* and *Archives II* albums, two CD collections that Andy had sanctioned and endorsed for sale through his US fan club. These contained performances by the Mk.1 and Mk.2 line-ups of the band, sourced mainly from bootleg recordings and BBC radio concerts. I have no particular problem with archival material being released. There is clearly a market for previously unreleased material and I would always do all that I could to assist in the production of such releases. If someone had spoken to me nicely I could have provided material of far superior quality to some of the recordings included on the album, some of which were poorly recorded by audience members with hand-held tape recorders. The whole project was promoted as being designed to beat the bootleggers at their own game, with the proceeds from the albums going directly to "the band". One would always naturally assume that to be the band which appears on the albums. In this instance, however, this turned out not to be the case and all of the proceeds were handed over to Andy Powell, I understand. There was never any proper accounting or royalty arrangements made for the musicians who played on the albums and to this date Andy had not seen fit to divide the proceeds from these albums amongst the other Mk.1 and Mk.2 members. The albums undoubtedly breached copyrights – our song-writing publishing was clearly not being paid, and appropriate licenses had not been obtained for the use of BBC material. I had no desire to be associated with this and the whole episode prompted me to start seriously questioning Andy Powell's morals. Of course the small amount of money that any of the original members would have made from the relatively minor sales of these limited edition albums would probably be less than the costs of taking legal action and so we all let it pass. With hindsight, this was a big mistake as our reluctance to actively oppose such a grubby deal effectively gave Andy Powell the green light to conduct similarly underhand deals in the years to come, safe in the knowledge that none of us would pursue him for our share of the profit. There is now a whole catalogue of albums out there for which licensing and legalities are at best questionable – album such as *Tracks* for example. However, despite certain misgivings about Andy Powell's conduct around this time, he and I began communicating reasonably cordially with regard to the upcoming 4CD set.

With regard to Wishbone Ash as a working band, the reunion period had truly reached its conclusion following the departure of Ted Turner in January 1994. Following my second split with the band in 1991, Andy and Ted had carried on for a couple of years with Ray Weston and Andy Pyle, but by the end of 1993 Ted had decided he'd had enough. He too was unhappy with Andy's business model and his methods of handling band finances.

TED TURNER: *We toured for a while and I did enjoy the company of Ray Weston and Andy Pyle. We played well together and I thought the album Live in Chicago was worthy. Eventually Andy saw the future one way and I saw it another. The main reason was musical differences. This coupled with his dubious business practices made staying with him untenable. This was no longer Wishbone Ash – not even close. I had no desire to serve the Andy Powell road show.*

RAY WESTON: *The last time the line-up of Andy, Ted, Andy Pyle and myself played was during the Total Recall tour across Canada, the US and Europe. It was a package tour along with Blue Oyster Cult, Uriah Heep and Molly Hatchet – Wishbone were bottom of the bill. We travelled by road in a van for thousands of miles. It nearly killed our one crew member and changed his whole perception of "the road". It was exhausting and the money was a joke. This brought about big tensions. I believe at the end of the tour Ted wrote Andy a letter telling him exactly what he thought of him. It was enough to drive the sanest person to craziness. I hadn't personally decided not to continue with Wishbone Ash. Andy faxed me to say he was continuing with a new American band.*

Around this time Andy began playing with East Coast US blues band Blue Law but, realising that there remained – and I quote – "a fan-base to exploit", he set about forming a new version of Wishbone Ash with him as the sole original member. Using American musicians Roger Filgate (guitar), Tony Kishman (bass/vocals) and Mike Sturgis (drums), Andy undertook a UK/European tour during the Spring of 1995 and was working on new material, written mainly by Roger Filgate and himself. The band had a further period of UK and European touring scheduled to begin in November 1995, commemorating the 25th anniversary of Wishbone Ash's first album. It was

Photo by David Moffitt

*25 Years tour –
with Mike Sturgis,
Roger Filgate and
Andy Powell, 1995.*

not long before the tour was due to start that Tony Kishman announced that he would not be joining the band on the road. Officially Tony was reported to be ill, but rumours soon began to circulate to the effect that he was signed contractually to a Beatles tribute show, from which he could not get release to join the tour. Either way, it left poor old Andy up shit creek without a paddle. There weren't too many people who would have been able to step in at such short notice, so guess who got the call?

When Andy called me and broached the idea of me coming back out to play again, I was at first reluctant. I don't think Andy would ever have chosen to have me back in the band and I believe it was only because he was in the position of having to possibly cancel a tour that he came to me. In addition, I had a number of other commitments, including a charity Christmas theatre production with the lovely BACCES (British Airways Cabin Crew Entertainment Society) at the Beck Theatre in Hayes for which I had been involved on the technical side annually for a number of years. I was also in the process of putting together my solo album. So initially I said "No, I'm busy". I simply couldn't see how I could possibly fit in a tour around my existing commitments. Eventually, after several conversations we figured out a way it could work by moving a few dates here and there. Unfortunately this also meant my solo album got put on hold as my time needed to be spent rehearsing Wishbone Ash material rather than mixing my own CD. That was no real issue to me – I would always put Wishbone Ash activity first in any case. So, I committed to joining Andy and his band on the *25 Years* tour.

Whenever you are faced with the choice of working again with people you know well, you are well aware of the potential pitfalls. Working with Andy again, I knew there would be some tricky moments, but in most respects we worked together fine. Roger Filgate and Mike Sturgis were both good men and I became very fond of them. Roger was a really nice, laid back kind of guy as well as being an incredible guitar player with a lot of creative ideas – I could totally understand why Andy got involved with him. Mike was an extremely gentlemanly, pleasant chap and a top class drummer. He was an American living in London and by strange coincidence he was living in Southfields just up the road from my place. One night after rehearsals I made the mistake of walking home with him and found out that Mike – who is quite tall with extremely long legs – doesn't do walking. It was more like marching and it was quite an aerobic walk from the studio in Putney back to Southfields that night. Both Roger and Mike had a very good understanding of what Wishbone Ash's sound was all about. Overall I was very pleasantly surprised and impressed by the band's interpretation of the music. Rehearsing with the band went very smoothly and stepping back into the old material was effortless. I was also pleasantly surprised by the quality of the new music that had been written by Andy and Roger, which was melodic and quite deliberately in the classic Wishbone Ash mould. Andy originally wanted me to sing a few of the new songs, although I only eventually ended up singing one on stage – a track written mainly by Roger called 'Top of The World'.

We kicked off the *25 Years* tour at the Bottom Line in London on 2 November 1995. It felt great to be back on stage playing Wishbone Ash material again and, as always, we were given a very warm reception. As the tour progressed and I got to talk to people after the shows, it was clear that people were very pleased to see me back on stage, playing the Wishbone Ash music which had been a backdrop to my life. The big question that was continually being put to me during the tour was as to whether or not I would be returning to Wishbone Ash activity on a more permanent basis. This was a question that I was not entirely able to answer as none of us knew precisely what the future held at that point. From my standpoint I was happy to be back playing Wishbone Ash music and would have been happy to have continued with this line-up, which I believed to be very strong. I firmly believe we could have taken things further with this particular blend of original members and fresh faces.

The terms under which I got involved in the *25 Years* tour were not ideal. Wishbone Ash, in both the seventies and during the reunion period, was always operated on an equal share basis when it came to splitting performance fees, merchandise profits and album royalties – the only exception to this rule being song-writing. When Steve Upton was managing the business side of the band, he never took commissions or insisted on any greater share of the takings. He did what he did for the overall good of the band and its members rather than for personal gain. The way Andy Powell ran his new version of Wishbone Ash, however, was somewhat at odds with the way the band had been managed in the past. Andy had set up his band very much as a personal family business venture. He was managing the band and paying the musicians a performance fee, effectively relegating the band members to the status of hired-hands rather than equity members. The remainder of the tour profits, both from performance fees and merchandise sales, was therefore Andy's to keep. Now, this may have been acceptable to Roger Filgate, Tony Kishman and Mike Sturgis, but as a founding original member, who had contributed creatively to the back catalogue of music off of which the band was predominately trading, I was never entirely comfortable with being paid a "fee" and treated as a "side-man" or a "hired hand". However, I'd been off the live scene for some time and was eager to get back on stage to play some Wishbone Ash music. Unlike Andy, I do not consider myself a businessman, and so I agreed to the offer that was on the table, figuring that if things went further than this one tour, Andy and I would be able to come to an amicable arrangement that reflected our positions as original members of the band.

During a break in the tour schedule we made an attempt to record some of the new material that we had been playing on stage. We worked at Element Studios, in Hampton Court – the studio that had been set up by John Sherry and was now being run by his son Jody. These sessions were strange for me. I had by this stage become quite used to being very hands-on in the production department, yet in this instance Andy and Roger were quite precious about what they saw as their "baby" and they clearly wanted to see it through to its conclusion without any outside involvement. It soon became apparent that they didn't want me getting

With Roger Filgate, Barnsley 1995.

Photo by Gary Carter

345

my sweaty mitts on it and that they wanted total control. That was a shame as I felt with my knowledge and experience in the production field coupled with my distinctive bass and vocal style, I could really have helped them achieve something that resembled an authentic Wishbone Ash album for the late nineties. I could have done a really good job on the bass lines and put a bit of attitude into it, but because Roger had already constructed the bass parts and had played them on earlier demo sessions of the songs, I think he really wanted to play the bass parts on the album himself. It soon became obvious that my involvement was not wanted. Although I did lay some parts down, eventually Andy suggested to me that maybe I could leave my Gibson Thunderbird bass guitar at the studio and let Roger record the bass parts playing my instrument. Initially I said to them "No, I don't let anyone use my instrument," but they were so desperate to get that classic Wishbone Ash sound that they wanted to get their hands on my guitar. They really were missing the point there because it's not the instrument that makes that classic Wishbone Ash sound, it's the man who's playing it. The real irony, of course, is that I rarely used the Thunderbird on any of the classic Wishbone Ash studio recordings – it was basically my stage instrument. I was amused by their complete naivety. Reluctantly, I left my guitar there for a couple of days and let them get on with it. I was later told that very little, other than the drum tracks, was used from the Element session with pretty much everything else being replaced at a studio in Connecticut.

Following the *25 Years* tour, I went back to my studio to continue work on my solo album as well as the material for the 4CD set for Repertoire. Meanwhile, Andy Powell made various suggestions during interviews to the effect that the new Wishbone Ash album could feature contributions from both Tony Kishman and myself. This was not to be and Andy, Roger and Mike completed work on what would become the *Illuminations* album in Connecticut, with Tony later recording the lead vocals at another studio. I always refer to the album as *Eliminations,* as once again I had seemingly been eliminated from the proceedings. Certainly I had not been kept in touch with the way things were shaping up with the album or what was planned for the future and any information I gleaned was through the jungle drums – nothing new there!

Although I was not part of the *Illuminations* recording, I was invited by Andy Powell to perform with the band during the band's Autumn 1996 tour UK/European tour to promote the album, as there were certain shows that Tony Kishman could not make. The reality was that I ended up playing the entire tour, bar four shows which Tony flew in for. I was pleased to be playing with the guys again and I really enjoyed the musical and personal company of Roger and Mike. This time we had a little more time to prepare for the tour and I felt this line-up of the band was beginning to sound very impressive on stage. Unfortunately, behind the scenes, dealings with Andy were becoming increasingly difficult. Although I was once again hired on a "fixed fee" basis, this time Andy did agree upfront to give me an equal split on merchandising, although he later reneged on that promise, wriggling out of the deal on the basis of me having been selling my solo album *Walking The Reeperbahn* at the gigs and therefore having an income from that. As the *Illuminations* tour reached its completion I could sense that this

Back with my old mate Andy Powell, Barnsley 1995.

Photo by Gary Carter

little chapter in the Wishbone Ash story was nearing its end and it came as no surprise to me to hear through the grapevine that Andy had decided to use Tony Kishman for future touring into 1997.

That was not quite the end of this episode though. By this stage the Wishbone Ash Convention – or *Ash-Con* as it would become known – had become an annual event on the Wishbone Ash calendar. This was a prestigious event which would feature a live concert in the evening, preceded by a host of peripheral activities during the afternoon – rare video screenings, a questions and answers session with the band, meet and greets, etc. They were highly pleasurable events to attend and the evening concerts were always a highlight of the tour. You couldn't lose when you had a room packed full of the band's most loyal supporters. I had been part of the 1995 and 1996 events and had enjoyed the experience. Although I had not been invited to tour with the band during 1997, Andy did invite me to appear at the *Ash-Con* event in Mansfield in November 1997. I was asked by Andy to perform 'Master of Disguise' and 'Living Proof'. Now, 'Living Proof' I could have done standing on my head, but 'Master of Disguise' was a tricky one as we had never performed it live at that point and it took me a while to re-learn it, having not played it since the 1979 *Just Testing* album sessions. After all this work, I arrived in Mansfield to be told that we would not now be playing 'Master of Disguise' after all. Instead we would be playing a bunch of other old stuff, which I had not rehearsed at all. I ended up being on stage for almost an hour and because of my lack of preparation I was not altogether happy with my performance. The audience were very warm, as always, but I was not informed by anyone – either before, during or after the event – that the show was being filmed. The show was later released as a fairly poor quality video cassette, and no one ever had the courtesy to consult me about any royalty for the use of my performance – I wonder in whose pockets the proceeds from that one ended up? Not for the first time I found myself in a situation over which I had hardly any say or control. The plan had been changed at the last minute and important considerations were completely overlooked. This shoddy treatment is the kind of thing that leaves one feeling used for someone else's profit and is, well, just so bloody tacky. That was the last time Andy Powell and I were to play on stage together.

By the end of 1997, Roger Filgate and Tony Kishman had, for different reasons, decided they did not wish to tour. In Roger's case he had health issues which made touring quite arduous for him, while Tony wanted to concentrate on his Beatles tribute show and promote his then recently released solo album. Mike Sturgis had also announced that he would be

Photo by Gary Carter

Dublin 1996.

focussing on teaching in future and would only be available for a limited number of appearances. Once again Andy was faced with having a tour booked – for the Spring of 1998 – and no band to play it. With this in mind he put out a feeler to both Laurie Wisefield and myself about the possibility of a Wishbone Ash Mk.2 reunion. Steve Upton was even contacted. I was up for it in principle but told Andy that I did not want it to be on the basis of the previous two tours, where he was effectively paying me a wage rather than giving me a share in the profits as an equal split. Laurie also had similar concerns and we both felt that a reunion of one of our most prolific line-ups needed to be properly planned and managed and could only ever have taken place on an equity share basis. This was clearly not what was being offered by Andy and the idea never got past initial discussions. Andy wanted to continue being leader of the band and in full control both financially and creatively. He didn't want to give an inch – just in case he lost control, I guess. I am not the kind of person to settle for that on an ongoing basis and it would have been very much against the grain for me to be back in the band, yet employed by Andy Powell as a sideman. It wasn't that it necessarily offended my ego, but it just wasn't right. It is just not tenable for Andy Powell to be calling up any of the members of the classic line-ups and asking us to get involved on the basis of him being in control and paying the wages. It's an insult, and demonstrates a complete lack of respect. That was not the way the band worked in the seventies and even when Ted and I rejoined the band in the late eighties after some time away, it was certainly never a case of Andy and Steve, as the mainstays at that time, "employing" us. Instead we formed a new company to handle the reformed band's business on an equity share basis. What Andy was looking for was a band of "yes-men" who could step into his travelling show at short notice to help him fulfil his commitments and so he formed another new line-up which included the return of my old mate Ray Weston – who, somewhat ironically, I had been instrumental in getting into the band several years earlier.

> **RAY WESTON:** *I bumped into Mike Sturgis at the Cafe De Paris in London. He was playing with Wishbone and looking for a sub to fill in. I'm not sure if Andy calling me was connected, but he telephoned asking if I could take the chair for some UK dates. Mike was taking over as head of the percussion department at Guildford Academy of Music. My subbing went on a while longer! I could see it was very much Andy's operation by now.*

Since 1998 Andy's roster of musicians has included bassist Bob Skeat, guitarists Mark Birch, Ben Granfelt and Muddy Manninen, and drummers Ray Weston and Joe Crabtree. Ray remained with Andy until 2007.

> **RAY WESTON:** *Andy called me a couple of weeks after the 2007 German tour thanking me for my loyalty and contribution but telling me that he was looking for another drummer. I*

was fine with it. The fun was lost for me, and had been for a while especially after Ben Granfelt left. As well as being a great guitar player and writer, he brought energy and woke us all up! I was totally bummed when he left. I should have left then too.

Over the past few years Andy has taken his vision of Wishbone Ash forwards with a series of album releases and a busy touring schedule. Now, I have the utmost respect for Andy's musical ability and I do admire his work ethic. There are also some songs from his output that I have enjoyed – in particular some of his collaborations with Roger Filgate and Ben Granfelt. However, having said that, I do believe that the feel of the original band is often lacking and I would have to say that certain album releases have undoubtedly damaged the band's reputation and confused the public. In particular, the two albums of trance music released during the late nineties – *Trance Visionary* and *Psychic Terrorism*. For the uninitiated these releases feature "drum and bass" dance music tracks laced with loops and samples from Wishbone Ash's classic recordings and bear little resemblance to what most would regard as the classic Wishbone Ash sound. People have come to me and said they bought those albums because they were Wishbone Ash projects and were disappointed to find that the music bore no resemblance to the Wishbone Ash they knew and loved. I'm all for left field projects and experimentation to a certain degree but to put those albums out with the name Wishbone Ash on was one step too far for me. I also strongly believe that *Psychic Terrorism* ranks as the most disgusting album title I have ever heard. I was quite appalled to see such an offensive title like that associated with the name Wishbone Ash – it borders on evil. My voice was also used on one of the albums as a sample, without my permission. Andy didn't ask me if he could use my voice – maybe he felt he didn't have to. Once again, a distinct lack of respect was shown. I'm not one to bear a grudge but when you've been on the receiving end of this kind of treatment for so long, you do reach a point where you say "Enough".

CHAPTER FIFTEEN

Walking The Reeperbahn

WHILE THERE was no new Wishbone Ash recording project for me in 1996, I did manage to put together my solo album *Walking The Reeperbahn*. For this I decided to re-assess some of the recordings I had stockpiled over the years – in particular songs that had been recorded with my band the Wolf Gang. I also had some newer compositions that I had written and recorded since the second split with Wishbone Ash. The Wolf Gang recordings had been filed away for several years, but I wanted to take another look at them to see if there was anything there that could be worked with. Reviewing the music all those years later, it was clear there were some decent recordings in there that deserved to be available to the Wishbone Ash fan-base, who during my years not playing with the band had constantly requested some solo music. However, I didn't want to just release the recordings as they stood, as there were areas in which I felt they could be improved upon. In particular I was very keen to get Robin Berlin involved – a very tasteful lead guitar player who I had worked with on the Roy Hollingworth album – as, with all due respect to Stewart MacKenzie's interesting and atmospheric guitar work on the Wolf Gang tracks, the music also needed some orthodox rock guitar and I knew Robin could provide this missing link. I had also met a guy in Southfields called Steve Williams – a very respected drummer who had played with artists such as the Human League and Midge Ure. I got him to come down to my home studio to record new drums tracks on a couple of tunes which had originally been recorded to a drum machine. I also got my brother Glenn involved. Using Steve, Glenn and Robin's contributions, we were able to make the music sound a little more up to date and, in retrospect, I wish I had done that on more of the songs, some of which had been recorded as demos with me playing all the instruments. Having said that, despite these perhaps lacking a little in polish, they do have a certain feel, of which I am quite fond – technical quality is not always everything.

To a certain degree, the *Walking The Reeperbahn* album had the kiss of the eighties, mainly due to the use of the keyboard sounds of the day, which do tend to date it a little bit. The album dives off in a few different directions musically, but as a record of what I was doing during my spells away from Wishbone Ash, I believe it stands up well. Most of the music on there was not written with Wishbone Ash in mind and the instrumentation is different, but I still think it contains the same melodic and creative qualities that I brought to Wishbone Ash and I was glad to finally have this material available.

The album opened with 'Fire Sign', which was the Wolf Gang's version of the song I had originally recorded with Wishbone Ash during the *No Smoke Without Fire* sessions. Like many songs on the album, it had been recorded as a band – in this case featuring Ray Weston on drums, Stewart MacKenzie on guitar and Eryl Price-Davies on keyboards – at my home studio at 59 East Sheen Avenue, back in the early eighties. My studio was located around the corner in a room that was separate from the rest of the house. I also had a pretty decent sized bathroom upstairs in the house that we would use to record drums, with cables running in from the studio. That is where Ray played the drums on this track and others on the album – I can hear the ambience of that room on the recording. It was an unusual set-up in that the rest of us had no visual communication with Ray, but it worked really well. We approached the song a little different from the Wishbone Ash version, which was quite relaxed, whereas the version recorded with my band had a more up-tempo feel and featured synths, arguably making it a lot more modern and more in keeping with the time-frame in which it was recorded.

The title track 'Walking The Reeperbahn' was a much later recording, originally conceived and recorded as an instrumental during the early nineties. When I was having a meeting about the album release with my good friend and then manager Nick Lyne, we went through all the tracks to try to find a title. Nick quizzed me about all the songs and when we got to 'Walking The Reeperbahn', he said "That sounds interesting – could we have that as the album title?" to which I replied "Not really, because it's an instrumental." So he said "Couldn't you write a lyric for it? What is the Reeperbahn, anyway?" So I explained to him that the Reeperbahn is a great long street in Hamburg where all the music clubs are – Wishbone used to play there and the Beatles also played some of their most famous early gigs at the Star Club there – and it is also Hamburg's red light district. So Nick said "Great, that's perfect. For the cover we could have a picture of you talking to a couple of tarts." So, I went home and thought about it and then went into my studio try to figure out how I could write a lyric around the music that I'd already recorded. I thought it was going to be a tall order, but it actually wasn't that difficult. I thought back to times I had spent in Hamburg and remembered that the last time we had played there, I had talked to a girl who worked in a restaurant there. The band had arrived early, I got talking to her and we ended up going for a walk along the Reeperbahn. We didn't know each other, but by the time we'd gotten to the end of the Reeperbahn, she'd told me about her life and I'd told her about mine and we were getting on really well. After that she went to work, I went to do the gig and we never met again – it was just a brief meeting of minds. The lyric was written partly about that but also about the sights and sounds of the Reeperbahn in general. I refer to the fact that the Beatles started there and I also talk of the "thrill seekers" – the people who come from all over the place to the club district in search of a good time. Then of course there are the "hookers" – girls used to come from all over Europe to work there, the whole attitude to prostitution in Germany being more relaxed, with it legal and government sponsored and all the girls getting regular medical checks. When we used to play there we would talk to them and got on great with them. I've been back more recently and the Russian mafia have moved in and it's got quite seedy, but back then it was a fantastic place. In the last verse I refer to "Sex and drugs and rock 'n' roll", which you can't really avoid there. The closing line is "It's time to say gutun arbend", which literally means "Good evening". What I wanted to say was "Good night", but "Gute Nacht" wouldn't sing very well, sounding more like a barking dog. I had played all of the instruments on the track myself, but towards the end of putting the album together, just before we mixed it, I got Robin Berlin to put the lead guitar on, while Steve Williams provided live drums. I thought Robin played some fantastic lead guitar lines on that track, while Steve's drumming had a lovely feel – a very instinctive player.

'Hot Surrender' was a song I had originally wanted to call 'I Surrender', but at the time there was also a band called I Surrender, who I had done some production work with, and so I changed it to avoid confusion. Lyrically, it's quite a heavy song for me as it deals with the time when Susie and I had first met and had fallen in love. I was still married to Maurn at the time, and for a few years Susie and I tried to leave each other alone. I attempted to sort my life out and let her get on with hers and it wasn't until a few years later that we finally got together – there's a lot of emotion in there for me. This one was recorded by Eryl-Price Davies, Stewart MacKenzie and myself, originally with a drum machine. Again, we got Steve Williams to record live drums prior to mixing and he did a great job. I also got Susie's daughter Annalise to put some backing vocals on the song.

'My Brother' is a very simple song, built on a very basic structure – sometimes simplicity is beauty. It was written around the time that my brother Kim announced that he was going to get married. His bride to be, Kathy, was from a New York Italian family and we all knew they would one day live in the States. They did spend a few years in London, but eventually ended up living in Long Island. Kim was much loved in our family and we all knew that he was going to be moving away. The song displays mixed emotions, as on the one hand we were all pleased for Kim and wanted to be there at the wedding – for which we all travelled out to New York – yet at the same time we were all going to miss him. I played everything on that song – it's basically a rough demo, but it has a certain feel that I like.

1996

'Strangers' came from an idea by Eryl Price-Davies. He wrote most of the lyric, although I contributed to the chorus. It was recorded by Eryl, Stewart MacKenzie, "Brown Rice" Tim Broughton and myself and we did a lot of jamming on this one to try to get the feel right – it has some nice spontaneous freedom. There are two notes on the guitar after the first chorus that are very "Ennio Morricone" – they sound like something out of a spaghetti western. Stewart was great at putting in little touches like that – he was a very original player. This was one of the last recordings from the East Sheen Avenue days. It's quite a haunting song and one of my favourite recordings from that time.

'Psychic Flash to Ginza' is an instrumental I recorded during the early nineties. It started off as me playing a strange bass-line along with an early programmable Roland drum machine. It sounds nothing like a drum kit, but that is what gives the piece such an unusual feel. I added keyboards and had some melody ideas for a guitar part, which the piece was really crying out for, and I got my brother Glenn to play on it. He put down some wonderful guitar on what was the first time we'd played together on a recording since the Empty Vessels days. The tune attempts to capture the mood of a dream I'd had at home in the mid-seventies about being threatened and hounded by the police. I was trapped in a room and couldn't get out. This actually did take place about a week later on the other side of the world, in Japan – see earlier.

'You' was the original recording of the song that appeared on Wishbone Ash's *Strange Affair* album. This version was recorded by Eryl Price-Davies, Stewart MacKenzie, Ray Weston and myself a few years earlier and has some subtle differences. It's one of my favourite songs self-penned songs, although I was never totally happy with either the Wishbone Ash recording or this one. As explained earlier it's an important song for me, with a lot of emotional content that reflects the maelstrom that was my life at the time I wrote it.

'Passion' is really quite different for me, having an almost dance-like groove. This one comes from towards the end of the Wolf Gang period and was recorded by Eryl, Stewart, Tim and myself. In the eighties I was experimenting with synthesisers, drum machines and different grooves. Not being in Wishbone Ash allowed me the opportunity to try different things and I believe I gained positively from this as a musician. Once again Susie was on my mind when I wrote the lyrics, which are quite romantic and sentimental, which kind of adds a bit of balance after the bitchiness of the previous song. Being a Libran I always seem to want to balance things.

'Lean On Me' is a cover of the Bill Withers song, which I felt had a great sentiment – very human and positive. It's a song that has been recorded in a lot of different styles over the years, but I wanted to do a rock version of it. I think if you're going to do a cover you have to make it belong to you – there's no point in copying the original. Stewart plays a nice guitar solo on it – very melodic and probably the closest thing he ever got to a conventional guitar solo. I also think the drum and bass groove between "Brown Rice" Tim and myself is really nice and there's also a keyboard part from Eryl in there that's reminiscent of Marianne Faithfull's song 'The Ballad of Lucy Jordan', from her *Broken English* album, which I was always very fond of.

'Kelly's Away With The Fairies" has a crazy, bizarre lyric, full of little phrases just pulled out of the air. The song is a kaleidoscope of all the crazy things that were going on in my life around the time I wrote it back in the early eighties. This particular recording features Ray Weston, Eryl Price-Davies and Stewart MacKenzie, but we did actually re-record the track as an instrumental with Wishbone Ash for the *Nouveau Calls* album in 1987, where it took on the title 'Something's Happening in Room 602'.

'Where Will I Go When I Die?' – now there's a question! The track is not intended to be taken too seriously. It's just me having a little chat with my maker, and there are some quite comical lyrics in there. This recording was actually a demo from the early eighties with me playing everything. We actually did another recording of it with the Wolf Gang and, although it was of better quality technically, I felt the demo has a much better feel.

'The Naked Truth' is actually my original version of 'In The Skin'. It was written as 'In The Skin' just after I was sidelined from Wishbone Ash in 1980 and recorded by Eryl, Ray, Stewart and myself around 1982. Years later it was, of course, adapted by Wishbone Ash for *Nouveau Calls* and so when we came to putting out my solo album we changed the title. It was the first song I wrote after parting with Wishbone in 1980. It's about being out there on my own, feeling somewhat naked, which is both a challenge and, at the same time, exciting. The song does also have a spiritual dimension and represents freedom, as well as a certain degree of sadness and apprehension. As with all the songs on this album, it's a document of the time it was written in.

'Heaven Is' was basically a jam session recorded by Andy Powell, Steve Upton and myself during the *Here To Hear* sessions late one night. I wanted Andy to get a little Jeff Beck-y here and he really got into that spirit and plays some very nice guitar here. It's quite spontaneous and we only did a couple of takes at the most. We didn't use it on the album at the time and it never really found a home on a Wishbone Ash album, so I popped it on my album instead. A few years later it did actually get added to the CD reissue of *Here To Hear* but at the time of my album release it was still something of a lost gem that I felt would be interesting for fans to hear.

'Broken Down House' closes the album and was written about the place where much of the music on this album was conceived and recorded. It was an odd place but that's what I loved about it. When we first arrived there in 1978 the roof was leaking in about a dozen places – the place really was "broken down". I have fond memories of times spent at that house with Maurn and our first daughter Jessica, as well as working in the studio that I'd built there. The song is basically me laying down an idea that I had as a demo. I liked the sound of it and didn't really feel the need to re-record it, although Robin Berlin did add some lead guitar much later. The mix is quite busy, but that reflects the way the house was – spacious and with a lot going on.

I was really pleased to have *Walking The Reeperbahn* out. Although some of the music has a different feel to what many perceive as the traditional Wishbone Ash sound, I stand by the material for its melodic content and its relevance to the point in my life at which the songs were written. My songs generally reflect whatever is happening in my life at a particular time, and this album is an important part of my life journey. Generally it was well accepted and I think a lot of people enjoyed hearing me making music in a different context to Wishbone Ash. I would like to mention that the "working girls" on the album sleeve are in fact the lovely Yenka Honig, a friend of Susie's daughter Annalise, and Yvonne, a friend of Susie's niece, Nicola. To my knowledge neither has followed the oldest profession.

By 1999, I had become friendly with a guy who lived in Southfields called Keith Chapman – the creator of *Bob the Builder* and other children's television programmes. One night I was at his house and he introduced me to an old friend of his called Simon Burrett. Simon told me about his band – a blues/rock outfit called the Blue Bishops. He gave me a CD to listen to and invited me to a live gig. I enjoyed the energy of the band on stage but felt their CD didn't really capture this live energy. I offered to get involved in producing a recording session for them to see if I could help them capture the excitement of their live show. Around this time their bass player left the band and Simon asked me if I could play a few gigs with them to help them fulfil their existing commitments. I agreed to help, thinking that it would just be on a temporary basis, until they got a permanent bass player. Little did I know that this band would be part of my life for the next seven years.

With Simon Burrett of the Blue Bishops, 1999

Photo by Simon Redley

The Blue Bishops were a great bunch of guys and quite a diverse set of characters and players. Simon Burrett was a great slide player, Big Bob Sellins was a big grizzly bear of a man – another fantastic guitar player with a deep, gruff voice. John Fisher was a rock solid drummer and I particularly liked Geoff Grange, the band's front-man – a great singer who was particularly good on the harmonica – or "gob iron" as he called it. We did have some personnel changes along the way, with Bob Sellins eventually leaving and John Fisher being replaced by Justin Hildreth.

Geoff Grange hailed from Hartlepool and was a through and through English rhythm 'n' blues man. They don't come any better than Geoff and I particularly enjoyed his dry sense of humour. One day I was travelling with him down to the West Country to play a gig. We were driving along the A303 past Stonehenge when all of a sudden Geoff said "Look at that bloody mess those builders have left over there". I was laughing at that for days. It also turned out that we had a connection that dated back to the early Wishbone days. I'd been playing in the band for some time when, while travelling in the van, Geoff said to me "My brother used to work with Wishbone Ash". I said "Really? Who was that then?" He replied "His name's Alan but you probably know him as Granny". Granny was a brilliant bloke who had worked with us back in the seventies. I couldn't believe it, but then I looked at Geoff closely and I could see a resemblance.

Life on the road with the Bishops – touring in their van which was fondly known as the Turdis – was always great fun and, as Simon Burrett remembers, there were certainly many adventures along the way, particularly when we travelled into Europe.

> **SIMON BURRETT:** *Most of what I remember – when I actually do remember – is about the laughs. The band members have always shared a sense of humour – Martin was no exception. I knew Martin was a fully-fledged member of the Blue Bishops*

when he started carrying his own gear! A seasoned tourer, he has never been backwards in coming forwards with tales of the road, for the road, and hot tips and advice. One of his big things is passports. Every tour Mart would always remind us of the need to make sure we had our passports – not that we needed reminding. However, we would politely accept the advice for the umpteenth time without complaint. So there we are in the Fabulous Turdis, an ex-old people's home mini-bus from Burnham-on-Sea, rattling along towards Dover doing at least forty-five breathtaking miles an hour, when Mart realises he hasn't got his passport. Emergency stop! Everything is turned out – pockets, coat, jacket, cases unloaded and searched – no passport. A phone call reveals Mart's passport is still comfortably at home with its feet up in Guildford. That's where the good offices of my then wife Sue kick in. We managed to get her on the mobile in Herne Hill, where I was then living. She dropped everything, drove from South London to Guildford, picked up the offending item, then drove all the way to Kent to a lay-by just outside the port, where we met and she handed it over. By some miracle we made the ferry and the tour went off brilliantly. Mart never mentioned passports ever again. But we did, whenever we possibly could!

I didn't get involved vocally with the Bishops, other than singing back-up at live shows, for a number of reasons. Firstly, I viewed it very much as their band and me as a temporary member. Secondly, Geoff was a great vocalist and front-man in his own right and was perfect for the bands style of music. Simon and Bob also took turns on vocals. Once I got involved gig promoters were naturally keen to publicise my involvement and the Wishbone Ash connection in order to maximise on ticket sales and, after a while, quite a few Wishbone Ash fans would turn up at shows. Understandably they

Photo by Simon Redley

With Geoff Grange of the Blue Bishops, 1999.

would ask me to play Wishbone Ash songs. We talked about the possibility of putting in a couple of Wishbone numbers – songs like 'Jailbait' that would have sat well with the Bishops' bluesy repertoire – but to me it didn't seem right and we all agreed we didn't want to go down that road. Inevitably once we put a couple of Wishbone songs in, people would have wanted more, which would not have been fair on the other guys. The Blue Bishops was their band and I was happy to be involved as bass player and producer. I certainly didn't want to be seen to be taking over.

The Blue Bishops' album *Deep* was released in 2002. Although it was a studio album, I approached the production with a focus on trying to capture the band's live energy. I was pleased with the way it turned out. I think there are some great songs on there and some great playing from the entire band. We also had Martin Barre from Jethro Tull guest with us on one track – a really super guy and a fantastic player.

The Blue Bishops was never a full time band. Everyone else had other jobs and the band only gigged on an occasional basis, but I grew very fond of the guys over a period of time and, for me, working with them actually reawakened my love of performing live music. Over the years I had become more and more engrossed in studio work. Now, I love working in the studio, but when you haven't played live for a while, you do tend to lose a bit of perspective – you need both things really. However, as much as I loved the Bishops, there was always an understanding that my involvement was on a temporary basis. My first love remained the music of Wishbone Ash and it had always been my intention to eventually get a band together to perform Wishbone Ash music. That took me a few years...

The year of 2001 marked a big change for my family, as we relocated to Guildford, Surrey. The main reason for this was that Susie had started a business in Guildford and after a while it became apparent that commuting to work each day from south west London was going to be a pretty heavy ordeal. Susie's business, specialising in alternative medicine and natural remedies, would become a huge part of our lives, and I was fully supportive of her new career. In fact this is something I've always had an interest in and I would eventually become completely signed up to alternative medicine – herbal remedies, reiki, acupuncture, etc. In fact, these days I very rarely take pharmaceutical drugs at all. With prescription drugs there's always a price to pay – particularly the side effects and risk of addiction. Having lived and travelled in America, I've seen how it's become very much part of the American culture, due to the sheer power of the multi-national drug corporations, who brainwash people from birth to believe that if they have anything wrong with them then they need one of their products. The whole pharmaceutical industry is very cynical and I try to avoid it. I hardly ever go to the doctor and I avoid hospitals like the plague. In recent years homeopathy has got a pretty bad press but it's worked for me on a number of occasions. Alternative medicine is a whole subject in itself that I could talk about for hours.

SUSIE TURNER: *When I turned fifty I embarked on a huge adventure, opening a franchise of Neal's Yard Remedies in Guildford, Surrey. Within months I had realised the commute was crazy, and that our children would benefit so much from a move away from Southfields, where our neighbourhood had changed, with frequent causes for concern including the violent mugging of a female neighbour right outside our house. We found a home on a hill with endless views to the Surrey Hills and I dragged the boys, kicking and screaming, from the ghetto – Martin being one of them! We all adapted well to our Aga Saga and Martin discovered the many reasons why so many of his ilk have settled in the surrounding countryside. Drummers turned polo players, heavy rock guitarists opening garden fetes – it is a coming of age which makes some sense! I am in my shop most days and cannot envisage a time when I will not run a business. The whole family have embraced natural medicine to varying degrees – Martin is an absolute convert! We have therapy rooms and both enjoy regular massages and treatments from the wonderful friends I work with every day.*

In the summer of 2002, my brother Kim became ill with a chest cough which wouldn't go away. He came up to London for the first of many tests and was eventually diagnosed with cancer. Throughout the winter and early spring of 2003 he fought a noble battle with the support of a great team from the London Clinic as well as his many friends and family. His former wife, Kathy brought their daughters, Stevie and Jaimie, from New York to be with him and Sting very kindly lent his lovely home in Highgate so that everyone could be together and close to the hospital. Kim was upbeat and determined to win the battle and it was hard to believe he might fail until close to the end when he moved down to Rowcroft Hospice in Torquay, close to the home he shared with Joann, his wife. The care he received there was incredible and he passed away peacefully on 12 May 2003. A few days before he died Sting had visited at night, knowing he would be on the road for a while and worried that his old buddy might not be with us much longer. Sting sat at his bedside, although Kim was asleep most of the time by now. Trudie told us at Kim's funeral that Sting had returned in the early hours and sobbed in her arms, knowing he had just said goodbye to Kim. That really touched us all – Sting is a sensitive and caring guy and my brother was part of his life for many years.

Losing Kim was devastating to me – he had been my baby brother, my first experience of caring for a small child. We had shared a lot of music and family life and I was very proud of all his achievements with The Police and, later, Sting – not bad for a kid who left school with no qualifications. It took me a long time to come to terms with the loss and it is particularly hard to think of my Mum losing a son. She is always really brave, but I know she thinks about him every day. His daughters are both beautiful and successful and a real credit to their mum – he would be so proud of them. At the time, I thought that I had tip-toed through the mine-field and dealt with it all reasonably well, but no, I found out years later when the grief came pouring out, so painful but so important to express. Methinks us English folks are all a bit stiff upper lip and not the best at dealing with the "grief" emotion. I do believe his spirit is still with me and I know he watches and helps me to make the best decisions in my life.

In August that year Susie also lost her Mum to cancer and she and Mimi spent a lot of the summer in the US caring for her in her final illness. The following January, Susie's Dad also lost his battle with cancer. It was an absolutely brutal year – the attrition in our families was paralysing for a while.

As always the music was there to help the healing process and the spring of 2004 saw the release of *Lost Pearls,* a CD collection of previously unreleased Wishbone Ash songs, dating mainly from the *No Smoke Without*

Fire and *Just Testing* sessions. Andy Powell had located the masters of some of these recordings, while I also had some in my archives, and a deal had been struck with Talking Elephant records for a release of this long lost material. My involvement as producer of this project came about after Andy and his band appeared at Guildford Civic Hall during the autumn of 2003. On this occasion, Andy's bass player Bob Skeat had to pull out of the gig at the last minute due to his partner getting taken seriously ill. So here was Andy in Guildford, about ten minutes from where I live, in desperate need of a bass player. So what did he do? Call me? Not this time. Instead he called Graham Smith, the bass player from Wishbone Ash tribute band Ashbone U Wish. Ray Weston invited Susie and myself to the show. By this stage I didn't have any real desire to go to see the band but Susie suggested that we go down and have a look. As I walked into the Civic Hall I thought to myself "Wow, that sounds a bit more like the Wishbone Ash I know", and then as I looked at the stage I noticed the bass player had got himself a Gibson Thunderbird bass guitar like mine. Then as I looked closer I realised that it wasn't the regular bass player, but Graham from Ashbone U Wish. I actually thought he did a really good job, although as usual I ended up listening to a few songs before concluding that while it was nice to hear the songs played live, it didn't quite have the spirit that I felt it should and ended up heading for the bar. While there I got delayed by a fan who steamed into me saying "Martin, what do you really think of Andy's band? There's something missing, ain't there?" So I agreed "Yeah, I suppose there is something missing." Then he replied "I know what it is – it's YOU!" The things these punters come out with! I hung around after the show and went up to the front of the stage as everyone was clearing away, giving Graham the shock of his life when I shouted up to him "Oi, can I have your autograph, mate?!" After the show I went backstage to say "hi" to everyone, which was pleasant enough, and then as we were leaving the venue Susie casually dropped a little surprise on me – "I've invited everyone back to the house, darling."

That night at my place was when Andy started talking to me about the *Lost Pearls* project. They'd had somebody mix the recordings and it just didn't sound right, so Andy asked me if I would be interested in getting involved. I said "Sure, send it over to me and I'll have a listen". When they sent me a disc I just couldn't believe my ears. Somebody had sat in a studio and mixed these recordings that had DBX noise reduction on

Photo by Laureen Large

On stage with the Blue Bishops, 2005.

them. Now, DBX noise reduction is severe. It totally trashes the sound and leaves it very mid-rangy and compressed. The recordings basically needed decoding, which I knew I would be able to do, and so I said to Andy, "Send me the masters and I'll straighten it out."

All of the songs featured on *Lost Pearls* were essentially outtakes – songs that had not been proceeded with and had been left in various stages of completion. Most of them were unfinished and demanded a lot of work before they were useable. I had to muster all my "wizard" energy to make those tracks sound good - they required a lot of repair work. For example, in one instance on one of my songs called 'Football and Boxing' I even had to re-record the lead vocal because the lyric had only been partly written and by the third verse I was singing a load of rubbish. So here I was nearly 25 years after the original recording finishing off the lyric and re-recording the lead vocal. Obviously it's an album aimed more at the diehard Wishbone

Ash collector rather than the mainstream fan and I guess you have to be pretty committed to want to listen to an album of previously unreleased tunes. Overall I was pleased with the way the album came out. I even got the album finished in time to coincide with Andy's Spring 2004 UK tour.

With *Lost Pearls* completed I think Andy figured that having worked on the final unreleased Wishbone Ash recordings, I had done all that I could do as far as archival material goes and had therefore outlived my usefulness. Andy's been a fine weather friend in that respect – he only comes to me when he needs something – but at least calling him a "friend" is better than the way he refers to me these days, which is as the enemy and someone he is at "war" with!

At this point we entered into a whole new situation...

CHAPTER SIXTEEN

Phoenix Rising

I WOKE UP one morning during July 2004 to a nice little letter from Andy Powell's lawyers Walker Morris, demanding that I surrender to Mr. Powell my website domain name www.wishboneash.co.uk, which I had legitimately registered, and which offered an excellent array of historical information on the band's classic years as well as information on my activities and also other members of Wishbone Ash through the years. They requested that I sign an undertaking never to use the name Wishbone Ash in any capacity again. Furthermore they insisted that I pay their client's costs relating to this matter. I was absolutely gobsmacked by the sheer lack of soul displayed by Andy Powell. Just a few months previously, he had sat in my house drinking my wine, eating my food and playing my instruments and I had done him a massive favour in putting together an album in time for his tour. So what does he do? Turns around and stabs me in the back – which is the only way I can describe it – by threatening me with legal action. He has since denied ever taking legal action against me, but what else can you call a lawyer's letter making such unreasonable demands? I'd certainly never encountered anything like this in my entire professional career and really had no idea how to deal with such action. I spoke to various people about it and eventually, through my webmaster and long-time confidante Gary Carter, I was put in touch with Martin Darvill at QEDG Management. Martin was a lifelong fan of Wishbone Ash and was already managing another ex-Wishbone Ash member in John Wetton. Together with Gary's invaluable input as probably the leading Wishbone Ash historian and archivist, Martin helped me respond. During the course of meetings around this time, we also discussed the idea of me taking a Wishbone Ash band on the road. This was something that had been on my mind for several years and fans had certainly been requesting for me to start performing Wishbone Ash music again. In particular I was keen to explore the full extent of the band's catalogue, including songs that had never been played live before. However, this project had not yet come to fruition, mainly due to me not having access to the right musicians and the infrastructure needed to launch such a project in a fully professional manner. Martin was keen to help facilitate this and help get me back out on the road.

We responded to Mr. Powell's lawyer's letter stating that we would not be surrendering the domain name or complying with any of their requests. They then put in a complaint to Nominet – the UK internet domain name registry – claiming that my registration of the www.wishboneash.co.uk domain name was "abusive" and "misleading". Mr. Powell's team filed a complaint to which we were given the chance to respond, which we did. The Nominet procedure allowed Mr. Powell, as the complainant, to respond to our defence, which he did. This response, to which the procedure did not allow us the privilege to answer, contained a number of mistruths, which I thought was pretty low. We then entered into a period of "mediation" through Nominet, which basically consisted of a mediator calling me up and asking me if I would be prepared to surrender the domain name in return for a sum of money, to be negotiated. I responded by asking them to go back to Mr. Powell and tell him that I did not want his grubby money and that I would be fighting this on a matter of principle. So, off the guy went with a flea in his ear. With us unable to reach an agreement, both Mr. Powell and I signed an agreement that the matter would be passed to an independent expert adjudicator and that we would both be bound by his decision. Prior to reviewing the case, the expert was compelled to reveal to Nominet if he felt there was any factor which would prevent him from reviewing the case in an objective manner. To that end, he felt obliged to inform Nominet that he had seen Wishbone Ash perform live in the seventies and owned one of our albums. Both Mr. Powell and I had the opportunity to decline his involvement if either of us felt this would prejudice the case in any way, but neither of us had any problem with it – in fact, I thought better still that the person adjudicating knew a bit about the band's history. The outcome was that Mr. Powell's complaint failed, with the expert feeling that parts of the "evidence" presented by Mr. Powell were somewhat orchestrated and that what he was trying to do was use the Nominet procedure to carry out a fully fledged band name ownership complaint on the cheap, rather than in a court of law where it truly belonged.

I am not usually one to bear grudges, but the working relationship between Andy and myself, I am saddened to say, was changed forever by this confrontational and extremely unpleasant turn of events. Up to that point I had always been open to future collaboration and had, at the back of my mind, always thought that Wishbone Ash in one of its most recognised forms could re-group at some point in the future. Indeed this was another reason why I had held off forming a band of my own for so long. Sadly this unfortunate development was instrumental in me coming to the conclusion that any future work I did in this the context of Wishbone Ash would need to be done independently of Mr. Powell and that I needed to put together my own version of Wishbone Ash. It had also become obvious to me around this time, through a great many other signs, that my destiny still laid with the music of Wishbone Ash and that I would have been a fool not to act on this, especially as so many of the songs contain the emotional energy which had been my life.

With the whole Nominet enquiry behind me, I began formulating plans to form a new band. If I was to be forming a band to play Wishbone Ash music, it was important to me that the musicians involved had the right feel for the band's music, as I was very keen to get back to something that resembled the sound of the definitive years of the band – something I felt latter day line-ups had moved away from. I was not necessarily looking for big name players, but obviously the people involved needed to have the technical ability required to perform the music.

Through the Blue Bishops, I had met a man named Simon Redley. He was managing a British country singer called Lucy Diamond. Simon asked me to have a listen to what they had recorded and to tell him what I thought. I told him that I thought the songs sounded good, with commercial potential, as did the playing, but I did criticise the way her voice had been recorded and felt that overall the music needed a really good producer. After I'd offered my critique, Simon said "I feel exactly the same as you do, so how about you getting involved?" So, I got involved in some of their recording sessions and I could feel instinctively that this was important and was something I should do. I didn't really know why I was doing it, as it wasn't really my kind of music, but I found them interesting as people and I did quite a bit of work with them. One day I arrived at a session to be told by Simon that he had a pedal steel guitar playing coming down later that day. I asked "Is he an American?" Simon said "No, this guy is English." I thought to myself "English pedal steel player? I'll believe that when I see it" because the pedal steel is traditionally an American instrument. Anyway, this guy turned up at the studio and did an excellent job on the pedal steel. Then they asked him to play a lead guitar solo. He picked up a six-string and started playing away, again doing an excellent job. Later in the day I got talking to him in the control room and he said "Actually, Martin, your guitar player Laurie Wisefield is probably my biggest influence and actually got me playing guitar." So I replied "Really? That's interesting. So, you're familiar with Wishbone Ash's material then?" He said "Oh yeah, absolutely." So I said "Maybe you and I need to talk. Can you play the guitar solo in a song called 'Persephone'?" He replied "That's a tricky one". I said "Yeah, that's why I'm asking you." So he said "As a matter of fact, Martin, yes I can." So I replied "You and I definitely need to get together." This was my introduction to Keith Buck and effectively the birth of Martin Turner's Wishbone Ash.

KEITH BUCK: *I started playing guitar at the age of ten. My best friend Paul "Ginty" Johnson, who was then eighteen, taught me the basic chords and led me to a love of acoustic music and in particular Cat Stevens. After that I was self taught. My career had been a case of right time, right place, I guess. Also I do believe you make your own luck. I played in a working men's club band at age thirteen, earning enough money to buy my first Gibson SG guitar. I was then in various bands with and without my buddy Ginty and turned pro at the age of seventeen with a country trio call the Rouchelles. I took up the Pedal Steel guitar in 1978 and have continued a love affair with that instrument to this day. I then worked for various TV comedians/celebrities such as Duncan Norvelle, Jim Davidson, etc, doing cabaret session work in theatres while also working on original music with Sally Barker, who is a very successful progressive folk-rock singer (we even supported the original Wishbone Ash during their reunion). After that I had a spell with Alvin Stardust, touring and doing TV work with him for two years.*

Wishbone Ash were one of my favourite bands as a young teen. Live Dates was a template for my learning alongside anything by Free and in particular Paul Kossoff who I loved, but a major turning point in my guitar style was in 1976 when I got to see Wishbone for the first time at Leicester De Montfort Hall on the New England tour. It was Laurie Wisefield who totally blew my mind. I just loved his playing and still do to this day. He had so much of everything I loved about the guitar in his style. He played so tastefully and he also looked amazing. I never got to meet him but would have loved to. I also loved the albums There's The Rub and New England at that time.

Martin was helping produce a modern country album that I was playing guitar and pedal steel on. I knew he was going to be there and was excited to be meeting him. It all went very well. He was really nice to meet – I was a fan.

At that first meeting with Keith, I told him of my plan to put together a band to perform Wishbone Ash material and he said he would love to be involved. We agreed to meet up at some point in the future to discuss things further. However, before we even had a chance to get together, Keith called me up and said "Martin, I don't know why I didn't think of it before, but there's a guy called Rob Hewins, who I work with occasionally. He is a really good drummer, loves your music and would be perfect for this project." So I said "Hold on a minute, Keith. You and I haven't even got together yet and I'm really fussy about drummers." Keith said "Believe me, Martin, this guy would be able to do what is required". Then he called me again and told me of a guitar player he worked with called Ray Hatfield.

Martin Turner's Wishbone Ash Mk.1, Liscombe Park, 2005 –
with Rob Hewins, Keith Buck, and Ray Hatfield.

Photo by Michael Inns

In theory we had the basis of a line-up right there, but I thought to myself "Hang on a minute, this is all coming at me too quickly, let's take it steady." I had always imagined that it would be a tricky job to put a Wishbone Ash band together. The guitar harmonies, for instance, are fairly involved and some are quite similar to others, which does require a functioning memory – so, probably not a job for weed smokers then! I was probably a bit surprised at how easily it all came together and with Keith's help it soon seemed that the road lay before me – I just needed to recognise the signs and make the correct turns.

KEITH BUCK: *Whilst on holiday in Malta I had a telephone conversation with Martin where I said I could find the right people to put the band together and asked "Do you want me to have a go?" He said "Okay." I then called Rob Hewins, who I knew could eat the job alive, and also Ray Hatfield, who I knew to be a reliable pro as well as a great bloke. Rob knew the style very well and Ray and I had already played together for a few years. Even to this day we find it telepathy to play together – it is so easy*

RAY HATFIELD: *I first picked up a guitar at the age of eleven when my older brother came home from school with a cheap Watkins Rapier a friend had swapped with him. He didn't get on too well with the guitar but I loved it from day one and soon began trying to play the hits of the day by bands like T-Rex, Slade and Alice Cooper amongst others. Some of the older guys on the street played guitar at that time and we all swapped licks and ideas and played together in various line ups over the next few years. It seemed there was always some great band or guitar player I'd not heard of in those days and we'd all be recommending stuff to each other. It was a great* *time and place to be learning the guitar. Wishbone Ash had a big influence on me. Andy, Ted and Laurie are amongst my favourite guitar players of all time. I still listen to them often. At the age of twenty-three I studied classical guitar taking Grades 5, 7 and 8. I went on to teach for several years but unfortunately classical and electric guitar don't mix very well for me, and I don't play much nylon string stuff these days. Perhaps I will return to classical guitar later in life. All through my teens and early twenties I was in and out of various hard working bands playing some originals, but mainly covers in the pubs and clubs of the Midlands and north. We would play three or four times a week and had great times on the road at the weekend. I kept body and soul together at that time with a combination of teaching, busking and playing in hotels and restaurants. Around 1986 I joined a band called Arctic Chartre from Derby who wrote great pop tunes and sounded and looked a bit like Duran Duran. We came second in the Melody Maker battle of the bands and were signed up by Gerry Bron of Bronze Records. We recorded at Roundhouse Studios, London at weekends and in down time but were eventually dropped by him. We were so deflated as a band we broke up shortly after.*

Around this time I became involved in producing music, sound effects and occasionally voice-overs for the gaming industry whilst also playing the local circuit. It was also around this time that I heard and introduced myself to Keith Buck when he played one night in my local. We immediately hit it off having grown up to an almost identical soundtrack and became very close friends. When the opportunity arose a few years later to work together we developed quite an understanding on both acoustic and electric which of course helped in the early stages of Martin Turner's Wishbone Ash.

A little later I drove up to the Midlands, where all the guys lived, to meet with them. As I was driving into the area where Keith lived, the first road I went down was called Dryden Road. This immediately reminded me of Dryden Chambers which, in the early days of Wishbone Ash, was where John Sherry had his office. I thought "Is this John, looking down at me from the big gig in the sky, giving me guidance, or is it just coincidence?" Then I turned the next corner and I was in Tennyson Road. Now, 'Tennyson Lines' was a much loved song that I'd recorded with Roy Hollingworth – another rock 'n' roll departee whom I had worked with and was very close to. So I'm thinking "This is getting freaky – this is clearly a very relevant moment". I went into Keith's house and he introduced me to Rob and Ray. I really liked the three of them as people and it was clear they knew a bit about Wishbone Ash music and had a wealth of experience. We didn't actually play much at that first meeting, but agreed to get together to rehearse a few songs. A little later we met up at Rob Hewins' place where he had a rehearsal situation set up. He played an electronic drum kit and we all played through earphones, using little processors rather than big old amplifiers, so that we could play in his front room without causing the walls to crack. We played a few tunes and we all found ourselves laughing out loud at how much like the original Wishbone Ash it sounded, without us ever having played together before. Clearly Rob could play Steve Upton's drum parts perfectly and Keith and Ray certainly had the guitar parts down. It really was effortless and it was clear from the off that we were looking at something that felt natural and had that elusive spark of magic.

RAY HATFIELD: *Rob and I both got involved when Keith Buck recommended us to Martin and we did a sort of combined audition/rehearsal at Rob's studio where we played about four or five tunes together. I remember Martin talking passionately about how he wanted to form a band that could recreate the original Wishbone Ash sound and feel. I remember very early on, Keith and I were travelling back home together and played a CD Rob had mixed of the previous get-together. We both* *realised that Martin's distinctive voice and very unorthodox bass playing would make any two competent guitar players sound like our idea of Wishbone Ash. He's a huge part of what makes it sound authentic.*

KEITH BUCK: *I worked out all the guitar parts, being careful to keep all the Ted Turner and Laurie Wisefield parts for myself! I got together with Ray and we worked though the parts and got though about ten of the main songs. We then ran though them with Rob and then invited Martin up to see what he thought. His exact words after the first practice were "I guess we got a band then!" It sounded great from the first time we played 'The King Will Come' – my favourite – and the vocals also were good as we all sing. Martin seemed very happy with what I had done, so we rehearsed every week for a few weeks with Martin staying at my house and then we presented it to Martin Darvill and Gary Carter at Liscombe Park*

First studio concert with my new band – Liscombe Park October 2005.

Photo by Michael Inns

Liscombe Park, October 2005.

Photo by Michael Inns

We rehearsed intensely throughout the Summer of 2005 both at Rob's house, and also at Martin Darvill's studio at Liscombe Park, Buckinghamshire, where we were able to set up with full kit. The experience was extremely rewarding on both a musical and personal level, with a positive vibe not unlike the early days of Wishbone Ash. Collectively we had a great time revisiting many of the classics from the vintage days of Wishbone Ash, recreating the essence of many songs, some of which had rarely or never been performed live. By the Autumn of 2005 we were ready to start gigging. We previewed our live set at an intimate studio concert in front of a small audience of friends and family at Liscombe Park, followed by a couple of warm-up shows in Measham and Sutton, designed to showcase the band in an intimate setting, ahead of a tour early in 2006. The reaction to the shows was very warm and everyone who saw the band seemed to really enjoy it.

> **KEITH BUCK:** *The first gig I remember being great fun with a great reaction. Also to be able to play with Martin in my home town of Measham after being a fan all my life was a thrill. Even though the gig was a low-key warm-up it was still a great moment for me.*

There was a lot of activity behind the scenes as we prepared to launch the band. I have always maintained that if you want to get anywhere is the music industry you need a solid professional team in place. Some artists prefer to run the business side of things themselves, but personally I'd rather entrust others to take care of that side of things, leaving me free to concentrate on what I do best. Martin Darvill quickly proved to be an extremely capable manager, well versed in all areas of the business. Don McKay came on board as our booking agent while Gary Carter – who had been involved with Wishbone Ash for many years – not only continued to maintain my website, providing that important link between the band and its fans, but also assisted with many other behind the scenes duties. In the early days we also had Laureen Large – who had been involved behind the scenes with the Blue Bishops – assisting us in the PR department, and a little later our concert sound engineer Mick came on board. This transformed our live sound considerably, as it makes such a difference having someone behind the desk who knows the music inside out, rather than relying on in-house engineers – many of whom are young guys who have little understanding of the subtleties that are contained within the music of a band like Wishbone Ash and whose approach to live sound is very much based on sheer volume. On a few occasions where Mick has not been available we have been delighted to have my old friend Mark "Hobbit" Emery behind the controls.

> **MARK EMERY:** *I treasure the days that I had with Wishbone. They were very important days of my life. Working with Martin again recently on occasions has been a real pleasure and if I can be of any assistance in the future, I would be happy to be so. I wish Martin and his band the very best of fortune in the future.*

Compiling the set-list for our first tour was challenging, as there was so much material there to choose from. There are a lot of considerations to take into account when putting a set together and it's important to achieve a balance of mainstream crowd favourites as well as some lesser heard material for our most ardent fans. In our earliest rehearsals it quickly became apparent that we were able to play virtually any song from the back catalogue and get it sounding decent. This was down to the guys alongside me and frankly there are songs that even the Mk.1 and Mk.2 Wishbone Ash line-ups would have been hard pushed to reproduce on stage. Of course the gear we had access to in the seventies was crude in many respects when compared to the mind-boggling array of eletro-gadgetry available now. One big plus with my new band was the vocal ability within the band – Keith, Ray and Rob all had a broad array of talents and were all singers in their own right, and so we were able to reproduce effectively the vocal harmonies from the recordings.

We undertook our first proper UK tour in February 2006, a mix of clubs and small theatre shows. The band was really starting to gel by this point and I have great memories of those shows – launching the band into the public arena and re-connecting with the Wishbone Ash fan-base. Highlights included a packed gig at the Borderline in London as well as a fantastic show at the Roadhouse in Birmingham, where we were joined by none other than my good friend Ted Turner. It's always a pleasure to play with Ted. Even after all these

Photo by Ian Burgess

Keith Buck, Cardiff 2007 – I will be forever grateful for the part he played in helping me form MTWA.

Ray Hatfield, Southend 2006.

years and him having not done a great deal of live work in recent times, he still has that magic touch – the ability to send a shiver up your spine with his playing, particularly when he improvises and hits just the right pattern of notes. That's what makes him a great guitar player. I just wish he'd done more over the years, but instead he got into playing golf! I think Ted really enjoyed playing with the band and he said to me after the show that he'd played with Andy Powell not long before but had felt the spirit and vibe was lacking, yet when he played with our band he found it full of vitality and life. Coming from Ted, I took that as a real compliment. Ted has his own recollections of this show:

> **TED TURNER:** *A cold February evening in my home town, both Mart and I were struggling with a touch of flu. Enthusiasm generated the music. The band members are all cool guys and they are fans of Wishbone. It is obvious they are enjoying their time together with Martin. This created a warm atmosphere for us to share and for them and the audience to see us together*

again. Some things just are – it takes little effort to connect with someone with whom you feel close. Martin and I have such a relationship, and for me this was a real pleasure, like putting on an old shoe. Funny because he now looks like one (laughs)! I remember feeling nervous not having performed much but from the first note I returned to a special place. Sitting backstage listening to others play our music puts it in a different light – interesting how others interpret the music. Subtle changes they make puts focus on the original arrangement and structure for each piece. It is a labor of love on their part. It shows. They are doing a fine job.

RAY HATFIELD: *I remember how it felt when Ted Turner stood on stage with us at The Roadhouse in Birmingham and I got to play the twin guitar part in 'Standing in the Rain.' That was a fantastic feeling. To make it even more special, it was my wife's birthday so my family were there to hear it all as well. Most of that gig later came out on CD and I think the feel-good factor shows.*

KEITH BUCK: *It was a boyhood dream come true for me to stand on the stage with both Turners in Birmingham. I guess that was my favourite gig. Coming from listening and learning in my bedroom to standing with Martin and Ted was a long journey, but I respected them and still do. I loved that moment in Birmingham.*

Ted has appeared with my band on a couple of occasions since and we both keep open the possibility of future live or studio collaborations, should the right set of circumstances present itself.

TED TURNER: *We have proven that working together brings works of quality. I am open to developing new music with Martin. Who knows what is "around the corner"?*

Photo by Maria Lundy

With Laurie Wisefield – Liscombe Park, 2011 –
It's always a pleasure to meet up with my ex-band mates.

Laurie Wisefield has also stated his approval of the songs we were involved in together continuing to be performed on stage and, like Ted, does not rule out the possibility of us working together in the future.

> **LAURIE WISEFIELD:** *It's great the music is living on with whoever is playing it, and that there are people who still want to hear it. I think, above all, there was a lot of integrity in our music and that comes through. As for any reunions, I would never say never. However I always tend to look to the future, so going back to recreate something we have already done and achieved is not especially exciting to me, but something new – much more of a possibility.*

We recorded a lot of material during our shows of 2005/06 for a two-volume live album release. *New Live Dates Vols. 1 and 2* basically comprised of our full live set from that first tour. Much of the material came from the Birmingham show, including Ted's guest appearance, with additional material from other gigs and even a few tracks from our studio concert at Liscombe Park. The albums were designed to give people a taste of what we were all about – a souvenir of the live shows for those who were there

Photo by Laureen Large

Magic night in Birmingham – Ted Turner joins MTWA for the New Live Dates recording – Feb 2006.

as well as something that we could provide to promoters in order to secure work in both the UK and abroad. In that regard, I believe *New Live Dates* served us well, and stands as a useful record of the beginnings of Martin Turner's Wishbone Ash, capturing the raw live energy of our early live performances. The albums contained a diverse range of material – from set list standards such as 'Warrior' and 'Living Proof', through to previously overlooked tunes like 'Silver Shoes', 'Diamond Jack', 'Say Goodbye' and 'Baby

The Angels Are Here' and many others making a first time appearance on a live album. The album also introduced our friend Howard Johnston as sleeve designer and I felt Howard did a really nice job of re-interpreting the classic *Live Dates* themes in a fresh way, making for a very pleasing package. Overall I felt *New Live Dates* looked, sounded and felt like a Wishbone Ash album should.

The only black cloud surrounding the launch of the new band were the "wrecking tactics" employed by Andy Powell and his team. Andy's biggest bone of contention was my use of the name "Martin Turner's Wishbone Ash". A lot of thought was put into choosing the name of my band, and everyone concerned knew that no matter what we called the band, promoters would always attach the words Wishbone Ash to their advertising in order to get as many people through the door as possible – that even happened with the Blue Bishops and the Wolfgang, even though those bands did not play Wishbone Ash music. We felt the best way to describe what we were offering was to use the name Wishbone Ash, but qualify it by using my name as a prefix, leaving those who purchased tickets under no illusion as to what they were going to be getting – i.e. my interpretation of Wishbone Ash music. Andy, however, was absolutely incensed that I'd dared to use the words "Wishbone Ash" within the title of my band, feeling that he had an exclusive right to do so. He felt that we were causing "confusion in the marketplace". How can that be when the title of my band gives a pretty good clue as to who is going to be onstage? Contrast this with the marketing for some of Andy's concerts over the years – I have been sent handbills for concerts of later line-ups stating "Original Wishbone Ash" or "1970s Line-Up" and I have lost count of the number of times that images of myself and the classic line-ups have been used to promote shows on which we were obviously not appearing. Of course, I and the other core members believe it is Andy who is confusing the market place, and he should have called his band "Andy Powell's Wishbone Ash". That's what it is – no confusion there.

Andy's people would contact promoters, telling them that he owned the name Wishbone Ash 100% (untrue!) and that I had no right to perform under the name (also untrue!), but many venues and promoters were clearly intimidated and refused to book us for some time. The reality proved to be that most Wishbone Ash fans were happy to support both bands performing the music and there was clearly room for both Andy and myself in the marketplace. Sadly, Andy didn't see it that way.

For a brief period we reached a "gentleman's agreement" with Andy whereby we would agree to appear as "Wishbone featuring Martin Turner" and, in return, he would agree to certain terms that included, amongst other things, him adding a clear and distinct link to my website on his site and removing the rancorous comments from some of his supporters which were present on his fan forum. He also agreed not to discuss publicly the specifics of the agreement – a clause he contravened the very next day after the agreement had been signed by disclosing the deal at a fan Convention event, prior to an agreed joint announcement date. Several months on, it became apparent that we had been somewhat tricked into making this "gentleman's agreement" and that Andy had no intentions of adhering to his part of the bargain. Instead he appeared to be encouraging a battle of the bands, even declaring that he was at "war" with us on his website – an insult, in my opinion, to those in the world who really are at war and, especially, those who have lost loved ones in conflict. In the end, the "gentleman's agreement", simply didn't work. As such, we reverted to our original chosen name of Martin Turner's Wishbone Ash, as we had said upfront we would do should the agreement fail to be adhered to. Andy Powell has since gone to press with the total mistruth that we changed the name from Wishbone featuring Martin Turner to Martin Turner's Wishbone Ash. That is not so – it was Martin Turner's Wishbone Ash from day one – something we informed Andy of privately as a matter of courtesy as far back as 2004 and still have documentation of.

On stage during the first MTWA tour - Southend, 2006.

Andy Powell bases his claim for exclusive rights to the name Wishbone Ash on his registration of the name, for his own use, as a trademark in 1998. In order to register a trademark, you need to be the original user of the mark. In the case of Wishbone Ash there were four original users – Steve Upton, Ted Turner, Andy Powell and Martin Turner – and one further equity member, Laurie Wisefield. Andy's 1998 registration was made without the consent of the other original users – in fact, without even informing us – and the registration only came to light in 2004 during the Nominet enquiry. While Andy's registration prevents third parties from using the name, it does not prevent use by any co-owner who possesses residual rights to the name. We can all use the name, as we all co-own shares in it – legal precedent going back to the core members who had equity participation. I am constantly reminded of other bands who exist with only one founder member. All examples I'm aware of are different to Wishbone Ash in that other bands have had written agreements regarding use of the name. The name is bought and sold – rights forfeited – and so in many band's cases, one man may own the name outright if he has bought the shares of the other members. In the case of Wishbone Ash, this simply did not happen and there has never been any agreement regarding the name. None of the other core members of the band – Steve Upton, Ted Turner, Martin Turner and Laurie Wisefield – ever gave away or sold their rights. Andy Powell has never paid a penny for our shares and his claim to sole ownership is akin to co-owning a house with three brothers, allowing one brother to remain in the house rent free, and then finding out he is claiming he is the sole owner of the house by virtue of his continued presence. Andy may presently hold the registered trademark, but he is not the sole owner of the name. I am often asked why I chose not to put my share up for sale and I respond that Wishbone Ash is my life. I've never wanted to do anything else and, contrary to what continues to be reported elsewhere, I've never voluntarily left the band. On the contrary, I have always made myself available for Wishbone Ash projects, be it live or studio work.

In an attempt to rectify the trademark issue in a way that none of our rights – including Andy Powell's – went unprotected, Steve, Ted and I proposed to Andy that he should admit us as co-owners of the trade mark. Laurie's rights would also be protected as the only other core member as even though he is not a founder, he was an equity member and therefore owns a share – unlike all subsequent members who have been salaried and were never co-owners of the name. We were all astounded when Andy refused to admit us onto the trade mark he had registered, because the only option available to us would then be to have his registration overturned on grounds of "bad faith", being that he had registered his trademark without seeking consent of all the owners of the name – this could result in the name not being trademarked or protected at all. So, here we are into years of legal procedures at unnecessary cost. It is all going on as I write, and those of us involved are amazed that Andy doesn't agree to do this sensibly. At the end of the day there are five owners of the name. That is a fact, and any other registration is irrelevant.

In addition to his registration of the Wishbone Ash trademark, there have been numerous other business transactions throughout recent years that have given the other core members of Wishbone Ash great cause for concern – in particular, various misrepresentations concerning the licensing of past Wishbone Ash material dating back over a number of years, the full extent of which only really came to light during the Nominet case. Neither Andy's "bad faith" trademark registration nor him being the sole original member in the band that presently performs as "Wishbone Ash" gives him any legal or moral license whatsoever to sign away rights to our collective material or conduct business deals on behalf of the core members, which has been the case on several occasions. There is a whole catalogue of releases out there featuring material performed by the original members, which has been released without our required consent. Andy may well feel he has the right to "exploit" the existing fan-base but he certainly has no right to exploit or otherwise abuse the original band members. We retain the right to exercise control over all co-owned material, on both artistic and business levels and Mr. Powell has denied us this right on several occasions. His moral fibre therefore has to be seriously questioned. The rich body of work we created together back in the days of group democracy and equity membership is not only Andy Powell's lifeblood, but also the lifeblood of the other original members and their families. Does the housekeeper have the right to sell the family silver? We were also astounded to discover that he was using Hipgnosis designs without authority – unlike the use of Hipgnosis designs on our products, for which we have obtained proper licensing and pay an agreed royalty to Storm Thorgerson and Aubrey "Po" Powell, the copyright owners.

We remain willing to talk with Andy and my management – which now also represents Steve, Ted and Laurie, as well as fellow bassists John Wetton and Trevor Bolder, in all Wishbone Ash related matters – has been trying to facilitate this for some time. Andy, however, has to date declined to enter into meaningful negotiations or respond to our not unreasonable request for clarification regarding various seemingly dubious deals, of which pages of examples were sent to him and his lawyers. We were all incensed that it seemed he was also going to labels claiming he had sole rights to our jointly owned Wishbone Ash copyrights. All we want is for Andy to make good the numerous abuses of our jointly owned copyrights. It is somewhat counter-productive of Andy not to communicate with us as he too could benefit greatly were we to form a united front with regard to our shared legacy of recordings. For example, master recordings of our classic albums are owned by Universal – the largest record label in the world. Andy has made it very clear he will not discuss any joint approaches to Universal with respect to our back catalogue. That is a shame, as united we could have a greater influence over album re-issues, marketing opportunities and even possibly look at buying back copyrights to the recordings we created together. My team has an excellent relationship with Universal, Hipgnosis and the major industry players in general, but it would appear that Andy thinks he alone should be seen to be "flying the flag". The rest of us disagree and the consequence of Andy's refusal to join us in our efforts to deal with worldwide abuse of our rights has enabled such abuse to be more prevalent and we are all less financially rewarded than we should be. It has also resulted in Universal being reluctant to get involved in any further reissue programmes while there is such a lack of cohesion between Andy Powell and the other core members of the band. It is a great pity Andy has turned down olive branches relating to jointly protecting the interests that we will always share – the huge creativity of our recorded legacy. Andy fails to see that the ugly dispute aired in public damages the Wishbone Ash brand as a whole. It is ridiculous after our long history that he is seemingly too cowardly to address the outstanding issues. It could all be straightened out in a couple of direct meetings and would probably not require the involvement of Kofi Anan.

Despite the negativity from certain quarters, my band kept a busy schedule with touring. Certainly I was not going to allow Andy Powell's legal posturing to cast a dark cloud over my legitimate musical activities and, as far as I was concerned, I was in this for the long haul. At our shows I was constantly being told by fans I chatted to along the way that they felt we were playing the Wishbone Ash catalogue with the sound and feel that they remembered from the early days of the band and that was extremely motivating and encouraging.

We did, however, have a minor setback along the way towards the end of 2006 when our drummer Rob Hewins broke his collar bone while playing football on astro-turf, something I had requested he avoided doing for precisely the above reason. He was unable to play for a few weeks, leaving us without a drummer and an impending schedule of UK and European shows to play. Needing a drummer to fill in at short notice, I called John Fisher, who I had played with in the Bishops for a few years, although he had parted company with them shortly after the *Deep* album and was by now playing in the band Audience as well as teaching percussion at Canterbury University. John was an excellent drummer and a very accomplished musician overall and was my first choice to fill in for Rob. Thankfully, John was able to get involved and set about learning our whole set in just a few days. We managed to squeeze in just one rehearsal in my studio before the first show and, given the time restraints enforced upon us, John did an excellent job musically and also fitted in with the band very well socially – he got on with everyone and we all liked him immensely. Sadly, within a few months of working with us he got extremely sick and eventually died of cancer in 2008, which was extremely upsetting for all concerned. I am extremely thankful for having had the opportunity to reconnect with John and play some Wishbone Ash music with him, and he did tell me that he got a lot from the experience as well.

Overall the period surrounding the launch of Martin Turner's Wishbone Ash was a very positive time and I was mightily pleased that the elements had all fallen into place. I was extremely happy to be back on the road playing the music that had been such a big part of my life.

CHAPTER SEVENTEEN

Through The Looking Glass

TOURING WITH Martin Turner's Wishbone Ash allowed me to fulfil a long standing ambition – to perform the whole of the *Argus* album on stage. The original band performed most of it, but never played 'Leaf and Stream' and quite often left out the acoustic introduction to 'Time Was'. Back in the seventies it was actually quite difficult to perform quiet, acoustic-based music on stage, with the limitations of the sound technology of the day, whereas today this is much easier to do. Before we announced an *Argus* tour we decided to get together to rehearse the material, just to make sure we were actually able to pull it off. Prior to going to Liscombe Park to rehearse the music, my manager Martin Darvill said to me "While you are rehearsing the album in the studio, wouldn't it be a good idea to record it?" I had a think about this and decided that if we were going to record *Argus* in the studio, then we should not just lay it down as a "live in the studio" recording, but actually take it on as a fully considered recording project. So, I went back to my band and announced to them of my plan to re-record *Argus,* at which point their jaws dropped and they all said "You can't do that!", to which I replied "Excuse me, why can't I do that?". They responded "Well, it's a classic album!" I explained to them that I believed the recording could benefit from the modern technology available and eventually we all agreed to take it on as a project. I think there was a bit of concern in the camp as to how close to the original we should make the new recording. My thinking was that since the original album was much loved, I wouldn't want to stray too far from that and, as such, we only indulged ourselves in a few embellishments, in particular on 'Leaf and Stream'. We were also delighted to have Asia's John Wetton and Geoff Downes join us on 'Throw Down the Sword'. We had a couple of great days in the studio with them as they laid their individual parts down. I really like Geoff's style of keyboard playing – he has a really cool rock 'n' roll vibe about him that you don't usually get with keyboard players. I was also pleasantly taken aback by how well the voices of John Wetton and myself blended. Thank you, gents – was great to have you on board.

Re-recording *Argus* went pretty smoothly. Strangely enough the biggest problem was getting the right bass sound. I thought I would be able to do it on the Gibson Thunderbird but once we got in the studio it became apparent that it was quite a different sound to that on the original album, which was played on a Rickenbacker, so I tried a number of different Rickenbacker basses during the sessions. I borrowed one from John

With John Wetton during the recording of Argus: Through The Looking Glass
- Liscombe Park, 2007.

Photo by Gary Carter

Wetton and tried that. It was a lovely old instrument but needed some fairly radical work on it – obviously I didn't want to start messing with someone else's instrument. Nick Beggs (Kajagoogoo/Steve Hackett) was working at Liscombe Park and brought in his Rickenbacker, which sounded very clean and didn't have the growl I was looking for. Eventually our friend and fan Tony Clark very obligingly supplied me with his Rickenbacker, which sounded more in the ballpark and was the guitar I played on most of the new recording.

Re-recording *Argus* was my first experience of recording a studio album using the digital computer recording system Pro Tools. I'd always been very much an analogue recording man, although I had used digital systems such as Otari Radar, and so recording with Pro-Tools was a whole new experience for me. When I took the recordings home to my studio to listen to them, I felt that while they had been very well recorded, they did have a tendency to sound very clean and clinical. In terms of sound, I felt that was way too far from the original 1972 album, which had been recorded on 16-track analogue equipment. My studio at home is primarily set up for mixing and is full of old analogue equipment, so I decided to mix it there in order to get some warmth into it and get rid of the sterile quality that goes with modern digital recordings. I think I eventually managed to achieve the right balance between the warmth of the original album's sound, combined with the quality of a modern recording. Achieving that balance was not an easy process and it took a fair amount of time. I think a lot of people regard me as being a bit of a perfectionist when it comes to recording. I don't think I am, although maybe I set my standards high and am not fast, but there is always a point that I reach where I believe the mix sounds just right. I can always feel that and won't give up until I reach that point. I'm not searching for audio nirvana, but I do recognise when something sounds right and I tend to take my time in order to hone it down. I'm not usually willing to quit until I get things as I want them to sound. It's a bit like sculpting – making an audio sculpture to me is the finished mix, the demo is a mere sketch and the initial recording the painting.

Once we got the album sounding nice, we then had to consider the title for the album, as well as a cover design. Initially Howard Johnston experimented with re-colouring the original sleeve design, but the original album designers Hipgnosis, who retained the right to veto any adaptation of their work, were not keen on this as a concept. We had no desire to offend the original designers, with whom we by now had an excellent working relationship, and instead Howard came up with a fresh design based loosely around the original warrior theme.

As for the title, *Argus: Through The Looking Glass* is a reference to looking in a mirror at a reflection, which is essentially what we were doing with the new recording. Obviously this was somewhat borrowed from Lewis Carroll's *Alice Through The Looking Glass*. Now, Lewis Carroll – or Charles Dodgson, to give his real name – just happens to be buried in a graveyard just a few yards from where I live. I often walk through there and one day I decided to visit his grave and ask his permission to use *Through The Looking Glass* as part of our album title. I got the distinct impression that he approved. That's my story and I'm sticking to it!

Before we embarked on the *Argus: Through The Looking Glass* project, a lot of people advised me that no matter what we did with the re-recording of the album, we would get shot down in flames. If we had recorded the album exactly the same as the original, people would inevitably have asked "What was the point in doing that?" Yet if we were to make too many changes, we would have been lambasted for having the audacity to interfere with something that was regarded in an almost reverent manner – in other words, you're damned if you do and damned if you don't. Certainly I had no desire to set the new recording up as a replacement for the original version or to imply that it is in any way superior. It was more of a case of "This is our version – we think it sounds lovely and want to share it with you". When the album came out the general reaction to it was very positive and very few people criticised it. The album was also instrumental in helping the band achieve greater recognition and legitimacy within the world's media and industry.

During the time between the recording sessions of *Argus: Through The Looking Glass* and its eventual release we did undergo a change in personnel. Keith Buck – who had effectively put the first line-up of my band together and to whom I shall be eternally grateful – announced to us early in 2008 that he had decided on a change of course and had accepted an offer to tour with Eagles tribute band Talon, primarily as a

Ray Hatfield – A fabulous touch on the guitar and a very creative musician

Photo by Lee Milward

pedal steel player. At the time Keith and his partner had a new baby on the way, and Talon were offering a higher level of work than we could offer him at that point in time. I can totally understand Keith's decision to move on and I have the utmost respect for him – he has a great work ethic and his guitar playing in my band was always extremely solid, with a great feel for the material, particularly the tunes from the Laurie Wisefield period.

> **RAY HATFIELD:** *I was of course sad to see Keith leave, but with a young family it was absolutely the right thing to do when the offer from an established band with a full diary of gigs came along. As his friend first and foremost that was the advice I gave him at the time. I've been along to see Talon a few times. They sound fantastic and are a perfect example of how to run that type of show.*

Keith was extremely gentlemanly about his resignation and even introduced us to his eventual replacement, Danny Willson – another highly experienced player from the Midlands.

DANNY WILLSON: *When I was about seven years old my brother and I were each given four-string plastic Beatles guitars for Christmas. A couple of years later I was given a proper guitar with six strings and made of wood. My very earliest influences were the songs that made up the top twenty from the mid sixties onwards. We used to religiously tape Pick of the Pops every Sunday evening using my Dad's reel to reel tape recorder and then spend just about every evening after school playing and singing along. I never had any tuition at all apart from a chord book or two, so everything was learnt by listening and working stuff out. By the age of ten I'd done my first gigs, playing at school and family gatherings.*

I remember a school friend playing me Wishbone Ash's newly-released Argus album when I was 14. I was immediately smitten by the songs, arrangements and lyrics, but most of all by the guitar and bass playing. And, wow, the sound of those twin guitars playing in harmony! Within a year I'd saved enough paper round /pocket money / gig money to buy a Flying-V copy and an Orange amp. I listened to, absorbed and then learnt all the Wishbone stuff from that period, and in fact I'd have to admit that virtually every note I've played since has been influenced in some way by Ted, Andy or Laurie.

After playing semi-professionally throughout my teens I turned professional, at the ripe old age of nineteen, joining a fairly well-known Leicester band called Kipper. We gigged all over the UK and had a very healthy fan base and a bulging diary. In those days a well-run pro band could quite easily play every night of the week if they wanted to. Following a change of image and direction we changed our name to Brooklyn and gradually progressed to doing original material influenced by such diverse bands as Yes, 10cc and Thin Lizzy. After securing a low-budget record deal we recorded an album and two singles in 1980, which unfortunately sank without trace. Oh well, we tried, and at least we made a decent-ish living and had plenty of fun. Incidentally, we often played 'Jailbait' in those days, and even more bizarrely, one of our regular followers was a talented young chap by the name of Keith Buck!

After Brooklyn ground to a halt in 1981 I played with various bands semi-professionally, the longest running of which, at around 10 years, was a covers trio called The Chase. Again, we had a great following and had so much fun, which was just as well really as we definitely weren't getting rich! Then in 1995, totally out of the blue, I was offered the lead guitar job in Showaddywaddy which led to fourteen years of relentless worldwide touring and recording as part of an incredibly professional and slick outfit. I thought that job would see me through to retirement but then I had a phone call from a certain Mr Buck. I've known Keith since the late seventies and we've always shared an interest in classic Wishbone Ash, so when he'd decided to move on from MTWA he kindly thought of me and suggested giving my number to Martin. Thanks Keith! Martin called me a few days later and we chatted for an hour or so and it all seemed to just fall into place. I was in! I had a pretty intense couple of weeks trying to get all the guitar parts and vocal harmonies into my head, whilst at the same time still doing gigs with Showaddywaddy. I did manage to find time one afternoon to pop over to see Keith for a bit of fine tuning, and Ray came over to my house a few days before my debut to make sure our parts worked well together.

Due to the lack of time available – due to us already touring with Keith, and Danny being out on the road with Showaddywaddy – there was no time for a full band rehearsal prior to Danny's first show with us in Penzance, although Danny did come along to our show in Dudley a few days earlier to get the overall feel of the set, as well as joining us for 'Living Proof'. Come the night of his first full show, Danny certainly rose to the occasion, playing a near flawless set with only the soundcheck for a quick run-through of a few of the songs. This is typical of Danny's positive attitude and boundless enthusiasm. Danny has his own memories of his first show with the band.

> **DANNY WILLSON:** *It was a smallish, friendly and informal arts centre type of gig, just perfect for my debut. Ray, Rob, Mick and I had a good laugh going down to Cornwall, especially when Ray managed, on the instructions of his sat-nav, to get his Volvo wedged at the end of a miniature street in Penzance with no room for manoeuvre. We thought we'd need a crane to winch us out but eventually, after an arm-aching thirty-seven-point turn, the car was freed without so much as a scratch. The gig itself went very well as I recall and considering I hadn't rehearsed with the band at all I think I played quite well with very few apparent nerves. Afterwards we all went to a bar for a few pints, which was fun, before going back to our seafront digs. It was a tough call filling the shoes of Keith Buck who was, and still is, a firm favourite with the fans, but the fact that I was quickly accepted was very reassuring and greatly helped to build my confidence.*

Danny brought more of a performance aspect to the proceedings, adding to the vocal sound as well as keeping us amused with his sense of humour.

> **RAY HATFIELD:** *Danny is a wonderful guitar player and very experienced at playing with live bands. He therefore fitted in very quickly. In my opinion he is one of the finest voices ever to grace a Wishbone line up and I love to hear him sing. Another*

of Danny's assets is that he's very upbeat and good company on the long trips we do. He has an extrovert personality and brings humour to everything he does.

With Danny now in the line-up, I was keen to add some contributions from him to the upcoming *Argus Through The Looking Glass* album, and so just before final mixing, we went back to the studio to add the icing on the cake. I felt it important that when the album was released, in October 2008, that it featured all members of the current touring line-up in some capacity.

DANNY WILLSON: *The album was virtually finished by the time I'd joined, so I wasn't involved in any of the main recording of it. However, it was decided that I should at least be present on the CD in some small way so I was invited down to Liscombe Park Studios for a whirlwind day of guitar and vocal overdubs, some of which were used on the final product. It was left to Martin to sort out whose parts to use and listening back now it's hard to tell which bits are mine or Keith's. The final result was great, with some really excellent performances from the lads.*

With Danny Willson, Stevenage 2009.

Photo by John Price

KEITH BUCK: *I enjoyed the Argus recordings. I remember being torn about keeping the parts faithfully and not straying too far from the original parts as, in my view, they could not be improved upon. Although I did not copy the solos note for note, I did keep a respectful nod to the originals. I was also happy that Martin left most of my playing on the recordings, as I was leaving the band as it was being finished, so most of my rhythm parts and nearly all my solos are still on the album.*

Our *Argus* tour of 2008/09 represented a transient period for the band. Danny came highly recommended by Keith and was available to perform the majority of the shows we had lined up. However, he was still under contract to Showaddywaddy and this initially resulted in a few clashes of schedules. Keith was very gracious and offered to fill in where he could. We also had Maurice Douglas filling in on a number of dates . This could have resulted in a somewhat messy situation but I actually enjoyed the contrast in playing styles between the different guitar players – each player bringing something different to the party. Keith always had a great feel for the music, while Maurice Douglas was also a very talented guy, who writes great songs and is a pleasure to work with – although I can never understand a word he says, because he's from Ashington, Northumberland!

KEITH BUCK: *I would always help out in the future, if asked. I have maintained a good relationship with everyone and, of course, I still love the songs*

RAY HATFIELD: *I remember when Keith stood in for Danny at the 100 Club in London and turned up with a car borrowed from his daughter, a guitar borrowed from The Guitar Workshop, Danny's amp and a lead and plectrum from me. He then proceeded to play the best gig I've ever heard him perform. Those of us who know him would just say that's typical, except that he turned up on time.*

DANNY WILLSON: *As you can imagine, there were times when things were so complicated, I was afraid to open my diary. In fact I think I managed to be in both bands for well over a year and, surprisingly, for the majority of that time I was very lucky in that there weren't too many gig clashes. Where dates did overlap we were fortunate to be able to call on Geordie lad Maurice Douglas who did a sterling job whilst I was off in my pink jacket! At one point in October 2008, MTWA had a month-long theatre tour booked at the same time as a Showaddywaddy Irish tour. This proved to be a bit of a headache but was resolved when the Showaddys kindly allowed me to find a suitable dep for their tour. In fact the "dep" turned out to be very suitable indeed and eventually took my place full time and is still with the band. Eventually I took the difficult decision to leave the safety-net of Showaddywaddy on the grounds that it was probably time for a change of musical direction. It had also dawned on me that I was causing both bands to be in a state of limbo without a stable line-up – I was aware of the unfairness of the situation. I agonized over the decision for what seemed like months and it became the main topic of conversation as we travelled to and from gigs. So yes, it was a huge step to take, but fortunately it all worked out for both bands and I'm glad to say I'm still big friends with my old mates, the "Creped Crusaders".*

Photo by Rob Holt

Danny Willson, Nottingham 2008 – Danny brought a great "performance" aspect to my band – a highly talented player and singer.

I counted myself very fortunate to have such a rich pool of talent I could draw from. This kept us in good stead for what was a very busy period of touring, including appearances on the *Classic Legends of Rock* tours alongside our friends Focus. These tours gave the band a chance to play in front of capacity theatre audiences across the UK, introducing the band to a lot of new people in the process. The *Classic Legends* tours were a highly pleasurable experience, being extremely well organised and promoted. These excursions also took us back into many of the venues that the original band had played back in the seventies and eighties. Wishbone Ash music has always leant itself very well towards being performed in a theatre situation.

On a sadder note, 2008 also saw the passing of our PR assistant Laureen Large. I always try and tell myself that it is one of the strange mysteries of life that we all have our appointed time to leave this world. However, when Howard Johnston called me to tell me the news of Laureen's passing, I was shocked and saddened, as were the rest of my band. On a lighter note, I recall my youngest daughter Melody picking up my mobile phone one day and announced that there was a girl calling me by the name of Large Laureen (surname showed up first on my old phone!), and I will always fondly remember her this way. She was a large personality in so many ways - generous, large hearted,

Photo by John Price

On stage during the Classic Legends of Rock tour - St. Albans, 2009.

honest, helpful, and with a large enthusiasm for music and the people involved. Rest in Peace, Laureen. Everybody needs a friend – you were a good one.

Although 2008 was a busy year, the personnel changes were not quite over and the tail end of the year saw us parting company with Rob Hewins. I was immensely fond of Rob's creative energy. The way he played drums was very much in the style of Steve Upton, which was exactly what I was looking

Photo by Rob Holt

Rob Hewins - An extremely talented all-round musician. I have the highest regard for his musicality.

for and Rob is also an extremely talented engineer and producer in his own right, as well as a multi-talented instrumentalist, extremely capable on both guitar and keyboards. His voice was also the perfect match for mine, not only tonally, but also in the way he was able to track exactly what I was singing, as I have a tendency to drag notes across the tempo, which is part of my personal singing style. A lot of people I have worked with have difficulty working with that, but Rob was always able to stay with me vocally. This was great for live vocal harmonies, which we were able to pull off very effectively. Rob was a great asset to the band both musically and vocally but, I think, had quite different aspirations for the band on a business level to what had already been formulated. We were not really in a position to offer him what he was seeking career-wise and this resulted in a certain amount of uncertainty all round, and eventually did lead to a parting of the ways. I retain great respect for Rob's musicality and would only wish him well in all future endeavours. Like Keith, he remains a friend of the band.

> **RAY HATFIELD:** *I remain in regular contact with both Rob and Keith and play with them whenever the opportunity arises. I was recently very proud to play a bit of slide guitar on the CD Out of the Blue that they recorded (with Paul "Ginty" Johnson) to raise money for Cancer Research UK. It's a great CD and a charity that's very close to my heart.*

> **DANNY WILLSON:** *Rob is that rare breed of drummer who is extremely musical in every way. He's a whizz in the studio, plays guitar and keyboards, and is a great singer to boot. His drumming has a real sense of dynamics, and his sympathetic but authoritative style has a wonderful knack of making other musicians squeeze more out of themselves. Thankfully he actually lives only two miles away so we do still get to play together fairly regularly*

Rob would be a hard act to follow and I am known to be choosy when it comes to drummers. Enter Dave Wagstaffe, who came on very strong recommendation from my manager Martin Darvill and having already played a couple of shows with us during the Spring of 2008 that Rob had been unable to perform. The experience of working with Dave had been a pleasure. An extremely pleasant chap and very reliable, he is one of those guys who, if you were in the trenches in the first World War, you would be glad to have beside you – a true team player with an extremely positive attitude, and a wealth of experience gained throughout a lengthy career.

> **DAVE WAGSTAFFE:** *Music was always being played in our house by both my Mum and Dad's records by Frank Sinatra, Lonnie Donegan, Nat King Cole, Elvis and Bill Haley, and my Grandmother's by Josef Locke and Benjamin Gigli and other big tenor voices from her day. My own first big influences were undoubtedly The Shadows, Cliff Richard's backing band. They were the first band I was taken to see live when I was ten, and at the time they were still called The Drifters with*

Jet Harris on bass and Tony Meehan on drums. Tony was my first drum hero, and then equally his successor Brian Bennett. I was brought up with all the sixties pop bands and was a fan of many but in particular the Beatles, Stones, Kinks, and Yardbirds. I'd also discovered an album by classical guitarist Andres Segovia of Bach pieces for guitar which I would attempt to play by ear on my beat-up old acoustic guitar, which must have sounded dire. I did go for classical guitar lessons some years later, but my first attempts at making music collectively was with my school pal Dave Green – he on home-made drums and me on guitar. We both must have thought we could do each other's job better – we switched and it seemed to stick. I didn't have any serious tuition until many years later with jazz teacher Joel Rothman, mainly to learn to read, and in the process realised how much other stuff I didn't know. I was offered to have lessons as a teenager with some local old teacher, so I went to see him playing in some hotel gig, but I thought he was a bit ropey and never bothered. There wasn't then the plethora of tuition material that there is now – DVDs, internet and college courses. You can learn a huge amount of technique now in just a few years, and there's no doubt that being self-taught is a much lengthier process. So my main source of inspiration was from records, TV and live shows.

My first bands were local semi-pro ones where we were living at that time in Skegness, and the last band there was with my pal Dave Green again. We attempted to relocate to London but we had a bad accident en route and trashed the van, which seemed to kybosh that idea. I moved down to London shortly after with my brother Steve, who for six months kindly drove me around to loads of auditions, until I got a band together with another Skeg musician Mick

*Pearl (later of Streetband and Q Tips with Paul Young).
We formed a blues rock band and blatantly stole the band's
name from the album of a band we admired – Argus. The
band existed for several years touring with bands like Thin
Lizzy, Pink Faries, Brinsley Schwartz, The Equals and many
others. The material we recorded at the time (1972/73) was
eventually released on the Audio Archives label many years
later. Since then I've been involved with countless other
bands and projects, among them jazz rock band Anaconda,
NWOBHM band Gaskin, prog bands Quasar and Janison
Edge and world music artist Cyrus Khajavi's band Kooch.
I've also worked intermittently with Oliver Wakeman since
2001 and also with UK prog band Landmarq since 1990,
squeezing in between them odd sessions with John Wetton,
Ken Hensley, Davy O' List, Peter Banks and others. I had a
fun year or two with tribute band The Illegal Eagles and a
stint with The Downtime Big Band which I had to let go on
joining MTWA.*

*In the early seventies I was a big fan of much of what was then
called "progressive rock", which encompassed a broader scope
of bands than it does these days and before I heard Wishbone
Ash, I was a fan of Colosseum, Led Zeppelin, Jethro Tull, The
Nice, Mahavishnu Orchestra, ELP and similar bands. On
hearing the first Wishbone Ash album I thought they were
superb. I think I saw them live first at the Reading Festival.
I thought Steve Upton was one of the best rock drummers
around at the time, having his own style, great feel and good
technique. His playing on the first two albums particularly
was pretty adventurous for those times, then he simplified his
style down somewhat for Argus. I got side-tracked away from
Wishbone album-wise after that album, but still saw them
live from time to time and always enjoyed them.*

I've known MTWA manager Martin Darvill for a long time,
and bumped into Martin Turner socially up at Martin
Darvill's house, and we went that evening to see him doing a
gig with the Blue Bishops. When previous drummer Rob was
unable to make a couple of gigs, Martin Darvill asked me if I
was free to help out, which I was delighted to do. Rob is such
a multi talented chap – he plays every damned instrument,
and well too, sings great and is a recording engineer to boot
– and a hard act to follow indeed. I holed myself up in my
studio and played along to the CDs for weeks. The first gig was
in Glasgow and then down to Newcastle, and we had to pick
up Maurice (Douglas) from the latter on route going up. My
main memories are having a good bit of camaraderie with
the band throughout and the usual mix of excitement and
nerves on a first gig. Both shows seemed to go pretty good and
I felt pretty confident, but I had put in a lot of homework.

And so we entered the second phase of Martin Turner's Wishbone Ash. Throughout the existence of my band to date, Ray Hatfield has been loyal to the cause. I'm immensely fond of Ray – he has got a fabulous touch on the guitar. Although he generally uses a pick, he is equally capable of playing finger-style in the way that Mark Knopfler does. He's a very versatile player and gets a wonderful sound. Ray was given a pretty difficult task in that when he joined the band he inherited most of Andy Powell's guitar parts and I think he has done an excellent job in interpreting Andy's guitar lines in a way that is faithful, yet fresh. Ray is a very creative musician who is always coming up with interesting ideas at sound-checks and rehearsals and this bodes well for new material from the band – this creativity is well displayed on his 2008 solo album *King Of The West*. Ray is also a wonderful guy to be with – he has a great sense of humour and can be quite mischievous at times, although never at anyone else's expense. He really does help keep a lovely atmosphere within the band.

DANNY WILLSON: *I'd watched Ray play and sing many times during the years before either of us joined MTWA, and was always struck by the fluidity and bluesy tunefulness of his playing. From the very first notes we played together in my bedroom studio a week before my debut gig I knew everything was going to be just fine. It was effortless, and the fact that we get on so well and share the same sense of humour made it all the more fun. His superb solo album is chock-full of tasty guitar licks not to mention his beautifully gruff (in a good way!) singing. He's also a master of the slide guitar and the.... ukelele! He's a great all-round musician and, let's face it, anyone who can pull off the epic 'Sometime World' solo whilst still managing to inject his own personality into it certainly ain't no slouch when it comes to guitar-slingin'!*

Ray and Danny, Stevenage 2009 – our guitar duo keep us amused with their humourous antics on and off the stage!

Ray and I already had a rapport of sorts before joining the band, so it really didn't take long to develop it further. Plenty of good humour and mickey-taking en route to gigs saw to that! We'd met quite a few times when he gigged at my local. In fact I'll go as far as saying just about anyone could develop a rapport with that loveable rogue. You'd have to be made of stone to resist Ray's good-natured bonhomie. He's the vital ingredient that gives this band such a cosy feeling – I hate him!

The balance we have in the band currently is very strong. There are no stresses and strains – everything fits together nicely and there is a great team ethic, not to mention a shared sense of humour that helps keep us sane. While we all remain serious and committed as regards the quality of our performances, we equally feel that it's important not to take yourself too seriously all of the time. Certainly some of Danny and Ray's antics have been the cause of much amusement, both on and offstage. I will never forget the night that Ray, during the middle break-down section in 'Phoenix', stepped up to the front of the stage and proceeded to play a spoons solo! We were all in absolute hysterics and just about managed to retain our composure to complete the track. The audience loved it and needless to say the spoons made a nightly appearance for quite some time after.

DAVE WAGSTAFFE: *Martin, Ray and Danny are all lovely chaps, and that goes for our faithful sound engineer Mick too. I think their musicianship speaks for itself and Ray and Danny work so well together despite having very different individual styles. And what can you say about Martin Turner? He was always one of rock's top players for me, and the author of some of rock's most classic and memorable songs. They are all good fun to be around, and the banter on the way both to gigs, and at gigs, is always very entertaining!*

Photo by Maria Lundy

Dave Wagstaffe – A true team player with a highly positive attitude and a wealth of experience.

As happy as I was with my current band, I had not overlooked the fact that the period of 2009/10 marked the 40th anniversary of the formation of Wishbone Ash and that, understandably, many fans were hopeful of the occasion being marked with a reunion of the original band members. I would very much have liked the opportunity to get together with the original guys one more time and, in fact, my management were in receipt of an excellent offer from one of the biggest UK concert promoters for a series of shows including an appearance at London's Hammersmith Apollo – or the Odeon, as I will always fondly remember it – on the basis that the line-up must include at least three original members. Steve, Ted and I felt it was only really worth doing if it was the entire original band – including Andy Powell. Unfortunately negotiations proved problematic, largely because we were in dispute with Andy over both his registration of the Wishbone Ash trademark, as well as various copyright issues. This necessitated us appointing my manager Martin Darvill to negotiate with

Andy in order to resolve the various outstanding issues, so as to pave the way for reunion discussions to take place. Andy later went on record as saying that my manager refuses to let him talk to me or the other original members directly, but that is absolute rubbish as it was most definitely Andy that I met a couple of years back at his lawyers office, when they asked if I could attend a meeting in order to hopefully resolve some of these issues. As I sat waiting in the reception, I spotted Andy and his missus on the other side of the room. I found it amusing that Andy appeared somewhat embarrassed to say "Hello" and so I thought I'd break the ice. I walked over to where they were seated, extended my hand and said "Andy, me old mate - fancy meeting you here," in an attempt to lighten the mood. Sadly little was achieved at the meeting as Andy and his assembled advisors adopted a stance of "No negotiation".

I'm always willing to talk with Andy about music, but when it comes to business issues, I prefer to leave it to those who know the business side best. Steve, Ted and myself were all willing to work with Andy for a series of reunion concerts – all we were asking was that Andy drop his legal threats and engage in meaningful discussions with our representative concerning outstanding matters. Andy did not appear to want to do that, which is a shame, as once lawyers get brought in things start to get very polarised. Everyone ends up spending a lot of money fighting each other and very rarely is there an absolute outcome. What is the point in giving a lawyer thousands of pounds to build a conservatory on the back of his house? It was simply untenable to enter into a reunion situation against a backdrop of litigation and dispute.

Throughout negotiations it became obvious that Andy felt quite miffed that anyone other than himself would be contemplating putting a Wishbone Ash reunion together. In my mind, it didn't matter who had received the offer – it just happened to be my management in this instance, which was not surprising given that they manage a number of high profile rock artists and as a consequence have an excellent working relationship with high level industry contacts, labels, promoters, media, etc. The involvement of a top promoter, who would have put adequate time and resources into promotions and advertising, could have made this a top event that would have raised the overall Wishbone Ash profile. Perhaps Andy saw a reunion as a threat to his incarnation of Wishbone Ash. That was never the intention and any reunion did not have to be at the expense of either Andy's band, or mine. On the contrary, both would have benefitted from the extra exposure of a high profile reunion project.

Negotiations with Andy dragged on for the best part of a year, throughout which time he requested a confidentiality agreement from my management – a not unreasonable request we duly obliged with. Then, low and behold, Andy decided to announce on his website that his current band was playing a 40th anniversary show at Shepherd's Bush Empire in May 2009 and that he was publicly inviting the other original members to join his band on stage for a performance of *Argus* – something I had already been doing for months. Furthermore, he did this without even having the courtesy to consult us first as regards our availability for the planned date or to discuss any aspect of the proposed performance. We felt totally insulted by this as it seemed to me to be a Machiavellian plan to make us an offer that we would obviously refuse so that he could paint the picture that he had offered a reunion and we had rejected it. This, of course, was the exact opposite of the reality, which was that many months earlier we had made a fair offer to Andy that would have been on the basis of the original band onstage for the full duration of the performance and on the basis of a four-way split of profits and merchandising between the four original members – I would make an educated guess that his offer to us would not have been so reasonable. Sadly this course of action finally put the mockers on any reunion of the original band. I was furious as well as disappointed, not so much for myself, but for the sake of the fans – the people who would have been overjoyed to have seen the original band stood on stage together one last time to celebrate a milestone in our careers. Such was my anger that in a phone interview with Dave Ling of

Classic Rock magazine, when asked what I thought of Mr. Powell's offer, I infamously replied by saying that "Andy Powell can fuck off if he thinks the original band is going to play support act at one of his gigs". The context of this quote was a jokey response in reference to the notion of Steve, Ted and myself being bounced into a reunion show being 100% controlled by Andy and his version of Wishbone Ash. Of course, that one throwaway remark got taken totally out of context and was used as the main headline for an otherwise positive and non-contentious article.

My management, PR and website staff have all continually instilled in me the need for diplomacy at all times and have constantly advised that any outpourings of emotion would be exploited by those who have something to gain from in-fighting. "Always be statesmanlike and don't wash dirty linen in public," I was implored. "You'll only appeal to the lowest common denominator if you slag off in public. You will be misquoted, and the vast majority of the public do not want to read about private disputes in the press." Certainly I would agree that there are always matters that are best kept private, and most of the time I temper my natural instinct to be candid, but now and then it has simply been a necessity to speak my mind, purely due to the series of mistruths that have been published elsewhere.

I remain saddened that we were unable to regroup as the original line-up to celebrate our 40th anniversary. Look at Genesis, The Police, Led Zeppelin, Black Sabbath, ELP – all were able to enjoy successful reunion concerts, but in the case of this Wishbone Ash reunion, despite the fact that the original band are all still alive and able to perform, it appeared to me that it was cleverly prevented from happening.

CHAPTER EIGHTEEN

Life Begins

WHILE THERE was no reunion of the original band to commemorate the 40th anniversary of the formation of Wishbone Ash, I was more than happy to mark the occasion throughout 2010 with my band's *Life Begins* tour, as documented on our recently released DVD and double CD. We put together a new set list for this occasion and dusted off many lost gems from the deeper Wishbone Ash catalogue resulting in a career-spanning show that seemed to please casual and hardcore fans alike. We also had the honour of Ted Turner joining us on stage at the inaugural *High Voltage* festival in Victoria Park, London on 25 July 2010. I thought the organisers of *High Voltage* did something fantastic and long overdue. The capital city, which had produced so many great artists over the years, had never really had a classic rock festival. In Victoria Park, they found a really nice site, the facilities were good, as was the organisation – it was a fantastic event and it was a pleasure to be involved. We appeared early on the Sunday afternoon, and a crowd of thousands gathered to watch us perform *Argus* and other favourites from the old days. I stayed on site for the entire weekend and took the time to watch a lot of the bands. It was also great to meet up with several bands that we had appeared with back in the seventies such as headliners Emerson, Lake and Palmer and ZZ Top. It was great to see ZZ Top again. I always loved them and they used to do a lot of gigs with us in the

With Dusty Hill (ZZ Top) and Bernie Shaw (Uriah Heep) and wife Radka at High Voltage, July 2010.

early seventies. I bought their first album and loved Billy Gibbons' guitar and voice. I always used to enjoy talking to Dusty Hill, who to me always looked like he'd just got off a horse in Texas, having just come off the prairie where he'd been lassoing steer – a real authentic cowboy! He is a great character and I really enjoyed meeting up with him before their show for a chat about the old days. No less than five members of the wider Wishbone Ash fraternity were there, either to perform or as invited backstage guests – Ted Turner, Laurie Wisefield, John Wetton, Trevor Bolder and myself – and we all took great pleasure in swapping anecdotes and sharing memories of experiences from times gone by. Overall *High Voltage* was a first class experience – a full blown rock show on a big stage, just like the old days – the only difference being that we were blessed with blazing sunshine all weekend – a rarity at UK open air concerts.

It was great to play with Ted again and I was equally delighted for Ted that he had been able to record and release some new music in the form of his 2010 solo album *Eclektic Value*. It's always a pleasure to hear Ted's voice, guitar and song-writing and I hope we will hear more from him in the future.

TED TURNER: *Several years ago I switched from recording my music on a digital audio workstation to a computer. Paul White, editor of Sound on Sound magazine recommended that I should try using Logic – the music program offered on Apple. He felt the control, the precision one has over the music – also the loops library within this system – was the best way to work for a songwriter / musician. I tend to agree. Eclektic Value was a big workload. How times have changed – one sixty year old man sitting in a room by himself with a laptop computer and a guitar, starting with a blank screen and producing a complete album ready for sale. This is how technology can enable the artist – a future that eliminates the middleman, allowing the artist to have control over one's own work. All recordings were done "inside the box". This is to say no additional software or production equipment was used to improve the sound, only what is in the Logic program – an example of how much can be done with so little – a real important message to get across and demonstrate; this was a consideration from the start. Before my passing, I want to leave something of merit – a legacy. I do not want just to be remembered for my work with Wishbone.*

We continued touring into the next year with our *Live Dates 2011* tour, delighting in be able to continue taking Wishbone Ash music to fans old and new, adding new territories to our touring circuit all the time. We played some pretty major shows during the year of 2011 – including festival appearances alongside bands such as Santana and Jethro Tull as well as theatre dates with our friends Uriah Heep and Argent. Our date-sheet presents us with a wide variety of situations to perform in, ranging from plush theatres to sweaty rock clubs, and from intimate arts centres to major festivals drawing thousands of people. Every situation is valid and offers something different for me as a performer. I love the intimacy of the performing arts centres – where we usually find ourselves performing to a mature audience of discerning music fans who want to sit down and listen carefully to every detail of the music. At the same time it's also important not to get too sterile and the clubs are great in that respect. Even in my advancing years, I still get off on playing to a hot and sticky room packed full of people singing and dancing and generally having a good time, reminding us of the true spirit of rock 'n' roll. Then there are the package tours and the festivals – a chance to introduce our music to a wider audience and share the experience with some of our contemporaries within the music business. I love all aspects of our live work and am simply grateful that, over forty years since the band's commercial peak, there are still so many people who want to pay hard earned money to listen to Wishbone Ash music in a live setting – some people remembering the songs from their youth, others discovering them for the first time.

I've met lots of guys in bands over the years and some of them enjoy touring and some don't. Personally, I'm a natural and take to it like a duck to water. I find it incredibly stimulating and right now am enjoying it as much as ever. I still have a hobo-like spirit and probably always will. It's like being a gypsy or pirate. You waltz into town and entertain people for an evening and then off you go to the next place. Then you come back a year or so later and do it again. I spent a long time off the road and right now I'm making the very most of the opportunity I have been given to do it all again. I haven't reached the slippers and hot water bottle stage yet – I'm rocking on. To be a wandering minstrel you are always on the fringe of society, hopefully reflecting back what you observe and experience. It's a strange and unpredictable way of life with great highs and lows. I was born to it, have tried to escape and live a "normal" life, but I know I have to submit to my fate. I am nowhere near ready to retire yet, although these days I do appreciate the balance between life on the road and my role within the home and I am equally adept at taking on household chores when the need arises as I am at nailing a mix in my "dungeon", as I call my studio. Away from music I enjoy the ordinary stuff – walking with kids and dogs, falling over, finding wild berries or mushrooms, looking at the sun at dawn through the mist (even saw sunspots once doing this!), moon and star gazing, lighting fires when it's cold, using a chainsaw to facilitate this, going to gigs, football or banger racing, visiting friends and family, cooking up huge dinners for family, etc. When I've had too many weeks of dark dingy hovels surrounded by electrical magnetic devices, I'll go charging out into the wilds and roll in the mud to earth myself and make cathartic contact with mother nature – a.k.a. gardening – if somewhat hap-hazard and freakishly.

SUSIE TURNER: *The thought of Martin and myself retired and tripping over each other in the kitchen fills us both with horror. Martin will always be involved in music – if not touring with a band, then in the studio with one or other daughter and, in time, the grandchildren. Both grandsons (my eldest daughter Annalise's children) in Florida are musical and I can imagine both Dulcie and Heidi – Jessica and Grace's daughters respectively – singing with Pa, as they call him, before too long. It is important for Martin to have a studio and he spends happy hours in there on a daily basis. It is his "shed" – every British bloke needs one! He keeps very different hours to me and will disappear to the studio after dinner, often until 2am. These are his most productive hours. I prefer to be in bed with a book by 10.30! I am up with the sun – he prefers to see it rise as he goes to bed, especially in summer!*

Martin is in an advanced stage of evolvement domestically. If I shine at the Aga, he positively gleams at the kitchen sink! With classical music playing at stadium volumes he will polish the granite as if he were about to perform brain surgery on it, rather than merely prepare his porridge and crumpets! The rest of us merely don our sunglasses for protection and retire from the area. It is no contest – he is the champion of super cleaning, a lifetime gift from his Mum! Same with the ironing, a skill acquired in dressing rooms, of necessity, and honed to perfection.

We have a large organic woodland garden which Martin tends on a sporadic basis. It will run amok for several beautiful, chaotic, colourful months then he dons his gloves, takes up his chainsaw and is out there until he can no longer see his victims, scalping every living thing to within an inch of existence! I am always alarmed, rescuing whatever I can for vases; he is almost unerringly right and the garden thrives and gives us endless pleasure. He retires to a deep bath of Seaweed and Arnica bubbles, swearing he has overdone it and needs to not do that again. Next day he's out there again, a triumph of optimism over experience which sums up his attitude to most things. He loves to chop wood and fills a log shelter every summer, which warms us through the winter – another of his passions being huge open fires.

Martin enjoys driving and has owned many cars over the years. His various touring vans have been great fun and he loves his van almost as much as his studio, spending hours cleaning it after every sortie.

My children all vary in how they regard me, both as a father as well as my role within music. Annalise – Susie's eldest daughter, whom I am not related to but have acted as her father for many years now – was able to come along and see me perform back in the Wishbone Ash days. She was always pretty wild, rock 'n' roll, etc and is a singer herself. She has been living in the States for the last twenty years or so but we maintain good contact. She used to sing backing vocals for me in my studio when it was in the IRS building on Kensington Park Road and she was working next door at the restaurant 192. In more recent times I have jammed with her band B-Movie in the States. Her guy Sean is a very cool drummer and all round musician.

Jessie was just about old enough to catch some of the Wishbone Ash re-union gigs, so she got to see her Dad in action back in the day – I can still remember the look of amazement on her face. She is definitely a one-off with a pronounced personality and also sings in a band called Q Tone. She was my first born and I have always had a very easy relationship with her – she's pretty much like a female version of me in some respects. I have also been able to do some recording with her.

Photo by Evelyn at Sage Arts

Grace.

Grace – Jessie's younger sister with the natural platinum blond hair – was too young to come out to see the original band but has come along to a few London gigs to see me perform with my band in recent years. Gracie has two small children so it is not so easy for her to get along to shows. Amazingly she also sings and dances with a Rugby Cheerleader team but motherhood does put restrictions on how much she can do at the moment. She is a rough diamond with a lovely voice and a wacky personality – mad as a box of frogs at times, but immensely lovable. I have also recorded vocals with Gracie.

Andrew, Susie's son by Andy Summers, has also been to quite a few shows. He is into "drum and bass" dance music and works with his crew, Vicious Circle. We are both Librans and have given each other practical help with recordings and studio stuff now and again. I have recorded my youngest daughter Melody's vocals for tracks that Andrew has put together with her and the combination seems to work pretty well. He has got into some of

Andrew at home in Guildford, moonlight serenading on the smokers' patio!

the old Wishbone Ash albums over the last year or two and its funny to have him tell me how much he likes some of the seventies music as he discovers it. By return, he turned me onto Muse, whom I've grown very fond of – them being West Country lads like meself.

Tom – well, what can I say? When he was young he was very impressed with my mate Nick Lyne, his Godfather, a "business man" in a suit who had a very smart office. It was easy to see that Tom needed this kind of role model and I was happy for Nick to come over and generously share his time. I don't think young Tom got what I am about and his sense of the formal probably suggested that I was a bit "dodgy". Tom is a pretty "straight" guy, does not mess with drink and drugs, is extremely discerning with relationships and is into golf, cars and football, playing in a team with our old friend Kid Jensen's son Viktor. He is about as fit and healthy as a chap can be and although I wish sometimes that he was not quite so fastidiously well behaved and would maybe benefit from letting his hair down, I also know that we all, as a family, rely on his keen brain and his input when things get pear shaped.

He does actually remind me of how I was at his age – rather cerebral, but a bit less rock 'n' roll, more healthy and squeaky clean. Conceived on bonfire night, his initials are TNT (Tom Nicholas Turner) and he does have a bit of a short fuse – do not mess with Tommy, mate!

Melody (Mimi) – or Mini Minx as I call her – has always wanted to be a singer from a young age. Like me, she is a bit of a belter and sings loud – I know because I've recorded her voice quite a bit. She is at a point where she needs to be out there working with

Photo by Susie Turner

Tom graduating with a 2:1 - proud moment!

people her own age, and is doing so right now. As I've already said, I was her daytime carer when she was a tiny soul and I therefore know her well. When she was very young we had a family "ding dong" where everyone was giving her a hard time about having told a fib. She was standing her ground and mouthing off and then ended up going off to her room. She put a big hand written note on her bedroom door saying: "Do not come in – I hate you all. Love Mimi" Ah, bless!

I have always tried to keep a communication path open with all of our children and anything they wish to discuss is on the menu – sex, drugs, relationships, or whatever they want to talk about. My kids have always been encouraged to express their feelings and I have great respect for their two different Mums – one busy, proactive and well versed in natural medicine, and one calm, wise, with a well developed insight into the human condition. I have been available to rescue kids at any time of day or night when they have been in trouble or stuck some place. There are times when everyone in our house is screaming at each other - i.e. getting it off their chest. To more sedate folks who happen to witness such goings on I'm sure they may well be taken aback, but as far as we are concerned that is family life and it's all done with a sense of humour. I really do care for them all as people and I think we all benefit from being part of an extended family, and they all get on well with each other too. I tend to regard them as friends rather than offspring, and then eventually along came grand children. Oh, 'tis a wonderful thing, the family.

Then of course there is Mum, who is still going strong. She was born in 1924 and so she is shrinking and really getting up there in years now. I do not see her as often as I would wish nowadays – only when I get to Torquay, as she does not enjoy travelling far anymore. I do however enjoy chatting with her at length on the phone which always starts with me saying "'Ello, my dear" in a broad West Country accent. I am always amazed at the strength of her spirit, her keen independence and the wisdom that she can introduce me to on occasion. In short, she is a very wonderful and much loved lady in our family.

Melody Rose
Photo by AlexP.com

So, it is a healthy balance of family and career these days. On the latter, I still feel the same way about performing music as I did in my twenties. The big difference now is that I'm not such a hooligan as I was in my younger days. I don't feel the need to drink and drug and go after crazy women like I did as a young man, so things are a bit more drama-free. Back then I couldn't get enough of it and would be out every night,

Photo by Evelyn at Sage Arts

B-Movie gig, Sarasota, Florida - I get to jam with my girls - Jessica, Annalise and Mimi.

no matter where we were in the world, and had an insatiable urge to go out for a drink and have a chat with people and end up dancing the night away. But you can only do that for so long. Back then it was scotch and coke before a show. These days it's a bottle of J_2O and some Neal's Yard Remedies!

I still have many ambitions that I want to fulfil within music. I still have the urge to travel. I have always felt that the music of Wishbone Ash transcends language barriers. Whether we went to South America, Australia, Japan, Europe, the music received the same passionate response from people. Whether they were able to understand the lyrics or not, they picked up on the emotional content within the music. One of the things about travelling the world is the wisdom that you pick up along the way. It doesn't matter what country you are in, what the culture or religion is, people over the world are basically the same – they enjoy a drink, a chat, some music and a laugh and are friendly towards people who visit their country from foreign shores. It's only the megalomaniacs who want power and money who cause all the problems in this world.

There are many places I have yet to visit and would love to go to - Tibet, Thailand, India and China for example. One of the places I would love to go to more than anywhere is Russia. I was brought up with Classical music and have a deep love of Russian composers such as Tchaikovsky, Rachmaninov, and Shostakovich. I think those influences can be heard in some of the melodies and guitar parts that I've written over the years. Russian music has had such a great influence on me and so I would be interested to see and feel the place where that music came from, as well as discover what impact our music has had on the Russian people.

Creatively, I still have much to say. I have had a wonderful time over the past few years re-discovering the wider catalogue of Wishbone Ash music and taking this to the masses. There is still more that can be done on that front, I believe. My focus so far has been on reproducing the music as faithfully as possible. When I go to see an artist live, I want to hear the songs as I remember them from the records and I believe that is true of the Wishbone Ash audience too. I believe we have achieved a nice balance in capturing the familiar sound of the classic Wishbone Ash line-ups, yet at the same time providing just enough scope for my musicians to step out and put their own stamp on the music. I am extremely pleased with what we have achieved to date but as we move forwards we begin to discover new ways of interpreting the music. For example, in 2011 we were invited to appear at the *Acoustic Festival of Britain* in Uttoxeter. There was a strict proviso that we were not to use electric guitars, full drum kit or big amplifiers and that was a challenge in itself. Wishbone Ash was known for its twin electric guitars, so how would the music sound stripped of that trademark? And what would the audience make of it? These were concerns I had when we committed to playing this show, but I needn't have worried. Once we got into rehearsals there were smiles all round as we discovered new qualities within the music. Playing acoustically gives you the chance to put more emphasis on vocal harmonies, get playful with the arrangements and allow the guitarists to get into whole different areas such as finger-picking. We thoroughly enjoyed the experience to the point where we actually introduced a four-song acoustic section into our regular rock shows during the *Live Dates 2011* tour and are now even considering recording some Wishbone Ash songs reinterpreted in an acoustic style, as well as playing some more acoustic concerts at some point in the future. It's still Wishbone Ash music, but with a different flavour – there's more than one way to skin a cat!

Then there is new music. My band and I have a wealth of ideas we would love to develop and get down in the form of a new studio album from Martin Turner's Wishbone Ash. To date, we haven't had the chance to bring these plans to fruition, although we did make tentative steps towards this during 2011, with some initial recording sessions. At this stage in my career, I make no apologies for devoting so much of my time to the band's live work as well as my family, and as yet we haven't been able to work a new album into the timeframe available to the band. Gone are the days when everyone lived near each other and devoted twenty four hours a day

Rehearsing acoustic material at Liscombe Park, 2011.

Photo by Gary Carter

to creating music. That was a wonderful period in my life but things are so much different now – everyone is older and have their own commitments and a day to day communal approach to music is near impossible. Of course, we live in an age where you don't actually have to be in the same room to create music – so much can be done by exchanging files by internet and recording with computers. Personally I find all that a little bit sterile and much prefer the situation of having the organic interplay of a group of musicians gathered in the same room, bouncing ideas off each other and spontaneously contributing to each other's material. That is the situation that allowed us to transform my original song material for *Argus* into what everyone now knows as the album. That is the spirit in which Wishbone Ash wrote and recorded *New England* – everybody together, chipping in and encouraging each other's creativity. It is in that environment that I would prefer to work up a new studio album and that is why it will take time. I am not the type who is happy to just slap it down and chuck it out, nor am I the perfectionist control freak some would have you believe. I just know when things sound right or not. I accept that sometimes I am slow, but I deal in quality not quantity.

So here I am in 2012 – nearly fifty years into a career in music that started with those semi-pro bands as a teenager in the sixties with my brother Glenn and, later, Steve Upton on drums. As a kid growing up through the fifties, I can remember clearly the shadow of World War II and the massive impact that it had on everyone as people struggled through the post war greyness and gloom that imperceptibly drifted into the sixties where our generation – the cold war, nuclear age children – morphed into young adults with such a surge of youthful energy and freedom. Rock 'n' Roll music was such an important part of our coming of age and as the dam burst and the technological revolution gained momentum we struggled to stay on the back of the bronco that had been released. Many who would dive in and go too far fell by the wayside but those of us who survived can surely only be amazed at just how much the world has changed at this point in human development. During our lifetimes the struggles of capitalism, communism and religious fundamentalism are maybe not that new, but the explosion of the internet age and the global awareness that goes with it, together with people's ability to move around our planet is unprecedented. It seems to me also that scientific discoveries about our world, about infinitely tiny particles and, conversely, about the immensity of our universe, are taking us to the borders of time and space. We live in a truly dynamic time.

I am glad to have survived the journey. It is rewarding to be able to continue to bring joy to so many people throughout the world, through the music that my band-mates and I cobbled together all those years ago. It has been no easy road, but I remain proud of my accomplishments within music and the recorded legacy of music from the definitive line-ups of Wishbone Ash. While we can all be wiser after the event, I would actually change very little and any negatives are by far outweighed by the positive achievements and the life-shaping experiences gained along the way. Every event along the road has played a part in getting me to this point where I am now content with my life on both a musical and personal level. I remain grateful to all those who joined me along the way to create the music and take it to the masses – in particular Steve Upton, Ted Turner, Andy Powell and Laurie Wisefield. We shared a dream, turned our ambitions into reality and made a lot of people very happy in the process. I would also like to express my gratitude to all of the people worldwide who have shown their love and been so supportive of our creative endeavours. Let's also not forget all those who have worked hard behind the scenes to make it all happen – the managers, agents, wives and girlfriends, record companies, publicists, producers, designers, road crews, etc, etc, past and present - bless 'em all.

If you made it this far through my ramblings - well done, and now it's time for me to get back to the music.

The journey continues...

Once In A Blue Moon

Friday 31 August 2012, Liscombe Park Studios, Buckinghamshire

SINCE MY return to the live stage in 2005, I have been overwhelmed by the level of love and support that has been shown by our friends and fans. For some time we had wanted to show our thanks, in a meaningful way, to those who have made MTWA possible.

Back in the Spring of 2012, my webmaster and long-time confidante Gary Carter suggested the idea of an intimate "studio" concert, attended by a small invited audience of friends and loyal supporters. The twist, however, would be that rather than playing the standard set we had been playing on the road during our *No Easy Road - Live Dates 2012* tour, we would instead play a unique set that would revisit some of the songs that have been in the MTWA repertoire but had not yet appeared on any of our live product, providing us with a chance to record these songs in a live setting for future release.

The initial idea was met with positive reactions from both my band and management team and we felt this would be a nice way of giving something back to those who have supported us – a free concert on the band's "home ground", so to speak. The last day of August 2012 was pencilled in and, given that the event was taking place in the Summer, we all thought it would be a lovely idea to stage the event outdoors in the studio grounds – weather permitting, of course!

And so the Garden Party was launched with an announcement on my website. The response was considerable and requests for tickets by far outweighed the limited number of places available.

There was no master plan to stage a "reunion" of any description, but we thought it would be a nice idea to invite Ted Turner, Steve Upton and Laurie Wisefield to this gathering of friends and fans. There were all invited on the basis that there would be no expectation of them to perform, but should they wish to do so we would be happy to have them involved – my band has always had an "open door" policy when it comes to guest appearances from members of the original Wishbone Ash line-ups.

Although Ted had already played with my band on several occasions, he initially thought he wouldn't be able to make it this time, because he had family stuff happening. Steve, however, was coincidentally going to be in England for a family get together around the time of the event, and said he would love to come along. We were all thrilled to bits to hear this as it had obviously been a long time since Steve had attended any Wishbonian gatherings. Once Steve had said he was going to be there, Ted said he would definitely be coming too.

> **TED TURNER:** *When I heard that Steve was going to attend I thought to myself "How many opportunities will we have that the three of us will meet", so I jumped on a plane.*

We also heard from Martin Darvill that Laurie, who was now playing with Snakecharmer, who are also managed by QEDG, was also interested in coming. All this unfolded quite spontaneously during the weeks leading up to the event, which now began to take on a life of its own.

Come the day of the show we were blessed with beautiful sunny weather. Maria Lundy at QEDG had done a fantastic job in organising the event, taking care of the planning and logistics – the work that goes on behind the scenes in organising an event like this is considerable, so a big thanks to Maria and the team at QEDG is due. My band had, as always, worked hard in rehearsals to pull off the varied selection of back catalogue gems and we even tried out a brand new MTWA song on the audience in the form of 'Mystify Me', one of several songs we plan to record for a studio album shortly.

We brought Ted onstage to play on 'Valediction', 'The King Will Come', 'In the Skin' and 'Why Don't We', much to the delight of the crowd. As a player, Ted is one in a million. Even though he has not been out there performing a great deal, he still has that passion and has never lost his special touch and ability to improvise.

Ted's appearance may not have been a total surprise to the audience, given the number of times he's already played with us, but I don't think anyone truly expected to see both Laurie Wisefield and Steve Upton called up to the stage. While we'd had a brief rehearsal with Ted the previous day, Laurie's performance of 'Living Proof' was totally unrehearsed and jammed on the spot. Typically, Laurie played flawlessly – he is such a technically gifted and accomplished musician, having played with so many different people over the years. Both he and Ted are very special players, for different reasons.

Our last song of the evening 'Jailbait' was one of those rare occasions where both Ted and Laurie played on stage together. They had done it once before, in Walthamstow back in 1991, but this time around I think they really hit it off musically, establishing a great rapport as players as they traded licks with each other. Ted later commented to me on how much he enjoyed playing with Laurie and echoed similar sentiments on his website.

> **TED TURNER:** *It was a real pleasure to make contact with Laurie. For me, we have crossed paths in the past but never really connected. Standing by the side of the stage listening to him play revealed his subtleties, finesse and feel as a player – very tasty – so playing 'Jailbait' was a very natural affair. We played well together.*

While Steve had already told us he would not be playing, it was a truly emotional moment when he also joined us on stage to take a bow. This clearly meant a lot to those in attendance. As someone who has been detached from the Wishbone Ash scene for many years, Steve was clearly quite overwhelmed by the degree of love and respect that was shown towards him. Over the years I have always conveyed to Steve just how much the music still means to people and how enthusiastic the audiences are, but that is something that is hard to discern from a distance. It doesn't actually have a great deal of impact until you're confronted by it and witness it first-hand. I met with Steve for dinner the next day and he did express to me that he had been genuinely moved by the occasion and had enjoyed sharing in the experience.

So there we were – Steve, Ted, Laurie and I all together in the same place for the first time in over two decades. It was as if it had been written in the stars and, of course, it was a blue moon that night as well! It was also great to see former associates and crew members such as Mark "Hobbit" Emery, Chris Runciman, Terry Finn and Rod Lynton – all important characters in the early Wishbone Ash story – as well as original MTWA guitarist Keith Buck. There was a truly wonderful atmosphere on and off the stage that evening.

> **TED TURNER:** *This was a very special day. To come face to face once again with the original road crew was memorable - memories I shall not forget. A day filled with affection, friendship and love. It was great to see everyone looking well, hearing the stories about their own interesting journeys.*

Naturally, since the Garden Party event, many fans have expressed that they would love to see Steve, Ted, Laurie and myself playing some shows together at some point in the future. There seems to be quite a lot of interest in that particular configuration of players – a hybrid of the Mk.1 and Mk. 2 Wishbone Ash line-ups, if you like. Prior to the Garden Party, I would probably have said that I would have thought it highly unlikely that the four of us would perform together, as it would obviously be a rather unusual line-up, with Ted and Laurie having never been in the band at the same time. However, after the Garden Party experience, I was able to see that this could work, and see no reason why we could not get together to play some shows at some point - not at the expense of my band, but more likely as a one-off reunion to mark a special occasion. However, I'm always hesitant to quote Steve, Ted or Laurie and would not want to alienate them by putting into the public domain any ideas that may have been discussed.

One thing is for sure, the Garden Party certainly reminded the four of us that we do have a very special rapport both as musicians and as people – something that our audience clearly picked up on that evening. I am glad we had the chance to spend some time in each other's company once again – both musically and socially. Some bands never get that chance and I truly hope we get the opportunity to do so again at some point in the future...